CLARA SCHUMANN

Clara Schumann, age 38, Munich. Photo by Hanfstaengl, 1857.
Robert-Schumann-Haus, Zwickau, DDR.

CLARA SCHUMANN

The Artist and the Woman

Nancy B. Reich

Cornell University Press

ITHACA AND LONDON

First published 1985 by Cornell University Press.

LIBRARY OF CONGRESS CATALOGING IN PUBLICATION DATA

Reich, Nancy B.
    Clara Schumann, the artist and the woman.

    Bibliography: p.
    Includes index.
    1. Schumann, Clara, 1819–1896.   2. Pianists—Germany—Biography.   I. Title.
ML417.S4R4   1985   786.1′092′4 [B]   84-45798
ISBN 0-8014-1748-1

45,891

Printed in the United States of America

*The paper in this book is acid-free and meets the guidelines
for permanence and durability of the Committee on Production
Guidelines for Book Longevity of the Council on Library Resources.*

In memory of
Haskell A. Reich
1926–1983

Contents

PART I: *The Life of Clara Schumann*

PART II: *Themes from the Life of Clara Schumann*

Illustrations

Preface

Though much has been written about Clara Schumann, she is still, more than 165 years after her birth, known to us only through the eyes and minds of her own era. She is viewed even today as her nineteenth-century contemporaries saw her—as a saint or "priestess," as a dedicated wife, mother, and musician. In seeking a modern approach to this great artist, I have examined new sources and reexamined the old. This study has deepened my regard for the artist and woman; it has also convinced me that she is worthy of the truth. Such a quest calls for the tools of musicological scholarship, the insights of psychology, and sensitivity to the history of women and their place in nineteenth-century musical history.

All of her biographies, even the most recent (published in English, French, German, Danish, and several other languages—testimony to the continuing interest in Clara Schumann), have been based on Berthold Litzmann's *Clara Schumann: Ein Künstlerleben*, published between 1902 and 1908, and on her correspondence with Johannes Brahms, which was published in 1927.

Litzmann's three-volume, 1,459-page biography, written under the supervision of Marie, the eldest Schumann daughter, and authorized by the Schumann family, is a major source for scholars of nineteenth-century music, and indeed has been a major source for my own book. Litzmann, a literary scholar and friend of the Schumann family, sifted through thousands of letters and all of the diaries of Robert and Clara Schumann as well as court orders, travel notebooks, household books, old programs, music autographs—all the papers that Robert Schumann meticulously filed and treasured. The two volumes of letters exchanged by Clara Schumann and Brahms between 1853 and 1896, to which Litzmann alone was granted access, remains a precious record of the lives of two great musicians. Litzmann's objectivity, understanding, and warmth were in no way reduced by the Teutonic thoroughness with which he performed his task. The many

English admirers of the art of Clara Schumann eagerly awaited translations of the letters and of Litzmann's biography; they were published almost simultaneously with the German editions. Unfortunately, Grace Hadow's admirable translations of the biography (1913) and letters (1927) are sharply abridged versions of the originals and thus omit many details vital to a complete understanding of the woman and her time.

A review of the original sources, moreover, reveals many nuances overlooked by Litzmann, who omitted much information, perhaps to protect the persons involved or perhaps because he believed it was not worth consideration. The translations suffer even more, less from the language conversion than from the shortening of the biography by one-third and of the correspondence by half. Hadow hews close to the facts, but so much is omitted that serious readers cannot depend on the translations. The same can be said of many other translations of Schumann sources. For these reasons, I have used only the German publications and provided my own translations for all material quoted. All citations are to the German works. (The *Memoirs* of Eugenie Schumann are the only exception, for reasons made clear in the bibliography.) I was most fortunate in being able to consult the first volume (1832–38) of the recently published critical edition of the letters of Clara and Robert Schumann, edited by Eva Weissweiler. Wherever possible, I have referred to this volume rather than to Litzmann's edition, as it offers an unabridged transcription of the correspondence. The volumes covering the later years are not yet available, and as I was unable to consult the surviving original letters, I have relied (cautiously) on Litzmann and on Wolfgang Boetticher's *Robert Schumann in seinen Schriften und Briefen* for quotations from letters after 1838.

A remarkable series of scholarly publications of Schumann documents from the archives of Robert-Schumann-Haus, Zwickau, has been appearing since 1971. These documents, meticulously edited according to contemporary scholarly procedures, have changed the course of Schumann research. Readers are no longer limited to family-authorized publications or to studies flawed by the prejudices of their editors. Through the courtesy of Martin Schoppe and Gerd Nauhaus of Robert-Schumann-Haus, I have had the good fortune to study many of the documents—the household books and "marriage diary," for example—before publication, and to read others, including the diary of Clara Wieck and the Wieck and Schumann family papers, whose publication is scheduled many years hence. I have also examined many hundreds of letters stored in archives in Europe and the United States, as well as published collections of correspondence involving the Schumanns. As a consequence I have gained an enormous respect for Litzmann but also an added dimension of understanding of the woman who was artist, wife, mother, teacher, editor, and a creative partner of Friedrich Wieck, Robert Schumann, and Johannes Brahms.

Since the reader may obtain from Litzmann (or the Hadow translation) a day-by-day chronology of Clara Schumann's life, I have not attempted to duplicate this detail or repeated many of the legends familiar to readers of the Schumann literature. Although Part I is organized chronologically, I have focused on what I see as key issues in the life of Clara Schumann—her close bond with her father, her relationship with her mother, her education and the development of her unparalleled career, her agonizing struggle for independence, the choices she was forced to make between family and career, her responses to motherhood, the changing balance in her family life, and her strategies for coping with the illness, suicide attempt, and hospitalization of her husband. During the forty years left to her after his death she built and maintained a career in Europe and England second to none. This rich life I have treated in Part II, where four major areas of her life are explored in detail: her friendships, her creative work, her life on the concert stage, and her activities as a teacher. In each of these chapters I have attempted to answer the many questions raised by musicians in regard to her contributions and influence, to offer information that has not previously been available, and to place Clara Schumann in perspective in the musical life of the nineteenth century. Readers may be surprised to see Brahms relegated to one chapter in her life; it was a most significant chapter, to be sure, but it was not the consuming central relationship that so many people have suspected.

My search for materials for this biography began inadvertently: in 1973 I came across the unpublished correspondence (1858–96) between Clara Schumann and Ernst Rudorff, who had been her student for a short time and who later taught her daughter Eugenie. There were many ties between Frau Schumann and the younger man. As head of the piano department of the Berlin Hochschule für Musik, Rudorff was a member of the inner circle of musicians and friends on whom she most depended. The Rudorff correspondence was a starting point; from there other collections of published and unpublished correspondence gave me insights to the personality and character of Clara Schumann not yielded by Litzmann.

Major sources for this study are listed in the bibliography, but a few documents, published and unpublished, which have been particularly meaningful must be mentioned here. All the papers and materials in Robert-Schumann-Haus, Zwickau, particularly the unpublished diaries of Clara Wieck, offer the researcher a wealth of previously unknown information—names, places, dates—as well as a new perception of the character and personality of Clara and of Friedrich Wieck, her father. The letters of Friedrich Wieck, edited by Käthe Walch-Schumann and not available in their entirety until 1968, provide a clearer picture of the man, a figure not treated with particular sympathy by Litzmann and never revealed in his true light. Joseph Joachim's correspondence with Brahms, Rudorff, and Clara Schumann, the letters of the Joachim family, the Schumann family correspondence, the Ferdinand Hiller correspondence, and the correspondence between Clara Schumann and Ernst Rudorff have illuminated music and concert life of the nineteenth century as well as the personal relationships of all involved.

Some of the letters that proved most significant to me appeared in articles in long-forgotten German music periodicals: the wonderful letters of Clara Schumann to Emilie Steffens (Chapter 6), for example, and her letter to Selmar Bagge (Chapter 10). Other writings from well-known volumes over-looked by previous biographers—a description of Clara in 1854 by Hedwig Salomon (Chapter 7), a letter of Clara to Emilie List about her sixteenth-birthday party (Chapter 4), an indignant letter to Hiller about her treatment in Düsseldorf (Chapter 7), a letter from Amalie Joachim to her husband in 1872 (Chapter 8), and entries from Ruppert Becker's diary (Chapter 7)—reveal a more human Clara Schumann, a woman who comes to life through her own words. These documents have been translated, most for the first time, and many are given in their entirety.

Students of women's history know that female influences, even in the lives of prominent women, are usually overlooked. This has certainly been the case in studies of Clara Schumann. Robert Schumann plays an inordinately large role in most biographies of Clara Schumann written by both men and women. And the place of Clara Wieck's mother, Marianne, and her signifi-cance in the life of the young pianist has never been explored. Indeed, Marianne is virtually ignored by Litzmann once she has borne Wieck's children and left his home. Perhaps the early divorce was an embarrassment to the Schumann family and thus to Litzmann. It is my hope that with this study Marianne Bargiel has been restored to her rightful place in the story of her daughter's life. In this task I was aided by Herma Stamm-Bargiel, who kindly shared pictures and family documents of the Bargiel family with me.

Locating the compositions of Clara Schumann has not been an easy task, but here, too, the archives at Robert-Schumann-Haus have provided valu-able materials. The collection of autographs and prints of Clara Schumann's music in Zwickau and the exciting discovery in the Staatsbibliothek, Berlin, of her song autographs collected into one notebook (listed in the appendix), as well as Robert Schumann's instrumentation of the last movement of her concerto, enabled me to date her works and prepare a more complete cata-logue of her works than any that has appeared previously.

Musical examples in Chapter 11 are taken from the first editions of Clara Schumann's works and from the Dover reprint (1972) of *Robert Schumann's Werke*, edited by Clara Schumann (Leipzig: Breitkopf & Härtel, 1879–93). Example 5 is from *Johannes Brahms: Sämtliche Werke*, edited for the Gesellschaft der Musikfreunde, Vienna, by Hans Gál and Eusebius Man-dyczewski (Leipzig: Breitkopf & Härtel [1926–28]). Examples 6 and 7 are from Schumann, *Impromptus*, H. J. Köhler, ed. (Leipzig: Peters, 1979), 29.

The spellings of names and musical titles varied considerably in the nine-teenth century. Clara Schumann, for example, always spelled her name with a *C* whereas Robert Schumann used both *C* and *K* in writing his wife's name. I have attempted to establish consistency in the spelling of names by using the spelling given by the individual himself or herself or in official documents of the period.

In their search for great women of the past, feminists have rallied round the figure of Clara Schumann. It must be pointed out, however, that she was not a feminist in the modern sense of the word. She had little interest in women's rights or the struggle for recognition that other creative German women were just beginning to launch in the mid–nineteenth century. She concentrated on her own career and her many obligations as she endeavored to reconcile the conflicts that inevitably arise when a woman steps out of her conventional place.

Clara Schumann was always her own person, perceiving herself as an artist who was a woman, and eternally grateful for the art that was to sustain her through a lifetime of tragedy and triumph.

NANCY B. REICH

Hastings-on-Hudson, New York

Acknowledgments

M y profoundest gratitude goes to Anna Burton, M.D., for her friendship, continuing support and sympathy, and the stimulating and fruitful collaboration we have had over many years. An accomplished musician and practicing psychoanalyst, she was a true silent partner in the creation of this book. Dr. Burton never spared herself in helping me think through and understand problematical situations and questions that arose during the course of my research. Her wisdom and penetrating insights have informed every page of this book.

I gratefully thank the many colleagues in both Europe and the United States who have aided this endeavor: Martin Schoppe and Gerd Nauhaus, who generously opened the archives at Robert-Schumann-Haus, Zwickau, to me and who have been helpful in every possible way; Hans Joachim Köhler, Leipzig, and Renate and Kurt Hofmann, Hamburg, for enlightening conversation; R. Klaus Müller, Käte Pittasch, Leipzig; Brigitte Berenbruch, Bonn; Helga Heim, Hamburg; Maike Holling-Suhl, West Berlin, whose friendship and devoted interest have made my research in Europe so gratifying and productive; Janina Klassen, Kiel; Maria Párkai-Eckhardt, Budapest; and Peter Cahn, Frankfurt, who have generously shared information with me; and Eva Weissweiler, Cologne, who kindly sent me her transcriptions of Clara Schumann's letters to Bettina von Arnim.

I thank also Imogen Fellinger, whose family connections with the Schumanns go back several generations, for her guidance and assistance, and Herma Stamm-Bargiel, who provided me with copies of unpublished sketches of the Tromlitz family, shared information about her Tromlitz and Bargiel descendants, and kindly gave me permission to reproduce the picture of Marianne Tromlitz.

I am very appreciative of the hospitality and kindness of Johannes von Gottberg, who granted me access to the Rudorff archives and gave me

[14

permission to quote excerpts from letters of Clara Schumann to Ernst Rudorff.

Among friends and colleagues in the United States, warmest thanks to Marianne von Recklinghausen Bowles and Gabriele Wickert for their expert assistance with translations, and to Adrienne Block, Gary Golio, Maryanne Joyce, Gladys Krasner, Karen Miller, Susanna Reich, Judith Tick, and Rachel Wade for unflagging encouragement, counsel, and assistance over many years. I have had stimulating and provocative conversations with Dr. Peter Ostwald, who was writing his Robert Schumann biography during the years I was working out ideas about Clara Schumann, and I thank him for his interest and encouragement.

I am grateful to Rufus Hallmark, Mildred Parker, and to my colleagues at the Stanford Center for Research on Women, especially Susan Bell, Karen Offen, and Marilyn Safir, for helpful suggestions. To Ralph Locke and Jurgen Thym for information about the Dickinson Collection, many thanks.

I have used the facilities of many libraries and archives and appreciate the gracious assistance of the following individuals and music libraries in the United States: Ruth Hilton and the New York University Music Library; Rigbie Turner and the Pierpont Morgan Library, New York; Bernard Wilson and the Newberry Library, Chicago; and the staffs of the music libraries of Columbia University, the Eastman School of Music, Harvard University, the Library of Congress, the New York Public Library, Queens College, Stanford University, the University of California at Berkeley, and Yale University.

I thank colleagues in European libraries who have been kind and helpful: in England, the staff of the Music Division of the British Library; in West Germany, the Stadtgeschichtliche Sammlungen, Baden-Baden; the library of the Hochschule der Künste, West Berlin; the Staatsbibliothek Preussischer Kulturbesitz, Musikabteilung and Handschriftenabteilung, West Berlin; the Staatliches Institut für Musikforschung, Preussischer Kulturbesitz, West Berlin; the Musikbücherei Schumannhaus and the Stadtarchiv, Bonn; the Musikwissenschaftliches Institut der Universität, Cologne; the Heinrich-Heine-Institut and the Universitätsbibliothek, Düsseldorf; the Stadt- und Universitätsbibliothek, Frankfurt am Main; the Staats- und Universitätsbibliothek, Hamburg; the Kestner-Museum, Hannover; the Bayerische Staatsbibliothek, Munich; and the Landesbibliothek, Stuttgart. In the German Democratic Republic, I have had kind and patient assistance from the staffs of the Deutsche Staatsbibliothek, Musikabteilung, Berlin; the Universitätsbibliothek, Leipzig; and Robert-Schumann-Haus, Zwickau. I also thank the staffs of the archives of the Gesellschaft der Musikfreunde, Vienna, and the Biblioteka Jagiellońska, Kraków.

Many thanks to Margit McCorkle and the staff of the Brahms Cataloging Project for placing their library and working papers at my disposal in Vancouver.

Acknowledgments

To Alan Lippert and Michael Lippert for technical assistance, and to Mi-Won Kim for preparing the musical examples, much appreciation. I am deeply grateful to Barbara Salazar of Cornell University Press for her patience and expert guidance.

Portions of Chapters 1 through 4 have appeared in substantially different form in *The Musical Quarterly*, Summer 1984. I am also grateful for the cooperation of Breitkopf & Härtel, Wiesbaden, publishers of Berthold Litzmann's biography of Clara Schumann and his edition of the letters of Clara Schumann and Johannes Brahms, and I thank the following institutions for permission to publish excerpts from letters and to reproduce pictures in their possession: Deutsche Staatsbibliothek, Berlin/DDR, Musikabteilung; Robert-Schumann-Haus, Zwickau/DDR; Staatsbibliothek, Preussischer Kulturbesitz, Musikabteilung, West Berlin; Schumannhaus, Bonn; Heinrich-Heine-Institut, Düsseldorf; and the Newberry Library, Chicago.

I acknowledge with thanks a grant for college teachers from the National Endowment for the Humanities, travel grants from the Deutscher Akademischer Austauschdienst, and the Penrose Fund of the American Philosophical Society, and assistance from the Faculty Service Commitee, Manhattanville College.

This book could not have been written without the steadfast encouragement, faith, and devotion of my late husband, Haskell A. Reich.

N. B. R.

Chronology

1785	Birth of father, Friedrich Wieck, August 18.
1797	Birth of mother, Marianne Tromlitz, May 17.
1810	Birth of Robert Schumann in Zwickau, June 8.
1816	Marriage of Marianne Tromlitz and Friedrich Wieck, June 23.
1817	Birth of Adelheid Wieck, August 10 (d. May 12, 1818).
1819	Birth of Clara Josephine Wieck, September 13.
1821	Birth of Alwin Wieck, August 27.
1823	Birth of Gustav Wieck, January 31.
1824	Birth of Victor Wieck, February 22 (d. January 2, 1827).
	Mother leaves Wieck and children, takes infant, May 12.
	Clara spends summer with mother; returns to father September 17.
	Clara begins formal piano lessons, October 27.
1825	Divorce of Marianne and Friedrich Wieck, January 22.
	Marriage of Marianne Wieck and Adolph Bargiel, August.
1828	Robert Schumann arrives in Leipzig; studies with Wieck.
	Marriage of Friedrich Wieck and Clementine Fechner, July 3.
	Clara plays at Gewandhaus as assisting artist, October 20.
1829	Robert Schumann leaves Leipzig to study in Heidelberg, July 4.
1830	Clara gives private concerts in Dresden, March 6 to April 7.
	Schumann returns to Leipzig; studies and boards with Wieck family.
	Clara gives first Gewandhaus concert as solo artist, November 8.
1831	Clara and father begin concert tour to Paris, leaving Leipzig end of September and returning May 1, 1832.
1832	Birth of Marie Wieck (half sister), January 17.
	Solo concerts in Leipzig, July and September.
	Local concert tours with father to Altenburg, Zwickau, Schneeberg, November. Schumann joins them in Zwickau.
1833	Concerts in Leipzig, January, February, April, and local tours to Chemnitz, Karlsbad, and Schneeberg.
1834	Schumann becomes editor and publisher of *Neue Zeitschrift für Musik*.
	Ernestine von Fricken arrives in Leipzig; studies and boards with Wieck.
	Birth of Cäcilie Wieck (half sister), July.

17]

Concert tour with father and Carl Banck to northern Germany (Hamburg, Hannover, Magdeburg), November 11 to April 1835.

1835   Robert Schumann begins courtship of Clara Wieck.

1836   Death of Schumann's mother. Robert meets Clara secretly in Dresden, February 7–11.

Tour with father to Breslau, February to April.

Tour with father to Naumburg, Jena, Weimar, November.

1837   Secret engagement of Clara and Robert, August 14.

Concert tour with father to Berlin, Hamburg, Bremen, February to May. Clara meets with mother in Berlin.

Schumann asks Wieck for Clara's hand, September 13. Suit rejected.

Concert tour with father to Vienna, October 15 to May 15, 1838.

Clara named Royal and Imperial Virtuosa.

1838   Schumann leaves Leipzig for Vienna, September 27.

1839   Clara leaves for Paris without father, January 8. In Paris from February 6 to August 14.

Petitions Court of Appeals for permission to marry without father's consent, June 15.

1840   Clara in Berlin with mother from September 1839 till marriage.

Concerts in Berlin and tours with mother in north Germany.

Court consents to marriage, August 1.

Banns posted, August 16.

Last concert as Clara Wieck in Weimar, September 5.

Marriage of Robert Schumann and Clara Wieck, September 12, one day before her 21st birthday.

1841   Death of Adolph Bargiel, February 4.

First concert as Clara Schumann, Gewandhaus, March 31.

Birth of Marie, September 1.

1842   Concert tour to Hamburg with Robert, February 14. Schumann returns to Leipzig; Clara to Copenhagen, returns April 26.

1843   Birth of Elise, April 25.

1844   Concert tour to Russia with Schumann, January 25 to May 30.

Clara named honorary member, St. Petersburg Philharmonic Society, March 5.

Schumann and Clara to Dresden, October.

Family resettles in Dresden, December 13.

1845   Birth of Julie, March 11.

1846   Birth of Emil, February 8 (d. June 22, 1847).

Vacation trip with Robert to Norderney, July 6 to August 25; miscarriage?

Concert tour to Vienna with Schumann and two eldest daughters, November 23 to February 4, 1847.

1847   To Berlin for performances of Schumann's oratorio *Das Paradies und die Peri* and several concerts, February and March.

Death of Emil, June 22.

To music festival in Zwickau with Robert, July.

1848   Birth of Ludwig, January 20.

1849   May revolution in Dresden.

Birth of Ferdinand, July 16.

1850	Concerts in Leipzig, Hamburg, and Bremen with Robert Schumann, February 5 to March 29.
	Decision to leave Dresden for new employment in Düsseldorf made March 31.
	Genoveva premiere and concerts in Leipzig, May 18 to July 10.
	Arrival in Düsseldorf, September; many concerts.
1851	Birth of Eugenie, December 1. Clara continues concertizing and teaching.
1852	"Schumann Week" in Leipzig; many concerts at Gewandhaus.
	Concerts in Düsseldorf and neighboring cities.
	Vacation in Scheveningen, August 12 to mid-September; miscarriage.
1853	Concerts at Lower Rhine Music Festival, May.
	Brahms arrives in Düsseldorf; meets Schumanns, September 30.
	Schumann dismissed as music director of Düsseldorf orchestra.
	Concert tour to Holland with Robert Schumann, November 24 to December.
1854	Concerts in Hannover with Robert Schumann, January 21–30; visits with Joachim and Brahms.
	Robert Schumann attempts suicide, February 27. To hospital at Endenich, March 4.
	Birth of Felix, June 11.
	Clara Schumann begins concert tours, October to December.
1855	Concert tours, January through July and October through December.
1856	Concert tours to Vienna, Prague, Budapest, January through March. First concert tour to England, April 18 to July 6.
	Clara sees Robert Schumann for first time in two and a half years, July 27.
	Death of Robert Schumann, July 29.
	Clara begins concert tours, October 28 to December 25.
1857	Continues concert tours. Resettles family in Berlin, October.
1863	First season in summer home, Baden-Baden.
1869	Marriage of Julie to Count Marmorito, September.
1870	Ludwig pronounced incurably ill; institutionalized in Colditz.
	Ferdinand called up to serve in army during Franco-Prussian War, returns September 1871.
1872	Death of mother, Marianne Bargiel, March 10.
	Death of Julie, November 10.
1873	Marriage of Ferdinand to Antonie Deutsch, August 13.
	Baden-Baden house sold. Resettles at 11 In den Zelten, Berlin.
	Friedrich Wieck dies, October 6.
1877	Marriage of Elise to Louis Sommerhoff, November 27.
	Begins work as editor of Schumann's collected works.
1878	Resettles in Frankfurt; begins work on faculty of Hoch Conservatory.
	Fiftieth jubilee as concert artist celebrated in Frankfurt and Leipzig, October 24.
1879	Death of Felix, February 16.
1883	Begins work as editor of Instructive Edition of Robert Schumann's piano works.
1885	Death of Alwin, October 21.
1887	Ferdinand hospitalized. Clara assumes responsibility for his six children.

1888	Final concert tour to England, February–March.
	Sixtieth jubilee celebrations in Frankfurt, October 26.
1891	Final public concert in Frankfurt, March.
	Death of Ferdinand, June 6.
1893	Death of Clementine Wieck, December 27.
1896	Clara Schumann suffers stroke March 26 and dies May 20.
1897	Death of Johannes Brahms, April 3.
1899	Death of Ludwig, January 9.
1916	Death of Marie Wieck, November 2.
1928	Death of Elise, July 1.
1929	Death of Marie, November 14.
1938	Death of Eugenie, September 25.

Abbreviations

AfMw	*Archiv für Musikwissenschaft*
AmZ	*Allgemeine musikalische Zeitung*
Bds	Deutsche Staatsbibliothek, Berlin/DDR
Briefwechsel	Clara and Robert Schumann, *Clara und Robert Schumann, Briefwechsel*, vol. 1, 1832–1838, ed. Eva Weissweiler (Basel: Stroemfeld/Roter Stern, 1984)
Diary	Diaries of Clara Wieck, RSH
Dwight's	*Dwight's Journal of Music*
Grove	*The New Grove Dictionary of Music and Musicians*, ed. Stanley Sadie, 20 vols. (London: Macmillan, 1980)
Hb	Robert Schumann, *Tagebücher*, pt. 3, *Haushaltbücher* (1837–1856), ed. Gerd Nauhaus, 2 vols. (Leipzig: Deutscher Verlag für Musik, 1982)
Jugendbriefe	Robert Schumann, *Jugendbriefe von Robert Schumann*, ed. Clara Schumann, 2d ed. (Leipzig: Breitkopf & Härtel, 1886)
Litzmann	Berthold Litzmann, *Clara Schumann: Ein Künsterleben nach Tagebüchern und Briefen*, 3 vols. (Leipzig: Breitkopf & Härtel, 1902–8)
Md	"Marriage diaries" of Clara and Robert Schumann, 1840–44, RSH
Memoirs	Eugenie Schumann, *The Schumanns and Johannes Brahms: The Memoirs of Eugenie Schumann*, trans. Marie Busch (New York: Dial Press, 1927)
MGG	*Die Musik in Geschichte und Gegenwart*, ed. Friedrich Blume, 14 vols. (Kassel: Bärenreiter, 1949–68)
MQ	*The Musical Quarterly*
ML	*Music and Letters*
MT	*The Musical Times*
NBMz	*Neue Berliner Musikzeitung*
NmZfB	*Neue Musikalische Zeitung für Berlin* (this title was used for a few issues of *NBMz* in 1847)
NZfM	*Neue Zeitschrift für Musik*

Abbreviations

Quellenwerk   Georg Eismann, ed., *Robert Schumann: Ein Quellenwerk über sein Leben und Schaffen*, 2 vols. (Leipzig: Breitkopf & Härtel, 1956)

RSH   Robert-Schumann-Haus, Zwickau/DDR

Rudorff-Archiv   Rudorff-Archiv: Privatarchiv v. Gottberg, D-3216 Salzhemmendorf-2, West Germany

Wgm   Gesellschaft der Musikfreunde, Vienna

PART I

THE LIFE OF CLARA SCHUMANN

CHAPTER 1

Prelude: The Wiecks
of Leipzig

On January 9, 1838, a poem, "Clara Wieck und Beethoven," appeared in the *Wiener Zeitschrift für Kunst*.[1] Written by Franz Grillparzer, Austria's leading dramatic poet, the verse linked the name of the great composer with that of a young woman who had just given her third Viennese recital at the age of eighteen. Grillparzer's response to her performance of Beethoven's Piano Sonata Op. 57, the "Appassionata," reflected the wild enthusiasm the young pianist aroused in Vienna.

Clara Wieck had arrived in the Austrian capital from her native Leipzig with her father, Friedrich, in December 1837. From her first concert on the fourteenth in the Musikvereinsaal to her last appearance in April, when she played for the emperor in the Burg, she was greeted with the kind of adoration the Viennese reserved for artists of the rank of Niccolò Paganini and Sigismund Thalberg.[2] Music lovers fought to buy seats in the overcrowded halls where she played; critics vied with each other in expressions of admiration. At her fourth concert, frenzied applause recalled her to the stage thirteen times. Princes and barons invited her to play at their palaces and showered her with jewels and treasure. The empress herself let her satisfaction be known with a gift of fifty gold ducats.[3] Recalling Clara's reception, Eduard Hanslick, the Viennese critic and music historian, described her as "not a wonderchild—and yet still a child and already a wonder."[4]

On March 15, 1838, she received the greatest honor Austria could bestow: she was named *Königliche Kaiserliche Kammervirtuosin* (Royal and Imperial Chamber Virtuosa), a distinction without precedent for an eighteen-year-old who was, moreover, a Protestant, a foreigner, and a female. The emperor had agreed to make an exception for Clara Wieck. On March 21 the emperor dubbed her *Wundermädchen* and assured her that he had made the award with the greatest personal satisfaction.[5]

Who was Clara Wieck? How did this slender, oval-eyed daughter of an unknown Leipzig piano teacher and music dealer manage to reach such heights of artistry? The question is still more intriguing when we consider that this girl, born in an age when musical talent in a female was regarded only as an asset in the marriage market, subsequently built a glorious career that spanned sixty years, a career that influenced the concert and musical life of the nineteenth century. Acknowledged as the peer of Franz Liszt, Thalberg, and Anton Rubinstein, she was a thorough professional and a working wife and mother, managing the manifold problems of career, household, husband, and children. At twenty-one she was married to a major composer; at thirty-seven, a widow with seven children, she became involved in a lifelong relationship with another composer. Furthermore, the indefatigable Clara composed music (twenty-three published opus numbers), taught, and edited the authoritative edition of the *Collected Works of Robert Schumann*.

This remarkable woman was a creative partner of three men: Friedrich Wieck, Robert Schumann, and Johannes Brahms. The first, her father and sole teacher, much maligned for the role he was later to play in the romance between his daughter and Robert Schumann, was a self-made man and self-trained musician, obsessive and ambitious. Convinced that gender was no handicap in the race for artistic greatness, he gave Clara the instruction and musical understanding that carried her beyond the ranks of the merely gifted to a position in the constellation of the great nineteenth-century virtuosi. His discipline and pride in her achievements provided the practical sense and stability that sustained her through personal and artistic crises. Wieck firmly believed that his pedagogical genius alone was responsible for the creation of the young pianist who generated such excitement in Vienna in 1838, over-looking entirely the role of Clara's mother, the girl's own remarkable talents, and the series of circumstances, at once tragic, auspicious, fortuitous, and predictable, which went into the making of the "Queen of the Piano." Wieck was at first, of course, the dominating figure in her life, but Clara soon grew to be the more significant, and he eventually shone only in the reflected glory of her light.

FRIEDRICH WIECK, 1785–1873

Friedrich Wieck, the youngest son of a merchant in Pretzsch, a small town about forty-five kilometers from Leipzig, was born in 1785 into a family with declining fortunes and very little interest in music.[6] Always passionately fond of the art, he studied where he could. At age thirteen he was given the opportunity to attend the Thomas-Schule in Leipzig, but was forced to return home after six weeks because of illness. A weak and sickly youngster, he remained in Pretzsch until 1800, when he went to the Torgau *gymnasium* to prepare for the university and his eventual goal, the ministry. In Torgau and later at the University of Wittenberg, where he matriculated in 1803, his musical education was haphazard. His only formal piano lessons were some six hours with Johann Peter Milchmeyer, who was in Torgau for a short time to give lessons to the wife and children of a well-to-do townsman.*

When Wieck completed his theological studies at the university and had preached the obligatory trial sermon in Dresden, he left theology and turned to the traditional occupation of the German university graduate who had neither money nor connections: he became a *Hauslehrer*, a private tutor in the home of a wealthy family. Over the next nine years he worked for several aristocratic families in Thuringia. His first position was with a baron von Seckendorff in Querfurth, where Adolph Bargiel, the music teacher of the Seckendorff children, became a close friend. Bargiel will appear again at a critical point in Wieck's life.

Conscientious, observant, and intelligent, Wieck was a perceptive teacher. He understood the latest thought in educational psychology (dominated, at that period, by Jean-Jacques Rousseau and his *Emile* and such educators as Johann Basedow and Johann Pestalozzi) and applied it successfully to his students. The young teacher speculated on such concepts as individualized learning and the critical role of motivation in teaching. And, like other progressive educators of his time, he placed great importance on regular physical exercise in the open air. His daughter's musical education, which was to begin in 1824, was influenced by his reading and experiences as a *Hauslehrer*.

In keeping with the rationalist spirit of the time, the young man insisted that the goal of moral training should be to educate the child to be a good person. Religion should not be a matter for the mind but should come from the heart, he wrote. He was particularly concerned with *Ehrtrieb* (which can be loosely translated as a striving for a higher state) and how it could be used as a positive force by the teacher. He cautioned that great care had to be exercised so that *Ehrtrieb* would not degenerate into mere ambition, a passion for glory, vanity, boastfulness, and malicious pleasure in denigrating others. Consistency, however, was not one of Wieck's virtues. In view of his later preoccupation with his daughter's musical career and bitter anger at her, his own *Ehrtrieb* seems to have been easily sullied by ambition.

Wieck came to music late. During his years as a tutor, he had little exposure to events in the musical world; his experience was limited to small-town musicians and church choirs, perhaps a performance of a neighboring nobleman's *Kapelle*. He did not attend a large-scale public concert until he was well into his twenties.

---

*It was a fortunate meeting: Milchmeyer (1750–1813), pianist and teacher, was a figure of considerable prominence to be teaching in Torgau. In addition to a treatise published in 1797, *Die wahre Art, das Pianoforte zu Spielen*, he was the editor of a collection of piano works. He held the title of *Hofmechanikus* to the elector of Bavaria because of a specially constructed piano he invented. See Ernst Ludwig Gerber, *Neues historisch-biographisches Lexikon der Tonkünstler*, 4 vols. (Leipzig: Kühnel, 1812–14), 3:428–29.

Since symphonic and choral works were performed only in a few large German cities in the early years of the nineteenth century, opportunities to hear a Beethoven symphony or a Haydn oratorio simply did not exist in the provincial centers where Wieck was working. In 1811 the young tutor heard, probably for the first time in his life, orchestral works by Beethoven, Louis Spohr, and Mozart, and the Haydn oratorio *Die Schöpfung* (The Creation). His copy of the program, preserved by his family, testifies to his attendance at the second German *Musikfest*, a two-day music festival in which forces from a number of Thuringian towns joined to play large works.[7]

Where and when Wieck learned enough theory to compose and enough about piano technique to set himself up as a teacher are still not clear. Yet by 1815 he was confident enough to dedicate and send a group of his songs to Carl Maria von Weber. To Wieck's delight, the composer took the time and trouble to write a detailed criticism of the works.[8] After publication, the songs were reviewed in a Leipzig journal, the *Allgemeine musikalische Zeitung*.[9] Some shortcomings were noted, and Wieck was advised to study voice because his vocal lines were "unnatural" and hard to sing. At the same time, however, the critic noted that the songs showed "some indications of talent." Wieck must have been gratified to see that his work was taken seriously and that a career in music appeared to be possible.

Wieck left his tutorial post and, applying his keen intelligence, energy, soaring ambition, and native talents to music, undertook a new vocation at the age of thirty. In 1815 he was established in Leipzig—with the financial help of a friend—as a piano teacher and owner of a piano store and music shop.

Although the actual date of his settling in Leipzig is not known, it must have been well before the April 19, 1815, issue of the *Allgemeine musikalische Zeitung*, which referred to him as "the popular Leipzig music teacher." Wieck's business—which he kept going until 1840, when he moved to Dresden—was called a *Piano-Fabrik*, usually translated as "piano factory." The enterprise was not a piano factory, however, but a store in which he rented and sold pianos, and tuned and repaired them as well. The term *Fabrik* was justified in part by his explanation that he stood behind every piano he sold.[10]

Leipzig was the natural place for an ambitious man to establish himself. Located in a flat basin at the confluence of several rivers and the crossroads of ancient north-south and east-west roads, the city had no natural beauty to recommend it, but from the time of its founding in the twelfth century it had been an important trading and cultural center. Though situated in Saxony and subject to its ruler, Leipzig was governed by a town council of middle-class citizens, mostly merchants and manufacturers, which had considerable political and fiscal independence. The semi-annual trade fairs that for more than five centuries had drawn buyers and sellers from all over Europe gave the city a cosmopolitan air and international renown. Leipzig's musicians were always particularly busy during the fair, for visitors enjoyed musical

Leipzig marketplace. Engraving in author's collection.

interludes in their business affairs. The founding of the university in 1409 and the establishment of the printing industry in 1480 contributed to the city's importance as an intellectual and cultural center.

In settling in Leipzig in 1815, then, Wieck had established himself in the right place at the right time. It not only was a metropolis with a strong commercial and middle-class tradition but one in which music had always had a special position and musicians a favored status. In 1841 a citizen wrote, "In our Leipzig, music . . . the interpreter of all human feelings, was held in high esteem and cultivated with an unmistakable preference."[11]

An active musical life had been recorded in the city since the thirteenth century. Music composed for daily and ceremonial events and performed by town-appointed musicians was described as early as the fifteenth century, and by the seventeenth century private citizens and university students had joined together in a *collegium musicum*, one of the first in Germany. Cultivation of the musical art was well established when Johann Sebastian Bach was employed by the town council in 1723. Unlike Dresden, the nearest large city and the royal seat of Saxony, with a courtly musical tradition and court-sponsored musical activities, Leipzig was a commercial center whose musical life served the needs of middle-class families.

The unusual interest and pride in church music, the traditions associated with the university (where music had been taught as a discipline since its founding), and the musical activities of the middle class encouraged the growth of such institutions as the Grosse Concert, a concert organization created by merchants in 1743, and its successor, the Gewandhaus Concerts, founded in 1781. The Gewandhaus Concerts, in which Clara Wieck was to play more frequently than any other pianist, was governed by a directorate of twelve townspeople, six from the learned professions and six from the mercantile community. In an age when most European musicians were household servants who performed for their aristocratic patrons and invited friends, the establishment of a concert hall in a commercial building and the administration of the concert organization by a group of middle-class citizens was an augury of the coming century, when concerts would be open to all who could afford the price of tickets.* From its inception the Gewandhaus was the leading musical organization in Leipzig. Other musical groups performed in the city, but the Gewandhaus concerts were and remain a unique Leipzig institution.

Theater and opera productions had never flourished in the serious Leipzig community as they did in the court cities of Dresden and Weimar. Until a Leipzig city theater in which both dramas and operas were produced was

---

*In *Geschichte der Gewandhausconcerte zu Leipzig vom 25. November 1781 bis 25. November 1881* (Leipzig, 1884), 15, 251, Alfred Dörffel points out that the name of the building in which the concerts were held reflects the fact that cloth (*Gewand*) was sometimes stored there, but that it actually was a multipurpose building that also housed the city library, with its magnificent collection of manuscripts.

founded in 1817, audiences in the commercial center were entertained by visiting troupes from Dresden. But Wieck attended the theater regularly, and saw to it that his daughter knew the great dramas of Lessing, Goethe, and Schiller as well as the popular operas of the day. The young girl heard an astonishing number of operas; by the time she was twelve she had seen almost every work presented in Leipzig, including operas by Mozart, Beethoven, Weber, and Rossini.*

Printing establishments had existed in Leipzig since the invention of type. At the end of the eighteenth century, eighteen general presses, each employing seventy to eighty people, affirmed the status of literacy and education in this region.[12] A typical Leipzig event that Clara attended was the *Gutenbergsfest,* on June 24, 1840. Processions, music (by Felix Mendelssohn), speeches, fireworks, a great dinner for 3,000 people, and the unveiling of Johann Gutenberg's statue celebrated the three hundredth anniversary of Gutenberg's invention of movable type. Toasts were drunk while music was printed on presses set up in the great square.[13]

In 1815, the year Wieck came to Leipzig, the city, which then had a population of 35,000, was recovering from the upheavals of the Napoleonic Wars. Parts of Saxony had been occupied by French troops, but at the so-called Battle of the Nations, fought on the flat meadowlands surrounding the city, the French were decisively defeated. Peace was restored and commercial life resumed.

Several concerns in Leipzig were already catering to the prosperous musical amateurs, but there was always room for another aspiring dealer. In his store in the Hohe Lilie not far from the main square, Wieck taught, kept his shop, and lived from 1818 to 1821.† An enterprising businessman, he sold and lent music, music books, and periodicals. In addition to pianos, he sold a keyboard instrument known as the physharmonica and such contraptions as the *Handleiter* (wrist guide), trill machines, finger stretchers, silent fingerboards—all devices intended to speed up music learning and teach correct habits to the large numbers of eager middle-class keyboard amateurs.

By the 1820s Wieck was traveling to Vienna regularly to buy pianos. He became friendly with the piano manufacturers Conrad Graf and Andreas Stein, corresponded with the pianist Carl Czerny, and met Beethoven.[14] Wieck impressed Leipzigers with his energy and ambition, and it was assumed he would go far.

Acting with his customary confidence and optimism, Johann Gottlob Friedrich Wieck made a practical and desirable marriage on June 23, 1816.

---

*According to entries in her diary, Clara saw, among other works, Weber's *Oberon,* Mozart's *Zauberflöte,* and Cherubini's *Wasserträger* in 1827 and Spohr's *Faust* in 1828. In 1831 she saw Beethoven's *Fidelio,* three operas by Rossini, and operas by Hummel and Mozart.

†The house, built in 1695, had originally been a guesthouse and later housed a wineshop called Reiche'sche Weinstube in der Lilie. It was still standing before World War II but no longer exists.

The bride was his student Marianne Tromlitz, the high-spirited nineteen-year-old daughter of Christiana Friederike, née Carl, and Georg Christian Gotthold Tromlitz (1765–1825), the cantor in Plauen, a town in southeast Saxony, near what is now the Czech border. Marianne's grandfather, Johann George Tromlitz, a leading flutist, composer, teacher, and flutemaker, had played solo flute in the Grosse Concert and was well known in Leipzig and other German musical centers.[15]

MARIANNE TROMLITZ WIECK BARGIEL, 1797–1872

It is clear that Marianne Tromlitz was an uncommonly talented young woman. In the first year of her marriage, Madame Wieck was singing solos at the weekly concerts in the Leipzig Gewandhaus. A review of Mozart's Requiem, which had been performed on December 15, 1816, referred to the soprano soloist, Madame Wieck, as the young wife of a local piano teacher, and praised her voice and "skill, confidence, and diligence." On March 13, 1817, she sang a solo at a Gewandhaus performance of the Beethoven Mass in C, and she performed in other works on March 27 and April 6, 1817.[16] Wieck was already acquiring a reputation through the talents of a family member. His prestige as a businessman and piano teacher rose with each performance Marianne gave.

To achieve and maintain a successful career, Marianne could not neglect the piano. She continued to study (perhaps with their friend Adolph Bargiel), supervised the household, and assisted Wieck by taking on students in voice and piano. Since she was the skilled pianist in the family, she taught the advanced students. Between household tasks and concert engagements (she was the first of Wieck's students to perform at the Gewandhaus)[17] she gave birth to five children. The first, Adelheid, was born in 1817, a few months after Marianne's first Gewandhaus appearance. Her second child, Clara, was born September 13, 1819, some sixteen months after the death of Adelheid in Plauen. Marianne continued her career after Clara's birth, and on October 18, 1821, appeared with the Gewandhaus orchestra, this time as a pianist, playing Ferdinand Ries's Concerto in E-flat. Her work was not interrupted by the birth of a third child, Alwin, on August 27, 1821, and of still another son, Gustav, on January 31, 1823. Marianne performed at the Gewandhaus in October 1822 and November and December 1823. Her November performance of John Field's Second Piano Concerto was reviewed in the *Allgemeine musikalische Zeitung* in July 1824.[18] By the time the review appeared, Madame Wieck had had one more child, Victor, born February 22, 1824, and had departed the bed and board of Friedrich Wieck.

On May 12, 1824, Marianne Tromlitz Wieck returned to her father's home in Plauen, taking with her her infant son of three months (who did not survive his third year) and her oldest child, Clara, then not quite five years

Marianne Tromlitz shortly before her marriage. Drawing, inscribed to a friend. Courtesy of Herma Stamm-Bargiel.

old. Saxon law assigned the three older children to the custody of the father, since they were legally his property.[19] Wieck permitted Marianne to keep Clara until her fifth birthday, but four days after that date, on September 17, the child was returned to her father in Leipzig. An appeal from the heart-broken Marianne begging Wieck to meet her in September so that Clara could be delivered "from my hands to yours" was ignored.* Johanna Strobel, Friedrich's maid, was sent to fetch the child in Altenburg, a town halfway between Plauen and Leipzig. A sobbing mother and grandmother accompanied Clara to Altenburg, and there she said good-bye.

Marianne Tromlitz Wieck and Friedrich Wieck were granted a divorce on January 22, 1825, and within a few months she was the wife of Adolph Bargiel, the piano teacher who had been Wieck's colleague in his first tutorial position. That she had been in contact with Bargiel through the years is clear from a letter from Marianne's father to Wieck.[20] Tromlitz acknowledged that his daughter might have behaved dishonorably, but chided Wieck for leaving Marianne alone with Bargiel so much. Wieck's driving ambition, vanity, and exploitation of his young wife never came into question.

The Bargiels remained in the vicinity of Leipzig for more than a year after their marriage, and Marianne was permitted to see her children during that time. Clara already dominated the family scene; there is no mention of her brothers in the querulous letter Wieck addressed to the mother of his children:

> Madam! I am sending you the dearest thing in life still left to me, with the proviso, however, that you say nothing, if possible, about what has happened, or that you express yourself simply, truthfully, and at the same time clearly, so that this guiltless, innocent, and natural creature hears nothing that could arouse her suspicions. Furthermore, you will give the child little pastry and make sure you do not condone any naughtiness. . . . When she practices, do not allow her to rush. I expect the most rigorous adherence to my wishes; if not, my anger will be incurred. 7 Nov. 1825.[21]†

Soon after this document was delivered, the Bargiels established themselves in Berlin, where Adolph took over the Logier Institute, a piano school established by Johann Bernhard Logier, a piano pedagogue who had a brilliant and influential but short-lived career in Berlin. The move to Berlin further limited Marianne's contact with Clara and her two sons. In December 1825 Clara suffered another blow. Johanna Strobel, the nursemaid

---

*The letter reproduced in Litzmann, 1:3–4, is identical with Marianne's note in RSH (5966-A2) except for one phrase italicized here), which for some unknown reason was omitted. The mother wrote, "Du bestehst darauf die Clara jetzt zu haben, nun sei es, in Gottesnamen, ich habe Alles versucht dich zu erweichen, *mag das Herz mir brechen*, Du sollst sie haben; jedoch meiner Mutterrechte begabe ich mich nicht" (You insist on having Clara now, so be it, in God's name, I have tried in every way to soften your stand, and *though my heart may break*, you shall have her; but I do not renounce my rights as a mother).

†Wieck addresses his wife in the formal manner, as *Sie*.

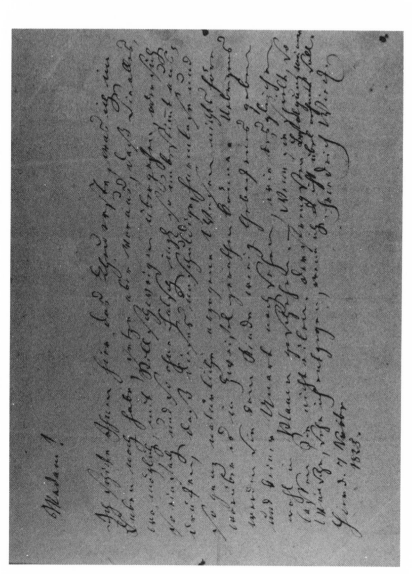

Friedrich Wieck's letter to Mariamne Wieck, Robert-Schumann-Haus, Zwickau, DDR.

who had been with the family since before Clara's birth, was dismissed and a new housekeeper installed. Thus within a year the five-year-old girl lost the two women to whom she was closest. Both were frequently vilified by Wieck; in later years he blamed any misbehavior on Clara's part on "contrariness" inherited from her mother and reinforced by Johanna.[22]

Clara corresponded with her "Berlin mother" and saw her from time to time, usually for short visits when Frau Bargiel was passing through Leipzig on her way to Plauen.* Life was not easy for Frau Bargiel. Divorce was uncommon and always threw a shadow on the woman. The young mother knew that she would lose her children if she left Wieck, but desperation forced the choice; the pressures of living with Wieck must have been unbearable. Though there is little written evidence about tensions or discord in the marriage, enough is known about Wieck to enable us to reconstruct the situation of his young wife. In the seven years of their marriage, she bore five children, practiced under his supervision, sang and played professionally, assisted him with piano pupils, helped with the business, and entertained his friends and business associates. Despite his rationalist education, Wieck's emotions often prevailed over reason. Harsh and stubborn, he dominated, controlled, and used those closest to him. His customers and students valued him and his skills because—it is very clear—he was a man of uncommon intellect and talent. There must have been a bond between the nineteen-year-old Marianne and Wieck at their marriage in 1816, but his demands and expectations, coupled with insensitivity, crudeness, and a cruel temper, drove her to flight. One surviving portrait of the young Marianne depicts a woman of strong character and determination, traits that Clara inherited in full.

Adolph Bargiel, the man to whom Marianne fled, was very different from Wieck, gentle, affectionate, and evidently undemanding.† Though he had more musical education and background than Wieck, he had less business acumen, and he suffered a series of blows in Berlin. The Logier Institute, which had been prospering, was forced to close in 1830 because of a cholera epidemic (all the students left the city). Soon thereafter he suffered a stroke from which he never fully recovered. He died in 1841, leaving Marianne with their four children. She was able to maintain the family by giving piano lessons in Berlin after his death and enlisting the aid of friends. (Robert Schumann was one of those who helped support her during those difficult years.) One of the children of her second marriage achieved musical prominence: Woldemar Bargiel, a composer, pianist, and conductor, later became a close friend and confidant of his half sister, Clara.

Intimacy between Clara and her mother was resumed only when she broke with her father, in 1839. Robert Schumann, who had enjoyed a close relationship with his own mother, got in touch with Marianne Bargiel. Thus Clara, at age twenty, rediscovered her mother and her mother's love. At that time she lived with her mother's sister when she was in Leipzig and with her mother when she was in Berlin. Thereafter she turned to her mother for help at crises throughout her life, and Marianne always responded warmly, immediately, and unselfishly.*

CLARA: THE EARLIEST YEARS

When Clara was born, in September 1819, her father chose her name. He fully expected that Clara—meaning light, brilliance—would be a great virtuosa, trained by him from birth. And indeed, both hereditary and environmental conditions favored such a development. The sounds of piano music were heard continuously in the Wieck house as customers tried out the instruments in the shop. Piano students came and went, and Marianne spent hours preparing for her performances.

The daily routine in the Wieck household included a walk of several hours, in which Clara joined when she was three. Wieck took it for granted that his daughter would keep up with the adults; fortunately, this sturdy child was able to do so. It was a routine that Clara loved and observed all her life; it was a daily necessity for her. Indeed, she attributed her health and longevity to this regular habit.

Aside from the musical activities of the elder Wiecks and the daily walks, very little is known about the first five years of Clara's life, but much can be inferred. An entry in her diary, which her father began for her when she was seven, reports the extraordinary fact that she did not speak—not even single words—until she was over four years old. Her father also recorded that she understood very little. Even when she finally began to speak, her parents assumed she was hard of hearing because she was so self-absorbed and appeared unconcerned with what went on around her. The myth that she was deaf and "slow" arose at this time, and seemed to be common talk in Leipzig.[23]

In the spring before she left home to spend the last few months with her mother, Wieck began, despite the "deafness," to teach her some little pieces by ear. She learned the music without difficulty; it was speech—words— that she could not hear. Soon after she returned from Plauen to live with her father, formal piano lessons with two other girls of her age commenced. At this time she began to speak full sentences, but the "deafness" did not totally disappear until she was eight.†

---

*That Clara ultimately understood her mother's tragedy is clear from the attitudes she held as a mature woman toward divorce and the custody laws. In May 1895, she wrote Brahms that a recently divorced woman acquaintance had fled the country in order to keep her eldest son; Clara Schumann approved (Clara Schumann and Johannes Brahms, *Briefe aus den Jahren 1853–1896* [Leipzig: Breitkopf & Härtel, 1927], 2:583).

†In view of the abilities that Clara manifested later, this may have been what Dr. Anna Burton terms "selective mutism," caused by emotional conflicts.

We may assume that there was a great deal of either angry talk or tense silence during Clara's early years. Wieck was not a man given to self-control. He characterized himself as caustic and blunt; indeed, he gloried in his "unceremonious" behavior.[24] His treatment of Gustav and Alwin was often cruel and physically abusive.[25] When Clara defied him, his bitter anger was never modulated. When in 1840 she refused to give up plans to marry Robert Schumann, Wieck sought revenge by sending defamatory letters about her to Berlin and Hamburg, where she was about to perform. The letters, which circulated among influential musicians and music lovers, described Clara as a "demoralized, shameless girl who has opposed her father in the most unnatural and shocking manner," and warned that other girls should be guarded lest they be "poisoned" by her.[26] And his efforts to besmirch the name of Schumann continued even after Clara had become Frau Schumann.

In view of Wieck's documented conduct toward his children, we may assume that Marianne, too, suffered his anger if she deviated from his expectations. And his expectations were onerous: his wife was to be artist and teacher as well as mother and wife, and was to submit to his will in all things. Considering Wieck's domineering personality and Marianne's tasks, the probability of normal and friendly communication between them in the eight years of their marriage seems small indeed. Johanna Strobel, the housemaid in whose care Clara was left and with whom she formed a close attachment, was described by Wieck himself as "not talkative."[27] Thus Clara did not hear much speech, the first requirement for learning to talk. And in all likelihood, her mother was not only overwhelmed by all her duties but probably too angry for the kind of patient exchange children need in order to develop speech. Clara's "deafness" and "self-absorption" may well have served as a buffer against the tensions in the house: it would be more comfortable to shut out words than to endure the sounds of displeasure and disapproval. Music, on the other hand, was not angry or threatening. It was safe. All her life it was to be a solace from which she could gain relief from pain and tragedy.

Left without a wife, Wieck turned to his five-year-old daughter as the instrument of his musical ambition. She was to show the world what Friedrich Wieck could do. The girl responded nobly.

Wieck did not remarry for some time. For four years Clara and her brothers lived in a motherless home under the care of her father and servants. During this time she studied with her father and rapidly gained attention as a child prodigy. Her brothers had neither her aptitude nor her compliant personality, and were largely ignored while Clara, the eldest child and only daughter, dominated the household. When she was nine, Wieck at last decided to marry again. On July 3, 1828, in the presence of his three children, he married Clementine Fechner, the twenty-three-year-old daughter of a pastor, Samuel Traugott Fechner.[28] Three days after the wedding, on what presumably was their honeymoon, Wieck, Clementine, and

Clara visited Dresden, where the child gave some private performances.

At the time of Wieck's second marriage, his business was firmly established and, thanks to his daughter (and his first wife), he already had a considerable reputation as a piano teacher. Clementine Wieck faced a formidable adversary in the person of her nine-year-old stepdaughter. To the two motherless boys she was undoubtedly a welcome addition to the household, but to Clara she was a rival, and for the most part an unsuccessful one. Clementine was in an unenviable position. Clara never relinquished her position as the star. Clementine remained at home with the other children and ran Wieck's business while he was off touring with Clara. All his energy and skills were devoted to his eldest child, the most gifted of his and Marianne's three surviving children. For years the household revolved about her and her needs: the silk gowns necessary for concerts, her own room, special pianos brought from Vienna. All the father's expectations centered on this daughter. The two boys, in contrast, having already lost their mother at the ages of one and three, were virtually booted out of the house as soon as they were old enough to survive on their own.

Clementine and Friedrich Wieck had three children. Marie, born in 1832, was groomed by her father to emulate Clara. She also played at the Gewandhaus and had a fairly successful career as a pianist, eventually receiving the title of *Fürstliche Hohenzollern Hof- und Kammervirtuosin* (Court Pianist to the Prince of Hohenzollern). She never achieved the fame and brilliant success of her older half sister, and her jealousy and hostility were poorly concealed in the book she wrote after Clara's death, *Aus dem Kreise Wieck-Schumann* (From the Wieck-Schumann Circle). Marie Wieck never married. Her father was her hero, and, unlike her half sister, she never withdrew her loyalty from him. The other two children of the second marriage did not live to adulthood.

Clementine Wieck was not a musician and from all accounts was possessed of great patience—two facts that undoubtedly contributed to the success of the marriage, which endured forty-five years. The relationship between her and her stepdaughter, on the other hand, was, as might be expected, always strained. With Clementine, Clara acted out emotions she controlled in her father's presence. (Clementine is rarely mentioned in the diary by either Friedrich or Clara, and when her name does appear, it is not always in a complimentary context. Clara commented on October 24, 1833, for example, "My little sister Marie seems to be a born singer since she screams when Mother—who sings off-key—sings. When I sing, she laughs and listens happily.") Wieck's letters to his wife in 1830, when he and Clara embarked on the first of many tours that were to take them away from home for several months at a time, indicate that Clementine Wieck was a woman of intelligence, culture, and capabilities. She managed the piano business during his absence, handled the correspondence, and above all, remained completely obedient.

The letters also reveal another side of Wieck: he had a sense of humor—

Marie Wieck, half sister of Clara Wieck. From Marie Wieck, *Aus dem Kreise Wieck-Schumann* (Dresden: v. Zahn & Jaensch, 1914).

earthy, at times even coarse—and no hesitations about expressing it. His humor, vivacity, and practical common sense, combined with his self-confidence and generally acknowledged talent as a teacher, explain how this otherwise formidable man could charm and gain the respect of the musical circles of Leipzig. His pedagogical principles, published in 1853 in a small book, *Clavier und Gesang*, were successfully applied to his docile and willing pupil Clara, and gained him worldwide fame.

CHAPTER 2

Clara's Career Begins

The girlhood diaries of Clara Wieck are an unparalleled source of information about her education, career, and the musicians and musical life she knew. Most significant, however, is what they reveal about Friedrich Wieck and the nature of the relationship between father and daughter. Until she was eighteen years old, almost every diary entry was written or supervised by her father. The title page reads: "My diary, begun by my father, the seventh of June 1827, and continued by Clara Josephine Wieck."* Thus Clara was seven years old when the diary, which was to be the "dearest companion" of her life, began.[1] The diary is visible evidence of Wieck's domination.† On May 24, 1831, he wrote in Clara's name, "From now on, I will write in my diary myself, whenever I have some time." But he made certain that she had very little time. Those sections that were written by Clara were examined by her father; he frequently made emendations and comments in the margins. Many of the entries in her hand were painstaking copies of the acerbic letters he wrote to associates, friends, and enemies, letters in which he made demands, threatened, castigated, denigrated, and denounced. Clara copied angry letters to the Gewandhaus directorate regarding her fees, letters to editors complaining about her reviews, arguments over money owed her father.

Wieck used the diaries as a way of communicating with and educating his child; he preached and philosophized. Information, praise, reproach, con-

---

*Litzmann gave the wrong date, May 7, 1827, on the title page of vol. 1 and omitted mention of other information that appeared on that page. On the lower part of the page is an inscription signed by Friedrich Wieck in Dresden and dated March 1859 which reads, "Notebooks 1–6 given by me to my daughter Clara Schumann and belonging to her." On the verso of the title page is a note written by Clara Schumann in Frankfurt on June 6, 1889: "When I die, I want my daughter Marie to receive all my diaries, since she is the oldest of all the sisters and brothers, and was ever my truest nurse and friend."

†Though Litzmann's biography is based on the diaries, he rarely distinguishes between the entries made by Wieck and those written by Clara.

demnation, exhortation are all clearly seen in his black, bold handwriting, but he persisted in using the first person throughout, as though Clara were writing; he even referred to himself as "Father." Most startling is the way he seemed to be taking over her personal identity.

A revealing entry written by Wieck in Dresden on June 17, 1834, reads: "Father arrived by express coach at seven in the evening. I flew into his arms and took him right to the Hotel Stadt Frankfurt." On February 28, 1833, he noted, "I played the 'Bravour' Variations of Herz (without rehearsal) and Hummel's D-Minor Septet in the 18th subscription concert. Everything was received with great enthusiasm." A few months later, on April 8, 1833 (Clara was then almost fourteen years old), we find, "My own concert in the Gewandhaus. The newspaper published a fine article about me." On the rare occasions on which he wrote as Friedrich Wieck, his daughter is referred to as "my Clara."

Only when Clara left home at the age of nineteen did the diary finally become her own. The last notebook, begun on April 23, 1838, accompanied her to Paris on her first independent tour and closed on September 12, 1840, the day of her marriage. Wieck retained possession of all her other childhood diaries until March 1859, when he finally handed them over to her. By the time he was able to part with this record of her early years, she was a forty-year-old widow with seven children.

A not unintended effect of this kind of diary keeping was a practical education: by copying his letters and reading his entries in her diary, Clara learned how to manage a correspondence and arrange a concert tour. She also absorbed—through her eyes, ears, and fingers—her father's attitudes toward money and success and something of his competitive personality and belligerent spirit.

The diary for 1838–40 is unique in that it furnishes an intimate record of her thoughts without her father's intervention. After her marriage and until 1844, the couple kept a joint diary, which is extant. And though, like many nineteenth-century diarists, Clara considered her journal a part of herself—it was at once a means of communication, a confessional, and a catharsis—the later ones, those from 1844 to 1896, cannot be found.*

In an 1831 letter to his wife, written during Clara's first extended tour, Wieck described a scene with a Frau Schmidt, the influential wife of a Weimar government official. She reproached him for allowing Clara to perform so much and not giving her time to play with other children. He replied angrily, "I have thought about education for twenty-five years and put my theories into practice. For the last seven years I have lived only for the education of my daughter. If, however, I still need advice, I will ask for it at the right time—and until then I decline to accept any."[2]

*Martin Schoppe, director of Robert-Schumann-Haus, Zwickau, believes that the later diaries were destroyed after Litzmann used them, presumably by order of Marie Schumann.

Wieck was justly proud of his skill in teaching. He had developed pedagogical theories during his years as a tutor, and his approach to his
daughter's instruction was carefully considered; it was a planned program
that included supervision of her every waking hour. From the moment Clara
was returned to her father's home, a few days after her fifth birthday, she
was in training.

Wieck began to work with her alone in the spring of 1825. She did not
learn to read music during her first year of instruction (though she learned to
write notes). Small pieces, written expressly for her, encouraged her to
concentrate on position, musical phrasing, and a "singing" tone, and provided a familiarity with the keyboard which accounted for the facility and
ease she kept to the end of her life. At the age of seven she was at the piano
for three hours a day—one hour for a lesson and two for practice.

Her meager general education was squeezed into the hours between the
piano and the daily walks. For six months beginning in January 1825 she
attended a neighborhood primary school run by a Demoiselle Marbach, and
then she was sent to the Noack Institute, a larger establishment, for perhaps
another year. Wieck deliberately limited her hours of school attendance; he
gave her a lesson every morning before school and often an additional one in
the afternoon. The months at the two primary schools constituted her only
formal education. Thus she lacked the usual opportunities for social intercourse with her contemporaries, obviously not an important consideration
for her father.

In *Clavier und Gesang*, the treatise Wieck wrote in 1853, he explained:

> My daughters always had a special tutor with whom I worked so that with
> just a few hours a day, their general education could keep pace with their
> artistic training and still leave enough time to exercise outdoors and
> strengthen their bodies, while other children have to sweat for nine hours
> a day on school benches and pay for this with the loss of their health and a
> happy childhood.[3]

Wieck's goal was to create a virtuosa. To achieve this goal, he wrote, "the
whole education from the earliest youth must be planned accordingly."[4]*
Clara learned what her father thought she needed to know—reading, writing, and, with private tutors, French and English, the languages required
for the concert tours Wieck expected to arrange for her. In addition there
were private lessons in theory and harmony with Christian Theodore
Weinlig, cantor of the St. Thomas Church, and composition with Heinrich
Dorn, director of the Leipzig Opera; she had lessons with outstanding teach-

*From the unpublished diary we learn more details: lessons in score reading and instrumen-
tation began in February 1831 (when Clara was eleven) and violin lessons with a Herr Prinz
began at about the same time. She began taking two lessons a week in counterpoint with
Heinrich Dorn in June 20, 1832, and in April 1833 she began a daily fifteen-minute voice lesson
with her father.

ers in the cities where she toured, studying counterpoint with Siegfried Dehn in Berlin, for example. She was sent to Dresden to study orchestration with Carl Reissiger, the kapellmeister, and voice with Johann Aloys Miksch, the renowned voice teacher. Wieck had her take violin lessons and study score reading with Leipzig teachers, and provided some sessions in religion to prepare her for confirmation at age fourteen. These lessons rounded out her education as Wieck conceived it. There was not much time for childish play or reading, but enough for many evenings of concerts, opera, and drama. Beginning at the age of six, she saw almost every opera mounted in Leipzig, and Wieck made a point of attending the opera in every city in which they toured. She prepared for these performances by studying the scores with her father.

Before she was nine, Clara was a member of the music circle that met at the Wiecks'.[5] In 1828 the group included Friedrich Hofmeister and Heinrich Probst, music publishers; Heinrich Marschner, composer; Dr. Ernst August Carus, a physician and music lover; and Gottfried Fink, editor of the *Allgemeine musikalische Zeitung*. A visitor recalled many years later, "Wieck's home was always the gathering place for local and visiting musicians and friends of music. Every composer and virtuoso who came to Leipzig found that the morning or evening gatherings there offered the best opportunity to play and to hear new things. The soul of the entire proceedings was Father Wieck, who, when he was in a good mood, sparkled with humor."[6] Robert Schumann, who arrived in Leipzig for a permanent stay in 1830, joined the Wieck circle and saw the family almost every day.

Frau Wieck did not take part in these musicales, but Clara, who was a more skillful pianist than her father, was very much in evidence, playing old and new works. The artist Johann Lyser, a friend of Schumann, remembered, "What could match those evenings when Francilla Pixis [singer and daughter of the composer Johann Pixis] and that *Wundermädchen* Clara sang and played together?"[7]

Wieck deliberately slowed the pace of public appearances. Clara played with professional musicians, but the first performances were at home and for Leipzig and Dresden friends.

With her first appearance at the Gewandhaus, on October 20, 1828, Clara, like her mother before her, brought Wieck into the public eye. Although her part in the concert was minor (she played a duet with Emilie Reichold, another Wieck student), she—and her father—were mentioned in the *Allgemeine musikalische Zeitung's* review of the concert:

> It was especially pleasing to hear the young, musically talented Clara Wiek [*sic*], just nine years old, perform . . . to universal and well-earned applause Kalkbrenner's Variations on a March from Moses. We may entertain the greatest hopes for this child who has been trained under the direction of her experienced father, who understands the art of piano playing so well and teaches with devotion and great skill.[8]

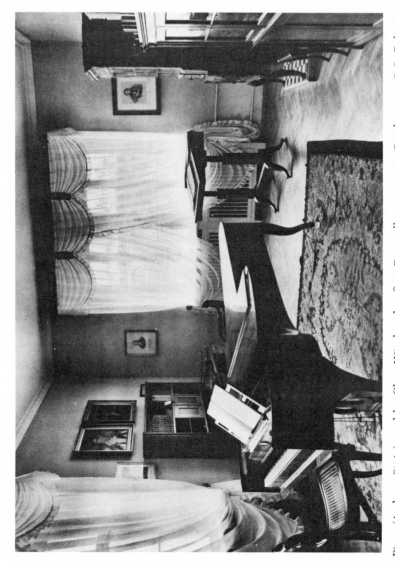

Piano (Andreas Stein) used by Clara Wieck at her first Gewandhaus concert, October 20, 1828. Robert-Schumann-Haus, Zwickau, DDR.

Clara's first appearances outside the familiar circles of her home took place in Dresden between March 6 and April 7, 1830. The ultimate purpose of the trip was clearly set forth by Wieck in letters to his wife: they were there to make connections that would enable them to play at court and to obtain introductions to the larger and more prominent Berlin and Vienna courts.

Father and daughter performed perfectly; Clara won all hearts and Wieck was besieged by requests to give lessons and share the secrets of his success. Moreover, he wrote his wife, the cognoscenti found it very "noble" of him to reject offers of public concerts. He was biding his time.

Clara was invited everywhere; aristocratic ladies vied with each other in bestowing rings, chains, and earrings on the ten-year-old child; older girls and titled ladies came to fix her hair. Wieck was careful to see that her head was not turned by the praise and compliments. "If I notice anything the least bit damaging, I will leave immediately, so that she can be in orderly middle-class surroundings. I am too proud of her unpretentiousness to exchange it for any wordly honors."[9]

So successful was the trip that Wieck seriously considered moving to Dresden, where he felt more appreciation would be shown for his talents. On March 19, 1830, he wrote to his wife:

> The sensation the two apes from the Leipzig menagerie are making here is not to be described. In Leipzig, they are too amazed and too nasty to understand the unique qualities of this goose among so many geese, to realize what an extraordinary child Clara is, and even less that your Fritz from Pretzsch could possess and educate this very same Clara. Everyone assures us that your two apes are the talk of the court and the town. It seems to have only the best effect on Clara because she is playing with a self-assurance that she has never shown before and she is, and remains, the Clara of old.[10]

The summer of 1830 was spent in preparation for her first solo concert in Leipzig, but the events of the year caused more than one change in plans. Repercussions of the July Revolution in Paris, the uprisings in Poland, and the subsequent disturbances in Dresden reached Leipzig; Clara's concert, originally scheduled for September, was postponed to November. Meanwhile, another event that was to have profound significance in Clara's life took place: in October a new pupil-boarder named Robert Schumann moved into the Wieck household. Schumann had returned to Leipzig after a short interlude in Heidelberg, where he had gone ostensibly to study law; now he intended to devote himself to music.

Political events and even the handsome new boarder were of lesser importance than Clara's first solo concert, which took place at the Gewandhaus on November 8, 1830. Wieck gave the Leipzig audience what was expected of a virtuoso artist, and secured the financial returns and the reviews he hoped for. Clara, "the eleven-year-old daughter of a local piano dealer and expert piano teacher," was hailed for her talent, industry, and excellent instruction.[11]

The success of the Gewandhaus concert and additional Dresden appearances spurred Wieck's ambitions. Convinced that Clara was ready for Paris, the center of the musical world at that time, he prepared to leave his pregnant wife and other children, his pupils, and his business and devote himself wholly to Clara's career.

His not unwilling daughter was set to studying new music and French to prepare for the big concert tour that would take her to Paris and, her father hoped, international renown. Father and daughter departed at the end of September 1831. Traveling night and day (Wieck would not part with an extra groschen merely for comfort), they jolted through Thuringia to Kassel and Frankfurt and thence through Darmstadt and Mainz to Paris, not to return until the following May.

Their first stop, only a day's trip by coach, was Weimar, where, through the efforts of a music-loving official, Clara played at private homes and stirred Johann Wolfgang von Goethe's interest. The great poet, who had heard many child prodigies in his day, was more than cordial and gave them an accolade Wieck had hardly dared hope for: a medal with his portrait and a note inscribed: "For the gifted artist Clara Wieck." Wieck's talents were not overlooked. In a written dedication, the great poet thanked him for his "masterly musical entertainment."[12]

Wieck believed that no musician had ever been so highly honored by Goethe (he was obviously unaware of the impact on the poet of the twelve-year-old Mendelssohn some ten years earlier), and asked his wife to be sure to tell Friedrich Hofmeister, the music publisher, that Clara had played at the Weimar court and *twice* for Goethe. He continually reminded her of the need to have Clara's success mentioned in the newspapers and requested that Hofmeister and Robert Schumann (already involved in musical journalism) do what they could about publicity.

They succeeded. A review from the Weimar correspondent appeared in the *Allgemeine musikalische Zeitung* in March 1832:

> Even in her first piece, the artist who is still so young reaped thundering approval that mounted to enthusiasm in the works that followed. And indeed, the great skill, assurance, and strength with which she plays even the most difficult movements so easily is highly remarkable. Even more remarkable is the spirit and feeling of her performance; one could scarcely wish for more.[13]

The journey progressed through Erfurt, Arnstadt, and Gotha with alternating fortunes. In some towns they found decent concert halls, good pianos, appreciative and knowledgeable audiences; others lacked one or more of these elements. In each situation, good or bad, however, Wieck had to perform the same chores—find lodging, provide himself and his child with food, cajole prospective patrons, make the proper contacts, rent the halls, try out the pianos, calculate which piece would have the best effect, publicize the event, and collect the money. And in each town Clara dutifully copied into her diary Wieck's letters to friends and foes, excoriating the provincial audiences and unresponsive patrons, commenting on fees, complimentary tickets, programs, and instruments. She was learning how to manage a concert tour; this practical education formed the basis of her own managerial skills later on.

The ambitious Wieck spent his remaining time writing. He believed he had something to say about piano playing—the fruits of twenty years of study—and, emulating Schumann, he penned a review of Frédéric Chopin's op. 2, variations on "Là ci darem la mano."[14]

This work of Chopin's youth was one of the staples of the young Clara's repertoire. Published in the spring of 1830 and first performed at the Gewandhaus on October 27, 1831, by Julius Knorr, a contemporary and friend of Robert Schumann, it was the subject of Schumann's first music review, probably his best-known literary piece.[15] At his first hearing of the Chopin work, Wieck realized its potential as a vehicle for his daughter, and he set her to work on the piece during the summer before her big tour. An entry in her diary, written on June 8, 1831, by her father, reads, "Chopin's Variations, op. 2, which I learned in eight days, is the hardest piece I have seen or played till now. This original and inspired composition is still so little known that almost all pianists and teachers consider it incomprehensible and impossible to play."

From Frankfurt, Wieck sent his review to Eduard Fechner, his wife's brother and a well-established artist in Paris, requesting him to give it to Chopin.* Chopin had his permission, he wrote, to edit the essay, translate, it, and turn it over to François-Joseph Fétis, the powerful editor of the *Revue Musicale*. Wieck assumed that his essay would serve as a brilliant introduction for them in Paris.[16] He proudly called the review, written in a high-flown style (in unconscious imitation of Schumann?), "a rhapsody" and "a fantasy." (He sent a copy to Frau Wieck with a note: "Schumann may read it. . . .True, it is not so poetic as his, but it is clear, strong, and rough.")[17] The fastidious Chopin was not impressed and wrote disdainfully to a friend, "One can die of the imagination of this German, who insists that his brother-in-law should send it to Fétis for the *Revue Musicale;* from this the good [Ferdinand] Hiller rescued me with difficulty by telling the brother-in-law that the thing is not clever at all but very stupid."[18]

In Frankfurt the Wiecks learned that Clementine had given birth to a daughter in January 1832. The new father responded by asking his wife what the child would be named (it was Marie) and remembered to express his concern for the health of mother and child in a few affectionate sentences.

---

*Litzmann mistakenly refers to Fechner as Wieck's cousin.

The bulk of the letter, however, described Clara's triumph at a concert of the Museum, the leading Frankfurt concert society. This was the sixteenth such event of their journey. She played so beautifully, he wrote, that the orchestra applauded at the rehearsal and at the performance, indicating their approval by tapping their bows in the stands, a real tribute from her older colleagues.

Though Wieck, feeling the strain of incessant travel, complained long and loudly of the lack of appreciation accorded his twelve-year-old treasure on this trip, she actually received glowing notices in almost every town. The girl herself seemed to flourish despite the tiring trip, and they pushed on.

As Clara made her way toward Paris, she practiced, studied new works, performed, composed, and took her daily walk. Still the dutiful daughter, she copied her father's letters into her diary, ostensibly to improve her handwriting. She studied French to prepare for Paris, but she was no longer a child—and perhaps never had been in the usual sense.

Wieck's boast when he told Frau Schmidt that Clara did not have time to play with dolls or other children reflected his sincere belief that his training gave her more happiness than the usual pleasures of childhood. Though he insisted that he cherished her childishness, her naturalness, her innocence, he exploited her musical gifts, treating her as a professional. Even in her first concerts, Clara played with the tone and musical understanding of an adult musician.

The impression she made on perceptive onlookers in Weimar was described in a letter by the tutor of the duke of Weimar:

> We heard the little Wieck of Leipzig—she's a veritable marvel; for the first time in my life I caught myself admiring with enthusiasm a precocious talent: perfect execution, irreproachable measure, force, clarity, difficulties of all sorts successfully surmounted—here are rare things at any age—but still one encounters them occasionally, and if little Clara had offered nothing more, I should have said that she was a machine, to play so remarkably, and I would have remained cold as a stone; but she is a musician, she feels what she plays and knows how to express it; under her fingers the piano takes on color and life; one takes an interest in her without wanting to, and if she does not succumb early to some lingering illness, she will not have much need of beauty in order to become a tempting siren. Poor child! She has a look of unhappiness and of suffering, which distresses me; but she owes perhaps a part of her fine talent to this inclination to melancholy; in examining closely the attributes of the Muses, one could almost always find there some traces of tears. [19]

The portrait of Clara sketched by her stepmother's brother in Paris in 1832 shows a thin-faced girl with a small chin and enormous dark eyes, her hair swept into a kind of chignon topped by a large, fluttering ribbon. Her head, held slightly to one side, seems too small for the elaborate off-the-shoulder

Clara Wieck, age 13, in Paris. Lithograph by Eduard Fechner, 1832. Robert-Schumann-Haus, Zwickau, DDR.

gown with huge puffy sleeves. A filmy net covers the decolletage and a frilly collar accentuates the neck and thin sloping shoulders. The waist is tightly cinched with a wide belt. Clara is wearing long, dangling earrings. Most striking is the wistful expression about her mouth and the unusual, slightly exotic eyes. The sharp, pointed chin betrays the child.

Within a year after her return from Paris, a description of Clara was published in the Hamburg journal *Caecilia,* edited by Johann Peter Lyser, a friend of Robert Schumann. A prominent feature of this short-lived publication was a six-page essay on Clara Wieck. Whether Lyser wrote the following description or whether, as Wieck speculated, it was based on a letter by Heinrich Heine is not known. That it was written by an astute observer, however, is clear:

> At first glance Clara seems to be a quite lovable thirteen-year-old girl . . . and one thinks no more about it—but, observed more closely, everything seems quite different! The delicate, pretty little face with the somewhat strangely shaped eyes, the friendly mouth with the touch of sentiment that now and then draws up in a somewhat mocking or wistful way, particularly when she answers. And the mixture of grace and carelessness in her movements—not studied, but it goes far beyond one of her years. All this—I confess it openly—stirred a quite peculiar feeling in me when I saw it. I know of no better way to describe it except as "an echo of Clara's mocking-painful" smile. It seems as though the child could tell a long story, a story woven out of joy and pain—and yet—what does she know? Music.[20]

Wieck was pleased, as always, by the references to his child, apparently disregarding the allusions to melancholy, tears, and pain.

The time spent in Paris—February 15 to April 13, 1832—gave Clara the cachet of Parisian concert, and it exposed the girl to new music, new manners, and new values, all of which she quietly absorbed. Yet she hardly made the impact on Parisian musical life her father seems to have envisioned. Though she and a Frenchwoman shopped hurriedly for the requisite new dresses and hats, the serious child with the awkward, aggressive father could not conquer the glamorous French capital. He wrote to his wife:

> You should see me at the soirees in yellow gloves and white neckband, speaking half German and half French and half despairing, hat in hand, from 10 in the evening till 2 in the morning, always pricking up my ears to make sure I will not miss anything. Child, you won't recognize your Friedrich again. You have never seen a more interesting sight.[21]

Wieck was determined to display Clara's talent and was willing to ignore the discomforts and financial costs of a Paris stay. But even the redoubtable Friedrich Wieck quailed at the thought of having to make himself understood in French. One senses from his letters that he is feeling distinctly uncomfortable in this center of Gallic fashion and grace.

"Our French doesn't help us at all, un pauvre allemand ne comprend pas un mot à Paris" he complained. "Everything is different here—everything! . . . One sleeps, eats, drinks differently." Worst of all, he had not been able to smoke in his carriage for four days on the way to Paris, and once there he could smoke only in his room. "Clara can never compensate me for what I am doing for her," he wrote.[22] This complaint may have been written half-mockingly, as far as the smoking was concerned, but it was a motif that ran through his relationship with Clara from that time on.

Wieck lamented that in Paris everything was done for superficial reasons, for the sake of appearances. Clara had to be dressed entirely in white and had to wear a new dress at each appearance—but the Parisians didn't care about cleanliness. "One small napkin is used for the whole week, and one glass of water is provided in the morning for washing." And, he adds, reminding us that he was traveling with an adolescent, "That suits our Clara just fine." He was overwhelmed by French customs; his pen failed him, and he promised he would have tales to tell when he returned to Leipzig. "You should see the life here. Ce n'est pas dire!"[23]

Without Eduard Fechner, Wieck's brother-in-law, they never could have made their way. He arranged Clara's first appearances at the Parisian salons of two wealthy music lovers, Madame Valentin and Madame Leo.[24] Through the latter, a patroness of many musicians, they met many eminent composers living in Paris that winter. Giacomo Meyerbeer presented them with tickets to his *Robert le Diable*, the spectacular audience-pleaser then reigning at the opera. Felix Mendelssohn, ten years older than Clara and later to become her fast friend, was already a sophisticated, well-traveled young man, not to be compared with the provincials from Saxony. Friedrich Kalkbrenner, the composer and pianist, admired the girl's playing but fell into a dispute with the quarrelsome father. The Wiecks found it difficult to establish a relationship with Chopin (they were not privy to the letter in which he had commented on the "stupid" review). Johann Pixis and Heinrich Herz, composers whose works Clara played, remained kindly but distant, but Niccolò Paganini, who remembered them from Leipzig, and Pierre Erard, the piano manufacturer, were friendlier and more helpful.

In Paris it was customary to play at soirées in the lavish homes of aristocrats or wealthy music lovers, await a newspaper mention, and then, at the right moment, schedule a public concert. Unfortunately, the right moment never came. First a Paganini concert at which Clara had the opportunity to be an assisting artist was canceled because of the violinist's illness. A concert at the music school of a friend, Franz Stoepel, on March 19 was a success, but the big concert arranged for April 9 at the Hôtel de Ville had to be held at Stoepel's small auditorium instead because of a cholera epidemic and few people attended. The Wiecks left Paris almost immediately after the last recital and arrived in Leipzig on May 1, 1832.

Friedrich Wieck, an astute businessman, prepared for Clara's appearances with great care. Although he believed in a dignified approach, he was not averse to capitalizing on the public interest in the young girl. At her concerts he peddled engravings of the portrait of her painted by Fechner, his Parisian brother-in-law. The engravings sold well and new ones were ordered in August 1832. (Clara noted in her diary that copies were sent to Robert Schumann and her "Berlin mother.")

Wieck never forgot the poverty of his childhood and never scorned an opportunity to make a thaler. For him money was a powerful source of security and he impressed its importance on his young daughter, conveying in many ways the lesson that money could be equated with love. From her earliest years Clara was rewarded with money for her playing and for learning quickly. All sums earned from concerts were noted in her diary by her father; he also recorded the costs of gifts he gave her, as on April 24, 1834: "Father bought me a large beautiful gold chain at Herr Struve for 45 reichstaler; it is worth 32 reichstaler in gold."

Wieck's interest in money was well known to everyone in Leipzig (Schumann referred to him as "Meister Allesgeld"—Master All-for-Money); businessmen appreciated his shrewdness. He worked out barter arrangements so that Clara could take French or theory lessons in exchange for the loan of a guitar or piano from his shop. Her father had contempt for payments in jewelry for his artist daughter; such gifts were immediately appraised and turned into cash. Those patrons who did not deliver the expected fees were roundly berated in letters that the child copied into her diary.

The money Clara earned at concerts was collected by Wieck (quite literally collected—he often stood at the door as the audience poured in) and invested in state bonds and in all likelihood in his business as well. From these funds Clara received rewards from her father when she played particularly well and small sums, perhaps eight groschen, after a concert—enough for a treat in a café. She paid for her own lessons if he was unable to arrange a trade with another teacher. As her father, teacher, and concert manager, Wieck believed he was entitled to the money she earned, and told her so in later years when Clara requested the return of money for which she had worked. Legally the money was his; social and economic restrictions on women remained in force longer in Germany than in most Western countries.[25] Wieck claimed, moreover, that he had a moral right to this money, since—as he pointed out in her diary and in the letters she copied—he had neglected the education of her siblings and given up other pupils so that he could devote himself entirely to her education and career. Though Clara may have felt some guilt over the treatment of her brothers, she was led to accept the situation as quite normal and natural. The attentions received,

[54

the marks of preference shown by her father, the applause of the audiences were gratifying. The realization that she might have been exploited occurred to her only in 1839, when the father she had loved and trusted refused her the thousands of thaler she had earned through her talents—and which he had, in the meantime, saved and invested. When she persisted in plans to marry Robert Schumann, she was informed that she owed Wieck money for the lessons he had given her. He also demanded that she share her earnings with her brothers and other family members. During the battle she told Robert, with some bitterness, that she had never received so much as a pin from her stepmother; she was always told to use her own money.[26] Even after a court had ruled in favor of her marriage and the banns were announced, Wieck kept the proceeds of her concerts. She was forced to bring suit to recover the money for which she had labored, but the matter did not go to court. After her marriage, it was finally settled through an intermediary.[27]

Clara's wistful, "mocking-painful" smile was the only outward manifestation of childhood unhappiness. The docile daughter occasionally exhibited "willful" or "contrary" behavior, which Wieck attributed to her mother and the influence of the maid Hanne. (Thus the two women she loved in her early years were similarly censured.) Her conduct was easily controlled by her father. For this child, to whom music and playing the piano were indispensable—perhaps even equivalent to love—prohibitions against playing or practicing were terrifying. Wieck punished infractions of behavior by withholding lessons or favorite pieces. Nine days after her first public appearance at the Gewandhaus, on October 20, 1828, the following entry was made in her diary:

> My father, who long had hoped for a change of disposition on my part, observed again today that I am just as lazy, careless, disorderly, stubborn, disobedient, etc. as ever, and that I am the same in my piano playing and my studies. And because I played Hünten's new Variations op. 26 for him so badly, and didn't repeat the first part of the first variation, not even once, he tore up the copy before my eyes, and from today on he will not give me any more lessons and I may not play anything but scales, Cramer's Etudes, Book I, and Czerny's trilling exercises.

On November 5 the instruction was resumed, after the "lazy and stubborn" child solemnly promised to change.

Possibly because of her sex and her moneymaking ability, Clara was never subjected to the abuse that Wieck unleased on his sons. Robert Schumann, whose own family life had been quiet and affectionate, described one episode in his diary on May 21, 1831:

> Yesterday I saw a scene whose impression will be indelible. Meister Raro [Wieck] is surely a wicked man. Alwin had not played well: "You wretch,

you wretch—is this the pleasure you give you father"—how he threw him on the floor, pulled him by the hair, trembled and staggered, sat still to rest and gain strength for new feats, could barely stand on his legs anymore and had to throw his prey down, how the boy begged and implored him to give him the violin—he wanted to play, he wanted to play—I can barely describe it—and to all this—Zilia [Clara] smiled and calmly sat herself down at the piano with a Weber sonata.

The horrified Robert added: "Am I among humans?"[28]

As a close observer of the Wieck family scene, Schumann also noted the interplay among daughter, stepmother, and father. When Clara was almost twelve, he wrote that he discerned "a trace of peevishness, capriciousness, and even a semblance of ill will in her conduct toward her stepmother." A year later he wrote, "Clara displays great obstinacy toward her stepmother, who is certainly a woman worthy of respect. The old man rebukes Clara, but nevertheless he is coming under her thumb more and more. She is giving orders like a señora—but she can also beg and cajole like a child."[29]

At fifteen Clara actively began to defy her father. On a concert tour to Magdeburg, Hannover, and other northern cities in 1834–35 the baffled father had a rebellious adolescent on his hands:

Clara now is often so inconsiderate, domineering, full of unreasonable opposition, careless, totally disobedient, rude, prickly, blunt, monstrously lazy, capriciously vain about rags [clothes] (we cannot even speak of other kinds of vanity because she no longer has the slightest interest in her art—and certainly no time to study—since she gets up at nine o'clock and isn't ready till half past ten, then receives visitors, is invited to dinner at noon, and in the afternoon is desperately unhappy if she should have to play, because then she is thinking only of the theater and—the gentlemen). In short, what is to become of her, God only knows—she certainly cannot remain at home. I will be irritated with her for the rest of my life; I can hardly enjoy anything about her without grief. A day doesn't pass when she doesn't vex me with all the things I mentioned. If I were not here, she would not perfect one single piece. She is so distracted that as a rule she doesn't even know if she is playing and her obstinacy about it all distorts her face. I will not be able to sell the pianos because she is so heedless that she is continually finding fault with them, complaining to other people about how hard they are to play and giving them a bad reputation.[30]

One can almost feel sorry for the father, surprised by the treacherous vagaries of the adolescent. She had not only been the proverbial apple of his eye; she had reigned over the entire household, and understandably so. Her concerts brought a sizable income; her labor attracted pupils and publicity for his business. Her talents gave him status and prestige, the means to travel, and opportunities to mix with great musicians, the rich, and the noble. Her concerts were his concerts, her reviews his. He shared in the tension, the mishaps, the success, the applause. A letter he wrote to his wife from Magdeburg tells part of the story:

> Listen, it is a miracle that the anxiety and anger I had last night didn't do me in. Just think, there were 600 people in the hall, unbelievably full because of Clara; the piano keys began to stick . . . in the Finale of the Chopin Concerto; fortunately, everything turned out well but it took much worry and lots of sweat to get through it. During the intermission I had to take the keyboard out in full view of the audience and fix the keys. It was all right—but when the staccato variations came in the second part, the whole damper mechanism and ten single keys stuck. What was I to do? Clara played, did not dare lift the damper (because it would not fall back down again), and so I pressed the single pedal during her performance, maybe 100 times, in full view of the whole audience. Yet Clara played like a god with unprecedented applause and unanimous bravos. I was bathed in sweat and had to rush back to the house, a half hour away, to change my clothes. Isn't it dreadful to have to live through something like that— especially after I had sworn to the music lovers here that I would have everything fixed and running as Graf and Bayer [well-known piano makers] did?[31]

Not the least of the shocks on this trip was Clara's developing sexuality. Wieck had asked Carl Banck, a young Leipzig composer and voice teacher, to accompany them, ostensibly because he was a native Magdeburger and could help with arrangements in that city. The primary purpose, however, was to divert Clara's mind from Robert Schumann, in whom she was show-ing unmistakable signs of interest. The lure worked. Clara flirted with Banck and with every other young man she met. For the first and probably only time in her life, she acted the coquette. The girl whose portrait was painted in Hannover has a mischievous glint in her eye—she looks out at us as if she knows her power. In Halberstadt she opened a ball. A day earlier, she gleefully reported in her diary that two men were fighting over her.

The tour continued for several months despite Wieck's overwrought con-dition. They returned home in April to face greater battles.

CHAPTER 3

Robert Schumann
and the Wiecks

When Clara and her father returned from Paris in 1832, they were eagerly awaited by Clementine, Alwin, Gustav, the four-month-old baby whom the father had never seen, and the former boarder, Robert Schumann. The young composer noted in his diary that Alwin and Gustav had run over to his rooms the instant Clara and Wieck returned.[1] In the days following, Clara's name appears in his diary with increasing frequency.

Born in Zwickau, a town of about 4,000 people in Saxony, some forty miles south of Leipzig, Robert was the youngest (and a late) child of a devoted family. The father, August Schumann, was a literary man who had prospered; beginning as the son of a poor country minister, he built a successful small-town career as bookseller, writer, publisher, translator, editor, and compiler of dictionaries and reference works. His wife, the daughter of a surgeon, doted on Robert. He showed musical talent early, and the parents turned to Johann Gottfried Kuntsch, a local music teacher, who offered much encouragement to the boy. Quickly outgrowing the knowledge offered by Kuntsch, Robert continued on his own, composing songs and piano works, directing, improvising, entertaining his family and friends, and making a local reputation as a musical talent.

His father, the major supporter of his musical and literary interests, died when Robert was sixteen, and although he had three older brothers—Eduard and Julius, in the family business in Zwickau, and Carl, a publisher and printer in nearby Schneeberg—he was placed under the guardianship of Gottlob Rudel, a friend and local merchant, who administered his share of his father's estate and advised Frau Schumann about Robert's future.* The two formed an alliance for a "practical" life based on the study of jurisprudence.

*An older sister, Emilie, born in 1796, had died in 1825 of a "nervous stroke," according to the death certificate in the family papers in Robert-Schumann-Haus, Zwickau. It was known, however, that she was mentally ill and had actually committed suicide.

Soon after his graduation from the Zwickau Lyceum—where he had been an outstanding student, highly praised for his industry and intellectual gifts—Robert arrived in Leipzig on a preliminary trip to enroll at the university and find lodgings. But the study of law was merely a cover for Schumann's real passions: music and literature. Friends reported that he rarely even approached the buildings where law lectures were held. His time was spent with music—playing and improvising on the piano, studying and listening to the music of Schubert and Beethoven—and walking and reading with friends.

One of the families in Leipzig with whom he was on visiting terms was that of Dr. Ernst August Carus, a physician whom he had known when Carus was director of a mental hospital in nearby Colditz. It was probably at a musical evening at Carus' home on March 31, 1828, that Robert Schumann met Friedrich Wieck and heard Clara play. Impressed by the child's musicality and technical prowess, he applied to Wieck for piano lessons, and studied with him until the following year. The Carus home remained the center of his musical and social life. The doctor's wife, Agnes, was an attractive young woman, with whom Robert frequently made music and with whom he was certainly in love. At eighteen, Robert was in love with every pretty woman he saw, including his three sisters-in-law. His letters and diaries chronicle adolescent enthusiasms for girls, poetry, music—all the emotions fervidly recorded.* He also enjoyed drinking (often to excess) and smoking, and, to add to the list of adolescent misdemeanors, was totally irresponsible about money. His letters to his mother and brothers are the typical calls for help of the impecunious student.

Robert convinced his mother that Heidelberg would be a better place to study law than prosaic, flat, and ugly Leipzig, but there, too, Schumann devoted more time to music than to law. Handsome, charming, gifted, spoiled, Robert played at studying law for two years before he eventually persuaded his mother to allow him to devote himself totally to music. In a well-thought-out letter he explains himself:

> My entire life has been a twenty-year struggle between poetry and prose, or if you like, call it music and the law. . . . Now I am standing at the crossroads, and the question "Which way?" frightens me. If I follow my guardian angel, he points to art, and, I believe, to the right way.[2]

Frau Schumann reluctantly agreed, but only after a correspondence with a man she felt that she could trust: Friedrich Wieck, Robert's Leipzig piano teacher. At Robert's suggestion, she asked for Wieck's opinion of her son's chances:

*Eugenie Schumann quotes from a letter of Robert: "The first thing I will look for in Heidelberg is a girl" (*Robert Schumann: Ein Lebensbild meines Vaters* [Leipzig: Koehler & Amelang, 1931], 91).

At the request of my dearly beloved son, Robert Schumann, I am taking the liberty to turn to you about his future. I am beset by trembling and deep anxiety as I write to ask you if you like Robert's plan, which is explained in the enclosed letter. They are not my opinions and I tell you openly that I am anxious about Robert's future. To *excel* in this art and be able to earn one's bread, much is necessary, as far too many artists before him have discovered—and even if his talent were truly outstanding, it would still be uncertain whether he could win approval and look forward to a secure future.

He has now studied almost three years, and needed many things— many; and now, just when I believed that he would soon reach his goal, I see him take a step backward to begin all over again; I see this just when he has reached the point when he could show what he could do, when his small inheritance is gone and he is still dependent on other people, and I wonder if he will get the approval he needs. Ah, I can't describe how depressed and unhappy I am when I think of Robert's future. He is a good person; nature has given him intellectual gifts for which others must strive with great difficulty; not an unpleasant exterior—enough capital so that he could study without cares—and of which enough could remain to live on respectably—and now he suddenly wants to enter upon a profession he should have begun ten years ago. Since you, honored sir, are a father yourself, you can well feel that I really am right and my cares are not without foundation. My other three sons are unhappy about this and all agree that I should not give in. I am the only one who does not want to force him to do something when his feelings lead him in another direc- tion—because it is certainly not honorable—after three vanished years— to begin again as an apprentice and throw away his few taler on something *unknown.*

Everything depends on your answer, the peace of a *loving mother, the entire happiness* of a young, inexperienced person who lives solely in higher spheres and does not wish to enter practical life. I know that you love music—do not let your feelings about Robert speak, but judge his years, his fortune, his strength, and his future. I beg you, I beseech you as a husband, a father, and a friend of my son, treat this as an honest man would and tell me frankly your opinion—what he has to fear—or to hope.

Please excuse the distractedness of my letter. I am so deeply affected by everything that I feel sick to my very soul, and have never found a letter more difficult to write than this one.[3]

Wieck's later attitude toward Robert Schumann when he presented him- self as a prospective son-in-law was doubtless colored by this emotional letter from Frau Schumann. But for the moment he took the opportunity to expand on his prowess as a teacher, to boast a bit about his daughter, and to assure Frau Schumann that in three years he could turn her son "into one of the greatest pianists now living." The hardheaded teacher understood the weaknesses of the young Schumann; he raised realistic questions and included some conditions for taking Schumann on as a student. First of all, Robert would have to follow Wieck's advice about practicing. He reviewed the history of the lessons Robert had already taken with him, in which Wieck had succeeded only "after hard struggles . . . in convincing Robert of the importance of a pure, precise, equal, smooth, clear, rhythmically distinctive and elegant touch." He complained of the irregularity of Robert's lessons and his propensity for excuses. "Has our Robert changed?" he asked. "Has he become more prudent, firmer, stronger, and may I say calmer and more manly? His letters do not bear this out."

Robert would have to take a lesson with him every day for a year. He pointed out that this requirement might pose a problem, since he would be out of town for varying periods on concert tours with his daughter. Would Robert be able to work alone? Wieck seemed doubtful, given the young man's previous lack of discipline.

Wieck declared that every virtuoso had to supplement his income by giving lessons, and he was even preparing Clara for that eventuality. Would Robert consent to live in this way?

Could Robert resolve, he asked, to study "cold theory" for two years and would he be able to work at exercises (as Clara did for several hours a day)? Admittedly, exercises stifle the imagination, he added, but that was one quality Robert had in plenty.

If Robert would not follow Wieck's advice, he could guarantee nothing. But, he assured Frau Schumann, if Robert succeeded in erasing Wieck's doubts—and he would give him six months to do so—he ought to be given the opportunity to try.[4]

Why would such a busy and ambitious man as Wieck undertake to work with a young man of such doubtful character? It is possible that the older man admired, even envied Robert. Robert's gifts appealed to the tough old teacher, and he was clearly eager for the opportunity to work with the imaginative young man, not only because he was a paying pupil or one who might bring him some renown, but because he relished Schumann's fantasy and playfulness, so alien to the serious, plodding young tutor that Wieck had been at the same age. Even during the early days of the struggle over Clara, when Schumann and Wieck had become adversaries, the father valued the composer and his gifts though he scorned the suitor.

Back in Leipzig, in the autumn of 1830, Robert was jubilant. He agreed to everything, moved into two rooms in the Wieck home, and became a member of the household. During the following eight or nine months he and eleven-year-old Clara took lessons daily and practiced intensely—she to prepare for her solo debut at the Gewandhaus and Robert to work toward a career as a performing musician. In the biography of her father, *Robert Schumann*, Eugenie Schumann described those autumn days as her mother recalled them:

Now a glorious life began. The mornings belonged to work, to serious study under Wieck's direction. . . . Evenings were the nicest time. Robert would fetch the children—Clara and her two brothers, Alwin and Gustav—to his room, and here he would become a child again with the children. He told them his best stories and played charades with them; he teased and frolicked and had the little boys taking turns standing on one leg—the one who could hold out the longest received a prize. Or he appeared clothed as a ghost, so that they ran from him shrieking; told the fearful Clara about doppelgänger, and about the pistol that he always carried with him, and she was the kind of child who believed everything he told her. . . . So, in this way, Robert was the biggest child of all and brought something of the sunshine of childishness to the serious life of his little friend. One can imagine how she loved him.[5]

Robert was soon dissatisfied with Wieck's tutelage and wrote his mother that he would like to go to Weimar to study with Johann Nepomuk Hummel. This was not a mere caprice; Hummel was a leading musical figure of the day—a student of Mozart, a rival of Beethoven, and kapellmeister at the Weimar court from 1819 to 1837. The name and reputation of the master undoubtedly lured Schumann, but he was also irked by his slow progress and by Wieck's insistence that he begin with finger exercises, "like a beginner."[6] His irritation was exacerbated by the daily example of the little virtuosa who achieved everything so effortlessly. He compared his playing with hers: "This whole morning everything went miserably. . . . Wieck sides against me, says I play the Herz variations like a dog . . . with Clara it just comes pouring out."[7] But when he mentioned his plans to Wieck, "in a light and casual way,"[8] a violent quarrel ensued; Wieck was threatening and ugly. Robert reported to his mother soon afterward that they were friendly again, but his diaries tell a different story. The Weimar plans had evaporated; the resentment lingered. Schumann treated Wieck with his customary respect, confided in him, worked with him, accepted his advice and hospitality; his true feelings were reserved for his journal. Here he recorded that Wieck was often hateful: "Meister Allesgeld has been gone with Zilia [Clara] for fourteen days now. His letters to his wife are the height of arrogance." He described his horror at the way Wieck mistreated his son, and on another occasion noted, "Wieck seems more dull, insipid, and arrogant every day."[9]

The contradictions that were to mark Schumann's relationship with his piano teacher began early. Wieck was more than a father figure; in Robert's eyes he seemed almost superhuman, and Robert desperately wanted this man's affection and approval. From Heidelberg, after only a few months of study, he wrote Wieck long poetic letters about himself, his music, and his enthusiasms (Franz Schubert and the novelist Jean Paul), and begged him to answer soon. And when he finally received his mother's permission to leave law and devote himself to music, his letter to Wieck was glowing and exalted: "Most respected one! Take me by the hand and lead me. I follow wherever you wish. . . . Trust in me; I will earn the right to be called your student."[10] In 1832, when Clara and her father had left Leipzig for a concert trip, Robert wrote: "You can hardly believe how I long for her [Clara] and both of you. I must always be among people who are above me. Among people who are my equals, or especially with people I cannot permit to judge me, I easily get proud and cynical." And in June 1832 he wrote to Wieck, "Every day in which I cannot speak with you or Clara is a blank in my Leipzig life."[11]

Many years later, in the midst of the battle with Wieck over Clara, Robert wrote a soul-searching letter to his beloved. He confided that he had "terrible hours of self-doubt" because of the way Wieck treated him: he had been "repulsed, insulted, slandered." But, he admitted, "I love and honor your father for his many great and noble qualities, more than anyone else can, except for you. It is a primitive, innate attachment on my part, a submission I feel toward him, as I do toward all energetic natures."[12]

If Robert could write these words in 1838, when he was already an established editor, critic, and composer, his need for Wieck must have been stronger still in 1831. Robert, at twenty-one, was still "finding himself." His indecision and unrest lasted well into his twenties, and the cyclic, seemingly unpredictable alternations of mood that remained with him to the end of his life had already made their appearance. Torn between his desires to perform, compose, write, and direct, continually running out of funds, reminded daily by Clara's skill of his late start as a pianist, he still turned to his mother for money, comfort, and security. Thus, when he was considering study with Hummel in 1831, he proposed that she leave her home in Zwickau and her other children and grandchildren to live with him in Weimar.[13]

He was also suffering from a "wound" of some kind during this time. Whether this was the trouble that affected his finger and ultimately forced him to abandon a career as a performer or some other illness is not clear.[14] Robert was overwrought much of the time. In September 1831 he wrote his brother Julius that he was in such a state of restlessness and indecision that he almost wished to put a bullet through his head. In a fit of hypochondria triggered by the cholera epidemic that was sweeping Europe in the early 1830s, he confided in his already nervous mother that he had written a will, "principally for your sake."[15]

Throughout this tumultuous year, Schumann was composing. His earliest attempts had been in Zwickau and Heidelberg, well before he had acquired any substantial formal training. In July 1831 he began to study counterpoint and thoroughbass (basic skills which he had avoided up to that time for fear they might inhibit his creativity) with Heinrich Dorn, director of the Leipzig opera, a man only six years his senior. (Twelve-year-old Clara began studies with Dorn in 1832.) The "dull" lessons, providing a discipline to which Robert had never before submitted (and sometimes lightened with champagne, according to his teacher), were not appreciated at the time: "I will never be able to get together with Dorn; he has no feelings, and what's more, has that East Prussian tone." But he admitted later that the theoretical studies were a good influence.[16] Dorn's recollection of Schumann was that he was an avid student and always produced more than was required of him. Robert was distressed when Dorn discontinued the lessons, but pursued theoretical and analytical studies on his own.

With the publication of his first compositions, the ties between Schumann and the little girl grew stronger. On Clara's return from Paris, he brought his *Papillons,* his second published work, to Wieck, who thought the music piquant and original and immediately gave it to Clara to learn. Disappointed at her first readings, Schumann described her playing as uncertain and wanting in understanding; he felt that the thirteen-year-old did not have full control over the work. Despite the "soulfulness" and "healthy enthusiasm" of her performance, he complained he missed a certain tenderness. But finally, on May 27, he wrote, "I have never yet heard Clara play as she did today—everything was played masterfully and also beautifully."[17]

For his twenty-second birthday, on June 8, Clara played two of his Paganini Caprices (op. 3) for him and also gave him a small gift she had brought from Paris. He was pleased by her attention but valued her performance above all, for by the time *Papillons* came out, Robert had given up the thought of a concert career, resolved to become a composer, and was turning to the young girl for performances of his work.

From this time on, Clara was the foremost interpreter of his piano works. A touching reminder of this dependence is a letter he wrote from Vienna a few years later:

> I am often unhappy, particularly here, because I have an injured hand. And I want to tell you it is getting worse. I have often cried to heaven and asked, "God, why did you do this to me—of all people?" It would have stood me in such good stead, especially now; music is so complete and alive in me that I ought to be able to exhale it like a whispered breath. But now I can scarcely play and one finger stumbles over the other. It is really terrible and has given me so much pain already. Now, you are my right hand and you, you must take good care of yourself so that nothing happens to you. I often think of the happy hours you will give me through your art.[18]

In contrast to Clara, who lived in a household of regular routines and controlled stability and concentrated on the career laid out so carefully by her father, Robert, nine years older, changed career plans several times, and suffered physical and mental crises that Clara was never to experience. He was haunted by the thought of insanity; fear of heights forced him to leave his fourth-floor room and move in with a friend on the first; he asked a companion to stay with him during the night. The deaths of his brother

Julius and, soon afterward, his beloved sister-in-law Rosalie deepened his anguish and fears, and he referred to the night of October 17–18, 1833, as "the most frightful" in his life.[19]

By December the mental anguish was over, possibly alleviated by a new and close friendship with Ludwig Schunke. In the new year, 1834, described by Schumann as "the most significant of my life,"[20] he began working on plans for a new musical journal, a project in which his musical and literary talents would be united. He and a group of friends, dubbed the *Davids-bündler*,* founded the *Neue Zeitschrift für Musik*, a weekly journal intended to counteract the conservative, "Philistine" tendencies of the musical world and the reactionary influence of such journals as the *Allgemeine musikalische Zeitung*. Only one of a group of editors during the first year (the others were Julius Knorr, Ludwig Schunke, Wieck, and Christian Ferdinand Hartmann, the publisher), Schumann was the busiest, conducting most of the correspondence, contacting potential contributors, editing articles, writing reviews, negotiating and planning. He continued to compose as well. A new phase of his life began when he decided to buy the journal and run it himself. (Schunke died in December 1834 and Schumann had a falling out with Knorr and Hartmann, but Wieck remained an associate for several years.) In 1835, after much maneuvering, he became the sole owner and director of the journal, which he was to edit for ten years.[21]

During these busy years, Schumann was briefly engaged to a young woman who had come to Leipzig to study with Wieck. Schumann announced her arrival in a letter to his mother dated July 2, 1834: "Two glorious creatures of the fair sex have recently joined our circle. One of them, Emilie . . . is the sixteen-year-old daughter of the American consul List, an Englishwoman [*sic*] through and through with keen sparkling eyes, dark hair, firm step, full of intellect, dignity, and life.† The other, Ernestine. . . ."[22]

When Ernestine von Fricken first came to Leipzig to study and board with Wieck, in April 1834, Clara enjoyed the thought of another friend close to her age.‡ Wieck, however, had evidently decided months earlier, in accor-

---

*May be translated as "Davidites." The term was chosen in celebration of the biblical hero. Included as members of the *Davidsbund* were friends, colleagues, and several mythical figures: Florestan, Eusebius, and Master Raro (characters who had appeared in 1831 in his essay on Chopin), who represented various aspects of Schumann himself. Florestan was bold and impetuous, Eusebius dreamy and gentle, and Master Raro mature and reflective. The latter name, which may have been a synthesis of Clara and Robert, also represented their teacher, Wieck. Many other *Davidsbündler* appeared under various pseudonyms in the essays and reviews Schumann wrote. Clara, for example, was known as Zilia, Chiara, or Chiarina; F. Meritis stood for Felix Mendelssohn; and Jeanquirit was Stephen Heller, the composer and the Paris correspondent for Schumann's journal.

†Emilie List, one year older than Clara, was one of the daughters of Friedrich List, a German political economist. Forced to leave Germany for political reasons, he had taken his family with him to the United States, acquired American citizenship, and returned to Leipzig in 1833 as the American consul.

‡Both girls celebrated birthdays in September. Ernestine would be eighteen that year and Clara only fifteen, but Clara's experiences as a touring artist made her mature for her age.

dance with his grand plan for his daughter's career, that she was to go to Dresden to work on French and English, study instrumentation with Kapellmeister Carl Reissiger, and take voice lessons from Johann Aloys Miksch. Clara viewed this arrangement as banishment from Leipzig and her friends. The letter she wrote Robert on his birthday, June 8, reveals her state of mind:

> Is this permitted, H. Schumann, to pay so little attention to a friend and not write to her even once? Every time the mail arrived, I hoped to receive a little letter from a certain Herr—Enthusiast, but alas, I was disappointed. I comforted myself with the thought that at least you would come here, but my father just wrote that you would not be coming because Knorr is ill.[23]

When she came home from Dresden at the end of July for the christening of her half sister Cäcilie, she saw Robert and Ernestine together and realized something was going on. An entry in her diary (written by Wieck) dated July 24, 1834, refers only to two young men she met in Leipzig. One was Carl Banck, "a highly cultivated musician and song composer and teacher, who has made my stay here very pleasant." Robert was perceptive enough to note in his diary that she returned to Dresden "sadly."[24]

Four years later she wrote to Robert, "When I returned to Leipzig, I was torn from my paradise. Ernestine barely spoke to me—she was mistrustful—for which I had truly given her no cause; Mother told me about a beautiful letter you had written her on Cäcilie's christening—and then I heard you were betrothed."[25]

Robert was convinced that he was in love with Ernestine von Fricken, who has been described as "physically luxuriant, emotionally strongly developed, and intellectually insignificant."[26] With a little aid from Henriette Voigt, an older, married woman of whom he was fond, and who evidently enjoyed matchmaking, he quickly persuaded Ernestine of his affection. Rumors reached her father, who wrote from his home at Asch to ask Wieck in alarm what was going on. Wieck's reply brought the baron von Fricken to Leipzig, and his arrival seemed to bring the affair to a head. When she left Leipzig on September 6 with her father, who was ill, it was clear that Robert and Ernestine had had an "understanding," and that in Leipzig she was regarded as his fiancée. Clara was not unhappy to see her go.

Eugenie Schumann, the youngest of the Schumann daughters, has told of a comment written by mother in the margin of Philipp Spitta's 1882 biography of Robert Schumann, *Ein Lebensbild Robert Schumanns*. Spitta had written, "As far as we know, a special affection [between Robert and Clara] first was apparent in the spring of 1836." Clara corrected the entry: "Already in 1833."[27] With the advantage of hindsight and awareness of the girl's preadolescent longings, we might date it even earlier.

Clara's relationship with Robert, whom she had first met when she was nine, had many elements: a mutual ongoing childish fantasy based on his stories, music they improvised and played together, shared memories and experiences, motherly concern, and girlish coquettishness. She was eleven when Robert lived at her house and she first enjoyed his attentions, his stories, and the childish games he played with her and her brothers— pleasures she had never before experienced. She placed his name on her list of those who were to receive copies of her opus 1, published in 1831. Opus 3 was dedicated to him (presumably with her father's permission) and sent off with this playful letter:

> Much as I regret having dedicated the enclosed trifle to you, and much as I wished that these variations not be printed, the evil has already come to pass and cannot be altered. Therefore, I ask your forgiveness for the enclosed. Your ingenious setting of this little musical thought will redeem the errors in mine.* I would like to request yours; I can hardly wait to make a closer acquaintance with it.[28]

When Robert left for a visit to Zwickau in 1832, Clara sent him news of Leipzig's musical life with the explanation "I just want to make you curious so that you will long for Leipzig." She needled the young composer: "Listen, Herr [Richard] Wagner has outdistanced you. A symphony of his was performed; it is as like Beethoven's A-Major Symphony as it is possible to be." She teased him about leaving his laundry in a carriage and wrote of saving a Christmas cake for him (which was not yet baked). The letter closed with a cautious neutrality: "Your friend, Clara Wieck."[29]

A childish letter? Perhaps, but this playful girl was asking for attention, chiding the man, toying with him. Coming from Clara Wieck, already a recognized artist, the reference to Wagner's success must have been like a twisting knife. But who could take her seriously? She was only thirteen.

By the time Ernestine von Fricken arrived in Leipzig, Clara viewed Robert as her special friend; when she realized the extent of the relationship between Robert and Ernestine, her reaction was typically adolescent. She flirted with Banck and let it be known (through her father) that she had fallen in love with a cellist in Magdeburg, knowing full well that this news would reach Schumann. His affections for Ernestine were cooling rapidly, however, and by the summer of 1835 the engagement, never formalized, was over as far as Robert was concerned. In the spring, while the ties were loosening, he was again seeing Clara daily. During this transition from Ernestine to Clara, Robert Schumann seems to have been emotionally attached to both young women. After receiving a birthday gift from Clara, he set off for Zwickau and Asch, Ernestine's home.

---

*Schumann had used a motif from her work in his op. 5. Her op. 3 is discussed in chap. 11.

Early in the fall of 1835 Clara celebrated her sixteenth and, according to her diary, "most brilliant" birthday with a group of her father's friends, all men, and several of them, to her joy, young. In a letter to Emilie List, after listing her many birthday presents (including "the complete works of Bulwer" from Schumann), she described the great day:

> In the early morning, about half past six, I received my things, and when I had looked at everything, I urged Father to get going, otherwise it would get too late. (We had, as you know, proposed to go to the Kuchengarten.) But Father said, "Just wait a little while longer. The others will come soon in order to go with us." . . . Just then . . . a servant girl came. She bore a beautiful wreath on a glass plate. I recognized her as Schumann's servant, took the plate from her, looking inside, and, imagine my surprise, found a basket with a porcelain handle and, in the basket, a golden cylinder watch. You cannot imagine my astonishment as well as my joy. You must certainly be wondering—as I did—the watch could not possibly be from Schumann alone? No, that was not the case. Indeed, it was from Schumann, [Dr. Moritz] Reuter, [Wilhelm] Ulex, [Louis] Rackemann, [Ernst] Wenzel, and [Ernst] Pfund. Immediately afterward we went—I with the golden watch—to the Kuchengarten, and there were the Stegmayers, who had placed a huge bouquet on the table. We weren't sitting long when the above-mentioned watch givers came, all adorned with "burning love" [the flower pelargonium]. You can imagine my embarrassment. I couldn't utter a word. . . . (The porcelain basket was from Herr Schumann alone.)
>
> At twelve o'clock, the six gentlemen (and Felix Mendelssohn as well) returned to dine with us. Now imagine my heroic courage: as we were drinking champagne, I stood up with the glass in my hand. Everyone was amazed, and I began and said, "Gentlemen, I cannot refrain from expressing my warmest thanks for the beautiful gift." . . . I must have seemed quite stupid. . . . After we ate, I played for Mendelssohn and he played also. Everyone left at 5 o'clock, but at 6, Dr. Reuter and Schumann came to fetch us for a walk. However, we danced until 8 and then went out walking.
>
> That was the famous sixteenth birthday. Oh, Emilie, if you only had been here. It was marvelous. I will not forget this day soon. We are saving a little post party celebration until you and Herr Banck are here again.[30]

Except for Felix Mendelssohn, the newly appointed director of the Gewandhaus orchestra, the guests were old friends of Wieck's and associates of Schumann on the *Neue Zeitschrift für Musik*. We may assume that Frau Wieck was present as hostess, but, as usual, she is not mentioned. Clara, though so often surrounded by adult men—friends, students,and walking companions of her father*—evidently still found it easier to communicate

*Note that Clara's guest list, presumably drawn up by her father, was all male. Guests at her fourteenth and fifteenth birthday celebrations were also chiefly men, friends of her father's. Even Clara's birthday parties were not her own.

Clara Wieck, age 16, in Hannover. On the piano is the solo part of the third movement of her Concerto op. 7. Lithograph by J. Giere, 1835. Robert-Schumann-Haus,
Zwickau, DDR.

with them through the piano than through speech. Her characteristic shyness in speaking explains her pride in finally being able to thank the gentlemen properly.

Schumann abandoned all principles soon after Clara's birthday; he assured her that all was over between him and Ernestine, that Ernestine was engaged to someone else. (She was not.) Recalling those months several years later, he wrote in his diary:

> Clara's birthday on September 13. . . . Clara's eyes and her love. . . . The first kiss in November. Then her trip to Zwickau at the end of November. I follow. Our meeting. . . . Break with Ernestine. . . . Clara's return to Leipzig. The poor Rakemann [another suitor of Clara's]. Lovely hours in her arms in the evenings in the Wieck house. Christmas 1835—New Year's Day 1836—break with Wieck. Complete separation from Ernestine.[31]

Clara was deliriously happy. She wrote to him later, "When you gave me that first kiss, I thought I would faint; everything went blank and I could barely hold the lamp that was lighting your way out."[32]

The kisses continued when they met in Zwickau in December on a concert tour Wieck had arranged. The engagement to Ernestine was over—although Ernestine did not know it until January 1836. (In 1838 she married the baron von Zedtwitz, to the great relief of Robert and Clara, and she was later generous enough to come to their aid in the legal proceedings between Wieck and Robert.) Lulled by Robert's attachment to Ernestine, Wieck did not realize what was happening for some time, but when his suspicions were at last aroused, his first reaction was to remove his daughter from Leipzig. He took her to Dresden on January 14 and remained there with her until February 7, when he had to leave on business. (Wieck was still renting and selling pianos.) Clara stayed on in Dresden with friends.

In the first flush of love, Robert persisted in the naive belief that Wieck would approve their marriage. Since Wieck admired Robert's compositions, had treated him as a friend, and had been a respectful collaborator on the *Zeitschrift*, he assumed Wieck would be happy to see his daughter and the promising young composer united. He went so far as to convince himself that he had been "chosen" and educated to be Clara's husband.[33] In ordinary circumstances, Robert Schumann was perceptive and showed unusual depths of sensibility and self-understanding for a young man, but in this situation he misjudged Wieck completely. Forgetting, or perhaps suppressing, his memories of Wieck's temper, jealousy, and possessiveness, he was astonished and hurt at Wieck's fury when the father learned that Robert and his friend Wilhelm Ulex had visited Clara in Dresden between February 7 and 11, while he was away. During that time promises had been exchanged and letters arranged. By the time Wieck returned, Robert was on his way to Zwickau to pay belated respects to his mother, who had died on February 4, and to take care of the will and other legal matters. (Unable to bring himself to attend the funeral, Robert had gone to see Clara instead.)

The struggle between Wieck and Robert for Clara which began after this incident was complicated by the fact that Clara and Robert both needed Wieck at this point in their lives. Schumann wanted to be both son and son-in-law to his old teacher. Yearning for the stability and firmness of an association with Wieck, he was shocked to find he could not have Clara and Wieck too. Clara knew she was in love with Robert but understood her father well enough to suppress Schumann's name in her diary; it appears occasionally and only in an offhand way in Clara's handwriting during the next few months. Music, her career, and the daily routines organized by her father still remained the center of her life. Within the next two years, however, she was to take the first faltering steps on her own. Wieck, selfish and supremely insensitive to those around him, proceeded impulsively and irrationally toward the estrangement that was to embitter his life.

Now, in February 1836, Wieck's rage erupted at Clara for the first time. He threatened to shoot Schumann if she should meet him again. He entered his thoughts on their deceitful behavior in her diary. All the insults, threats, and fury that she had seen visited on her brothers (and perhaps, in the dim past, on her mother) burst upon her now. From beloved pupil and protégée, source of all Wieck's artistic and personal gratification, she had suddenly become the enemy.

Wieck scheduled another long concert trip to keep her away from Leipzig and, except for a maid, was her sole companion on a concert tour to Dresden, Görlitz, and Breslau from February to April. It was a miserably unhappy tour, with Wieck in a rage from beginning to end. In Clara's diary he fumed at the miserly Dresden audiences, the inadequate pianos, weak orchestras, and dirty lodgings.[34] He sent Schumann an insulting letter informing him that all connections between him and the Wieck household were severed. For almost a year and a half Clara and Robert, for so long daily companions, did not meet or communicate in any way. Friends kept him informed of Clara's whereabouts and doings. Johann Peter Lyser, a close friend, described a concert in Dresden which he had attended:

February 24, 1836

There is not much more to tell you about Clara's last concert except what is expected: it was jammed, a Beethoven overture opened the concert, then Clara appeared—stormy reception—Now she played "Là ci darem la mano"—You know how! *Lieder ohne Worte* by Felix (give him three kisses for it), a Bach étude, and variations by Herz.

The audience applauded madly, the Old Man had a full money chest, Clara made her bows. . . .[35]

Since Clara's diary was still in part her father's, we have no direct knowledge of her feelings. Touring with her father, shut up with him for days on end in slow coaches and rehearsal halls, closeted in uncomfortable inns, she was forced to endure his attacks on Robert just at the point where a love long cherished and secretly hoped-for had seemed possible. Yet Wieck expected his daughter to carry on her concert career as she had always done, and she acquiesced. Her only contact with Robert was through his music: she played his Toccata and First Piano Sonata (in manuscript) for small private musical circles in Dresden and Breslau. Wieck apparently had no objection.

During this first, long separation, Schumann threw himself into work—composing, studying, writing—and an active social life. Among his close friends and companions were Mendelssohn, Ferdinand David (concertmaster of the Gewandhaus orchestra), the wealthy musical Voigt family, Dr. Moritz Reuter, Wilhelm Ulex (a music teacher), and the greatly admired English pianist and composer William Sterndale Bennett, who arrived in Leipzig at the end of October 1836. Schumann let his sorrows be known to all Leipzig and points south. To his sister-in-law, Therese, he revealed his soul: "Come soon and be a good sister to me; I have no one to give me womanly care." He described briefly what was happening between the Wieck family and himself. "I am in a critical situation and lack the calm and clear sight that would enable me to pull out of it. The way it stands now is that either I can never speak with her again or she will be mine entirely." Though he had many male friends, he missed a woman in his life. In December 1836 he wrote Therese, "Oh, remain true to me. In the deadly anxiety into which I fall from time to time, I have no one but you to turn to, you who seem to hold me in your arms and protect me."[36]

These were the years when Schumann was creating his best-known works, those impassioned piano pieces that include the *Davidsbündlertänze,* the *Fantasiestücke,* the Fantasie in C Major, and the three piano sonatas. A published copy of his Sonata in F-sharp-minor, "dedicated to Clara by Florestan and Eusebius," was sent to her in May 1836. Clara was not permitted to acknowledge receipt of the sonata, and soon thereafter Wieck insisted that all Robert's letters be returned. She obeyed.

In contrast to the festivities of the year before, Clara's seventeenth birthday, in 1836, passed under a cloud. It was the first such celebration in many years at which Schumann had not been present. Until the next big concert trip to Berlin and northern Germany, planned for the spring of 1837, she toured in the small nearby towns of Naumburg, Jena, and Weimar. At home she endured the close supervision of her father and stepmother.

The trip north, a prelude to even longer international tours, began on February 7, 1837, in Berlin, where Clara's mother, now Marianne Bargiel, lived. Immediately upon her arrival, Wieck took Clara to see her. "Here, Madam, I bring you your daughter," he announced.[37] The fact that Wieck himself recorded the words in Clara's diary tells us much about the man: he gloried in his power as he permitted a reunion between mother and child.

The two Wiecks saw Clara's mother and her ailing husband several times. Bargiel is mentioned briefly; Wieck's anger and contempt were reserved for Marianne. She was, he recorded in his daughter's diary, "far more rude, mean, deceitful, petty, and presumptuous than she had ever been." Unforgivably, moreover, she tried to "meddle" with the arrangements for Clara's concerts.[38]

In Wieck's correspondence there is no mention of Clara's feelings or reactions to her mother (or, indeed, about her relations with anyone else). Nevertheless, this must have been a time of thought and reconsideration for Clara. Though she had seen her mother briefly from time to time over the years, she had always been returned to her father and his influence. Now, almost adult herself and at odds with her father, she could begin to understand what had happened in Leipzig in 1824 and why Marianne had been forced to abandon her children. The Berlin visit gave her an opportunity to rediscover her mother, as it were, and from that time a genuine relationship developed between the two women. Within a few years Clara was able to turn to her mother for love and support.

Wieck's letters to his wife, Clementine, tell us much about the vicissitudes of touring in the 1830s, a great deal about Wieck, and very little about Clara.[39] His complaints were many: the high cost of food (which he partially circumvented by sending Nanny, the maid, out for dry rolls that they could eat for breakfast in their high-priced hotel room); the vast numbers of free tickets that Berlin concertgoers expected; the poor seats they were given for concerts; the problems with the censors and the bureaucracy; the surly Berlin serving classes; the supporting musicians who refused to cooperate on his terms in Clara's concerts; and not least, the high cost of postage.

His earthiness and vulgarity make themselves evident in the letters. Clara was taking lessons from Siegfried Wilhelm Dehn, a "formidable contrapuntist"—the kind of chap he had been looking for for a long time. "He will bring her to the point of writing circle canons; in a word, after twelve lessons, when she spits, she will spit up fugues." He damned the assisting artists, Carl Möser (the leading chamber musician in Berlin) and his "cursed" quartet, for having the temerity to ask for fifteen free tickets. He was proud of the way in which he outmaneuvered Möser and wanted all Berlin to know of his behavior.

Most striking in Wieck's letters is his attitude toward Clara: she is discussed as though she were an object on display. He was concerned about her health—but largely because a canceled concert would cause great inconvenience. The morning after her last Berlin concert, a triumph played in a hall filled to capacity, he sarcastically referred to "the queen," still sleeping at 6:30 A.M.

Wieck took great delight in routing his foes; the struggle with the "enemy" often seemed more important than Clara's playing. He was, of course, proud of her artistry and her talent at composition. He informed Clementine that publication of her collected works would be announced in the papers; that three publishers had bid for her Variations (op. 8) and Clementine was to ask Friedrich Hofmeister, their Leipzig publisher and close friend, how much he would give for them; Gasparo Spontini, the grand master of music in Berlin, not only wanted Clara to play privately for him but considered the Bellini Variations "the grandest and most beautiful piece of bravura music in recent times." But above all, Wieck felt successful because Clara's triumphs had "destroyed all the cabals."

Again and again we read of "victories"—victories over those who plotted against them, victories over the jealous Berlin dogs who would have done them in, victories over the poisonous music critics who doubted his daughter's genius. The reports of praise for Clara are laced with comments on the enemy. "Clara is the talk of the town and the other artists are butting their heads together in despair." After her first concert, on February 24, he boasted, "Triumph, triumph, Clara created a furor last night. Her masterly playing was rewarded by an hour and a half of thunder and formidable bravissimos—all the cabals have been destroyed . . . the public has decided—and *how* they have decided! Even Paganini did not have such accolades here."

All the concert arrangements were in Wieck's hands: he made the required rounds of visits to impress important people; he secured the permission of the police; he rented the concert halls; he borrowed or rented the pianos for practice and performance; he had posters and programs printed; he prepared publicity for the newspapers; he paid a visit to Mendelssohn's mother. "The amount of work is frightful," he wrote, but he did not forget to mention the many contacts he was also making for his piano business. Reviewers were commenting on his pianos along with Clara's performances. "Berlin will be a gold mine for us—and my business too," he wrote.

They moved on to Hamburg, where the "glorious Clara" was eagerly awaited. By the end of the concert trip, which closed in Bremen, both were exhausted. The weary travelers returned home on May 3 and were greeted by stepmother and Carl Banck at the outskirts of Leipzig.

Banck's proximity to Clara and her family plus the continued silence of the girl Robert loved drove Schumann wild. In the autumn of 1836 he began to have strong doubts. He wrote to his sister-in-law Therese, "C. loves me as warmly as ever, but I am completely resigned [to giving her up]."[40] During 1837 Schumann's spirits rose and fell in an alarming way. He wrote to Clara in January 1838:

The darkest time, when I knew nothing of you and tried to force myself to forget you, was about a year ago. Did you not think of me then? Our spirits must have been estranged at that time. I had resigned myself. But then the old pain broke out again—and I wrung my hands—and then I said to God on many a night—"Let but this one thing mercifully pass away, without my going mad." . . . I hurled myself to the ground and cried aloud—then I wished to cure myself, to compel myself to fall in love with a woman who had already half drawn me into her net.[41]

Several writers have speculated on the identity of this woman. Although musicians are mentioned (the British pianist Robena Laidlaw, for example, who passed through Leipzig about this time), he may have been referring to the Christel (or Charitas) whose almost daily visits to his room were noted in his diary. Robert certainly never entertained any idea of marriage to her, but she must have provided the female comfort and sexual gratification he craved, particularly at this time, when he was estranged from the woman he loved.

Banck's presence in the Wieck home and Wieck's persistent criticism of Robert almost succeeded in estranging the lovers. The possessive father, however, became characteristically agitated at Banck's friendly relationship with Clara, and, acting angrily and impulsively, he banished the young man from the house. Soon afterward Banck left Leipzig. Robert's diary notes, "Banck's departure from here—happier mood."[42] Within a few months the relationship between Clara and Robert was secretly resumed, this time on Clara's initiative.

While spending the summer of 1837 at the home of friends near Dresden, Clara was informed by her father that he had arranged a concert for her on August 13 in Leipzig. A few days later a conversation with Ernestine von Fricken, who was visiting in the area, evidently stilled her doubts concerning Schumann's previous relationship. Clara agreed to the concert but insisted on including three of Schumann's Symphonic Etudes in the program.* She then plucked up the courage to ask Ernst Adolph Becker, a mutual friend and a great admirer of Schumann's music, to convey a message to Robert, thus breaking the enforced silence of eighteen months. A swift and passionate exchange of letters through Becker followed. On August 13, the day of the concert, Robert wrote:

Are you still *firm* and true? As indestructible as my belief in you† is, yet the strongest spirit loses confidence when nothing is heard of the one who is loved more than anyone else in the world. And you are that to me. I have thought it all over a thousand times, and everything says to us, "It must be, if we wish it, and act." Write me just a simple "yes" if you will

*Litzmann mistakenly names the Sonata no. 1 in F-sharp Minor.
†The two were still addressing each other as *Sie*. It was not until October that the intimate *du* was used by both Robert and Clara.

give your father a letter from me on your birthday [September 13]. Just now he is well disposed toward me and will not reject me if you add your pleas to mine.[43]

Her answer, simple, beautiful, and positive, sealed the bond with Robert. For the remainder of their lives, they considered the following day, August 14, the day of their betrothal. In his diary Robert wrote, "A union for eternity."[44]

Clara Wieck had declared her intention to move away from her father and to the man she now hoped to marry. But a long struggle with herself and with her father lay ahead.

The famous courtship began with surreptitious meetings and secret letters. Their hopes were pinned on the formal proposal, written with Ernst Adolph Becker's help and advice, which was to be presented to Wieck on Clara's eighteenth birthday. With the letter Robert requested an interview and enclosed notes to Frau Wieck and to Clara. The interview was granted but Clara was never given the note. In a touching letter Robert formally asked for Clara's hand and implored Wieck, "with the utmost seriousness of which an anxious, loving heart is capable: bless us, be once more a friend to one of your oldest friends, and the best father to the best child!"[45]

Robert's self-confidence had been restored by Clara's yes and he was buoyed by the admiration and love of his many friends. To Robert's anxious queries, Becker replied:

> I do not know to whom I would rather have my daughter betrothed than a man whose heart is as true as yours, and who can write such études. I received them [the Symphonic Etudes] yesterday. . . . One cannot find anything more beautiful; I have reveled in them, undisturbed, all day. . . . For majesty and grandeur of thought, I know of no living person who can stand at your side.[46]

Despite Becker's confidence, it was another tear-soaked birthday for Clara, and Robert's interview with Wieck was a bitter and humiliating experience. "This coldness, this ill will, this confusion, these contradictions—he has a new way to destroy, he thrusts blade and hilt into my heart," he wrote to Clara.[47]

Robert believed that Wieck's interest in money was at the root of his opposition. Knowing what we do about Wieck, we can hardly doubt that he regarded Clara as a financial asset, but in all fairness we must acknowledge that other factors, many of them legitimate doubts that any responsible father might have, also figured in Wieck's resistance to the match. Gradually Schumann perceived that a great battle was beginning. "Eventually he must accept the idea of losing you. His obstinacy will shatter itself against our love. . . . Disabuse your father of his distorted views."[48]

Wieck could have chosen several courses of action, but, oddly enough, he began, and continued, a weak, often irrational offense. His behavior repelled many of their mutual friends, all of whom sided with the young lovers. His only ally was his wife. Though not a man of financial substance, Schumann had inherited a moderate legacy, had a growing reputation as a composer, was owner and editor of a successful music journal, and a man of intellect and undeniable genius, respected and loved by many. Wieck knew all this and, more than many other musicians of his generation, understood and valued Robert's gifts and adventurous musical spirit. But he doubtless recalled the revealing letter from Robert Schumann's mother and knew the un-disciplined and sometimes erratic early youth, the drinking and extrava-gance with money; he must have had an inkling of Robert's experience with women—Leipzig was a small town—and he was aware of the cyclic depres-sions and family history.* Yet in the battle over Clara, he chose to concen-trate on insignificant details (poor handwriting, soft voice, social maladroit-ness) and accusations about drinking to excess—a charge that may have been true in Schumann's earlier years but could no longer be substantiated. Wieck insisted that Robert did not have the money to support Clara in the style to which she was accustomed and that marriage would mean the end of her glorious career. The second argument shook Clara and created doubts that were to surface over the next two years. For the time being, however, she was in love and remained unconvinced by her father's arguments.

The letters exchanged between the lovers in the next few weeks are beautiful. Clara's letters, so prosaic in her later years, are here filled with poetry and warmth, tenderness and beauty. Robert's letters, always a joy to read, rise to new heights as the two pledge themselves to each other, even as Wieck is leading her off to Vienna and new triumphs on the concert stage.

*In "Schumann's Hand Injury," *MT*, 112 (1971), 1156–59, Eric Sams speculates that Wieck was aware that Schumann had sought treatment for syphilis and that this was the major (and unnamed) reason he objected to their marriage. In view of Wieck's character and the steps he took to prevent the marriage, however, it hardly seems possible that he would have failed to mention the disease if he had had even a faint suspicion that Schumann had it.

CHAPTER 4

The Break with Wieck

After the travails of the trips to Paris, Dresden, and Berlin, the success in Vienna was sweet indeed. Little was heard from Wieck about plots and cabals, and though he issued occasional curses at conditions and foes in the Austrian capital, his letters reflected less anger and hostility than did those from Berlin. Viennese charm had softened the old man—but not to the point of changing his mind about Robert. He had given permission for them to correspond while Clara was on tour, but she was so fearful that her father would read her correspondence that she secretly scribbled a few words at a time to her lover while standing at her bureau after long days of wearying performances.

The eighteen-year-old young woman had firmly declared her love for Robert but was still dependent on her father, emotionally, financially, and above all artistically. The effort to break with her father engendered extreme anguish. The situation was as monumentally difficult for her as any of the later crises of her tragedy-filled life, and in fact may have served to armor her against the impact of the devastating events to come. For Clara, the conflict between father and lover continued to the eve of her marriage, and even beyond.

Friedrich Wieck, the parent of this virtually motherless girl, was also the developer of her art and provider of the self-esteem that nourishes the artist. From the beginning, at a time when middle-class girls were expected to learn to tickle the piano keys prettily enough to amuse a husband but not to attract public attention, Wieck envisioned Clara as a musician—a great performer—and insisted that she could do anything a boy could do (and certainly do it better than his sons). He quoted with pride Goethe's remark "She plays with as much strength as six boys."[1]

Yet during the Vienna trip, which began in October 1837, a psychological separation from her father began to seem possible. Robert was more insistent; she had given him her word and her ring; the Vienna press and public accorded her more recognition than she had ever received before; and though Wieck's letters still refer to "our concerts" and "our feelings," Clara was gaining an independent identity. If a question remained in her mind about her future with Robert, she did not allow it to sully the triumphal days in Vienna during the winter of 1837–38.

Wieck viewed the trip to Vienna as his greatest artistic and financial triumph. Clara's success exceeded anything he had ever dreamed of. She was so immensely popular that Wieck worried through sleepless nights whether she could maintain her position and keep Vienna's hysteria at the high pitch her artistry had inspired. "All Vienna is saying that no artist has ever made a sensation like this," he wrote to his wife.[2] He marveled at the way the money rolled in. The Viennese were storming the box office and police had to be called in to restore order. Newspapers reported a new confection, "torte à la Wieck." In a letter to Robert on January 30 Clara described it: "Just imagine. They are serving 'torte à la Wieck' in the inns, and all my enthusiasts go and eat the cakes. They were recently advertised in the *Theaterzeitung* with the comment that they were an ethereal, light dessert that flies into the mouth of the eater. Isn't that a laugh?"[3]

In his usual fashion, Wieck gloried over the blows dealt to Sigismund Thalberg, the famed virtuoso, and other rivals. The triumphant Clara, he reported, aroused keen jealousy among other artists, who were losing their audiences to her, and among teachers, who were exploding with anger at her (his?) triumphs. "We have been vegetating in Leipzig," he wrote to his wife in the letter in which he enclosed the Grillparzer poem "Beethoven and Clara Wieck."* "Now comes the reward—now the whole world shall know there is only one Clara, a Clara at whose feet all Vienna lies."

The honors flowed so copiously that the reader (and Wieck himself) can barely keep up. He couldn't think of leaving; "Vienna would weep." The prospect of years of glittering success was exciting, but we sense that Wieck was beginning to feel some strain. While waiting to hear whether or not Clara would receive the emperor's award, he wrote, in an unexpectedly pessimistic mood, that it wouldn't help Clara in any case, because this was the last trip he would make. His health was affected by the rigors of concert life: the obligation he felt to stay in one place as long as money could be made, Clara's contrariness and obstinacy, the endless burdens and constant anxieties of concertizing—he could not take it much longer.

Once Clara received the imperial honor, however, Wieck cried for joy and hailed it as a vindication of all he had suffered.

> What a letter of recommendation this is! What a lesson to the envious pianists who have made a public spectacle of all my aspirations. We have borne it humbly and continued to strive—here is the reward. . . . Haven't I always, and rightly, soothed Clara by saying, "Have patience"? Now she has

*Described at the beginning of chap. 1.

the highest title; it is the greatest guarantee of safe-conduct in all of Europe. Now she understands the kind of steadfast resolution that is responsible for this. Would we be in Vienna if I had not battled the boors?

Clara was honored by musicians as well as by royalty: she received an autograph of Schubert's "Erlkönig" from a friend of the composer; editions were dedicated to her.⁴ Publishers fought for the privilege of publishing her works, and she was named an honorary member of the prestigious Gesellschaft der Musikfreunde.⁵

The Viennese reception was immensely gratifying to Wieck, and possibly as a result, his letters expressed more concern about his family; he teased Clementine, he sent kisses to his children. Feeling more secure and expansive, he directed Clementine to get bigger and better lodgings for the family. Clara, of course, was to have a room of her own in the new apartment; his children were to have rugs on the floor so they wouldn't be cold. But he spoke only of the two little girls—the children of his second marriage. Alwin and Gustav had not turned out well, he said, and would have to leave. His attitude toward the boys was unequivocal; he would not support them any longer. Gustav, just turned fifteen, was to be apprenticed to a piano maker. And if Alwin did not improve, Wieck wrote, he would be sent to an instrument maker in Pressburg. He warned that if either tried any "dumb tricks," they would go straight to prison (despite the fact that their sister was a Royal and Imperial Chamber Virtuosa).

The crimes of these dreadful youngsters were never spelled out, but it is obvious that, unlike Clara, who was earning "unheard-of" sums, they remained financial burdens. Clementine received her orders: "His [Alwin's] fate is irreversible—he must go—take the first opportunity [to ship him off] during the first week of the fair. He will never see his family home until he becomes a useful person." As for Gustav, Clementine was ordered to find an old suitcase for the boy so that he could set out on his journeys; "their father's home no longer exists for these bad boys."*

Wieck's thoughts also went out to Robert, whose talents as editor, publisher, and composer he enlisted in Clara's interests. Since it was necessary to keep in touch with Leipzig musical life, he requested every word printed in Schumann's *Zeitschrift*. Clementine was to ask Schumann to reprint the Vienna reviews, to publish the Grillparzer poem, to print up copies of reviews and the poem and send them all to Wieck for the Viennese press. Near the end of the trip it occurred to him that a sketch of Clara's life would also make good copy for the local papers. He directed (through his wife) that Robert write such a sketch and send fifty copies for distribution on concert

---

*Gustav was apprenticed to and became an instrument maker. Alwin eventually became a professional violinist and played in orchestras in Reval and St. Petersburg before he settled in Dresden in 1859.

trips. At the same time, he expressed resentment because Schumann had not thought to do so himself.

It seemed to Wieck that Schumann was not writing enough about Clara while she was busy playing Robert's works and building his reputation. "His *Carnaval* was performed by us for the great connoisseurs and created a great furor; since there is so much speaking, gossip, explaining, running, visiting, etc. here, his name as a composer will quickly become known. Clara also played the sonata [F-sharp minor] but it was not so well understood."

Though Wieck was clearly pleased with Clara on this trip, he made no mention of her feelings or reactions. Apparently she existed for Wieck's purposes, and as far as he was concerned, the triumphs were his.

Meanwhile, Clara and Robert, considering themselves engaged, carried on their clandestine correspondence. Elaborate plans were made so that she could receive his letters. To allay Wieck's suspicions, Robert was to address his letters to fictitious characters—now "BCDE," now "Herr Kraus"—in care of friends who were to send them on in fresh envelopes addressed to her, since Wieck knew his handwriting. Nanny, Clara's maid, was a firm ally, and picked up the letters for her at the post office. Robert did not understand why she did not write more frequently, and she explained that the only time she had to write was in the evenings when she was half dead with fatigue. Wieck would fly into a rage if he found her door locked.

There was much discussion of their future. Robert was dreaming, and Clara, the practical, experienced performer, sharply brought him back to earth, as she was to do often:

> I had to laugh at the place in your letter where you write, "and so we will return to our little house, laden with treasure." Oh, my God, what are you thinking of? Treasures cannot be acquired by instrumental art *any more*. How much one has to do in order to leave a town with a few taler! While you are sitting at Poppe's [a Leipzig coffeehouse] at 10 o'clock in the evening, or are going home, I, poor thing, am just arriving at a party, where I have to play to people for a few pretty words and a cup of warm water, and arrive home, dead tired, at 11 or 12 o'clock, gulp a mouthful of water, lie down and think, "Is an artist much more than a beggar"?

"Yet," she went on, in an impressive statement of faith from such a young artist—a statement that was to form the motto of her life—

> art is a beautiful gift. What, indeed, is more beautiful than to clothe one's feelings in sound, what a comfort in sad hours, what a pleasure, what a wonderful feeling, to provide an hour of happiness to others. And what a sublime feeling to pursue art so that one gives one's life for it.[6]

The covert correspondence was not entirely free of the conflicts that were agitating the girl. Clara's indecision tormented Schumann and undoubtedly contributed to his insecurities. At one point she wrote to Robert that she could sympathize with her father: "I am very upset when I see how miserable Father is when he thinks of losing me someday—I know my duty toward him and yet I love you endlessly." During all this time she was subjected to her father's continual threats of disinheritance if she married Schumann and began to react to them: "I no longer am so fond of my father, ah God, I cannot be so wholeheartedly loving, and yet I should like to be so—it is my father, after all, that I have to thank for everything."[7]

Many of her letters reflected her father's influence. The tone of this letter, for example, is strangely like Wieck's:

> I have also considered the future *very seriously* and I must tell you one thing: I cannot be yours until circumstances have entirely altered. . . . I require much, and I realize that much is needed for a proper life. Robert, test yourself. Are you in a position to offer me a life free from care? Consider that though I have been brought up simply, I have never had a care. Must I bury my art now? Love is all very beautiful, but, but—.[8]

Robert was beside himself, but he managed to point out with dignity that she should have brought up these objections before he asked her father for her hand. Though he recognized her father's pressure in her letter, he was hurt.

> And now, since you value my ring so little, I care no longer for yours, since yesterday, and do not wear it. I dreamed that I was walking by deep water—and an impulse seized me and I threw the ring into the water—and then I was filled with a passionate longing to plunge in after it.[9]

His dark words were a foreboding of the future: just before Schumann attempted suicide by leaping into the Rhine in 1854, he removed his wedding ring and threw it into the water. But in 1838 he was able to recover from the blow and gathered the strength to advise and comfort her. He was aware of the daily nagging and verbal assaults to which she was exposed. But Wieck, too, according to Clara, vacillated. On March 3 she wrote that she and her father had spoken of Schumann and that Wieck seemed to be prepared to accept him once more as a friend of the house. She optimistically assured her lover that her father was "quite kind." "He sees very well that I will *never* give my heart to another—and a father like mine would never consent to give my hand without my heart."[10]

Clara had misinterpreted her father's comments, perceiving them in her own way. She pointed out that it would be difficult to earn an adequate living in Leipzig and went on to sketch a glorious life in Vienna, where Robert could continue to compose and edit his journal and she could earn perhaps

2,000 taler through concerts and teaching. These earnings, added to his income of 1,000 taler a year, would enable them to live comfortably.

This was not exactly the way Wieck saw the situation. What he actually wrote in her diary on March 3, 1838, was:

> . . . spoke with Clara about Sch. and told her I will never give my consent to Leipzig, and Clara quite agrees with me, and assures me her view will also never alter. Sch. can maneuver, philosophize, enthuse, idealize as much as he likes; it is settled that Clara can never live in poverty and obscurity—but must have over 2,000 taler a year to spend.

Robert was happy to hear of a rational conversation, and his answer recalls his longing for a father:

> Now if only I could win the love and confidence of your father—whom I would so gladly call Father, whom I have to thank for so much of the happiness in my life, for his teaching—and also for grief—and to whom I should like to give nothing but joy in his old age, so that he should say, "They are good children."

Yet he was suspicious and added, "There can be no happiness in this relationship until your father . . . considers me the future son of the house."[11]

The constant rise and fall of their hopes did not weaken Robert's resolve, and before she returned to Leipzig she received a firm letter from him, asking her to set a date for their marriage and expressing grave doubts that Wieck would ever give his consent: "Since he has taken back what he promised so many times, he will do it again—in a word, I expect nothing from him, *we must act for ourselves.*" And he concluded, in a long letter written over about a week in April 1838, that they should settle on Easter 1840 for their marriage.[12]

The return to Leipzig, on May 15, 1838, marked the final period of the courtship but the conflicting emotions only became more intense. Though she never considered giving up Robert, doubts about the continuation of her career and guilt over separation from her father tormented Clara, and the reverberations of these feelings shook Robert again and again.

"If anyone asks if I have already seen you," she wrote to Robert in May 1838, "tears spring to my eyes."

> You are so near and yet I cannot see you. . . . I am suspended in heaven and immediately afterward am so unhappy because I cannot embrace you right away, you who are everything to me, you who have opened another world to me. . . . You are the ideal of a man, an ideal I have always carried in my heart.[13]

And on June 2, 1838, she wrote about their marriage:

83]

> It would be lovely if Therese could be with us the first weeks after our wedding. She could teach me many things that I cannot learn at home because my father does not want to see me anywhere but at the piano. How I would like to concern myself with household tasks now and then, but I would just be laughed at. . . .[14]

In April, while Clara was still away, Robert had written that although they were going to be in the same city for the summer, it might be best if they did not meet. He wanted a wife, not a girl for secret meetings and kisses. He had endured the situation for two years, he wrote, and he could hold out for two more years. The strain of plotting, of stealing a few minutes in order to get a couple of distracted words together, was too much to bear. "I am no longer a moonlight knight," he wrote, "If you yearn for me terribly, I will gladly come; otherwise we will refrain from meeting; it leads to nothing." But Clara could not restrain herself and they met frequently in the weeks she was in Leipzig. She even suggested visits to his room, but Robert decided it was too risky. "If anyone were to see you at my house, your father might do something dreadful. I cannot have you visit me now." Their notes indicate that they met often, however, perhaps daily.[15]

Complicated operations were set in motion for a visit of a moment or two. On June 8, Robert's twenty-eighth birthday, Clara wrote: "Be at our window at *exactly* 9. If I signal with a white cloth, walk slowly toward the old Neumarkt. I will follow soon after and go with you, since I have to fetch Mother at her mother's. *If I don't signal, it means she hasn't gone.*"[16]

Robert to Clara, an agonizing letter, June 20:

> I have such an urgent desire to see you, to press you to my heart, that I am sad—and sick as well. I don't know what is absent in my life, and yet I do know: you are absent. I see you everywhere, you walk up and down with me in my room, you lie in my arms and nothing, nothing is real. I am ill. And how long will this all endure?[17]

She could give no response. Visiting friends in Dresden from July 3 to August 7, however, she could write more freely. From the carriage that took her to Dresden she had seen Robert standing by, waiting to follow the carriage with his eyes.

> I saw you, two steps away from me, and could not get out of the carriage to throw myself into your arms. . . . As you came toward me, I felt as though I would fall into a faint because of the pain; everything turned black, and when I could see you no longer, my heart opened and the tears flowed so that I could not hide them. The feeling was indescribable.[18]

In the long August and September evenings of that year, 1838, Robert stood across the street from the Wieck home and watched the window for a glimpse of her shadow or listened for a few measures of his music as she practiced. She knew he was there.

Clara was beginning to be frightened by her feelings about her father:

> It has already come to this: I sometimes have frightening thoughts that I no longer love my father as I should. And when my beloved Robert is derogated, ridiculed, insulted, this arouses bitter feelings, this is the deepest wound. . . . The parting from Father will be difficult for me. I will have to struggle mightily, but *love will give me strength for everything*. When the time comes, *I will come too*. Father may perhaps disown me, oh my God, how dreadful, will it really go so far? God in heaven will forgive me then— it is indeed only love.[19]

Clara never accepted the anger she felt; guilt haunted her for many years. In July she wrote from Mayen, a suburb of Dresden:

> I forgive your anger at Father because I know you would forgive everything just as quickly if he would be friendly toward us. Your heart is so good that I cannot take [your anger] badly. I am his daughter and though I feel bitter at times, yet I still love Father so much. Believe me, he is good and believes he is doing this for my best interests. . . . He is very hard at times, and does not know the love that we cherish for each other, nor does he understand delicacy of feeling in such a situation, but believe me, when I am finally with you, he will gradually become favorably disposed toward me—he loves me too much to push me away from him forever. Be calm, my Robert, he loves you too; he just will not admit it.[20]

All his life Robert was to face the fact that Clara never really gave up her father, even in the face of the bitterest hostility, even when Wieck's behavior seemed insane. On the whole, Robert bore the situation well; his attitude indicated concern and understanding for Clara's need. But despite his surface dignity, he was frightened, shaken, and easily depressed. On August 1, 1838, he wrote, "You are attached to your father with great love and I respect you all the more for it. But Clara, if you were to give me up on his account! My blood runs cold. Forgive me. I am still so sick." On August 21 he complained, "Your father embitters my whole life, our entire love. He tramples everything underfoot; he worships only Mammon. What lies has he been telling Becker again? And you don't defend me at all? Enough of this . . . but all these slanders haunt me even in my dreams."[21]

Because of Wieck's rigidity and obduracy, the lovers were forced to resort to lies and deception. Even their friends were caught in the web. Ernst Adolph Becker, the courier of their secret letters, was put in one compromising position after another. While enjoying Wieck's hospitality in Leipzig between August 11 and 26, he was carrying notes between the daughter of the house and Robert. The Wiecks never suspected him, but they did suspect Moritz Reuter, the physician who was a friend of Schumann and of Wieck. Clara had to suffer the indignity of being searched for letters after Reuter visited the house. The lovers lived in constant fear of having their correspondence discovered. Her stepmother had warned Nanny that they had ways and means of finding out if Clara were writing to Robert. Clara begged him not to leave her letters lying around and not to mention anything that she had written. "For God's sake," she wrote, "*be careful;* the unfortunate consequences would be dreadful."22

Again, as in Vienna, Clara's anger at her father was entwined with her need and gratitude for his teaching. She felt she was indebted to him even for her love for music, her only solace when she was made miserable by his nagging and unreason. From Dresden in August she wrote:

> How love makes one so receptive to everything beautiful. Music is now quite another thing for me than it used to be. How blissful, how full of longing it sounds; it is indescribable. I could wear myself out now at the piano, my heart is eased by the tones and what sympathy it offers! . . . Oh, how beautiful music is; so often it is my consolation when I would like to cry. Yet we have my father to thank for this and will *never* forget this.23

In early September 1838, a few days before her nineteenth birthday, Wieck arranged a Gewandhaus concert, her first after the Viennese triumph. The next issue of Robert's journal brought a poem titled "Dream Picture," in which he praised Clara's playing as the acme of romanticism; it evoked images of Schubert songs: of the "Erlkönig" and "Mignon," of knights of old, of a pious nun. Robert pictured Clara as an elusive "angel child."24

The poem was for the public. Privately, the concert aroused in Robert a sense of the anguish he would experience many times as the husband of a concert artist, and for the first time he expressed ambivalence over his situation. To begin with, he had found it uncomfortable to attend because he resented having to share his glimpses of her with so many others. He sat quietly in a corner, watching his ring on her finger sparkle for him as she played, and felt completely left out. His true feelings are revealed in his letter of September 9, 1838:

> You played magnificently. The people don't deserve your [playing] . . .You are too dear, too lofty for the kind of life your father holds up as a worthy goal; he thinks it will bring true happiness. What difficulties, what a long way, how many days—and just for a few hours! . . . No, my Clara will be a happy wife, a contented, beloved wife. I consider your art great and holy. I hardly dare think of the happiness you will give me with it; but if we don't consider it necessary, you won't lift a finger if you don't want to, for people who aren't even worth playing scales for, isn't that so, my girl? Don't misunderstand me: you know I am an artist who believes you can

preserve art without our having to make long concert tours, indeed you will find in me a truly ardent musician, to whom it is all the same if you rush a little or hold back or play a little more elegantly—as long as it always comes from within—and it does with you.[25]

Soon after that concert, Robert left for Vienna. This trip had been conceived a few months earlier, when it occurred to Clara that it might be advantageous for Robert to visit the Austrian capital and perhaps eventually to move his journal there, particularly in view of her success there and Wieck's insistence that they could not remain in Leipzig if they married. Robert concurred and wrote to Vienna immediately. His plan was to enlist the help of Joseph Fischhof, the Vienna correspondent for his *Neue Zeitschrift* and professor of piano in the conservatory, and some of the influential people Clara had met in steering the project through the bureaucracy and intrigues of the music-loving capital. This was no easy task in a city where censorship was of a virulence unknown in Leipzig. As it turned out, the Vienna trip came to nothing as far as the journal was concerned but was of great importance in other ways: Schumann met Ferdinand Schubert, brother of the composer he had idolized, and discovered the great C-Major Symphony, which had been laid away with other priceless music manuscripts; he had more opportunities to hear vocal music, particularly opera, than had been possible in Leipzig; and he created a number of works in which the Viennese influence on both his emotional and musical life are evident. "Arabesque," op. 18; "Blumenstück," op. 19; "Humoresque," op. 20; and "Faschingsschwank," op. 26, were among the piano works composed in Vienna.[26]

Dreading his departure, Clara clung to him, begging for just one more meeting and still another, until finally Robert concocted an elaborate plot so that they could spend some time alone. He announced to his friends and landlady that he would be staying in Zwickau for two weeks before embarking on the final stages of the trip to Vienna. He did remain in Zwickau—but only until he received a message from Clara that Wieck had left town on a business trip. He then slipped back into Leipzig and stayed two days with a friend so that he and Clara could be together. Finally he left for Dresden on his way to Vienna.[27]

This separation engendered much anxiety and tension, and the letters between the lovers carried the seeds of a misunderstanding that was to break out in full force when Clara was in Paris. Moreover, Wieck was furious when he learned that the two were carrying out plans to meet the conditions he himself had laid down a few months before: that Robert was to leave Leipzig and establish his paper in Vienna and that Clara was to go to Paris alone. New conditions were established: Nanny, who was known to be sympathetic to Clara and Robert, was to be dismissed; Clara was to go on no more tours; and if she married, she was to "fulfill her duties to her mother" by sending Frau Bargiel the interest on her capital.[28] The demands were puzzling, as

Wieck had previously forbidden her to send anything to her mother.* More puzzling still was the announcement that he would not accompany her to Paris. Fearful, she turned to Schumann, who assured her that if worse came to worst and she had to leave her father's home, he would provide (indeed, had already provided) a fund on which she could draw. Yet despite Schumann's generosity and forethought and her father's senseless demands, Clara still wavered and Robert had to endure constant fluctuations in her mood.

"You are, forgive me, like a pair of children," he wrote on October 24, 1838. "You cry, he scolds, and it is still the same as ever. . . . You can't belong to him and to me at the same time. You will have to leave one, him or me."[29]

Though she protested that Robert was the one who mattered, Wieck's influence remained stronger. Without realizing the effect her words might have on Robert, Clara wrote of waiting until after 1840 for their marriage, if necessary, so they would be on firmer financial ground. Schumann's despair was so intense that Dr. Reuter had to remind her to be careful about what she wrote. Finally, on November 25, she wrote what he was longing to hear: "For your sake I will give up my father, whom I love more than anyone except for you. I will follow you without my father's consent. . . . That is a great deal for a feeling heart to do, difficult, but *I trust you*, my life will lie in your hands and you will make me happy."[30]

Alas, this was not to be her last word.

The trip to Paris became both a private and a public testing ground for Clara's independence, a frightening thought for her. Even Robert was hesitant at first and had to be convinced of the advantages to be gained from such a trip. As late as August he was writing to her: "About Paris, if I were in your place I would not act as if it means too much, nor would I talk about it too much either. Your father will certainly not stay home all winter. You cannot travel alone; I won't permit it."[31]

During the next few months Clara began to recognize the depth of her father's hostility. He would permit her to go to Paris without him, but he hoped for her failure and counted on her return from what he predicted would be an ignominious defeat. Fury at her defiance and independent spirit outweighed pride in her success; this man would be vindicated at any cost. But in counting on her need for him as teacher, father, protector, Wieck ignored all she had learned from that same source: practicality, self-confidence, and a particular hardheaded stubbornness. And so she decided to go.

Nanny, her only confidante, was not permitted to accompany her, and Wieck hired as chaperone Claudine Dufourd, a Frenchwoman whom Clara did not know. She left Leipzig with the stranger on January 8, heading

---

*Clara did send her mother money from time to time, since she knew that her need was great. After her September 1838 concert, for example, she sent her six louis d'or.

toward Nuremberg in a heavy snowfall. She planned to earn money by giving concerts along the way, as she had done on her previous trip with her father in 1832, and was gratified that despite her father's absence, her concerts in Nuremberg, Stuttgart, and Karlsruhe went well. Though she told herself that her father would come as soon as his business would allow, she was beginning to realize how well she had learned to carry on a career without him.[32] There were, of course, anxious moments as she sat in the carriage, writing to Robert. Addressing him now as Eusebius, now as Florestan, she described her headaches, her sleepless nights, and the responsibilities of the concert arrangements which were now hers.

The journey yielded two happy events: in Asch she learned that Ernestine was married and was willing to help Clara and Robert in any way; and in Stuttgart she found a traveling companion, Henriette Reichmann, a young woman of her own age who wished to study with her and was prepared to go to Paris to be with her. Henriette remained a friend for life.

The Paris the two young women and their chaperone were timorously approaching was still the musical capital of Europe: nineteen theaters and at least three concert salons presented opera, drama, vaudeville, ballet, revues, recitals, and other events daily. Giacomo Meyerbeer, one of many German composers Clara and Wieck had met on her earlier trip, was now the most admired composer in Paris, tsar of the opera, and, fortunately for Clara, a man easy to know. She was able to turn to him for advice, and although later Robert despised and castigated his music, he proved to be a reliable friend to Clara. She met other composers as well—Friedrich Kalkbrenner, Daniel Auber, George Onslow, and Jacques Halévy—but made little impression on them, nor did she care for the French composers (except for Onslow, of whom she became fond). Among the musicians she encountered were Charles Alkan, Pierre Baillot, Adolphe Adam, Luigi Cherubini, Johann Baptiste Cramer, and Anna de Belleville-Oury (a former competitor whom she branded "the most abhorrent woman in the world"), as well as Princess Christine Belgiojoso, a wealthy patroness. Through the Erard family, makers of musical instruments, she was introduced to many distinguished writers, including Alexandre Dumas and Heinrich Heine.

Hector Berlioz, whose *Symphonie Fantastique* had been analyzed, reviewed, and praised by Schumann in 1835, was introduced to her at the home of the Bertins, an influential Parisian publishing family. She described the meeting in a letter to Robert:

> He is quiet, has uncommonly thick hair, and is always looking at the floor, casting his eyes downward. He will visit me tomorrow. At first I didn't know it was he and wondered who this man was who continually spoke about you; finally I asked him his name, and when he told me I reacted with such happy astonishment that he must have been flattered. His new opera [*Benvenuto Cellini*] has been a complete failure.[33]

Berlioz, still struggling for a foothold on the perilously political musical paths of the French capital and burdened with an ill and incompatible wife and young child, had little time or inclination to help the young German pianist. She was not happy with his review in the *Journal des Débats* of her concert on April 16; he acknowledged her gifts as a pianist but damned her Scherzo with faint praise. Although she professed modesty about her creative abilities, she was accustomed to critical acclaim. She was taken aback by Berlioz' words, considered him hostile, and in her diary entry of April 18, 1839, described his review as "extremely malicious."

On her arrival in Paris on February 6, 1839, Clara had found good friends: Emilie List was there with her parents, and the mezzo-soprano Pauline García (later García-Viardot), whom she had met in Dresden the previous summer, was settled in the French capital with her mother and brother-in-law, the Belgian violinist Charles de Bériot, and making a great sensation.* Erard and Pleyel, the leading piano manufacturers, both pressed pianos on Clara, placing her in a predicament that she found difficult to handle: how was she to use the Pleyel (which she preferred) without insulting Pierre Erard?

There were many difficulties and disappointments in the big foreign city. It was several weeks before she was able to retrieve Robert's letters from the post office; she received no word from her father for even longer. Feeling completely cut off from her former life, she lamented to Robert that she was really alone for the first time in her life. But when Heinrich Probst, a friend and business associate of her father, and Eduard Fechner, her stepmother's brother, urged her to return home, she refused to leave and arranged to give concerts at the Conservatoire and the Erard salon. She wrote to Robert that she was considering touring in England for several months and returning to Paris in the summer to give lessons. She weighed the possibility of a tour in the French provinces before returning to Leipzig to marry at Easter 1840, with or without her father's permission.

She and Henriette Reichmann, accompanied by Claudine Dufourd (soon to be dismissed), took lodgings in the Hôtel Michadière, where Pauline García was also staying, but within a few months Clara and Henriette moved again, this time to share lodgings with the List family. Besides practicing, teaching, making her own concert arrangements, and playing in the right places, she and Henriette saw everything to be seen in Paris: the Tuileries, Nôtre Dame, the Palais Royal, the Invalides, the Pantheon, the stock exchange; they were caught on the streets during a political uprising (excitedly described in great detail to Robert); they attended operas, concerts, and ballets at every opportunity. Clara was not isolated in Paris and she managed to make her way, although it cannot be said that her presence was strongly felt. She found, probably for the first time in her life, much competition, and

*Bériot was Clara Wieck's assisting artist at the April 16 concert.

told Robert with some trepidation that all the pianists, male and female, were playing in Paris. But in March and April she arranged and gave several successful concerts, which were well reviewed in the Paris journals as well as in the Leipzig *Allgemeine musikalische Zeitung.*

The triumphs and praise, however, were not enough to sustain her. She needed her father's approval. Soon after she reached Paris, on February 14, she tearfully wrote to Robert:

> Just look, I have only you; you shall be my support. I have a father whom I love infinitely, who loves me, and yet I do not have the kind of father my heart requires. You must be all to me, my father as well, isn't that so, Robert? True, I have received letters since I have been here, but they are letters of a different sort. Not one loving word, like those that I so like to hear from you; they contain only cold advice, reproaches; my father believes himself to be unfortunate and that hurts me; I cannot feel any differently. I firmly believe that my father's heart will still yield, and in this belief, may our goal come closer and closer; when he sees us happy, he too will be happy.[34]

Within a few weeks Wieck read the reviews, heard from friends, and realized to his dismay that Clara was doing well without him. In an angry letter to Emilie List he declared his intention to deprive Clara of her inheritance, including the money she herself had earned, unless she gave Robert up, and threatened to begin a lawsuit against them both.

Robert's reactions to her reviews were ambivalent. He was proud of her (all of his letters to Paris are addressed to the "Royal and Imperial Chamber Virtuosa Clara Wieck"), and his advice demonstrated his confidence in her: "Don't leave Paris before you've had a *total* triumph. . . . Don't go to London before you're certain that your Parisian reputation has reached there. Those cities are the largest in the world. You are actually appearing in those places as a fully developed artist *for the first time.*"[35]

But he sent quite another message when he wrote:

> I am musing about our first summer in Zwickau as married folks. . . . First (another kiss), young wives must be able to cook and to keep house, if they want satisfied husbands, and you can have fun learning that from Therese; and then young wives may not make long journeys right away, but must take care of themselves and spare themselves, especially one who has spent the entire previous year working and sacrificing for her husband; third, we want to free ourselves from boring and curious visitors; fourth, we want to be able to take walks and I will show you all my boyhood haunts; fifth, you father could do us no harm. . . . [36]

Then the young man again reversed himself and wrote, "Write often and write long letters. Use your time to compose, play. *Don't be so retiring,* let them know what kind of artist they have in Paris."[37] A few days later he was still attempting to resolve his conflicting aims:

I have just read the letter in which you write, "If I remain in Dresden for one year I will be forgotten as an artist." . . . Clärchen, you are not really serious—and if you were to be forgotten as an artist, would you not be beloved as a wife? . . . The first year of our marriage you *shall* forget the artist, you *shall* live only for yourself and your house and your husband, and wait . . . just see how I will make you forget the artist—because the wife stands even higher than the artist and if I only achieve this much— that you have nothing more to do with the public—I will have achieved my deepest wish. Yet you still remain an artist. The bit of fame in the contemptible paper—I despise it.[38]

Robert's frustrations and ambivalence about her career continued. Even more threatening to his peace of mind was her protracted clinging to her father. Notwithstanding Wieck's threats, she urged Robert to placate him. In answer to Robert's reproach that she was too weak with her father, she replied on April 22, "My father . . . is to be pitied, and in my heart I often grieve over it; yet I cannot change it in any way. . . . Oh, Robert, forgive me if in the future a sudden melancholy overcomes me when I think of my father—but it is so painful."[39] Schumann may have found it even more difficult to accept Clara's reaction to a second and softer letter from her father, a letter from which the peremptory tone had vanished. Grasping at what she perceived as warmth, she wrote deeply and passionately to him of her feelings for Robert, what their relationship meant for her, and her longing for her father's blessing. She begged him to come to Paris, offering Emilie's help with the language for a trip to England.

Then in May, forgetting all her promises, she asked Robert to postpone their marriage, saying, in effect, "Father is right." She had just enough sensitivity to realize that Robert would have a right to be angry, but not enough tact to understand that the closing remark, "You are a man, Robert, are you not, and will not surrender to grief?" was equally insulting.[40]

Emilie List contributed to the hurt Schumann must have suffered; she sent him a letter presenting Wieck's side and informing him that Clara's health suffered under strain. If she wanted to keep her position as a virtuosa secure, Emilie wrote, she could give no more than one lesson a day, which might not suffice to support a household. Clara, she said, had two choices: she must either neglect her art and accept the cares of a housewife or have the means to survive without these petty cares and lead a free, independent life. "Therefore," she wrote, "I feel it would be far better if Clara gathered a small capital before she married." She ventured so far as to propose that Robert become a book dealer and publisher and take over the business of his recently deceased brother, Eduard. "Your art would not suffer," the young lady advised him, "and you would make enough money to satisfy Wieck."[41]*

*Emilie List was known to be sharp-tongued, and she meddled in Clara's affairs more than once. Though the two remained friends, there was occasional strain between them. Emilie never married.

Robert Schumann, age 29, in Vienna. Lithograph by Josef Kriehuber, 1839. Robert-Schumann-Haus, Zwickau, DDR.

Clara Wieck shortly before her marriage, age 20. Unfinished colored drawing, 1840. Robert-Schumann-Haus, Zwickau, DDR.

The thought of taking over Eduard's business had already crossed Robert's mind, but to receive such advice from Clara's friend infuriated him and might have caused a serious rift had he not received a letter almost immediately from Clara begging him to forgive her. "Tell me, my good, beloved Robert, what am I to do to restore your tender feelings toward me? Please tell me, I cannot be at ease when I know you are angry with me," she wrote when the full realization of what she had done struck her.[42]

Robert replied, "Just promise me not to entertain any more unnecessary fears, trust and obey me; after all, men are above women."[43] There is no doubt that Clara fervently agreed. Robert then sent her two letters, the first a dignified appeal to Wieck for permission to marry, the second a joint letter that was to be submitted to the Court of Appeals in Leipzig after she had signed it if Wieck withheld his consent. She did not hesitate; on June 15, she went alone to a notary in Paris, signed the letter, and sent it off.*

Clara's wavering seemed to be at an end, and as before, her decision was probably due to a blunder on Wieck's part. Just before she received the legal document from Robert, she had received a harsh letter from her father enclosing a list of conditions to which she was to agree. The conditions were absurd; Wieck had gone too far. She replied:

> Allow me to answer but one thing. I have not signed my agreement to your conditions and I tell you, I will never sign them, I have too much pride for that; besides, how could you think that I would sign a paper in which nothing but evil things are written of the man I love? You were not serious, and if you were serious, then I must say to you, you will never bring me to do such a thing.[44]

Robert's letter to Wieck read:

> Honored Sir:
> Clara writes that you yourself desire that we should come to a conclusion; I gladly offer my hand in peace. Let me know your wishes; I am happy and ready to fulfill them in any way I can. If by a week from today I have no word from you, I will assume that your response to my inquiry is a negative one.[45]

The answer, written by Frau Wieck, was brief: "Wieck does not choose to have any connection with Schumann."[46]

Robert forthwith presented the document with both signatures to the court and sent Clara money for a return trip to Leipzig, because a personal appearance was required.[47] Clara and Henriette left Paris the second week of August; they parted company a few days later in Stuttgart.

---

*Saxon law required the consent of the parents of both parties for any marriage, regardless of the age or rank of the children. (As an orphan, Robert was not obliged to obtain consent. Clara's mother gave her consent immediately.) If such consent could not be obtained, it was customary to appeal to the court.

The months in Paris had not brought Clara the great reputation she had sought, but they were of inestimable importance for her growth. Here she had lived, found and made friends, arranged, performed, and maneuvered in the muddy waters of Parisian musical life, composed, taught, survived— all without her father, and in a state of emotional turmoil that might easily have felled a lesser spirit.

On August 18, 1839, Robert met Clara in Altenburg, the city in which she had parted from her mother many years before. The lovers were together for a few days but entered Leipzig separately. Clara was apprehensive of her father's anger, but found that that problem had been taken out of her hands: her father's house was no longer open to her. She stayed with friends and relatives but soon left Leipzig to live with the Bargiels in Berlin. All her possessions—her clothing, music, piano, even her childhood diary—remained at her father's home.

The next year was to be the most difficult she had endured, even though her mother and Robert were nearby. To witness the genteel poverty of the Bargiels was a frightening experience. Marianne was obliged to give piano lessons while caring for four children, nursing a sick husband, and supervising a home. Clara realized that her presence, however much her mother welcomed her, was an additional burden for the Bargiels. Though Schumann gave Clara 400 taler in Prussian state bonds on September 3 (since Wieck had left her penniless), she felt helpless.* To add to her anxiety, she received several pitiful begging letters from Ernestine von Fricken, now widowed and also penniless.[48] Her discomfort turned to despair when she realized that Robert was experiencing a serious depression after the months of acting boldly and taking the initiative. He made no effort to disguise it in his letters to her:

> I beg you to whisper my name to the Almighty now and then that he protect me, because I can tell you that I am so depressed and worn out with pain that I can hardly pray. I am carrying a great burden of guilt—I separated you from your father—and this often torments me.[49]

On a visit to Zwickau in July, he was tortured by thoughts of death. "I am very sick now, weak physically and also mentally—from everything in my head. You must have noticed it from my letters as well. Everything exhausts me frightfully."[50]

Although Clara had endured many difficult moments, she had never known this kind of mental anguish. In Paris and now in Berlin, she reacted to emotional strain with such physical symptoms as pain in her fingers, shoul-

---

*From entries in Schumann's household books for 1839–40, we know that Schumann supported her for the entire year before their marriage. He sent money for all her needs—concert dresses, living expenses, and gifts for her mother, her stepfather, and even her brother Alwin.

ders, or arm, but even this discomfort rarely prevented her from practicing or performing. In January 1840 she gave a number of concerts in Berlin while suffering depression, aches and pains, fainting spells, and neuralgia, and found, to her surprise, that her audiences were unaware of her problems, that she played just as well as ever and received the same tumultuous applause. She was aware of Robert's history of depression but had never fully comprehended that she would have to deal with it. The realization was frightening, particularly now that she was dependent on him for emotional and moral support. It was easier to bear when he wrote and described his state: "I am often silent for days on end—without thoughts—merely muttering to myself."[51] But frequently he did not write or wrote coldly. She was in despair over one letter and wrote in her diary on January 15, 1840:

> Today a letter from Robert caused me to suffer one of the most painful hours of my life. He confirmed the fact that the court case may not be over before Michaelmas [September] and at the same time wrote that he would not prevent my returning to Father if I wished, etc. That was worse than a stab—at first it put me in a state of insensibility but then the tears came and flowed without ceasing. Oh, Robert, what an injustice you have done me.

On January 17 she wrote:

> My state of mind is indescribable—I cannot forget the words in Robert's last letter—they torture me. I have endured everything, I have lost my father, I have stood up to him in a court of law, what battles have I fought with myself, but Robert's love made up for all this. I believed his faith was immovable, and now he hurts me so much. I can barely calm myself.

She could not know at the time that Schumann was reacting to a "declaration" that Wieck had presented in court on December 14, 1839. It was too painful for him to describe the impassioned eleven-page document which was both malicious and libelous.* Although Schumann was able to prove the charges false, the situation was humiliating and expensive, and necessitated a further posponement.

The case dragged on, as court cases do. Wieck followed his declaration

---

*The eleven heated pages still seem to smoke with Wieck's unreasoning fury. He included nasty comments on Schumann's capabilities as a musician and composer, as journalist and editor; he wrote that Schumann could not help Clara with her career, since he was socially inept—could not speak clearly or write legibly; that he crippled his finger through his own stupidity; that he lied about his income; that he had been badly brought up and displayed an indescribable egotism and unlimited vanity; that he was a solitary drinker and drank to excess; and that he did not really love Clara—he wanted to use her for his own purposes and live off the money she earned as an artist. His daughter, he wrote, having been trained as an artist, was unfit to run a home; moreover, her special needs as an artist required her to have more money than a woman in ordinary circumstances would need. The document is in the Staatsarchiv, Dresden; a transcription by Georg Eismann is in RSH (5725-A3c).

with a formal five-page paper to which Schumann responded in an equally formal, lengthy, reasoned reply refuting Wieck's charges. Schumann's response was accompanied by supporting documents: an honorary doctorate from the University of Jena, an accounting of his income, letters from Ernestine von Fricken's father and other influential friends. The court was convinced and by July Wieck was finished, though he refused to acknowledge defeat. The court's consent for the marriage was conferred by default.

Schumann had answered Wieck's accusations with a suit of his own. On June 1, 1840, a "denunciation" was sent to Dresden, to which Wieck had moved, charging Wieck with slander and suing for the money Clara had earned on her tours. The suit for Clara's money was settled out of court but the slander charges were tried and resulted in a judgment against Wieck in April 1841. He was ordered to pay court costs and a considerable amount to the Schumanns.[52] In addition to the legal maneuvers, Wieck made several other last-moment attempts to bring Clara to her knees. In April 1840 he sent Alwin to demand that she pay for his violin lessons; soon afterward Wieck spread word throughout Leipzig that she would soon come begging at his door and sent maligning letters to Hamburg and Berlin just as she was about to appear there in concert. The foulest blow was his declaration that she was not playing well and would ruin any piano she used.[53]

He continued the assault on Schumann as well, spreading stories throughout Leipzig. The attacks were so virulent and his actions so irrational that Clara and many others thought he was losing his mind.[54] All the charges were lies, distortions, or half-truths, and thus easily disproved—but at a terrible emotional cost to the young composer.

In September 1839, Clara had asked her father for some of her earnings to serve as a dowry, but he refused, saying that if Robert really loved her, he would contrive to give her the money she asked for. The courageous young woman then resolved to provide her own dowry by giving concerts. Besides performing in Berlin, she traveled with her mother to Stettin and Stargardt, and later to Hamburg, Bremen, and Lübeck. By March 1840 she was able to write to Schumann, "I will tell you, though I don't like to speak about it, that I earned 970 taler, of which some went to travel expenses, purchases for me and Mother and the household, so that I now have 490 taler left. Are you satisfied? I am very happy about it and realize that in five weeks one could hardly ask for more."[55]

The tour brought her more than money; it was exhilarating to be on stage once more. She was distressed at Schumann's desire that she remain home during the first year of their marriage, and pointed out—as she was to do many times during their marriage—that she should earn money "now that I am young and have all my strength." There were some further uneasy moments in the months before her marriage when Clara proposed concert tours to England and to St. Petersburg, but Robert would not agree. She was quite prepared to face a lengthy separation, pointing out, in her practical

Friedrich Wieck, ca. 1853. From Marie Wieck, *Aus dem Kreise Wieck-Schumann* (Dresden: v. Zahn & Jaensch, 1914).

way, that she could not make as much money as a married woman as she had as a girl. Clara was dissuaded from the Russian tour only when she learned that Liszt would be there at the same time. She was not prepared to compete with him for audiences.[56]

Clara was clearly concerned about solvency. The possibility of having to use Robert's capital to set up housekeeping, she wrote in her diary on April 7, 1840, "pains me; I cannot look forward to the marriage in a happy frame of mind." But although she attributed all her anxiety to worries about money, other thoughts were undoubtedly troubling her. The attachment to her father had not lost its grip and the trauma of this separation was overwhelming. Outpourings of love for Wieck found their way into the diary during all the trials, both legal and emotional:

[August 24, 1839]   I think his fatherly love will triumph over his unreason.

[August 31]   My filial love and thankfulness can never cease.

[September 20]   Today I was overwhelmed by melancholy as I thought of my father. I regret everything so much, and yet was he not cruel? was he not terrible? Nonetheless I feel such an unextinguishable love for him— one friendly word from him and I would forget all the pain he caused me.

[September 26]   I feel so abandoned now; I belong to no one. When I see Robert, I want to cling to him.

[September 29]   Above all, I feel such great pity for Father, I cannot describe it. In losing me, he has lost all his hopes.

[November 11]   I would like to forget him (heaven forgive me), and yet cannot. I cannot suppress the childlike love I feel, and if I ever do, it breaks through stronger than ever and then I must weep. Yet it is a quieting thought to know that the feeling for my father has not disappeared and that is something I also want to preserve. On the one hand, he is to be pitied, even though, on the other hand, he has treated me so terribly.

Clara's letters during the months of touring in the winter of 1839–40 reveal patterns of behavior that were not to change. Like many other artists, she was nervous before a concert, rarely satisfied with her performance, and often depressed after the event. She often suffered lapses of self-confidence and physical symptoms. Schumann had little patience with her laments, pointing out that these reactions might have been deliberately encouraged by her father so that she would feel helpless without his presence. In a letter of February 1840 Robert also attributed to her father her fear of being forgotten if she married and stopped playing publicly.[57] As soon as Clara read this analysis, she realized how right he was; her mood changed instantly and she was ready to compete again. Lapses in self-confidence, however, were to occur again and again.

The conflicts of 1838–40 intensified Clara's jealous and suspicious disposition. The success of other artists troubled her. Camilla Pleyel, a beautiful and accomplished French pianist just a few years older than Clara, was in Leipzig while Clara was touring in the north with her mother. It was upsetting to learn that her father fawned on the coquettish young woman, worse when the Hamburg musicians sang her praises, unbearable when Robert praised Pleyel in his letters and in his journal reviews.

When, during one of Robert's very creative periods ("February is always a good month for me," he wrote),[58] he began to send her the songs he was composing, the first of the rich harvest of 1840, Clara's appreciation was clouded by suspicions she could not control. "How wonderful that you are composing so diligently," she wrote, "but as for the songs, it has occurred to me—is there perhaps some young nightingale in Leipzig who is inflaming you?" There was no reply to this question, but the letter that accompanied the songs should have been reassuring: "The songs are my first published ones, so don't criticize them too much. As I composed them, I thought only of you. Your eyes, you romantic girl, follow me everywhere, and I often think one cannot make such music without such a bride."[59]

Clara was never completely convinced, despite the passionate letters and the need for her he expressed in this letter of December 1838:

> It is from you that I receive all life, on whom I am wholly dependent. Like a slave, I should often like to follow you from afar at a distance, and await your slightest bidding. Ah! let me say it once more, come what may—I will whisper it even to whoever closes my eyes, "One alone has ruled my life completely, drawn me into her inmost being, and it is she that I have ever honored and loved above all."[60]

The young artist always had a lingering fear that she wasn't pretty enough or intelligent enough to keep Robert happy. During the last month before her marriage, other doubts assailed her. On June 17, 1840, she wrote in her diary:

> Oh, how I tremble, how my heart pounds—I have an unhappy character. Even my great love for Robert gives me unhappy hours—I often ask myself, can I make him as happy as I would like to, as he deserves? Won't family responsibilities put too much pressure on him? Will he be recognized? Oh, my God! These and so many thoughts torture me—if I were only his wife already!

Schumann was also tense during the summer. Like Clara, he had never been altogether free of jealousies and suspicions. His often vicious references to Wieck in the correspondence of 1839, his violent hatred of Carl Banck, and his fierce anger at the men who courted her in Vienna indicate his all-too-human fears. His continuing envy of Clara's friendship with Mendelssohn plagued him for years. His letters during the summer of 1840 filled with criticisms, recriminations, and admissions of jealousy even toward such old friends as Johann Verhulst, reveal the strains he felt.[61]

The times Clara and Robert spent in Berlin and Leipzig were the happiest during the long months of 1839 and 1840. They made music together, they walked, they talked—but not too much; it was easier to communicate through music or pen—and enjoyed their physical proximity.

The court's decision came in July 1840, and though they had to wait ten more days to learn if Wieck would appeal, they began to look for an apartment in Leipzig. Even during a summer that should have been completely happy, she was troubled. On July 19 she wrote in her diary, "I am trembling and quivering about the coming day with both joy and anguish. I have hardly any mind left; I feel continuous anxiety and have never felt more exhausted. If only heaven preserves my health!"

By August they learned that the court had ruled entirely in their favor. A concert tour to nearby Thuringian towns was planned just before the first banns were published. Her last concert as Clara Wieck took place on September 5 in Weimar.

The wedding on September 12, the day before her twenty-first birthday, settled the conflict between father and lover. She was now the wife of Robert Schumann.

CHAPTER 5

The Marriage

The marriage between Robert and Clara Schumann was unique in musical history. They were drawn together and remained together not only because of common musical experience, mutual emotional dependency, and physical attraction, but because their musical and creative needs complemented each other.

The early months of their marriage were the most joyful Clara had ever experienced. Her husband was both mother and father to the woman who had lost both: his tender, Eusebius side (the one she preferred) provided maternal warmth; his brilliant mind, creative genius, and sharp critical talent stimulated and inspired the young artist. And finally, her sexual fulfillment, after so many years of postponement, must have been an overwhelmingly joyful experience; the diaries and letters of this prudish age are silent on the subject.

Now that they were at last together, they began a journal, the *Ehetagebuch* (marriage diary), in which they vowed to write, alternating weekly. Though diaries and journals were common, a joint diary was unusual. For the Schumanns, however, such a venture was particularly apt, since both had difficulty expressing their feelings in speech. Clara's reticence may have stemmed from her early years of silence. Robert's inarticulateness probably began as social diffidence, awkwardness, lack of confidence, but it continued past adolescence, gradually worsened, and during his later years became at times total speechlessness. He always spoke best with his pen; writing was his mode of expression, for words as well as music, and the marriage diary was to be the primary avenue for intimate communication between the two. It remains an important source of information about their daily life in Leipzig and about their visitors, providing a record of the vicissitudes of their emotional life, their thoughts on the music they composed, played and heard, and "character studies of significant artists with whom we are in close contact."[1] Problems, complaints, fears—all were shared on the pages of the marriage diary.

For the next few months they kept to the plan of writing in alternate weeks, but as Robert became absorbed in his composing, the task became Clara's. Robert, who was extremely orderly, also kept household books, notebooks in which he entered household accounts and recorded his income, Clara's earnings, appointments, comments on music and people, and brief notes on his compositions and their dates. Over the years his note taking became increasingly compulsive. In 1846 he even began to record the dates on which he and Clara had sexual relations.

On December 5, 1840, Clara declared in the marriage diary, "We have been married a quarter of a year today, and it is the happiest quarter of a year of my life." There was, however, one "but" expressed: her sadness about the continued break with her father. The only contact between the two families was through lawyers and courts. The slander suit initiated by Schumann on June 2, 1840, was not settled until April 1841, when the court ruled against Wieck.[2] On February 27, 1841, Clara's piano was delivered to her—the result of distressful negotiations conducted by a go-between.[3]* In August 1841, however, just before her first child, Marie, was born, Clara was forced to ask their old friend Ernst Adolph Becker to intercede in order to collect the 43 taler Wieck had agreed to pay for the shipping of the piano.[4]

Wieck had given up his Leipzig piano business and resettled as a voice and piano teacher in Dresden almost a year before his daughter's marriage, ostensibly because he wished to work with Johann Aloys Miksch, who was nearing the end of his long career as a voice teacher.[5] The healthier air in that city may also have figured in his decision to move. It is more than likely, however, that he felt he had to get away from Leipzig, which seemed to be filled with Schumann's friends. Wieck ignored the birthday greetings Clara sent him in August 1841; the note announcing the birth of his granddaughter was answered with a rude letter.[6] He continued to spread rumors about Schumann and his daughter; during Clara's solo trip to Copenhagen in March and April 1842, he told people that they had separated.[7] They feared he would return Clara's money in worthless notes, if at all. Wieck had no compunctions about making public his contempt for Schumann (even at the risk of another libel suit) and referred to his son-in-law's Spring Symphony as the "Symphony of Contradictions."[8]

In May 1842, however, after premieres of both the First and Second (the latter was published as the Fourth) symphonies, Wieck initiated efforts toward a rapprochement. Wieck had always considered the creation of a symphony to be the mark of a *real* composer (one of his complaints was that Schumann had been talking about a symphony for years but had not yet

---

*Major Serre, an old friend who lived near Dresden, took on this task.

produced one); perhaps he weakened after Schumann composed two such works.

On a visit to Leipzig in May 1842, Wieck presented to a mutual friend a proposal for mediation of the differences between Schumann and himself. Schumann found the tone offensive, and no doubt recalling the gossip Wieck had spread during Clara's Copenhagen visit, he did not reply. Clara, however, met with her father during his visit and saw him with new eyes:

> I didn't see much of Father; he was busy from morning till evening with instruments and Marie, who had to test them all. I am so used to a quiet, peaceful life with Robert that I could no longer be with Father, even for a short time. This frightful agitation, this restlessness of mind and body doesn't permit him—or anyone around him—to secure any kind of tranquil enjoyment of life.[9]

Eight months after the unsuccessful attempt in May, Wieck tried again to effect a reconciliation with Robert. In a letter that Clara received on January 13, 1843, he said he was writing at the instigation of Clementine, his wife, "your best, noblest, truest, etc. friend." He admired Robert's diligence and creativity, he said, and hoped they would both visit him in Dresden, where his music studio and any other rooms in his home would be placed at their disposal for a performance of Robert's quintet. "The Dresdeners will come," he assured Clara, "if one attracts them with food or drink or music." He asked her to bring the baby along, reminding her that she would not have to pay for the baby on the train. Offering to meet them all at the railway station,* he assured her that there need be no discussion of the previous four years. "We have many other things to talk about." Wieck evidently wanted to wipe out the whole history of the conflict. He was so eager to see her, he wrote, that he would come to Leipzig if she could not get to Dresden. And he indicated some sensitivity about the reaction of other people to the Wieck-Schumann affairs. "Your husband will agree with me that we should not speak to anyone about all this. When people see us together, they will assume everything is all right."[10]

Robert's career was well under way; Clara, now a mother, was continuing to make headlines as a performer; and Wieck seems to have feared that he would be left out of their lives and successes. Clara grasped eagerly at this offer of reconciliation. She wrote a long and affectionate reply, dated two days after his letter, asking about his health and about her stepmother and stepsisters, describing her activities and Robert's new compositions.[11] Wieck visited her on February 3, 1843, and soon thereafter—two months before Elise was born—she went to Dresden, alone, to see her family.[12]

---

*A railroad line between Leipzig and Dresden, one of the first in Germany, was established in 1839.

This was the first of many short trips she made that year. After a private performance of the Schumann Quintet in Dresden on February 14, Clara wrote, "Father is now heart and soul [*Feuer und Flamme*] for Robert's compositions." Though she expressed great joy at the reconciliation, she was sick for three days on her return, possibly the result of the excitement and tensions of the Dresden visit.[13]

Schumann grumbled about Clara's visits to Dresden. Several times he was tempted to join her, but pride and memories held him back. The success of his oratorio *Das Paradies und die Peri* and its forthcoming Dresden production brought a note from Wieck directly to Robert:

> *Tempora mutantur et nos mutamur in eis.** With Clara and the world to consider we can no longer remain at a distance. You are yourself the father of a family—why do we need long explanations? We were always agreed as far as art is concerned—I was even your teacher—my verdict decided your career. I don't have to assure you of my appreciation of your talent and your fine and genuine endeavors. I await you in Dresden with joy. Your father.[14]

Finally, in December 1843, more than a year after Clara's reunion with her father, Schumann agreed to meet with him, and after the *Peri* performances in Dresden, Clara and Robert spent Christmas with the Wiecks. The reunion was cool, however, and the relationship remained perfunctory. Clara never regained her trust in her father, and both she and Robert suspected bad faith for years after the reconciliation.

One other conflict ruffled the idyllic early months of the marriage, and the emotions aroused led to much discomfort and suppressed anger. Clara craved and for the most part received from Robert love, warmth, approval, and musical and intellectual inspiration, but he could not give her what had been part of her life for many years—full participation in the musical world, the rush of applause, the adoration and admiration of an audience. Robert would have been happy to live quietly, to have Clara perform for him and perhaps some friends and provide a comfortable nest, like a conventional *Hausfrau*. For Clara, however, such a life was impossible, and the conflict permeated their married life. They rarely acknowledged this aspect of their relationship openly, but their children and friends were aware of it, and it is clearly revealed in their letters and diaries.

Schumann was, by and large, a devoted and thoughtful husband. He was generous and left the administration of the household to Clara: his household books record gifts and "extra" money for his wife almost every month; he registered his love and great pride in her playing and musicianship in the diary and in letters to friends. Yet her discomfort expressed itself in many ways: she was jealous of Robert's attentions to Amalie Rieffel, a student of his

*Times are changing and we are changing with them.

and the daughter of a friend; she was annoyed by her aunt Emilie Carl, her mother's sister, who she felt interfered in the running of the Schumann household; most distressing, and in the face of all evidence to the contrary, she had recurrent fears of losing Robert's love. In the entry of October 24 to November 14, 1841, she wrote in their diary:

> I have had several unhappy days in which I really tormented my poor husband—I thought he didn't love me as much as he had during the first year [of our marriage]. I know very well that he has many things on his mind which vex him. I was very irritable and because of this gave myself many troubled hours.

A year later, in November 1842, she wrote:

> An indescribable melancholy has taken hold of me for the last few days. I think that you don't love me the way you used to. I often feel so clearly that I cannot satisfy you and at times it seems to me—when you are tender— that it is only because of your good heart, which does not wish to hurt me.

The diary contains no response to these fears, and they seem to have subsided as her career took on larger dimensions.

During the Leipzig years they lived in an apartment on Inselstrasse, one flight up. Clara spent her time studying music, reading, playing (when it did not interfere with Robert's composing), entertaining visiting musicians, and keeping house with the help of several servants.* Almost every musician of note who passed through Leipzig visited them during the first year of their marriage. The list of visitors included Mendelssohn; the Dutch composer Johann Verhulst; their old friends Ernst Becker, Ernst Wenzel, and Moritz Reuter; the English composer William Sterndale Bennett; Walther von Goethe, the grandson of the poet; such local composers and publishers as Moritz Hauptmann and Robert Friese; the pianist and composer Adolph Henselt; the Norwegian violinist Ole Bull; the young pianists Amalie Rieffel and Harriet Parish, with their families; Heinrich Lichtenstein, a Berlin zoologist and music lover, with his family; and many others.

In a letter to her friend Dr. Adolph Keferstein, dated October 22, 1840, Clara described her situation:

> Allow me to send you a greeting and to present myself as a young married woman. Yes, we have finally achieved our greatest desire and enjoy great

---

*The wages of servants were exceedingly low. In the household books we read that Schumann reckoned on a little over 3 taler (plus frequent tips) for three months' wages for the serving girl. In comparison, the wedding ring cost 6 taler, two bottles of champagne cost 4 taler, the fee to the bookbinder for the special binding for *Myrthen*, the songs that were his wedding gift to Clara, was 3 taler, and rent for the apartment from September to Easter was 65 taler.

happiness. We love each other more every day and live only for each other. . . . We have so many musical pleasures now that our life is truly blissful. Moscheles was here last week and was honored by Mendelssohn in the Gewandhaus and by David, Kistner, etc., and we gave soirees in our homes.* It was a frantic time—something different every day. Now he has gone and we are awaiting Ole Bull, about whom I am very curious. He is an artist about whom many differing opinions prevail. Our Gewandhaus concerts have begun and have already given us two wonderful symphonies of Beethoven—the Eroica and the Fourth. Today there will be a Mozart symphony. In the soiree Mendelssohn gave to honor Moscheles, the Bach Triple Concerto was one of the works performed—played by Mendelssohn, Moscheles, and me.[15]

For a time the novelty of her situation satisfied her. In February 1841, the twenty-fourth week of her marriage, she wrote in the diary, "We are enjoying a happiness that I never knew. My father always mocked at the so-called domestic bliss. How I pity those who do not know it; they are only half alive." There was, too, intellectual and musical growth during this period which Clara valued. The two musicians analyzed Bach fugues together, read Shakespeare and Goethe together, and both composed, Clara with many reservations. Her first Christmas gift to her husband was a group of three songs on texts by Robert Burns and Heinrich Heine, composed in odd moments when her husband was out of the house and she could use the piano freely.

But there was another nagging problem disturbing the domestic bliss. In addition to Robert's responsibilities as editor of the *Neue Zeitschrift*, he was so engrossed in his composing that Clara made this plaintive entry at the end of January 1841: "Robert has been very cold toward me the last few days. It is true that there may well be a happy basis for it, and no one can appreciate all he undertakes as much as I do, yet at times this coldness, which I have not deserved in the least, hurts me." More and more she began to feel shut out of his creative life. The frustration was intensified, of course, because she was not herself performing and could not even use the piano when Robert was working. Even a room and a piano of her own could not meet her needs.

Robert, aware of the cost to her of his intense absorption, was not unappreciative: "I could never say enough about all the love shown to me with such a willing heart by Clara during this time [while he was composing the First Symphony]. I could have sought among millions [without finding one] who, like her, treats me with so much forbearance and consideration," he wrote in the February 14–21 entry of the marriage diary.

Today Schumann's early piano pieces are considered to be his greatest works: they were innovative, even revolutionary, a bold and exciting affirma-

*Ignaz Moscheles was a leading piano virtuoso and composer who had taught Mendelssohn and was his lifelong friend. Ferdinand David was a violin virtuoso, composer, teacher, and concertmaster of the Gewandhaus orchestra. Friedrich Kistner was a Leipzig music publisher.

tion of the new romantic spirit; technically brilliant without mere super-ficiality, they explored new harmonies, colors, and metric patterns, opening the way to the new German romanticism. Yet Schumann (and Clara) firmly believed that it was necessary to prove oneself as a composer by writing orchestral works in the larger, extended forms.* There may also have been some practical motivation for the new head of household: recognition as a symphonic composer would bring financial rewards as well as status. What-ever the reasons were—and there may have been many—he began sketches of symphonic works in the final months of his "year of song," and on January 23 threw himself into the creation of the B-flat (Spring) Symphony. She heard nothing of this symphony, which was composed and completed in a virtual frenzy—sketched in four days, orchestrated in ten—until it was performed for her and two old friends, Ernst Wenzel and Ernst Pfundt, on February 14, 1841.

Some of her frustration is evident in this two-edged diary entry of January 1841: "I must admit, my dear husband, I had not given you credit for such skill—you continually inspire me with new awe." This backhanded compli-ment must have irked the composer, who had been exposed to similar tactless comments from Clara in the past. In 1838, for example, Clara had responded to his expressed intention of writing string quartets with the question " . . . do you really know the instruments well enough?"[16]

At the completion of the symphony, Schumann forgot his irritation and paid homage to Clara's understanding:

Now, many sleepless nights are followed by exhaustion; what is happening to me is what might happen to a young woman who has just been delivered of a child—so light, so happy, and yet ill and weak. My Clara knows this very well, and is attending to me with doubled tenderness, which I will repay later.[17]

A concert on March 31, 1841, her first solo appearance since her marriage, was the great reward for her care and patience: it generated public acknowl-edgment of her husband as an important composer, provided the contact with the public that was so essential for her, and gave Robert the oppor-tunity to show his appreciation of her playing. The occasion was a benefit concert conducted by Mendelssohn for the Gewandhaus orchestra pension fund. In the history of music, this date is remembered as the premiere of Robert Schumann's First (Spring) Symphony, but in Leipzig the orchestral masterpiece was only one of many works on the program and was over-shadowed by Clara's reappearance in her native town.

*In a letter of September 28, 1840, to Camille Stamaty, a French pianist and admirer, Schumann described his *Kinderscenen* as "mere bagatelles," not to be compared with works in the larger forms (Wolfgang Boetticher, *Robert Schumann in seinen Schriften und Briefen* [Berlin: Hahnefeld, 1942], 347–48).

Robert considered it an "unforgettable evening," and added, "My Clara played everything like a master and in such an inspired mood that everyone was enchanted."[18] Clara described the concert in a letter to her friend Emilie List:

> I was received with such enthusiasm that I went pale and red; it did not cease even when I seated myself at the piano. (I have never yet heard anyone received like this, not even Thalberg.) You can imagine that this gave me courage since I had been shaking all over with anxiety. I played as I can hardly ever remember playing.[19]

Even before the March 31 concert, Schumann was deeply involved in new works, among them the Overture, Scherzo, and Finale, op. 52, the Phantasie in A Minor for piano and orchestra (later the first movement of the Piano Concerto), and the first version of the Symphony in D Minor. Plans for the oratorio *Das Paradies und die Peri* were under way, and once again Clara could not disturb him by practicing. "The more Robert involves himself with his art, the less I can do as an artist, Heaven knows! There are always interruptions, and small as our household is, I always have this and that to do and that robs me of my time," she wrote in the diary on May 9, 1841. She was unhappy, he felt guilty, but both agreed that his work had to take precedence.

Clara was not involved in the creation of any of his works, not even the work for piano that she later premiered. She was in a fever of anticipation and a little resentful on May 31, when she wrote:

> Yesterday he began a symphony once more. . . . I have not yet heard anything of it, but I see Robert's [creative] energy and often hear D minor sounding wildly from afar so that I already know it is a work created from the depths of his soul. Heaven is good to us. Robert cannot be any happier in composing than I am when he shows me such a work. Do you believe me, my Robert? You could well believe it.

Complaints were confided to the diary. On June 3, 1841, she wrote:

> My piano playing is falling behind. This always happens when Robert is composing. There is not even one little hour in the whole day for myself! If only I don't fall too far behind. Score reading has also ceased once again, but I hope that it won't be for long this time. . . . I can't do anything with my composing—I would sometimes like to strike my dumb head!

There may have been some comfort in knowing that the Phantasie was revealed to her first; she played it with the Gewandhaus orchestra at a closed rehearsal on August 13, a week or two before Marie's birth. The occasion was a prepublication run-through of the Spring Symphony. She was so agitated with excitement and joy over the symphony, the Phantasie, and the opportunity to play that she reported in the marriage diary on August 22 that she was ill for days.

Almost exactly one year after their marriage, Clara gave birth to her first and best-loved child, Marie. The published diaries refer to her pregnancy only in oblique terms. The delivery was not difficult, and the firstborn was joyfully welcomed by both parents. In the next thirteen years Clara was to give birth to seven more children, but later ones did not receive the whole-hearted reception conferred upon Marie. Clara conceived very easily, generally had uncomplicated pregnancies, and evidently made no attempt to prevent conception, though her husband must have been aware of some of the contraceptive methods in use at the time.

Schumann may have harbored some hopes that babies would put a halt to Clara's performances, but he did not reckon with her determination. The year 1842 brought a full-scale renewal of Clara's solo career. Once she realized that wet nurses were available, that the baby could be boarded with relatives, that an additional maid could be hired for a pittance, that motherhood did not necessarily tie her down, she wasted no time.* Clara composed, toured, played, and was feted as in the old days before marriage and childbearing. The schedule took its toll, but she knew she had to establish herself as Clara Schumann, pianist, as soon as possible. There was no lack of pianistic talent in the 1840s, and the twenty-two-year-old performer was already mindful of younger artists making their way to fame. Clara's fears of other artists were quite realistic. Notwithstanding the glowing comparisons of her playing with that of Franz Liszt, Sigismund Thalberg, and Camilla Pleyel, and the musical growth during her marriage, she could not compete with these virtuosi unless she remained in the public eye. Nor was she any longer a child prodigy or young girl. She greeted the news of the mushrooming career of the twelve-year-old Anton Rubinstein politely but with some trepidation. At the end of December 1841 she wrote to Emilie List that she had heard he was "supposed to be the greatest genius born in a long time."[20]

Conscious of such rivals' threats to her career, she accepted all invitations to perform. In all she gave at least fifteen concerts between January 1 and April 25, 1842. And all this activity created a grave crisis. In those years a woman, even a married woman, could not travel alone. Robert had to accompany her on most of the tours. He did not relish the role of traveling companion and manager, and though his works for both piano and orchestra were always performed on her programs, he was uncomfortable about leaving home and child, his editorial responsibilities, and the peace and quiet

*A wetnurse was hired for about six months for each Schumann baby. The expenditures are noted in the household books.

required for creative work. He was almost always ill in the weeks preceding their tours—a possible consequence of his conflicting emotions.[21]

The concerts in nearby Weimar in November 1841, in which Clara played solos in the first half and his new symphony was performed in the second, were gratifying to both. In accepting the invitation, Robert proudly wrote to the conductor, "My wife requests that her maiden name be omitted from the announcement of the concert; she wants to be called by my name, once for all, and I love her all the more for it."[22] But the decision to accept invitations from Bremen and Hamburg involved more problems. This would be a longer journey, and plans had to made for care of Marie, now six months old (she was sent to stay with Schumann's brother in Schneeberg) and for a replacement at the *Neue Zeitschrift*. Schumann was pleased with the conducting of Friedrich Wilhelm Grund, the leader of the Hamburg Philharmonische Gesellschaft, and he enjoyed his status as a recognized composer. An incident in Oldenburg, however, a duchy about seventy-five kilometers from Bremen, unnerved him. Robert's entry in the marriage diary tells the story: "February 25. Clara rode to the court and returned, overjoyed at her reception. The thought of my undignified position in such situations did not permit me to feel any pleasure." In short, she was the only one to be invited.

The difficulty was compounded by Clara's decision to accept a long-deferred invitation to play in Copenhagen, though her husband could not accompany her. Even Clara felt uncomfortable about the situation. Many months later, her guilt still had not subsided when she wrote, on May 30, 1842, a long explanation to her friend Emilie List:

> Yes, I really did go to Copenhagen alone (that is, without Robert, but with a lady from Bremen). . . .* As the time approached, Robert realized more and more the impossibility of leaving his paper in strange hands for perhaps another two months; the three weeks for which he had arranged were over, and so we decided to give up the journey; but I weighed the whole thing—I am a woman, am not neglecting anything at home, earn nothing, why shouldn't I use my talent for once to contribute my mite to Robert? Could anyone blame me for this? Or my husband for going home to his child and his business?[23]

Copenhagen was an overnight journey over the water—a frightening prospect for the landbound Leipzigers. Clara had many misgivings, particularly when illness and a storm forced a postponement of her journey from Kiel to Copenhagen. While she waited for the right weather for the boat, concerts were quickly arranged in Lübeck, Kiel, and Hamburg. Her Hamburg friends were astonished at her determination, she wrote in the marriage diary on February 18, 1842: "Several times my courage deserted me; I thought that heaven had sent me all these troubles to dissuade me from my

---

*Marie Garlichs, an old friend.

plans, but I thought of Robert, and my wish to contribute something and the joyful reunion after a successful journey. . . ." The reception in Copenhagen more than made up for her frustrations. She was there from March 20 to April 18 and performed seven times. She met Hans Christian Andersen, the composer Niels Wilhelm Gade, and the Danish royal family, enjoyed great acclaim, and earned large sums of money.

In all the marital disputes over her career, the question of money loomed large. They both knew she could earn more in one three-week concert tour than Schumann obtained from composing and editing in a year. Glorying in her skill as a performing artist and manager, this daughter of Friedrich Wieck never considered that her husband's pride might suffer. Independent, proud, and determined, she persisted in her professional career and savored both the money and the fame.

Robert's letters from Leipzig were melancholy, but she did not receive them until she was well into the Copenhagen triumphs. Though she wrote to Schumann daily, the separation proved to be an almost unbearable strain for him. The diary and household books are filled with such comments as "Miserable life," "Drank a frightful amount," "Leading a bad life."[24] He drank too much, borrowed money from friends, and wrote his wife:

Leipzig, March 13, [1842]
My dear Clara, do you still recognize this handwriting? What a mood I am in. I already regret having allowed you to part from me and I have to listen to the most unkind judgments about it. Your father is here now and running all over town. Early this morning Dr. Reuter told me about it—at first I was quite beside myself; now I have collected my thoughts and know that I have behaved as a proper family man and businessman. . . . You are probably arriving in Copenhagen this very hour. The weather here is mild, yet I am fearful; was it rough during your crossing? . . . It is really sad in our home; everything seems to ask, "Where is your good Clara?," even the flowers at the window. . . . Otherwise, nothing much has happened. . . . I found many letters when I came, but nothing of significance. My symphony is supposed to be given in Breslau on the seventh . . . and also in Dresden, just about now. . . . I am thinking of America again; you consider it too. Your mother in Berlin was very much in favor of it.

Leipzig, March 16
Still no news from you, my Clara. Have you forgotten me already? Yesterday I could hardly bear the melancholy that overwhelmed me. This desolation in the house; this emptiness in me! *Letting you go was one of the most foolish things I ever did* in my life and it certainly won't happen again. Nothing tastes good or right. On top of that, I am really not well at all—and am tormented by the worst cold—and without music. But if a letter came from you, I would be better. Reuter acts very peculiarly toward me, as if I had committed a crime in letting you go alone. So I scold him. . . . And then the dummies here think that one must travel over icebergs to get

to Copenhagen and that you are traveling by reindeer. . . . I will not let you go to Stockholm . . . or at least only if I can come with you. Do you play for small groups sometimes? That always makes an artist popular. . . . I intend to make up my mind about America by the end of April. Reuter urges it strongly. It depends on you.

March 24

. . . I am calmer now and a little bit more used to our lonely life. . . . May the sacrifice be worth it and bring you satisfaction as an artist. You are still so young and I can scarcely blame you for not wanting to be forgotten as an artist after working so hard in your youth—in a word—you can still enjoy giving people pleasure through your lovely talent. . . . What about America? It must be decided by the end of April.

Leipzig, April 1

I read your letters three, four times over, and know them by heart. Your handwriting looks so firm and steadfast . . . otherwise everything is quite still in our household. Emilie [the maid] is a diligent and unassuming girl . . . we really speak very little. She may very well consider me severe and morose. . . . I am rejoicing at the coming of spring. . . . Then we will discuss the future too. . . . Yesterday I laid out our whole position clearly for myself . . . on paper—with figures. . . . We don't have to worry at all; we still have enough money. But a change must take place this year. Don't write to Emilie [List] about America. The thought just occurred to me to write an acquaintance there who is also very musical. I shall get some information and wait for an answer. The step is too enormous. . . . Write to me right away about your concert, what you played, how you were received, send me the newspapers that have some words about you. I would like everyone here to know about it. . . . *I have to scold you, however: you write so little about yourself as an artist, where you have played and whether you were understood.*

April 14

Perhaps you are on the sea now. . . . The sky here is somewhat overcast, yet the weather is gentle and there is no strong wind. I hope it is the same on your boat. May our loving heaven lead us to each other soon. Your last letter with the news from the papers delighted me immensely, as do all your and my joys. It cheers me up, which I need. A few days ago I was frightfully angry. I'll tell you about it later. Listen, [August] Cranz [a music publisher] in Hamburg is a miserable fellow and a gossip. . . . He reported the dumbest blather to Hofmeister—who then told it to David—and now it is making the rounds, e.g., that I left you in Hamburg *sick*—that we ran up debts in Hamburg, that nobody liked you there, and all sorts of things like that. I was beside myself. . . . When you get to Hamburg now, . . . go to his wife and tell her calmly, but with all the pride of which you are capable, your and our opinions [of such talk]. Cläre, I beg you, play with all imaginable care and genius so that such shameful gossip will be disproved. Your honor as an artist is as dear to me as your honor as a woman, and I must and can rely on you in all things. . . .

April 22
I wanted to write to you yesterday, but was so sick with a horrible anger that I could not. Your father has told all of Dresden that we *were separated.* On many days, like today, for example, which is so wonderfully blue, one can laugh at such baseness, but on others it can embitter the heart and I have had many days like that.[25]

America seemed to offer solutions to many of their problems. By 1842 the New World had become both a refuge and a land of plenty for Europeans. Many Germans had already emigrated to the United States; others hoped to go for a short time, make a fortune, and then return. The Schumanns were toying with the latter idea, since many friends and acquaintances had already braved the Atlantic and returned prosperous and safe. Emilie List's father, for example, had fled with his family for political reasons and acquired U.S. citizenship. As a child, Pauline García had already had many adventures in the New World.* And well before the big German emigration of 1848, European artists were enthusiastically received and highly paid in New York, Boston, Philadelphia, Charleston, New Orleans. Reports of events in the United States appeared regularly in the German newspapers. In just a few years, Jenny Lind, introduced to the New World by the great impresario Phineas T. Barnum, was to be paid close to $1,000 a concert plus expenses for a staff that included companion, secretary, two servants, and a carriage.[26]

The Schumanns began to think about America during their trip to Hamburg and Bremen (the port from which many émigrés left). An American tour of a year or two, they thought, might enable them to earn enough money to live well for the rest of their lives. By March 6, 1842, however, Robert wrote his friend Theodor Töpken, "The American plans have receded into the background somewhat. The gulf that separates it from home is just too enormous."[27] But they continued to think about America as they searched for solutions to the problems of finances and competing careers.

Schumann was happiest when Clara could settle down for a few months, as she did on her return to Leipzig in April 1842, to the life he had envisioned before their marriage: *Hausfrau,* mother, hostess, student (she began together with Robert, to study the string quartets of Haydn and Mozart). Robert was working again, with feverish intensity and speed, in still another genre: this was his year for chamber music. Within a few months he wrote three string quartets and two works for strings and piano: the piano quartet and the piano quintet, both premiered by Clara. But, as before, Clara heard only faint and frustrating glimmerings of the music as he worked, and she was unable to practice or compose during that period.

Almost always a period of intense creation was followed by a depression during which Robert was unable to work. He referred to such episodes as "weakness of the nerves." On February 17, 1843, he wrote in the diary that

*In 1825, when Pauline was four, her father, Manuel García, took his family and an Italian opera troupe to New York City. They remained in North America until 1829.

Clara was giving him "tender care," though she was once again pregnant, expecting a child in April 1843.[28] Robert's depression, of short duration, was followed by another phase of violent activity. He accepted a position as professor of piano and score reading in the newly established Leipzig Conservatory of Music and took up his duties there in April 1843. At the same time he began work on *Das Paradies und die Peri* (completed in a few short months), and he continued his writing and editorial work on the *Zeitschrift*.

By 1843 Schumann was gaining some recognition for his orchestral works in European musical circles. His works were played in several German cities, and champions in Paris, Brussels, Amsterdam, Copenhagen, and Vienna saw to it that his pieces were performed for connoisseurs, if not for the general public. His status as a writer and critic was recognized as well. Despite this success, however, money was still a problem, and a teaching position represented a certain amount of financial security.

The Leipzig Conservatory was from its inception a school of the first rank. Founded by Mendelssohn during the period that saw the spread of professional music education, it drew students from the entire musical world. Edvard Grieg was one of the hundred Norwegian students who attended, and Arthur Sullivan was an early representative from Great Britain.*

Professional music training in Europe developed in the aftermath of the French Revolution. The Paris Conservatoire, founded in 1795, became the model for similar institutions in Milan, Bologna, Prague, and London. Up until the establishment of the Leipzig Conservatory, the first modern school of its kind in Germany, professional training was not organized. Most musicians learned from family members, were apprenticed to musicians, or studied privately with a succession of teachers. Clara Wieck's education, for example, with teachers from Leipzig, Dresden, and Berlin, was not unusual. (It *was* remarkable, of course, for a girl to undertake such systematic instruction in so many branches of the art, but she had her father's ambition and good pedagogical sense to thank for that.)

Schumann had joined in many of the preliminary discussions about the conservatory, but the moving force was Mendelssohn, who poured his time and organizational talents into the new venture. Schumann noted its founding in the marriage diary on February 17, 1843:

> The establishment of the music school (through Mendelssohn) will certainly be fine and productive; as a musician I look forward to its beginning. It will be, without doubt, a support for good music and will have a significant influence on the entire education of German youth. The teachers who

*The roster of foreign students is truly impressive. In the period 1843–68 there were, for example, a total of 109 students from Great Britain: 73 male and 36 female; 90 students from Russia: 67 male, 23 female; 85 students from North America: 68 male and 17 female; from South America and California (grouped together), one student. See Emil Kneschke, *Das Conservatorium der Musik in Leipzig: Seine Geschichte, seine Lehrer und Zöglinge* (Leipzig: Breitkopf & Härtel, 1868), 69–70.

have been named are Mendelssohn, [Ferdinand] David, [Moritz] Haupt-mann, [Christian August] Pohlenz, [Carl Ferdinand] Becker, and me. Later Clara will also teach when she, as they say, can offer lessons with some degree of regularity.*

Schumann hoped to teach composition as well as piano, but apparently he was not a successful teacher. When he was depressed or "melancholy," as he put it, he found it difficult to speak. Even at his best he was not a talker. Students complained that he would sit through a lesson or rehearsal and rarely say a word, even when there was a clear need for a comment or criticism.[29]

The premiere of *Peri* in December 1843 entailed additional respon-sibilities for the Schumanns. Though Clara did not hear the work until it was completed (she complained in the diary in April 1843, "Robert has com-pleted the second part of *Peri* but shared little of it with me"), she was called on to arrange the piano-vocal score and be with him at rehearsals. Rehearsals and the first performance were conducted by Schumann, making his debut as a conductor. Though he had avoided such positions in the past—probably because of his inexperience with the orchestra—he could not always refuse, and after accepting the challenge of conducting *Peri*, he was satisfied with his work. Gradually he accepted more offers and eventually assumed the musi-cal directorship of several musical organizations. He could handle perfor-mances without difficulty but his inability to communicate during rehearsals was a continuing handicap. Clara's first inkling of this problem came in a letter from her friend Livia Frege, the leading soprano in the premiere of *Peri*: "If only your dear husband could resolve to scold a little and to demand greater attention, everything would go better right away."[30] It was the first of many such appeals to Clara.

Though Clara did not take her place at the conservatory until later, her own professional activities did not cease. Maternal cares and pregnancy had not prevented her from performing at the Gewandhaus on October 2, 1842; on January 8, 1843, at a special Schumann matinee; and on February 2 and 9. After Elise's birth in April, she played twice more in Leipzig, and gave several concerts in Dresden. Though the trip to Dresden was short—only a few hours on the new railway that linked Leipzig and the capital—Robert's daily letters during her absences indicate his constant need for her and dependence on her:

[February 12, 1843] There is a strange silence in the house, but it seems to me that your dear spirit is everywhere. . . . I was very sorry for the poor papa; he was depressed. Marie is well; when she hears the word "Mama" she waves her hand sadly as if she knew you were gone.[31]

*Clara was in an advanced state of pregnancy at the time.

In September, both children were with her and the "poor papa" wrote:

> The weather was so beautiful. I thought of you often, especially last night
> at 6:30. When I don't have you, I bring out old diaries and read them.
> Yesterday I read yours from the Paris days until late at night. What an
> exciting life we led then—it often sounds like a novel to me. But there are
> also many beautiful memories, are there not? . . . Otherwise, everything
> is quiet around me. The sun shines full into the window, but the air is cool,
> the sky wonderfully blue. Today I finally wrote to Herr von Bielke [of the
> Weimar court] and the grand duchess and am glad to be free of that
> matter. I would have preferred to dedicate the quintet to you, but, I
> thought, princely roses are also not to be despised.* However, I intend
> the first opera to be yours.[32]

> [November 14, 1843]   Dr. Härtel was just here and offered me the edi-
> torship of the *Allgemeine musikalische Zeitung.* . . . I did not reject it right
> off because there is much to be said for it—but I did ask for time to think it
> over. . . . I just told Dr. Härtel that in any case I would not want to take
> over the editorship between New Year and July 1844, since I was going to
> be traveling with you and wanted to have a half year for myself, just for
> once.

A letter of November 19 shows his need for her counsel: "If only you were
here! . . . Drop me a line tomorrow, so I will know exactly where I am and
how long I can put off Härtel because I *absolutely* must talk it over with
you."[33]

Occasionally Schumann expressed some guilt about depriving his wife of a
full career as a musician. On Februrary 17, 1843, he wrote in the diary that
she had composed some fine songs and piano works. After she presented him
with a number of songs on his thirty-third birthday, he noted on June 28,
1843, that she seemed melancholy and added that he suspected it was because she could not buy him fine gifts. At the same time, however, he
expressed the conviction that she was happiest in her role as a mother. And
in the marriage diary, at least, Clara did not contradict him.

On January 25, 1844, the Schumanns started on another great journey to
the north, the journey to which Robert referred in November when he was
negotiating with Härtel. After initial reluctance and much vacillation, he
agreed to a Russian concert tour, not only for Clara's sake and the extra
income it might bring, but because he mistakenly thought it would give him
time to compose and the opportunity to refresh himself after the hectic
activities of the previous year. He felt unwell almost until the day they left,
and he had such ambivalent feelings about the trip that Clara, at her wit's
end, went to see Mendelssohn for advice.[34] Evidently Mendelssohn was

*The quintet was dedicated to her after all.

able to persuade Robert, for on January 6, he finally agreed to go. Marie and Elise were left with Robert's brother and sister-in-law in Schneeberg.

For Clara this trip was no sudden fancy. Clara had longed to tour Russia even before her marriage. In the fall of 1840 Schumann had announced Russian plans in a letter to Liszt, but Robert's work, Clara's ill health in the months immediately following the wedding, and above all the news that Liszt's Russian tour would coincide with theirs caused a postponement. In November 1840, Count Aleksei Fedorovich Lvov, director of the Russian Imperial Chapel, offered his help in any trip they should undertake, but advised against an attempt to compete with Liszt, an established favorite in Russia.[35]

Historically, St. Petersburg had always been a mecca for Western European artists. In the late eighteenth century Catherine the Great, herself a German princess, inaugurated a "glorious epoch" by inviting such Italian composers as Baldassare Galuppi, Giovanni Paisiello, Giuseppe Sarti, and Domenico Cimarosa to St. Petersburg. The Russian aristocrats, raised by English, German, and French governesses, denigrated Russian culture and depended on Italian, French, and German troupes for concerts, dance, and opera. Even during the repressive regime of Nicholas I (1825–55), literature and the arts flourished, and foreigners were greeted with passionate enthusiasm. Vladimir Stassov, a Russian writer on music, reminisced, "In those days, the Russian ruble had a very good clink to German ears; it was customary for such musical luminaries as Liszt, Thalberg, [Giuditta] Pasta, [Pauline García] Viardot, . . . and others to come."[36] Ferdinand David, the Leipzig concertmaster and a good friend of the Schumanns, had spent six years in Dorpat, a Germanic outpost in what was then Livonia, now Estonia (and part of the Soviet Union), as the first violinist of a resident string quartet at the estate of a wealthy baron (whose daughter he later married). Pauline Viardot had made a smashing debut with an Italian opera company just a few weeks before the Schumanns arrived in St. Petersburg. Clara's brother Alwin, later employed in the St. Petersburg theater orchestra as a violinist, was living in Reval, on the Gulf of Finland. And during their tour the Schumanns were assisted by two old friends, Adolph von Henselt and Heinrich Romberg, both well-known German musicians who had established themselves in Russia.

Clara, with her amazing stamina, had no difficulty with the rigors of a Russian tour in midwinter. She described several weeks of cold, exhausting travel by coach and sleigh through forests, over frozen rivers, huddled under furs and rugs, and stopping at uncomfortable and dirty inns. Arising at three o'clock in the morning in order to be under way by four, she gave solo concerts without supporting artists day after day in Königsberg, Tilsit, Riga, Mitau, and Dorpat (and intended to continue in this way, she wrote to her father).[37] They almost froze, but Clara, exhilarated and fulfilled, pressed on.

Robert did not fare so well. He fell ill in Dorpat and during the entire trip never fully recovered. Suffering from cold, fever, aches, and pains, from anxiety and melancholia, he did not consider the tour a success, despite several charming letters to his father-in-law. Three doctors who were consulted in Dorpat diagnosed "nerve fever." Clara described him as weak, sick, sad, and angry. He was insulted by a gesture of the baron von Liphardt, who had invited them to dinner in Dorpat. After Clara had played for the assembled guests, Liphardt pressed 150 rubles into his hand. Schumann was furious and Clara had to convince him it would be best not to return the money.[38]

He recovered somewhat and they went on to St. Petersburg, but there he was unable to accompany her on her rounds to visits to ministers, officials, and the court. (She went with Henselt.) On their way to Moscow they detoured to Tver (now Kalinin) in order to visit Schumann's uncle, a seventy-one-year-old surgeon who had emigrated to Russia forty years earlier. The journey to Tver was extraordinarily difficult and more than once Robert thought he would faint. He was still weak and suffering from attacks of vertigo when they arrived in Moscow. The worst of his physical sufferings gradually subsided but not before one frightening episode when he could not see and believed he was going blind. While he rested in their hotel room and wrote poetry (composing music was out of the question), his wife, animated and energetic, visited institutions and potential patrons, practiced, and gave several concerts.

Clara earned a great deal of money—close to 6,000 taler, of which almost 3,000 was clear profit—and was much acclaimed on the Russian tour.[39] She performed for the tsar and tsarina in the Winter Palace (which seemed like a "fairy tale in the Thousand and One Nights"),[40] gave many brilliant concerts, and on March 5, 1844, was made an honorary member of the St. Petersburg Philharmonic Society.

Though Schumann traveled to Russia primarily for Clara's sake, he was gratified to find that he was greeted respectfully by such influential connoisseurs as Count Mikhail Wielhorski and the grand duchess Helena, and letters and documents hint that he would have been welcome to stay on and continue his career there. But the flattering attention and compliments did little to overcome his severe depression.

A man who met the Schumanns at a soiree given by the composer and conductor Count Aleksei Fedorovich Lvov described them as he saw them that evening:

> Schumann was, as usual, silent and withdrawn the whole evening. He spoke very little and just murmured incomprehensibly to the questions put by Count Wielhorski and the host, A. F. Lvov. Something like a conversation developed with the famous violinist [Wilhelm Bernhard] Molique, who had just arrived in St. Petersburg a few days earlier, but it was carried on in whispers, without life and vivacity. Schumann sat mostly in a corner near the piano . . . with a sunken head, his hair was hanging in his

face, he had a pensive expression on his face, and it looked as if he were about to whistle to himself. Schumann, that night, exactly resembled the life-size statue by Donndorf.* Clara Schumann was a little more talkative; she answered all the questions for her husband. In her playing, she proved herself to be a great artist with masculine energy and feminine instincts in interpretation and execution, although she was only twenty-five or twenty-six years old.† But one could hardly characterize her as a gracious or sympathetic woman. They both spoke French with Saxon accents and German like true Leipzigers.[41]

It seems clear that Robert was in serious trouble, certainly the worst since his marriage. And it is equally clear that Clara did not face up to the situation. Practicing, performing, visiting, sightseeing, she was a self-absorbed concert artist on tour, and considered it her primary duty to carry on with her commitments. He, of course, could not bring himself to articulate his despair, and so, on their return, she was surprised to find that Robert had written in his travel diary, "Almost unbearable suffering and Clara's conduct!" She recorded this line in the marriage diary and added, "I know of nothing, but it seems to me now, as I read through the notebooks, that I frequently provoked Robert's anger though it was certainly never done intentionally, but only because of my own awkwardness and because I am slow. It often takes quiet deliberation on my part to understand what other, wiser souls may see in a moment."[42]

As Robert's illnesses and depressions became more frequent, it was difficult to overlook his obviously disquieting behavior. For a long time Clara simply assumed more responsibilities without acknowledging the situation. A few months after their return from Russia, Robert was so ill that he took to his bed, and she had to recognize that drastic action was necessary.

The return to Leipzig and reunion with the children brought mixed feelings to Clara. She had left the heady world of the glamorous star and had to function as wife, homemaker, and mother once more. Schumann had to make a decision about the journal. Ten years old, it had achieved international recognition and even some financial success, but the composer realized that his own creative work was suffering. His hopes, standards, and goals for the *Neue Zeitschrift* had remained high, and he put it aside with some reluctance but also with relief. In June 1844 Oswald Lorenz became the editor of the *Neue Zeitschrift* and Schumann severed his connections with the periodical.

In August 1844 Clara joined Robert on the faculty of the Leipzig Conservatory, but their teaching was interrupted when Robert suffered a severe physical and mental breakdown. They took a short trip to the Harz Mountains. Several other cures were attempted, but Robert became so weak that

---

*Adolph Donndorf created a statue of Schumann for his tombstone.
†She was in fact only twenty-three.

he could barely walk across the room. It was no longer simply a "nervous" condition; he had pains, he trembled, he wept, he could not sleep. Clara, by this time pregnant with her third child, abandoned plans for another concert trip and devoted herself to Robert and his health. They decided to visit Dresden, perhaps for better air, perhaps for diversion. He was very weak on the journey and in Dresden "there were eight terrible days. Robert didn't sleep at night, his imagination created the most frightening pictures, in the mornings I usually found him bathed in tears, he gave up completely," she wrote in the diary. Wieck's presence in Dresden was of no help and must have exacerbated the situation, as he tried to "rouse Robert forcibly."[43] They moved from a hotel to private lodgings and then took an apartment.

Clara fulfilled some concert engagements in Halle and Leipzig. After a rather precipitous decision to leave Leipzig permanently and settle in Dresden, events moved quickly. Their friends arranged a farewell musical evening for them. The Mendelssohn Octet was performed (twelve-year-old Joseph Joachim, Ferdinand David's prize pupil, was one of the players); Livia Frege, the first Peri, sang; and Clara played duets with Mendelssohn. After a public performance at the Gewandhaus on December 5 and a farewell matinee a few days later, the Schumanns bade farewell to Leipzig, the city where Clara was born, where her talent had been recognized and nurtured, the city where she had first faced the world as a concert artist.

CHAPTER 6

The Dresden Years

W hy Dresden? The Schumanns must have asked themselves this question often; certainly their friends puzzled over the move from Leipzig, the musical capital, to the baroque court city of Dresden. The years in the Saxon capital began in sickness and anxiety and continued through many illnesses and disappointments. During those years Schumann composed many of his great works, but the feverishly exalted creative periods were interspersed with serious depressions that forced his wife to take on increasing responsibilities. Clara's health and stamina carried her forward as she continued her own concert career, aided her husband artistically, emotionally, and financially, bore four more children during the five years they lived in Dresden, supervised a household that included three servants, gave piano lessons, and composed her best works. Clara Schumann's basic character changed little after adolescence, but the Dresden years fixed firmly the conscientious, dutiful seriousness mixed with some bitterness (and doubtless some anger) with which she performed her duties.

The move from Leipzig, the city they both loved, is difficult to comprehend. During the years Schumann had lived in Leipzig, the Gewandhaus orchestra had been brought to the highest level in Europe, the conservatory was off to a triumphant start, the Leipzig music journals circulated throughout the world, and Leipzig's music publishing houses maintained their reputation as the most prestigious in Europe. The libraries and multitude of readers were matters of pride for Leipzig's citizens. Schumann boasted, "Liszt, the spoiled darling of the aristocracy, arrived and complained continually of the absence of fine dresses and of countesses and princesses, so that I was annoyed, and told him that we too had our own aristocracy here, namely, 150 bookstores, 50 printing establishments, and 30 newspapers."[1]

Henry F. Chorley, an English traveler, described Leipzig as a quaint, cheerful, friendly town that had no court "to stiffen its social circles into formality, or to hinder its presiding spirits from taking free way. . . . It possesses a University to stir its intelligences, a press busy and enterprising, and a recurrence of those gatherings which bring a representative of every class in society in Europe together."[2] From Dresden, in October 1844, Schumann wrote a friend, "Leipzig remains the most important city for music and I would advise every young talent to go where one hears so much good music."[3]

The reasons for the hurried move were ostensibly related to Robert's health; Dresden was generally considered to have a salubrious environment. Situated on the broad and beautiful Elbe, ringed by gently rolling hills, it had better air and more scenic beauty than Leipzig. There was little commerce, industry, or manufacturing in Dresden in the 1840s. One has only to recall the imposing baroque churches and palaces, the royal galleries, the gardens and promenades, all vividly portrayed in Canaletto's paintings, to see instantly why Dresden, the seat of a kingdom for many hundreds of years, was known as "the Florence of Germany."

Schumann's doctor had originally recommended a trip to Dresden because other treatments had failed. And though Robert was ill and depressed during his first few weeks there, he decided to remain. It has been suggested that Schumann was offended because he had not been considered for the post of Gewandhaus director while Mendelssohn was away in Berlin, but as Schumann had never indicated any desire to take over a position that required so much administrative work and so many public appearances, this conjecture seems unlikely. Moreover, he had just given up the *Zeitschrift* (undoubtedly a traumatic decision) so that he could devote all his time to composition.

One can speculate on another reason for the move. Robert was ill, could not make decisions, was unable to conduct, teach, or even compose. Clara was pregnant again. Father Wieck was in Dresden. The recent reconciliation had obscured the bitter memories and they remembered only the father, the man of strength and character. At this juncture in their lives, they may have entertained the illusion that Wieck would serve as a protector in the new sanctuary.

Dresden had, of course, many pleasant associations for them. As a ten-year-old, Clara had given her first concerts outside the home circles here and had attracted the attention of influential and wealthy music lovers among the court circles. The estate of Major Serre and his wife, Friederike, at Schloss Maxen, near the city, had long been a refuge for the Wieck family; Clara had spent many vacations there. Other friends in Dresden included the Kaskels, whose home she had been visiting in 1836 during the first major conflict with her father over Robert; Carl Kraegen, a pianist, an old friend of her father and a great admirer of Robert's work; Wolf August von Lüttichau, the intendant of the court theater; and Carl Gottlieb Reissiger, now the kapellmeister, with whom she had been sent to study the summer Robert and Ernestine were engaged.

In Dresden, stylishness and luxury were highly valued; and though in the past Dresden had had its share of musical luminaries—Heinrich Schütz and Johann Adolph Hasse, for example—the Schumanns found that music took second place to literature and the plastic and graphic arts. Moreover, musical life was dominated by the tastes of the aristocracy, who traditionally patronized the court chapel and opera. Dresden was proud of the reputation of Carl Maria von Weber, who had been appointed kapellmeister in 1817 and was the first to develop German opera in that Italianate city. Richard Wagner, who joined the opera staff in 1842, was in Dresden during the first few years the Schumanns lived there, but Clara saw little of him.

The Schumann circle was small; it included Ferdinand Hiller, composer and conductor, their closest friend among the musicians; Wilhelmine Schröder-Devrient, a singer greatly admired by both Clara and Robert; and Franz and Friedrich Schubert, the Dresden concertmaster and his cellist brother, with whom Clara later instituted a regular series of chamber concerts. Aside from Hiller, however, they were neither welcomed by nor felt comfortable with the local musicians. Their closest friends were artists, painters, and sculptors. Schumann's music—romantic and "modern"—had few adherents in Dresden, and he made no secret of his low opinion of his musical colleagues.

Fortunately, Leipzig was only a four-hour train ride away, and Clara took frequent advantage of the proximity to her native town. Thoughts of Leipzig were always with them. A year after the move to Dresden, when they visited Leipzig for a concert, Robert wrote to Hiller, "The life and people here certainly do cheer us up considerably. Sooner or later, I really think we shall settle down here again."[4] They never did.

The Schumanns began a joint study of fugue and counterpoint in January 1845, after Robert's illness of the autumn, and continued through the next few months, ignoring the doctor's advice to stay away from music. During these few months his "nervous illness" waxed and waned. "Gloomy demons possessed me," he wrote to the Dutch composer Johann Verhulst on May 28, 1845. "Now it is better and I am working again, something that had been quite impossible for months."[5] But in that same May, Clara wrote in the diary, "Robert's nerve trouble will not lessen," and in July he himself wrote to Mendelssohn, "I have so much to tell you. What an awful winter I had with a terrible nervous languor accompanied by a host of terrible thoughts that nearly brought me to despair; but things look better now—music is again beginning to sound within me, and I hope to be recovered soon."[6]

From the beginning of the Dresden years to 1849, the Schumanns' letters and diaries read like catalogues of misery. He was not self-conscious about his illness or averse to Clara's discussing it. Indeed, much of our information about his mood variations comes from Robert's letters to friends. In September 1845 he wrote to Mendelssohn, "Hofrath [Dr.] Carus has recommended early-morning walks, which do me a great deal of good but I am not yet myself, and every day I suffer . . . in a hundred different places. A mysterious complaint—when the doctor tries to take hold of it, it seems to disappear."[7]

On December 3, 1849, during the negotiations for a position in Düsseldorf (which he accepted in 1850), he wrote to Hiller, "All this time I have been suffering from headaches, which kept me from working or thinking." And he added, in an oblique reference to Düsseldorf's insane asylum, "I have to be careful to guard against all melancholy impressions."[8]

Despite the ill health, the Dresden years were in fact very productive. Many of Robert's best-known works—the Piano Concerto, the C-Major Symphony, Album for the Young, the Concert Piece for Four Horns and Orchestra—stem from this period. Other great works of the Dresden years are not so well known today, but Schumann regarded them highly, pouring into them his talents and mastery—indeed, as he wrote, his "life's blood": *Genoveva*, his only opera; *Scenes from Faust;* and *Manfred*, the melodrama based on a poem by Byron. In April 1849 Schumann wrote Hiller, "This has been my most fruitful year."[9] By this time Schumann had eliminated all his literary work and other distractions, and with Clara's help was concentrating solely on composition except for the few hours a week devoted to a choral society he had organized.

Clara's public career slowed down somewhat during the Dresden years. There were many reasons: Robert's health and her obligations as wife and mother, her continuous pregnancies (at least four; she may also have had a miscarriage) during their five years in Dresden, the musical and political situation there, and her unfailing presence at and support of all Schumann's activities.

For most of 1845 and 1846, her concertizing was limited to Dresden and Leipzig, but the concerts she gave were outstanding events and she premiered works of great significance. She performed Schumann's Piano Concerto for the first time in Dresden under Hiller on December 4, 1845, and in Leipzig under Mendelssohn on January 1, 1846, the final month of her fourth pregnancy. (Emil was born on February 8.) Two months earlier she had premiered Adolph Henselt's new concerto (October 5, 1845), and in October 1846 she played Beethoven's Fourth Piano Concerto with cadenzas she had composed. All in all, she gave some twelve concerts in these two years. It is astonishing to read in the household books that on a vacation on the island of Norderney—a North Sea resort—she underwent "a change in her condition" (probably a miscarriage) on July 26, yet played publicly there on July 27, 1846.[10]

She put her entrepreneurial skills to use by organizing a trio in Dresden, and in October 1847 inaugurated a chamber music concert series, probably the first of its kind in that city. She also gave benefit concerts for friends and various causes.

Clara's income from tours and concerts during the Dresden years was not inconsiderable and helped pay for their rent and other basic family needs. There is no doubt that the profits from the Russian trip were a comfortable cushion during the first years in Dresden, when Robert was so ill; her concerts continued to be an important source of income. She earned 120 taler from the Norderney and Leipzig concerts in 1846, 320 taler (after travel costs) from the Vienna–Brünn–Prague tour in 1846–47, and 482 taler from two Berlin concerts in 1847.[11] In the years 1845–47, her husband's only income consisted of small amounts from his capital, from music publishers, and from occasional teaching. By 1849, however, Schumann was earning substantial amounts from the sale of his compositions (1,223 taler in one year),[12] so that her earnings were a proportionately smaller share of the family income.*

Both Clara and Robert began giving lessons in piano and composition soon after they settled in Dresden. Teaching grew into a satisfying source of income, so that by 1847 Clara could write, "I give two lessons nearly every day. . . . It is certainly quite a pleasant feeling to earn something daily."[13]

The first two Dresden years were also productive for Clara Schumann the composer. It was during this stressful period that her Preludes and Fugues, Trio in G Minor, and a number of still unpublished works were completed.

At the close of 1846 the Schumanns and their two oldest children left on an ill-fated tour to Vienna. Distasteful arguments with Wieck, who was in Vienna at the same time, and empty halls for their concerts created discomfort and anxiety. The critics were unsympathetic to Schumann's music, although Clara's playing was not faulted. On their return home, they found their youngest child ill, but they had to leave him and the other children with servants and take off almost immediately to prepare for a performance of *Peri* and several concerts in Berlin for which Clara was scheduled.

Probably the most remarkable incident of the Dresden years was Clara Schumann's heroic behavior during the May 1849 uprising. The insurgents expected that every able-bodied man would join them. Schumann's sympathies lay with the rebels but he was in no condition to fight. Clara hid him as long as she could, then had to flee through the back door with him and their eldest child, leaving the other children behind with the servants. She returned in the middle of the night with another woman, courageously walking through open fields to the embattled city, seven months pregnant (Ferdinand was born on July 16), facing squadrons of armed men, to rouse her children—ranging in age from a year and a half to six years old—and lead them to safety in the suburbs. The family remained away for about a month.

Curiously enough, this was a time of great activity for Schumann. While wife and children were sheltered by friends, he was writing feverishly (in a *Schreibfeuer*, as he put it), completing the Song Album for the Young, Songs

---

*The figures on pp. 669–83 of *Hb* indicate the continuously growing popularity of Schumann's music during his lifetime. Though the audiences were small, the music was selling.

Clara and Robert Schumann in Vienna. Lithograph by Eduard Kaiser, 1847.
Schumannhaus, Bonn.

from *Wilhelm Meister,* songs for men's voices, and a motet, and planning the cathedral scene for his *Faust.* Many other works originated in the months during and just after the May Uprising, an event in which Richard Wagner took such an active part that he was exiled from the Saxon kingdom. Political statements in the diary and letters during these months indicate that both Schumanns sided with the insurgents, but Schumann, unlike the extroverted, outspoken Wagner, was not a fighter. He remained a spectator and composed his music.

During his "nervous" times, Robert depended on his wife for psychological as well as artistic and financial support. When she went to Leipzig for the opening of the season in October 1845, he remained behind because, as he put it to Mendelssohn, "any disturbance in the simple order of my life throws me off balance and into a nervous and irritable condition. That is why I preferred to stay at home when my wife was with you in Leipzig—much to my regret. Wherever there is fun and excitement, I must still keep my distance."[14] And the troubled composer wrote to his wife while she was in Leipzig for the premiere of the Henselt concerto, "I am getting along tolerably well, yet I am in a perpetual state of agitation because I think of you continuously. . . . Did you arrive safely? . . . Do you feel strong?"[15]
Another letter to his absent wife shows dramatically his need for her:

> I had a bad night. I always feel so strained but this always gets better when you are with me again. Yet I feel how much I am lacking in health; I cannot tolerate anything. All the pains and joys of life disconcert me; it is an overexcited state of mind—if only it would change soon. I *cannot* work at all; all peace has left me and I search for it everywhere.[16]

In good times, too, he depended on her, not only as a wife but as a musician. Clara's superb skills and training were exploited in the arrangements for piano of his Overture, Scherzo, and Finale, the C-Major Symphony, the Faust scenes, and *Genoveva,* and she served as assistant conductor and accompanist for his Dresden choral group. She coached at rehearsals of his *Peri, Mignon,* and *Faust,* and, as we have noted, premiered all his great piano solos and vocal and chamber works in which the piano had a part.
Looking back almost fifty years, Marie von Lindemann, one of the women who sang in the Choral Society, described the close collaboration of the two Schumanns:

> I still can remember the influence that the superlative artist Frau Clara Schumann exerted on us as she accompanied our singing and developed our understanding of the music through her wonderful, thoroughly intelligent playing. One can imagine how, under this double leadership, all the powers we possessed would grow. . . . In each gathering, it was clearly seen that one spirit dwelled in both and this was even more evident when

it was our lovely task to bring a new creation of Robert Schumann to the ears of the public. With what calm, with what confidence he turned to his Clara to bring us closer to an understanding of his ideas through stressing every important tone, through intensifying the nuances. And how we saw her eyes flash with enthusiasm when the beauty of his music was appreciated![17]

Emilie Steffens, a favorite piano student of Clara's, spent much time with the family, in a sense filling the role of "wife" for Clara. According to Steffens, Clara practiced during the hours Schumann was away from the house, usually from 6 to 8 P.M., when he took his customary beer at a neighborhood tavern. Practicing ceased when he returned for supper at 8. Steffens remained in Dresden in charge of the children when the Schumanns went to Leipzig in June 1850 for the *Genoveva* premiere. The letters she received from Clara Schumann tell most eloquently of this woman's responsibilities and the conscientious manner in which she carried them out:

Monday, June 17, 1850
Dear Emilie,
The children are coming tomorrow afternoon at 2:30 and I would ask that either you or Pauline [the maid] wait for them at the train station; from there take a droshky and go with them to the house.* Take the suitcases with you in the droshky. You will find some things in the suitcases that I have sent back and in the dirty laundry there are some of my things. Please throw them in the big laundry. I am enclosing ten taler so that you will have enough money. I should very much like you to make out a small extra bill for the expenditures that I do not have my husband settle, such as the tailor, the seamstress, the handkerchiefs, etc. The laundry likewise.

Today I am asking you to send two things by return mail, namely, the book for which I have already asked; it is lying on my piano in a yellow paper cover and inside are some songs that I have written and also some small pieces of music paper, which naturally you should not send; then go into my husband's room, sit down at his piano, and stretch your right hand out toward the other package of music that is underneath in his music cabinet. There you will find copies of his *Lieder-Album für die Jugend.* Look for a clean copy and send it along, carefully packed, of course, so that it won't be damaged. Both things *right away,* please! . . .

June 24
About the opera . . . I believe that it is best that you come early Monday, in any case, since it is very possible that it will be performed on Monday though this will not be decided on before Sunday. Would you tell the others and write once more how many tickets I should order? . . . I hope

*The two oldest children had been taken to Leipzig for their father's birthday and were returning home.

Pauline is well again so that you will not have to bring a stranger into the house—that would be a very big nuisance to me. Lock everything up, lock up the key to the laundry room. . . .

June 29, 1850
I am writing today with a joyful heart after the second performance of the opera, which took place yesterday. I wished you could have been there. The performance was far better than the first. . . . God grant that the children remain healthy—I am worried about Ferdinand. Write to me again right away. . . . What does Julie want? I have ordered a charming baby doll for her—will she like that? Ludwig is getting soldiers and a nice picture book. . . . Also give Pauline notice for August 1 as soon as you get this letter. Don't neglect to do this before July 1.[18]*

In their conscientious attention to detail and their peremptory tone, these letters are reminiscent of Wieck's, with their exacting instructions and admonitions to his wife. In contrast to Wieck's arrogance, however, consider the selflessness exhibited by Clara. There is no trace of the narcissism one associates with a concert artist, a woman who was once the spoiled darling of the Viennese aristocracy. Her concerns are her children, her husband, the routines of a household that she manages with efficient determination. Here, writing from Berlin, she is the wife of a composer, dependent on the skills of others to do justice to her husband's music, suffering through the endless wrangles, temperamental outbursts, and intrigues of an opera premiere, awaiting the rising of the curtain with beating heart.

It is clear that Clara's career took second place to that of her husband during the Dresden years. She was apparently not aware of any resentment toward Robert, but her outbreaks of anger and bitterness over the reception of his music may have been sharpened by this buried frustration. The Vienna concerts of 1846–47 were a great disappointment to Clara, not because her playing was criticized (it was in fact praised) but because Schumann's symphony and concerto were coolly received. Eduard Hanslick, who was present, described the scene after a concert:

> The minutes passed in an uncomfortable silence, since each of us were depressed by the cool reception of the marvelous evening of music. Clara broke the silence first, complaining bitterly of the coldness and thanklessness of the public. The more we tried to soothe her, the more audible her despondency became. Then Schumann spoke the unforgettable words: "Calm yourself, Clara dear. In ten years it will all be different."[19]

And indeed, a change was evident in less time than that. By 1849, publishers were vying for his work. *Peri* was performed as far away as New York.

*The Schumanns were planning to move to Düsseldorf in August.

On September 18, 1849, Schumann could write to Franz Brendel, who later took over the editorship of the *Neue Zeitschrift*, that he was "quite content with the recognition" he had been receiving.[20] But the composer, feted and honored in so many other places, was virtually ignored in Dresden. Clara fumed and raged at the lack of respect received in their home town. She referred to the Dresden audiences as *Klötze* (klutzes) with no spark of life— dull, boring, conservative people. When the attendance of the men in the Choral Society dropped, she wrote angrily, "That is the Dresden feeling for art—now that there are only a few more Wednesdays that we will be here, they have stopped attending." And a few days later she wrote, "It isn't a taste for art that drives people here to make music, but, at the most, an interest in people, or just ordinary curiosity." She saw the Dresden musicians as hypocrites: "This is altogether a fine group—first they embrace each other as 'dear colleague' and 'darling' and then they would like to scratch each other's eyes out."[21]

Her father's presence in the town must have added to the discomfort of living in Dresden. Wieck, now well established as a piano and voice teacher, had been helpful when they first arrived in the difficult autumn of 1844, but Clara soon found she could manage better without him and was angered by his arrogance. When her father criticized Robert, she defended her husband, who still was unable to express verbally his deep-seated anger at his father-in-law. They spent the first Christmas in Dresden together but the two families still found themselves far apart on many issues. Clara concertized with her half sister Marie several times but had misgivings about her talent: "She plays well, but not extraordinarily well."[22]

An argument with Wieck in Vienna in 1846 aggravated their relationship. The major difficulty seemed to lie in Wieck's prodigious self-assurance and egoism; he could permit no contradictions and could not acknowledge Schumann's success as a musician. The disagreement centered on his voice students, and culminated in his refusal to allow Marie and Minna Schulz, a favorite student, to participate in Schumann's Choral Society. The animosity grew so extreme that they even suspected he had a hand in some unfavorable reviews in Vienna. By 1850 his name had all but disappeared from the Schumanns' diary and letters. He was not invited to the premiere of *Genoveva* in June, whereas Marianne Bargiel was a frequent and welcome visitor. Clara never broke completely with her father, but by the time they left Dresden, the emotional attachment had withered.

During the Dresden years Clara gradually assumed a new role, that of Schumann's defender and protector. Both husband and wife were probably unaware of the extent of his growing dependency. Because of his recurring illnesses and his total self-absorption when he was working, she began by participating in and then taking over many of his responsibilities, a situation he seemed to accept willingly, though it is difficult to imagine he did not feel some resentment. He was not unappreciative of her help and praised her openly and publicly. Though he doubtless preferred to think her principal role was that of mother and wife, Schumann encouraged her professional activities and took pride in her talents and achievements. Twice he went to great lengths to have her compositions published as a birthday surprise for her. He informed Heinrich Dorn, their old teacher, that Clara had published a volume of fugues, and added that he wished Dorn could get to know them. To the pianist and composer Ferdinand Hiller he wrote in 1847 that when he visited he would hear Robert's new trios and Clara's as well.[23]

His letters to friends are filled with expressions of tenderness for his wife and family: "She is a gift from above," he wrote to Mendelssohn in October 1845. "There is no doubt that she really deserves affection and encouragement as an industrious and hard-working artist, and indeed as a woman too." "My two girls are dear angel-children, my wife the same old dear," he wrote to Verhulst in 1844, and to Mendelssohn in 1845, referring to his own poor health, "But I daresay better times are coming, and when I look upon wife and children I have joy enough."[24]

Whenever he was able, he acted as manager and made concert arrangements—the role once filled by her father. In a letter outlining his considerations before accepting a job offer in Düsseldorf he asked Hiller, "Would there be anything for my wife to do? You know her, and that she cannot be inactive."[25]

Robert understood his wife. No matter how busy she was with her husband and his work, with her children and their needs, she required her own artistic activity to be truly content. At the end of July 1847, after a year that included concert tours to Vienna and Berlin, a Schumann festival in Zwickau, the death of her youngest child, and the start of a new pregnancy, this woman wrote in her diary: "I am lazy, but I cannot help it because I am always ill and terribly weak. Oh, if I could only work, that is my one sorrow."[26]

CHAPTER 7

Düsseldorf and the Death
of Robert Schumann

Clara Schumann's conduct during the last years of her marriage raises many questions. Did she become overly directive during the years in Düsseldorf? Did she neglect her husband during his hospitalization? Why did she wait two and a half years before visiting him in the institution where he died? A reexamination of the available material permits us to view these difficult years in perspective and goes far toward explaining her conduct.

The position offered Robert in Düsseldorf—music director of the Municipal Orchestra and Chorus, with responsibility for ten concerts and four church music services yearly—was accepted with many reservations. The warm greeting in the Rhenish city dispelled their doubts, but the good feelings were of short duration on both sides.[1] In contrast with the reception in Dresden, the Schumanns were treated with great respect, but objections to the composer's conducting style rose almost at once; discipline in the chorus was lax, attendance at rehearsals dropped, critics murmured, and by the end of the first season it was clear that there was general dissatisfaction with the new director, though esteem for his creative work had not lessened. Clara was defensive and raged in her diary and in letters to friends about the loose character of the Rhinelanders, their lack of taste, and the "intrigues" against their music director. As early as April 1851 she complained to her sister-in-law that Robert was unappreciated and announced their plans to leave Düsseldorf.[2] Throughout the three remaining years they made frequent futile inquiries about other positions. There were no offers, no places to go—and so they remained. The Düsseldorf years saw Schumann's deepening mental illness, his suicide attempt, and the tragic closing of his life; for Clara it was the beginning of a forty-year widowhood, the inauguration of close friendships with Joseph Joachim and Johannes Brahms, and a renewal of her concert career.

From the outset of their arrival in the new city, Clara Schumann was honored not only as Schumann's wife but as an artist in her own right. She was Düsseldorf's premiere pianist and played with the orchestra under Schumann's direction as well as in solo and chamber music concerts. As the soloist in the first orchestra subscription concert on October 24, 1851, Clara, like her husband, was greeted with a flourish of trumpets. She was delighted by her enthusiastic welcome but dismayed by Robert's angry reaction after the concert, when Ferdinand Hiller chivalrously proposed a toast to her rather than to him. This incident signaled the start of many misunderstandings. Tensions grew and many bitter tears were shed, but they never prevented her from continuing either her full support of her husband or her own professional career.

During their first session in Düsseldorf Clara appeared as soloist only occasionally, but letters and newspaper reports reveal that she was not forgotten; her influence and reputation as a musician were growing. There was ample professional recognition during the Düsseldorf years: a glorious Schumann Week in Leipzig honored both husband and wife in March 1852, a few months after the birth of their seventh child, Eugenie; the post brought urgent invitations to perform in England; Clara gave brilliant performances at the Lower Rhine Music Festival in May 1853, in which her long-lasting association with Joseph Joachim, now a mature artist, began; gala concerts with Robert launched her popularity in Holland, where she gave twelve concerts between November 26 and December 20, 1853, and appearances in Hannover in January 1854 strengthened her relationship with Joachim. She gave concerts on every trip she took, even those that were officially vacations. Visits to and from old rivals—Camilla Pleyel in Brussels in August 1851 and Liszt, who came to Düsseldorf in September—were reminders of her days on the stages of Europe. And within a few months she had a "little colony" of students who came from all over Germany to study with her.[3] Finally, in January 1853, the Schumanns moved into a new apartment on Bilkerstrasse, in which she had her own piano in a room where she could practice without disturbing her husband. In this room she began to compose again, and within three months in 1853 she wrote pieces that were to be her last works: Variations on a Theme of Robert Schumann, Three Romances for the Piano, Three Romances for Violin and Piano, and Six Songs, op. 20 through 23.

Although long concert tours were not possible because of the many young children and the continuing pregnancies (one pregnancy between the births of Eugenie and Felix ended in a miscarriage in August 1852), Clara performed in Düsseldorf and the neighboring cities of Bonn, Cologne, and Krefeld as frequently as she could. The scheduling and arranging of the concerts were entirely her responsibility and the details she attended to were staggering. Why did she undertake these additional tasks? A letter to Wilhelm Joseph von Wasielewski, a friend and violinist with whom she often played, tells part of the story:

135]

January 20, 1853
I have another question to ask of you today, dear friend, about which
Robert knows nothing, and I ask that you frame your answer in such a way
that it seems like more of an inquiry from you, or, if something stands in
the way of realizing my wish, then just do not answer at all. It concerns a
soiree in Bonn, about which we once spoke last summer and for which I
have had a great desire because, first, it would give us the pleasure of
playing with you and Reimers* again (I am thinking, naturally, of the
Quintet [op. 44]), and then it would also perhaps yield a small income. You
know well that there is not very much here and our household requires
much! (This is between us, dear J. v. Wasielewski, is it not?) . . . .[4] †

In addition to her own professional activities and the obligations to her
growing family, her diary shows an increasing involvement with her husband
and his duties, an involvement that Schumann both encouraged and resented. Though it was customary in Düsseldorf for the conductor to accompany the chorus at rehearsals, for example, Clara took over this task, partly
because of Robert's finger injury and partly because he had come to depend
on her support at the piano.

Clara identified completely with her husband and took as personal affronts
any criticism of his work. To her letter to Wasielewski she added a post-
script: "Excuse my terrible writing, but I am so agitated today, unfortunately again by an insult that was directed at Robert, that my hand is trembling.
But don't let Robert know that I mentioned it to you." Frederick Niecks,
who personally knew many of their Düsseldorf colleagues, writes, "She
watched over him, she placed herself between the outside world and him,
and prevented, as far as possible, those rubs which tortured his sensitive
mind."[5]

In March 1852, after describing a rehearsal of the Choral Society at which
the behavior of the women singers was so undisciplined that it made her
"blood boil," she wrote in her diary, "There is nothing I would like better
than for Robert to withdraw entirely from the Choral Society, for the position is not worthy of a man of his stature."[6] But she participated willingly in
each rehearsal of the chorus and never suggested that the hackwork at the
piano during rehearsals hardly befitted her rank as a concert artist.

Her responsibility for the family and greater personal strength were recognized on November 7, 1853, when a committee from the city administration informed Clara (not Robert) that in the future Robert would conduct
only his own works; all other conducting responsibilities would be taken over
by Julius Tausch, the assistant director. Clara reacted violently in her diary:

*Christian Reimers, cellist.
†These and other confidences paved the way for Wasielewski's 1858 biography of Schumann,
which Clara disavowed and refused to read. Perhaps she felt some guilt for having undermined
the image of Schumann as master of the house.

> This was an infamous intrigue and an insult to Robert, which forces him to give up his position entirely, as I told the gentlemen immediately, without having spoken to Robert. . . . I cannot say how angry I was and how bitter it was for me not to be able to spare Robert this outrage. Oh, they are low-minded people here! Vulgarity rules, and those men who mean well . . . draw back, condemning but doing nothing. What would I not have given to pick up and leave immediately with Robert, but when one has six children, it is not so easy.[7]

Though she reacted to the insult as any loyal wife would have done, she did not perceive that the manner in which it came—through her—was equally insulting.

Schumann had never been an effective conductor, should never have been offered the position, and should not have accepted it. Friends always knew he had problems in this kind of executive post, but neither he nor Clara (who must have been aware of his problems) acknowledged any weakness on the podium.* After his first attempt at leading an orchestra in Leipzig, he proudly wrote Clara of what he perceived as success, but his letter was received at the same time as the gentle admonition from Livia Frege, "If only your dear husband could resolve to scold a little . . ." † Schumann gave up the Men's Chorus in Dresden ("I found too little real musical aspiration, and did not feel suited to it, nice people though they were"),[8] and despite some critical enthusiasm for the Dresden Choral Society, it was known that he had difficulty holding that group together. He depended increasingly on Clara, who would communicate the conductor's wishes to the chorus from her place at the piano.

The conducting responsibilities in Düsseldorf were heavier and his weaknesses more severe and more visible, and the strain on him and his wife was correspondingly greater. When Schumann was away or ill, Julius Tausch, his deputy, took over. At first this arrangement suited Schumann, and he asked that Tausch continue with preliminary rehearsals because, as he wrote to the committee, "for a creative artist, after his day's work, it is too great an irritation to direct the preliminary studies of an amateur choir."[9] But when the chorus preferred Tausch for all rehearsals, Clara, who had never liked Tausch (and who was displaced as pianist by him), took the new arrangement as a personal affront. Her suspicions were aroused and she saw it as a "plot."

In 1852 Schumann's condition deteriorated rapidly. He suffered great physical and mental anguish during the 1852–53 season, and although he conducted one concert at the Lower Rhine Music Festival in May 1853, it

---

*In a letter to the Austrian critic Eduard Hanslick written on January 19, 1859, she was still resolutely denying that Schumann had any special problems as a conductor and blaming his difficulties in Düsseldorf on his illness and "intrigues." See Hanslick, *Aus neuer and neuester Zeit* (Berlin: Allgemeiner Verein für deutsche Literatur, 1900), 320–21.

†See chap. 5, at superscript 30.

seemed clear to everyone—except his wife—that he did not have the energy to continue as municipal music director and certainly did not have the strength to withstand the accusations and counteraccusations, threats of dismissal, and charges of intrigue that were flying back and forth. His symptoms were alarming: he was more taciturn and withdrawn than ever, he had attacks that resembled mild strokes, he had no strength or stamina, and worst of all, he suffered from auditory hallucinations in which certain tones sounded incessantly—torture to anyone and a special horror for a musician. Effective conducting was out of the question, though he continued to compose and write. Berthold Litzmann refers to "a certain apathy and dreaminess" as well as "a peculiar and noticeable difficulty, from time to time, with verbal expression."[10] Wasielewski, more specific, describes a noticeable increase in difficulty with speech. "More than ever, all musical tempi seemed too fast. . . . His physical bearing had something weighed down about it, and despite declarations of friendliness, a real apathy was evident in his intercourse with others."[11] Other problems were insomnia and an embarrassing (for Clara) fervor for table tapping—a parlor game in which spirits from the other world were supposed to manifest their presence by rapping on a table. Ten-year-old Elise was expected to assist with this new enthusiasm.[12]

One cannot help wondering how a musician of Clara's stature could defend Schumann's conducting when his incapacities were so clear. Perhaps she harbored the natural (but vain) hope that if she ignored the signals of mental illness, they might disappear. Burdened with six children and a household, teaching and performing, the thirty-two-year-old woman probably avoided thinking about the situation; to acknowledge it would have been to acknowledge the need for action. Berthold Litzmann, her greatest apologist, wrote, "The warding off of each and every criticism that was directed against him was the only protection against critical or skeptical agitation in her own soul."[13]

The situation was made even more difficult by a change in Schumann's behavior toward her. He was now frequently nervous and irritable and increasingly critical of her playing. Niecks reports two incidents in which she was denigrated, both times as a woman artist: once Schumann asked Tausch to replace Clara in playing his quintet because, Schumann explained, "a man understands that better," and on another occasion he had Tausch "relieve her" as the accompanist of the chorus, "since the pianoforte drumming tired her too much and was more suitable for a man."[14] As early as November 9, 1850, Schumann blamed her playing for the cool audience response to his D-Minor Trio, faulted her performance of Beethoven's *Appassionata* Sonata (a work she had made her own as early as 1838), and told her that her accompaniment of the singer was "terrible."*

---

*It is possible that this criticism was a projection of his own inability to function well, as reviewers and friends reported no diminution of her artistry.

To her diary she poured out her feelings after that evening in November:

> What grieved me so frightfully was that I had played with all my strength, given it my best, and thought to myself that it had never gone so well, and so it was even more bitter to hear, instead of a friendly word, only the most bitter, discouraging reproaches. I hardly know any more how I should play. Though I took great pain to accompany the singer in the most sensitive and responsive way, Robert said my accompanying was terrible! If I did not have to use my playing to earn some money, I would absolutely not play another note in public, for what good is it to me to earn the applause of the audience if I cannot satisfy him?[15]

We may wonder at this artist's desperate need for her husband's approval; her history gives some insight into the problem. From childhood on, Clara equated approbation of her playing with love. Her early performances had secured the love and attention of her father, the one parent who was left to her. During the early years of the courtship, audience approval compensated for the lack of her father's support. Her performances in Berlin revived the opportunities to regain her mother's attention and love. Thus, for Clara, Robert's criticism was tantamount to a withholding of love. As far as we know, however, she never acknowledged to herself or revealed to her husband any resentment of his criticism. Tears fell, but the anger she was probably feeling (and suppressing) was directed at the ungrateful Düsseldorf audiences rather than at the man who was causing it. She treasured every bit of praise he gave and guarded him more zealously than ever.

Despite the illness and strains generated by the official position, Schumann was composing throughout the Düsseldorf years. Her diary describes the joy his music gave her: "I have no peace; I must try Robert's new sonata immediately"; "I am burning with impatience for it"; "overpowering"; "sweeps one away to the wildest depths"; "It has been a long time since I have been so affected by music."[16]

Many of her comments, however, reveal a curious conflict of emotions. She reported in her diary that while Schumann was composing this Trio in G Minor, op. 110, which made a "powerful impression" on her, he allowed her to hear nothing at all of his work. When, on October 27, 1851, she was finally permitted to listen to it, she wrote:

> How wonderful is such an incessantly creative, powerful spirit; how I glory in the fortune that heaven has granted me sufficient intellect and feeling to comprehend this heart and soul so completely. Often a terrible anxiety comes over me when I think that I, among millions of wives, am the one who is so blessed, and then I ask heaven if it is perhaps too much happiness. The shadows cast by material cares cannot compare with the joys and the blissful hours that I enjoy through the love and work of my Robert.[17]

The months that began in September 1853 were fateful. Clara's birthday—her thirty-fourth—and their thirteenth wedding anniversary were celebrated in great style. After elaborate preparations, Schumann, who was feeling particularly well at this time, arranged an excursion and the following day presented his wife with a new piano, piled high with newly composed music. Again her "hunger" for his music was appeased, though she had "a feeling akin to sadness." She was frightened by the frenzied pace at which he had been working and by the great expense of the new piano. In her diary she wrote, "I cannot express very well what I feel, but my heart was filled with love and respect for Robert and thanks to heaven for the great happiness that overwhelms me. It may be presumptuous to say it, but is it not really true that I am the happiest wife on earth?"[18]

At the end of that month, however, the "happiest wife on earth" found she was pregnant again and that a long-awaited trip to England would have to be postponed once more.* This time she was able to express her feelings quite clearly; on September 30 she lamented, "My last good years are passing, my strength too. . . . I am more discouraged than I can possibly say."[19]

On the same day Schumann wrote in his diary: "Herr Brahms from Hamburg," and the following day, "Visit from Brahms, a genius."[20]† The arrival of the twenty-year-old composer was described, many years later, by Marie, the Schumann's eldest daughter, at that time twelve years old:

> One day—it was in the year 1853—the bell rang toward noon; I ran out, as children do, and opened the door. There I saw a very young man, handsome as a picture, with long blond hair. He asked for my father. My parents went out, I said. He ventured to ask when he could come again. Tomorrow, at eleven, I said; my parents always go out at twelve. The next day at eleven o'clock—we were in school—he came again. Father received him; he brought his compositions with him and Father thought that as long as he was there, he could play the things for him then and there. The young man sat down at the piano. He had barely played a few measures when my father interrupted and ran out saying, "Please wait a moment, I must call my wife." The midday meal that followed was unforgettable. Both parents were in the most joyful excitement—again and again they began and could not speak of anything but the gifted young morning visitor, whose name was Johannes Brahms.[21]

Brahms had turned up at the Schumann home at the urging of Joseph Joachim. The impact of the Hamburg musician on the Schumann family was stunning. In words befitting an oracle, Schumann described Brahms as a "young eagle . . . a mighty Niagara . . . the true Apostle."[22] By October 13, Schumann, who had not written a literary essay in ten years, completed "Neue Bahnen" (New Paths) for the *Neue Zeitschrift*, in which he hailed the

*The Schumanns' last child was born June 11, 1854.
†Two days later, on October 3, he added, "Clara's certainty": Clara was pregnant again.

young composer as "springing forth, fully armed, like Athena from the head of Zeus; a young man over whose cradle graces and heroes have stood watch."[23]* He urged Breitkopf & Härtel to publish the young composer's first efforts.

Schumann had always given generously of his time, talents, and advice to other composers, but never before had he reacted so enthusiastically. "Robert loves him and takes great pleasure in him, both the man and the artist," wrote Clara in her diary on October 30. They saw Brahms almost every day during October, playing music, walking, talking, reading together. Although Clara had not always shared Schumann's enthusiasms, this time she took equal delight in the young man's music. The sonatas that Brahms brought with him had a masterful sweep and freshness that captured the imagination of both Schumanns. Brahms's presence may have helped the couple recapture the joy and excitement of their early days in Leipzig, when they were at the center of new musical thought. For a moment, perhaps, they were able to recapture a sense of the sureness of their musical direction and forget the troubles in Düsseldorf. Brahms, who referred to Schumann as "the Master," may have been embarrassed, but he accepted the praise gratefully. He left Düsseldorf on November 2, a few days before the delegation visited Clara to announce the reduction of Robert's responsibilities.

The Schumanns did not devote themselves exclusively to Brahms during October 1853. Throughout the month they had critical confrontations with committees from the orchestra society. On October 19 Schumann noted in his household book, "Conference. Shameless people."[24] Several disastrous rehearsals and concerts were conducted by Schumann in the church and for the orchestral subscription series. They entertained many out-of-town visitors, including the French artist Jean-Bonaventure Laurens and his family (Laurens sketched portraits of Brahms and Schumann at this time); Bettina von Arnim and her daughter, Gisela; Joachim, who came briefly on October 14 and then again at the end of the month to play with the Düsseldorf orchestra and give a recital with Clara. There was much music making with Albert Dietrich and Ruppert Becker, young local musicians, as well as with Brahms. Throughout this time, Clara, pregnant again, continued to concertize locally, teach, practice, write letters for Robert, make the necessary arrangements to play in Cologne on November 8 (Beethoven's Fifth Concerto) and Bonn on November 12 (chamber works), and supervise her six children and the household.

The difficulties that culminated in the delegation's meeting with Clara on

---

*Schumann may have had second thoughts about his excited response. In a talk to the Robert-Schumann-Gesellschaft in Zwickau on June 6, 1984, Gerd Nauhaus reported that he found a letter to Georg Wigand, the publisher of Schumann's *Gesammelte Schriften* (Collected Writings), requesting that "Neue Bahnen" be omitted from the collection. The article did not, in fact, appear in the first edition published by Wigand in 1854, although it has appeared in subsequent editions of the *Gesammelte Schriften.*

November 9 were never officially resolved;* the Schumanns did not remain in Düsseldorf to attempt to work anything out. After a rather high-handed letter to the concert committee dated November 19,[25] they left on November 24 for a concert tour in Holland which turned out to be a heart-warming success. In Düsseldorf the arguments and discussion over a possibly broken contract continued, but in the end the mayor, Ludwig Hammers, in a noble gesture insisted that Schumann's salary for 1854 be paid whether or not he conducted. Hammers was also instrumental in ensuring that Schumann's salary was continued even after he was hospitalized.[26]

Clara gave ten highly appreciated concerts in the three weeks of the Dutch tour. Her husband received a laurel wreath and the couple was serenaded. A short tour in January 1854 to Hannover, where they were welcomed by Joachim and Brahms, was a pleasant contrast to their uncomfortable position in Düsseldorf. Schumann was cheerful and talkative, Clara noted in her diary, but she added that Brahms seemed unusually quiet and Joachim more serious than usual.[27] Could they have noticed something disquieting in Schumann's behavior?†

By February 10, when the final breakdown began, they were back in Düsseldorf. With great alarm Clara noted increasingly frequent auditory hallucinations, headaches, and sufferings beyond anything she had ever seen. Dr. Richard Hasenclever, a friend and member of the chorus, attended him until it was thought necessary to consult another physician, a military doctor named Böger.

A witness to Schumann's last days was Ruppert Becker, Wasielewski's successor as concertmaster of the Düsseldorf orchestra. The young violinist—the son of their old friend Ernst Adolph Becker, their confidant and adviser during the battle with Wieck—described the situation in his diary:

> February 14
> Today Schumann spoke about a peculiar phenomenon that he has noticed for several days now. It is the inner hearing of beautiful music in the form of entire works! The timbre sounds like wind music heard from afar, and is distinguished by the most glorious harmonies. Even as we were sitting at Junge's [a restaurant], his inner concert began and he was forced to stop reading his newspaper! God grant that this doesn't mean the worst. He spoke of it, saying, This is what it must be like in another life when we have shed our corporeal selves. Most significant that these strange phenomena appear now, at a time when Schumann has not composed for eight weeks or more.

*Frederick Niecks, *Robert Schumann* (London: J. M. Dent, 1925), 272–82, offers what seems to be a reasonably complete and fair discussion of these events.

†A letter to Joachim dated February 6, 1854, in which Schumann wrote of a "secret message between the lines," could not have allayed Joachim's fears that Schumann was disturbed. See *Briefe von und an Joseph Joachim*, ed. Johannes Joachim and Andreas Moser, 3 vols. (Berlin: Julius Bard, 1911–13), 1:153–54.

February 21

What I had not dared to think would happen has happened! Schumann has been insane for several days now. I learned it first yesterday from Dietrich, who told me that Frau Schumann would like someone to come in order to free her from the continuous watching. So I visited him today but it would not have occurred to me to think he were ill if Dietrich had not assured me of it. I found him quite as usual. I conversed with him for a half hour and then took my leave. Frau Schumann looks as if she is suffering as she never has before. If the situation doesn't change, the worst is to be feared. She is in the eighth month of pregnancy [actually the fifth or sixth] and has not closed an eye since his illness. The poor, unfortunate woman! During the night she sits by his bed and listens for every movement.

February 24

I visited him at noon and Frau Schumann asked me to go walking with him. During the hour I spent with him he spoke quite rationally, except when he told me that the spirit of Franz Schubert had sent him a wonderful melody that he had written down and on which he had composed variations.[28]

By the night of February 26 Schumann was insisting that he must go to an insane asylum, "as he could no longer control his mind and could not know what he might do during the night." Doctors and assistants were summoned, and for the first time in ten days and nights Clara did not sit with him. "The next morning," she wrote in her diary, "he got up but was so profoundly melancholy that I cannot possibly describe it. When I merely touched him, he said, 'Ah, Clara, I am not worthy of your love.' *He* said that, he to whom I had always looked up with the greatest, deepest reverence."[29]

That day Marie was given the task of keeping an unobtrusive eye on her father while Clara spoke with Dr. Hasenclever in another room. Marie later told what happened:

The last time I saw my father was on the day on which he left the house to take his life. I had been called, since my mother had to speak with the doctor. I was supposed to sit in my mother's little room and pay attention if my father, who was in his room nearby, needed anything. I sat at my mother's writing table for a while when the door of the next room opened and there stood my father in his long, green-flowered dressing gown. His face was quite white. As he looked at me, he thrust both hands in front of his face and said, "Oh, God." And then he disappeared again. I sat as if spellbound for a short time, and then I realized what I was supposed to be doing. I went into Father's room. It was empty, and the doors, those to my parents' bedroom and those that opened from there to the hall, were wide open. I rushed to my mother, the doctor was still there, and then all the rooms in the house were thoroughly searched. It was clear my father was gone. Now they sent people out for him, but my mother told me to go to Fräulein Leser, to tell her what had happened.* When I went out to the street I saw a large noisy crowd of people coming toward me, and as I came closer I recognized my father, supported by two men under his arms, and with his hands in front of his face. I was terrified, and sobbing aloud I ran through the streets to Fräulein Leser, to whom I told everything and who immediately arranged that she and Fräulein Junge [her companion] would come back with me. We found my mother in the greatest anxiety. She had seen Father coming, the doctor and Fräulein Leser attempted to calm her, and then the doctor insisted that she go to Fräulein Leser. An attendant was procured for my father and a few days later he was taken away in a carriage. We children stood upstairs at the window and saw him get in. The carriage was driven into the courtyard to avoid being seen out in the street. Dr. Hasenclever and the attendant climbed in after him. We children were told that our father would soon return to us quite recovered, but the household servants who were standing near and watching cried.[30]

They were never to see him again, although he lived on for two and a half more years at a hospital in Endenich, a suburb of Bonn, a short journey from Düsseldorf. Periods of peace and clarity alternated with episodes of anxiety, depression, and insanity.

By the time Schumann's rescuers got him back to his house after his suicide attempt, Clara was no longer there. The doctor had urged her to go to the home of a friend, for her own sake as well as Schumann's, and she did not see him during the five days he remained in Düsseldorf, though she sent him flowers and messages. In her diary she described his departure in the carriage but she herself did not witness it. She remained at the home of her friend Rosalie Leser until after he left. The doctor's injunction against seeing him continued throughout the years of Schumann's hospitalization, and we learn with astonishment that she did not see her "passionately loved" husband until two days before his death, when he was so weak he could neither move nor speak.

Once Schumann was at Endenich, the doctors forbade her to visit him, ostensibly because they feared that reminders of the past would provoke renewed anxiety and agitation. Schumann, guarded by a male nurse with whom he seemed to be on good terms, was observed secretly by friends and relatives who then reported back to Clara. For many months Schumann did not even ask for or about her (though he knew she was pregnant), and the doctors evidently thought it best to prohibit all communication between the two. Brahms, who spoke with the doctors in December suggested that her letters to the doctors might be too "overexcited." He advised her to tone them down so that the physicians could see that she was stable and realistic and so perhaps permit direct contact with Schumann.[31] Finally, in September 1854, Dr. Peters, the hospital's assistant director, asked Clara to

*Rosalie Leser, blind friend of Clara Schumann.

write to her husband, who seemed somewhat improved, because, the doctor explained, Schumann was beginning to doubt the existence of his family. She wrote immediately and as frequently as possible thereafter, always assuming that their correspondence would be read by the staff.

Between September 1854 and May 1855, Schumann wrote eight letters to Clara. They varied greatly: some were warm, loving, and rational, others brief, enigmatic, and confused.[32] Then the letters ceased. In September 1855 Dr. Franz Richarz, the institution's director, wrote her saying there was no hope for a complete recovery. If she continued to write to her husband, the letters have not survived.

For the first ten months Schumann saw no one other than the hospital staff. Clara received weekly reports from the doctors but was requested not to visit. Finally, in December 1854, Joachim was permitted to speak with him, and thereafter Schumann had some face-to-face visits with Brahms and the writer Bettina von Arnim as well. Frau von Arnim, sister of Clemens Brentano and wife of Achim von Arnim, had met the Schumanns through Joachim, and Clara was flattered by her offer to visit Robert. In an emotional letter dated April 13, 1855, Clara thanked her in advance and told her that she had written to prepare Schumann for the visit. The visit, which took place in late April or early May, actually caused Clara much grief.[33] The older woman described a desolate, cheerless place and recommended that the patient be returned home to his family. This advice contradicted everything Clara had been told by the doctors, and in great alarm she sent Joachim to assess the situation. He reported that Schumann was very agitated and no change was made.

The medical position is puzzling, in view of the fact that Dr. Richarz had the reputation of being particularly humane and progressive; his patients were treated with respect and rarely put under constraint.[34] Moreover, Schumann seems to have been given special attention, probably because of his reputation and because Clara paid the fifty-taler monthly fee promptly. He had his own suite of rooms with a piano, and after his initial recovery he walked daily in the garden. By April 1854 he was taking long walks, accompanied by his nurse-attendant, into Bonn and the surrounding area. Richarz's hospital was a private institution in a parklike setting. From the large, pleasant rooms that are presumed to have been Schumann's, mountains can be seen.

Despite Dr. Richarz' excellent reputation, Schumann's friends and family always felt some uneasiness about the treatment and regime at Endenich. There were times during the course of the two and a half years he spent there when Schumann seemed quite well. Bettina von Arnim evidently saw him during one of those periods.

To add to Clara's uncertainties about Endenich, Schumann himself made several troubling remarks about his stay there. In a letter to Joachim and during a visit from Brahms, Schumann whispered that he would like to get away—"away, away from here."[35] Everyone offered advice, including

Brahms's mother, who ventured to say she thought Schumann would be better off at home with his family, or at the very least should try another doctor or cure.[36] In the spring of 1855 and again in March 1856 Brahms made several trips to inspect other hospitals but was disappointed in both the institutions and the doctors he investigated.[37] At Joachim's urging, Clara went to speak with Dr. Richarz in May 1855 to discuss the possibility of a move, but he convinced her that the patient was in no condition to make a change.*

More puzzling than the doctor's prohibition of her visits is the fact that Clara did not challenge it. There is no simple answer to this enigma. There are many possible reasons. First, Clara was basically a dutiful and conscientious woman. True, she had defied her father to marry Robert, but the decision was, as we know, extraordinarily difficult for her, and she vacillated for many years before she was able to disobey her father. Her ordinary mode was to follow the instructions of those who were in positions of authority. Though she had doubts about the doctors at Endenich and was frequently uneasy about their directives, she did not question their authority.

Second, she certainly must have felt inadequate to deal with mental illness. Relatives of mental patients, particularly those who are suicidal, frequently feel guilty. Though Clara was not officially informed of the suicide attempt, she suspected it almost immediately. The news had spread rapidly throughout the musical world.† Everyone knew. Albert Dietrich, a close friend in Düsseldorf, wrote Joachim that he was sure she knew the truth.[38]

Third, Schumann's depression was so deep and his sense of isolation so extreme that Clara was apprehensive about seeing him. The man she knew was no longer there. Added to the fear was the anger and resentment she must have felt when she found he did not want to see her or their children.

Fourth, the fear, expressed in her diary and in letters to friends, that in a moment of insanity he might, as he himself suggested, harm her or the children or himself was not unrealistic.

Fifth, the growing relationship with young Brahms originally brought her relief from engulfing melancholy and then gradually brought her a happiness she had never before experienced. It was inevitable that some feelings of guilt emerged when she realized what was happening.

Sixth, she received a sense of comfort, exhilaration, and power from the successful concert life she had resumed—indeed, felt she was forced to

---

*They met in Brühl, some fifty kilometers north of Bonn.

†In far-off Boston, the suicide attempt was reported on April 22, 1854, just two months after the event, in a sympathetic statement: "The melancholy report of the insanity of this great composer appears to be confirmed, although we get no direct and full accounts. Foreign papers contain a paragraph, under the head of Düsseldorf, his last place of residence, to the effect that he had escaped his keepers and thrown himself into the Rhine, but that he was saved. His case, however, was considered hopeless. . . . Probably the overexcitement of an active brain, always intensely busied with the conception and execution of new musical creations, was the true secret of his lamentable state. [*Dwight's*, 5 (1854), 22].

resume, in order to pay for Schumann's hospitalization and support her family.

During the first few weeks of his hospitalization, Clara was desperately anxious to see her husband and get some information about him. She begged Wasielewski, at that time music director in Bonn, to inquire after him daily and send her news about Robert's condition. On March 10 she wrote:

> Oh, dearest friend, what are you inflicting upon me by not writing a word about my husband! Today is the sixth day that he is in Endenich and I know nothing, not a word! Oh, what a sorrow this is for me! My heart breaks when I have no idea of how he is living, what he is doing, if he still hears the voices, in short, every word about him is balm for my wounded heart! I don't ask for any kind of decisive word, just how he sleeps, what he does during the day, and whether or not he asks after me, *that* I am certainly entitled to know. Oh, my dear friend, don't do this to my heart— leaving me so completely without news. If you yourself cannot go . . . pay someone, charging it to me, and have them go to ask.[39]

She poured out her feelings on paper but made an effort to control herself in front of her children. On May 7, 1854, Brahms's twenty-first birthday, Hedwig Salomon, an acquaintance from Leipzig, stopped in to see her and recorded her impressions:

> My longing to see Clara Schumann prevailed over my shyness toward this celebrated artist. We came to Schumann's kitchen first, from there went to the children's room, where the nurse asked us to wait because "the Frau Doktor" was playing just now but we could listen from outside. The playing sounded grand, serious and powerful; we could not understand how she could play like that at this time. When the piece was over (I didn't recognize it though it was familiar), she came out; she looked so pathetic that it was difficult not to embrace her immediately. She was altered, looked old and jaundiced, but not broken or tearful. We avoided talking about the misfortune; she asked after friends and why her father had not written for so long. Then she . . . struggled against tears and burst out in bitter sobs. "If I didn't have the firm hope that my husband would be better soon, I wouldn't want to live anymore. I cannot live without him. The worst is that I may not be with him and he has not yet asked for me, not even once during the whole time." She could barely bring out these words, they were interrupted by convulsive sobs and her lovely eyes looked at me in an unspeakably sorrowful way. "But don't think," she continued, "that my husband is so bad. You would hardly notice that he was ill, he can carry on the deepest conversations, and is totally clear about his situation; he went to the institution voluntarily so he could return to us all the sooner."[40]

Two young men were at the piano in Schumann's room. Brahms had been playing his C-major sonata for Clara and Julius Otto Grimm. As he played,

Hedwig Salomon noted, Clara became cheerful, appeared transfigured and young. It seemed to do her heart good, but she praised Brahms only with smiles and a handshake.

On April 2 Clara asked Wasielewski to suggest that the doctor write on Mondays rather than Sundays because

> on Monday mornings I give piano lessons at court early and always receive his letter just before I go there, and that is terrible because I am always so upset after the letter that I break out in audible sobbing, and that is awful for me. If he cannot write regularly on Monday, then let it go and better not say anything about it because I would rather endure it all than lose a word.[41]

In the terrible days after February 27, Clara turned to friends for support: her blind friend Rosalie Leser and Leser's companion, Elise Junge, were at her side from the beginning; Clara's mother came posthaste from Berlin; the young Düsseldorf musicians Albert Dietrich and Julius Otto Grimm and the two young men who had been closest to Schumann in the last few months, Brahms and Joachim, arrived almost immediately. Brahms came on March 3, announcing he was there to help her in any way he could.

Clara's greatest solace was music and her piano. The presence of the young musicians and Brahms's unwavering loyalty supplied sorely needed support. She did not have the heart to give public concerts (pregnancy alone would never have stopped her), but she did resume teaching two days after Schumann left, and she played with Brahms and Dietrich or Grimm daily, first only her husband's music and then that of other composers. In the course of the next two years she saw Brahms almost every day when she was at home and corresponded with him when she was touring. Brahms stayed on in Düsseldorf, composing a bit, trying to make some money by teaching, and helping Clara's housekeeper and the servants with her children. The friendship with Brahms sustained her while Schumann was in Endenich; only gradually did she perceive that it had turned to passionate love.

Clara Schumann remained in Düsseldorf with her children until after the birth of Felix, her eighth and last child, in June. Soon after, a period of touring and concertizing began. The extent of her restlessness can be seen in her schedule for the last six months of 1854:

July	Berlin	Julie brought to stay with Marianne Bargiel
August	Ostend	Vacation; Clara plays several concerts in Brussels and Ostend
October 16	Hannover	Concert at court
October 19	Leipzig	Gewandhaus concert
October 23	Leipzig	Gewandhaus concert
October 27	Weimar	Concert under Liszt's direction
November 3	Frankfurt am Main	Concert
November 4	Frankfurt am Main	Concert
November	Düsseldorf	Short visit to see children

November 13	Hamburg	Three concerts with Philharmonic
November 15	Altona	Concert
November 16	Hamburg	Concert
November 18	Lübeck	Concert
November 21	Bremen	Concert
November 23	Berlin	Concert
November 29	Breslau	Concert
December 1	Breslau	Concert
December 4	Berlin	Concert with Joachim
December 7	Frankfurt an der Oder	Concert
December 10	Berlin	Concert with Joachim
December 16	Berlin	Concert with Joachim
December 20	Berlin	Concert with Joachim
December 21	Leipzig	Concert with Joachim
December 22	Düsseldorf	Home for Christmas

The year 1855 opened with concerts in the Netherlands in January; in Danzig, Berlin, and Pomerania in February and March; and at the music festival in Düsseldorf in May. During the autumn of that year she toured with Joachim again. In 1856 she made even more extensive tours: Vienna, Budapest, and Prague early in the year, and from May to June the long-postponed trip to England, where she gave twenty-six concerts in two and a half months.[42]

She could not remain at home; her disquiet was not assuaged by the concert tours, and she took frequent trips: to hear Beethoven's *Missa Solemnis* in Cologne, to attend a performance of her husband's *Manfred* in Hamburg, short vacations alone, with women friends, and with Brahms. Often weak, exhausted, prone to anxiety attacks about Robert, she was buoyed by the enthusiastic reception of her audiences and by Brahms's adoration (though they were rarely, if ever, alone). Obsessed by her pain and by her perceived need to support her family, she rejected all offers of financial aid from friends and set out again and again, despite pleas to stop from Brahms and others. Her need to keep moving was desperate; she felt relief from grief only when she was working.

Her art gave her more than solace: performing for audiences provided the love Schumann had withheld, and though his letters from Endenich were now filled with praise and admiration for her playing, actual applause was more gratifying. Mixed with the pleasures of concertizing were the ambivalent feelings confided to her diary and in letters to friends. On the one hand, she desperately wanted her husband back again; on the other, she could not face seeing him mentally ill. After hearing from Dr. Richarz on September 10, 1855, that Schumann's situation was hopeless, she wrote in her diary:

> What a thought, to see him, the most zealous of artists, mentally weakened, perhaps, or far more likely, prey to the most terrible melancholy? Do I want to have him *like this*? And yet, should I not want to have, most of all, the person back again? Oh, I don't know what to think any more; I

have thought it all over thousands upon thousands of times, and it always remains just terrible.[43]

She was proud that she could earn the money to pay the doctors' bills promptly but resented the burden and considered sending Robert to a less expensive state institution.[44] The news that Robert was again composing and writing letters to his friends was welcome, but she and Brahms were concerned that his letters would reveal his mental condition.[45] She responded immediately to his requests for music paper but knew that the work in Endenich was not worthy of him and later suppressed much of it. For those closest to him—Brahms, Joachim, and Clara—the image of Robert as a man revered, respected, and loved slipped gradually into that of a pitiable figure and a source of embarrassment.

In 1854 there was no financial necessity for Clara to go on tour. Schumann's salary continued until 1855, and offers of help from wealthy friends and music lovers in Leipzig and Hamburg came pouring in. She rejected Härtel's offer to give a benefit concert in Leipzig for her and her children, saying, "I will never allow anyone to give a concert for me. That I will do for myself when it is necessary."[46] Paul Mendelssohn, her banker and brother of Felix, sent her a check with a tactful note as soon as he heard of the events of February 1854. She consented to hold it in case of need but returned it within a few months. Between 1854 and 1856, Clara added 5,000 taler to the Schumann family capital, more than Robert's Düsseldorf salary over a four-year period.[47]

Schumann never learned of the full extent of her professional activities. She was just completing an English tour in June 1856 when a telegram from Endenich reached her. Schumann was totally debilitated, though he was still conscious. Before the final days, Clara went to Endenich twice—on July 14 and July 23—but did not see her husband. Though she was prepared to see him on the twenty-third, Brahms (who had accompanied her) and the doctors persuaded her not to go into his room because his appearance was so shocking. Only when they realized that he had no more than a day or two to live was she permitted to see him. Clara spent July 27 and 28 with her husband; she was calm and controlled and able to describe in her diary what she saw: "For weeks he had had nothing but wine and gelee*—today I gave it to him—and he took it with the happiest expression and in haste, licking the wine from my fingers—ah, he knew that it was I."[48]

On the afternoon of July 29 she and Brahms slipped out to meet Joachim at the railway station. The three returned about an hour later to find that he had died in his room, quite alone. She could feel only relief at his release. She wrote in her diary:

---

*Probably calves'-foot jelly, given to invalids.

His head was beautiful in death, the forehead so transparent and gently rounded. I stood at the body of my dearly loved husband and was calm; all my feelings were of thankfulness to God that he was finally free, and as I knelt at his bed I had such a holy feeling. It was as if his magnificent spirit hovered above me, oh—if he had only taken me with him! I saw him today for the last time—I placed some flowers on his brow—he has taken my love with him![49]

Schumann's illness and the cause of his death have been subjects of much controversy. The symptoms he presented were puzzling and a medical diagnosis was as difficult in 1856 as it is now in retrospect. He may have been suffering from hypertension in addition to the cyclical variations in mood (often viewed as a manic-depressive disorder) which he experienced from late adolescence on. But in view of the weakness, headaches, vertigo, ringing in the ears, and the later suicide attempt and hospital record, it is difficult to ignore the possibility that he had syphilis, a diagnosis that the physicians of the time could not make with any certainty. One widely accepted theory is that the illness was a late nervous-system effect of syphilis, acquired many years earlier, well before his marriage. The presumption that the infection was latent is offered as an explanation for the failure of Clara and their children to become infected.

Ostwald's recent diagnosis, in modern psychiatric terms, is that Schumann had a major affective disorder, personality disturbance, many physical problems and psychosocial stresses, all aggravated by inadequate medical treatment. He suggests that the actual cause of death was self-starvation.[50]

Clara was carefully shielded from any hint of syphilis. She and her family tended to believe, with Drs. Richarz and Peters, that his death was caused by a nervous condition aggravated by overwork.

CHAPTER 8

The Later Years

In her place of prominence, the young widow seemed to provoke either great loyalty or downright hostility. Despite her modesty, simplicity, and unpretentiousness, she seemed to her children, friends, and audiences to be larger than life. On stage and off, she had a sense of self that never deserted her: as mother, teacher, and pianist she rarely lost her dignity and self-possession.

Throughout her lifetime she was described as a "priestess," and the appellation seems appropriate not only because of her consecration to her art but because of her characteristic solemnity. Sober and earnest, she was often teased for her serious demeanor. Dressed almost always in dark colors, she did not condescend to court her audiences by cultivating an appealing stage personality, by personal display, or by playing popular music. There were periods when the once-slender woman gained weight, but she never seemed bulky or awkward; her erect, dignified bearing made her appear taller than she was. Although she had an expressive, pleasant face with large, beautiful dark-blue eyes, she never thought of herself as attractive. At the age of eighteen she made derogatory comments on her own appearance, writing to Robert from Vienna that she could not understand why all the lovesick swains came flocking round.[1] In 1842, when she was compared to a leading Danish actress whom she resembled, she declared, "We have similar features and figures, but she is pretty whereas I am ugly."[2] Even as a young unmarried woman she found it difficult to act playful, coy, or flirtatious, and though her father urged her to put on a pose, if necessary, for box-office considerations, she was incapable of emulating the flirtatious Camilla Pleyel, for example, about whom she wrote, "At this point, half of her art consists of coquetry; now I really understand why Father was always so unhappy that I was not coquettish." But she comforted herself with the thought that the real connoisseurs "will like me as I am."3*

Her students found her fussy about details, very strict, but capable of real warmth and generosity. She demanded no more of them than she did of herself, and when she insisted on conscientious rehearsals for each concert, even if her students had played the music in public only a few days earlier, they knew this was her own practice. In his memoirs the baritone and conductor Sir George Henschel wrote:

> Her art she took very much in earnest . . . . Whenever Madame Schumann and I, as was frequently the case, were the soloists at the same concert and she accompanied me in her husband's songs, we would invariably have a rehearsal of the songs some time before the concert, even though perhaps we had done the same songs only a week before, somewhere else.4

To her friends—male and female—she was often peremptory, demanding, and even controlling, but her open mind, integrity, stability, and rectitude won their loyalty. These qualities were inherent in her performances. Amy Fay, a young American who studied piano in Berlin in 1869, wrote home after she first saw Madame Schumann, "Such *noble* playing I have never heard."5 Reviews of Clara Schumann's concerts always stressed her solidity and objective "classical" playing.

Despite her many triumphs and brilliant career, observers always noted the sadness that seemed to pervade her spirit. Even when she was a child, her melancholy look struck those who observed her. And during the years of artistic triumph and marital happiness, a lingering remnant of sadness remained visible. During Robert's final illness and after his death, friends and children often saw her in tears. Liszt's description after she played in Weimar in 1854 was published widely: "To the moist, youthful lustre of her eyes, there has succeeded a fixed and anxious look. The flower crown, once so loosely woven in her hair, now scarcely hides the burning scars which the holy circlet has impressed so deeply on her brow."6

It was on this occasion that George Eliot met Clara Schumann. Later she described Clara as "a melancholy, interesting creature. Her husband went mad a year ago and she has to support eight children."7

The young Clara had met tragedy early in life; her defenses against loss

---

*In the same entry, Clara noted that she had heard from Frau Mendelssohn, the mother of Felix, that Pleyel "had bewitched all the men in Leipzig . . . she had accompanied [Wilhelmine] Devrient in the "Erlkönig" [Schubert's song] so beautifully that the singer was completely eclipsed. . . . Each movement she made was contrived: at the end of a work, she remained with the orchestra, spoke with the musicians, bowed again and again in a childlike way as though she could not understand why she received so much applause and then sat herself down at the piano and played another piece."

evolved in early childhood as she learned to cope with the loss of her mother and nurse, the divorce of her parents, and the tyranny of her father. During her adolescence she was rarely granted the opportunity for normal carefree times, high spirits, and laughter. She often expressed regret that her letters to Brahms were too often recitals of woe and sorrow, and she resolved many times to "ban sad thoughts to avoid making life so hard for the children."[8]

On August 20, 1869, she wrote in her diary that she admired and envied the "lightheartedness" of Pauline García-Viardot, and she added, "Everything is always so merry there [in the Viardot home], as if there were no sorrows in the world."[9] An observer described her appearance after Schumann's hospitalization as "careworn and sad" and added, "she appeared just so years ago when she was a young girl. She never had a childhood. Her father was determined to make a virtuoso of her, and the joyousness of youth she never knew. Even then her countenance showed her secret sorrow."[10]

As she was buffeted by continuing disasters, the melancholy was transformed into a relentless sobriety and severe self-discipline. Doing one's duty, she once told Eugenie, is what brings happiness.[11]

Making music was, as always, her solace. Without it she would not have had the strength to endure the illnesses, deaths, and tragedies that were the regular companions of her life. Ever thankful for the professional activities that could relieve her sufferings, she once wrote to Avé-Lallemant, a conductor and old friend in Hamburg: "It often seemed to me—and still does—that when I played, my overburdened soul was relieved, as if I had truly cried myself out."[12]

Her children took great pride in their mother but also suffered from the divided life she led. The triumphant star, the renowned teacher, the successful editor and composer was unable to give her children the emotional environment they needed.

MOTHERHOOD

Even before Robert Schumann died, his children were dispersed—as they were to be for many years. Marie and Elise, aged fifteen and thirteen, were at boarding school in Leipzig; Julie was in Berlin with her grandmother; Ludwig, Ferdinand, Eugenie, and Felix were in the Düsseldorf apartment in the care of Bertha, the housekeeper. Brahms, who occupied a room in the same apartment house, helped with the children while Clara was away on tour. The arrangements Clara made for the welfare of her children after Schumann's hospitalization were not unusual in nineteenth-century Germany. Wealthy families frequently sent their children to boarding schools for a proper upper-class education. Middle-class parents generally entrusted the care of their chidren to servants, though the mother might spend some part of each day with them, partly to instill proper moral and ethical values and partly to set an example of proper feminine behavior for the girls. The father provided the financial support, and, occupied with this important duty, spent little time with his children except for formal occasions or by prearrangement. Families celebrated such occasions as Christmas, birthdays, name days, and confirmations together but might not dine or vacation together. Like many other families in their situation, the Schumanns had two or three servants—a maid, a cook, and perhaps a general housekeeper who took major responsibility for the household under Clara's supervision. During Schumann's lifetime—and for his time, Robert Schumann was an unusually devoted father—the parents frequently left the children with friends, relatives, and servants when they went on tour or on vacation trips.

In those few European families in which the mother was a performing artist, the experience of the children differed little from that of the Schumann children. Occasionally they were taken along on tours with servants to care for them; more often they were sent to boarding schools. The younger children of Pauline García-Viardot, for example, generally accompanied her and her husband on their rounds of European opera houses, but the eldest daughter, Louise, was often left home in the care of a grandmother or maid—and resented it.[13] The six children of Margarete Stockhausen, a singer and the mother of Julius Stockhausen, Clara's "glorious singer," occasionally toured with her and their harpist father, but beginning at the age of seven, Julius spent most of his childhood in boarding schools with his younger siblings.

Clara's own mother departed from the traditional mothering role not only by her ultimate surrender of her three children in order to divorce their father but also by cultivating her musical career while bearing and nurturing eight children. The second and more conventional Frau Wieck was never a model for her stepdaughter. As a child, Clara knew her primary task was to play the piano, the only activity that brought her her father's love and admiration. She returned to this priority when her husband died. She had, of course, never given up the piano but simply added household tasks and motherhood to what she considered her basic responsibility.

During the fourteen years of their marriage, the Schumanns lived four years in Leipzig, six years in Dresden, and four years in Düsseldorf. In each of these cities Clara established a home with the needs of children, composer-husband, and performer-wife in mind. In each home she practiced, performed, composed, and taught, despite the demands of her children, the illnesses of her husband, and the discomforts of childbearing. Between 1840 and 1854 Clara Schumann gave at least 139 public concerts, and during those years she was pregnant almost continuously. At a time when respectable ladies were expected to remove themselves from public view when their pregnancy became obvious, Clara continued, like her mother before her, to teach, practice, and perform, sometimes up to one week before the birth of a child. Though she had several servants and a wetnurse for each child, the pressures on the artist-mother must have been immense.

Clara Schumann's feelings about motherhood progressed from enthusiasm to ambivalence. Marie, born in 1841, was welcomed wholeheartedly and pronounced "a great blessing,"[14] as was Elise, born in 1843, and perhaps Julie, born in 1845. By the time there were four children, however, Clara began to express grave doubts about her role as a mother. In May 1847, when she may have just become aware of a fifth pregnancy, she wrote in her diary:

> What will become of my work? Yet Robert says "children are blessings" and he is right, because without children there is indeed no happiness, and so I have decided to face the difficult time that is coming as cheerfully as possible. Whether it will always be like this, I don't know.[15]

As the family grew, she became increasingly resentful. Ludwig's birth, following the death of the infant Emil, may have offered the grieving mother some consolation, but the prospect of still another child (Ferdinand was born eighteen months after Ludwig) caused her great distress.[16] The Schumanns evidently did not practice birth control, and comments in the household book gradually change from "great blessing" to "Clara's new fear" and "frightening expectations." Entries in the household book: "change in Clara's condition and her joy—good effect of the bathing" suggest that the termination of the pregnancy in Norderney in 1846 was welcome.[17]

For the most part, Robert Schumann enjoyed the role of paterfamilias. In September 1845 he wrote to Mendelssohn to congratulate him on the birth of a second child. "We are looking forward to a similar event, but I always say to my wife, 'One cannot have enough.' It is the greatest blessing we can have on earth." To Verhulst he wrote in April 1848, "I possess great treasures in my own home, such a dear wife, such satisfactory children. We have got a boy now too; his name is Ludwig and he is the delight of his mother." To his friend Eduard Krüger he wrote on November 20, 1849, "Our house is very merry. Five children are running about and already beginning to listen to Mozart and Beethoven."[18] His *Jugendalbum, Liederalbum,* and the three sonatas of op. 118 were written with his children in mind. Characteristically, he kept detailed notes on their growth and progress in his "Little Book of Memories."[19]

Though Robert Schumann was aware of his wife's need to continue her professional activity, it never occurred to him to alter his daily pattern to give her the time she needed. He did not, of course, participate in the details of child rearing and household management, and it probably never occurred to Clara that he might have done so. Always conscientious, she never shirked what she regarded as the woman's responsibilities, but she must have felt underlying resentment as she went about her homemaking duties and practiced only when her husband, the composer, would not be disturbed. Once Schumann became ill, however, and the household had a clear need for funds, his wife assumed the combined burden of career and financial responsibility more than willingly.

In July 1856, on tour in England after two and a half years without sight of her husband, Clara received the telegram that notified her of Schumann's extreme weakness. On July 4 she returned to the Continent, but instead of rushing straight to Endenich or perhaps going immediately to Düsseldorf to see her children, she detoured from Antwerp, where Brahms met her, to Ostend in order to show her young friend the North Sea. On July 6 she returned to Düsseldorf, where her four youngest children were waiting for her. As we know, Schumann died on July 29, two days after Clara was finally permitted to see him.

After the funeral in Bonn, the two eldest children were informed of their father's death in a letter from Clara. Two weeks later, Clara took Ludwig and Ferdinand along on a month's vacation in Switzerland with Brahms and his sister, Elise. But by October there was further dispersal: Ludwig and Ferdinand, eight and seven years old, were sent to a boarding school in Bonn. "I felt terrible, but it is certainly in their best interests," Clara wrote in her diary on October 18, 1856.[20] The two youngest children, five and three, remained with the housekeeper. Brahms left Düsseldorf in October, just as Clara Schumann began the round of concerts for the new season.

In the years that followed, the health and well-being of her children were constantly in her thoughts, and she expended much time and energy directing their school and living arrangements. ["You wouldn't believe how difficult it is to bring up so many children so that each one is educated to be a capable human being,"] she wrote to her friend Emilie List in 1860.[21] No detail was too small for her concern, as we can see from this request in a letter to Ernst Rudorff, a former student and family friend, who was helping with arrangements for seventeen-year-old Ferdinand in Berlin: "I ask nothing more for him than a small room to sleep in and where he can also work on Sundays and evenings, and a simple but hearty diet; at noon he should regularly have as much meat as he wants, as he is growing frightfully fast."[22]

A stream of instructions and admonitions flowed by mail to housekeepers, governesses, music teachers, and the children, but she was rarely with them for birthdays, confirmations, or even Christmas holidays, and they suffered grave illnesses, even death, without their mother's presence. Despite Clara Schumann's regular, meticulous instructions concerning her children, it seems clear that she was not sensitive to their emotional needs and that her primary concern was with the professional tasks and duties that supported the family: teaching, practicing, learning new works, keeping up with an enormous professional and personal correspondence, and, of course, her concerts, which involved ten months of travel each year.

Clara Schumann was proud to be an artist but did not encourage any of her children to follow in her footsteps. Gender had no place in this decision. Each child was given the best musical education Clara could afford; each daughter was given the opportunity to develop enough skill to be able to teach and support herself if necessary. Recalling her own years as a child prodigy, she felt strongly that her children should experience as normal a childhood, family life, and education as was possible under their peculiar circumstances. Moreover, she believed that if any of her children were to attempt a life as a professional musician, the burden would be especially great because of the responsibility of the Schumann name; for this reason, Clara discouraged—often tactlessly and sometimes callously—Felix's interest in a musical or literary career. She realized dimly that she might be doing him an injustice and belatedly attempted to make up for her severity by teaching her grandson Ferdinand and offering to aid him in his ambition to become a music teacher. Three of her daughters and several grandchildren and great-grandchildren had careers as piano teachers but none was a concert performer.

In the sorrowful days and months following Schumann's death, the young widow accepted—almost eagerly—the responsibility of providing for her family. Outsiders may have pitied her, but she soon realized that the life of an artist, even with all its trials and tensions, brought her a fulfillment that motherhood could not match. Most of her contemporaries assumed that financial need was her only reason for living as she did: the good mother was sacrificing her comfort to provide for her little ones. Only Joachim and perhaps a few others understood that concertizing brought this artist satisfactions she could never achieve by remaining at home with her children. Few considered what life was like for the daughters and sons of Clara Schumann.

Marie Schumann, 1841–1929

Marie, the firstborn, was the favorite of both her parents. Of all the children, Marie seems to have had the happiest and most secure early years. Schumann noted her musical skills and other charms in his "Little Book of Memories," and he spent more time with her than with any of the other children. Beginning at the age of five, she was often delegated to take her mother's place on daily walks with Schumann, especially when Clara was recovering from childbirth or otherwise indisposed. Clara, twenty-two when Marie was born, also felt exceptionally close to her eldest daughter and confided to her diary in June 1870 that she found her greatest happiness as a mother in the friendly relationship with Marie. When she was away from home, it was Marie she missed most. In 1868 she wrote in a memorable letter to her eldest daughter, "My dear, dear Marie, if you only knew how dear you are to me, how my whole existence is bound up with yours . . ."[23] The life of the favorite became consumed by her mother's life. Never marrying, she remained with her mother until Clara's death.

As the oldest, Marie began to take over household tasks early, but she also vacationed and toured with her mother more than did any of the other children. All major decisions were first discussed with Marie. When Clara accepted a teaching position in Frankfurt, Marie became her assistant; when her mother retired from teaching, so did Marie. Their students reported that Fräulein Marie (perhaps fifty years old at the time) sewed the collars on her mother's concert dresses; she also wrote most of the letters that Clara dictated during her recurrent attacks of rheumatism and bursitis. She accompanied Clara to Vienna in 1858 and 1860, to Paris in 1862, to The Hague in 1863, to Russia in 1864, and to England thirteen times. What Louis Viardot did for Pauline García-Viardot and Otto Goldschmidt did for Jenny Lind-Goldschmidt, Marie did for her mother. In fact, Clara Schumann's career might not have survived without Marie's efficient, patient service. In 1871 Clara Schumann changed her will to reflect her appreciation of Marie's help, acknowledging the sacrifice that had prevented the eldest daughter from pursuing her own career. (The will was revised several times: in 1882, in 1889, and once again in 1891, after the death of Ferdinand.)

In addition to serving as assistant teacher, secretary, seamstress, and companion, Marie acted as surrogate mother; at the age of twenty she was put in charge of their Berlin apartment so that the younger children would have a home while their mother toured. Marie went to see Julie in Divonne in 1867 and to visit Ludwig in the mental hospital in 1870; she sat up with the dying Felix in 1879; she visited Ferdinand when he was hospitalized for morphine addiction in 1887 and represented her mother at his funeral in 1891. Clara bequeathed her diaries to Marie, and after Clara's death Marie became the guardian of the Schumann tradition and the Schumann legend.[24] Both of Berthold Litzmann's books (the biography of Clara and her correspondence with Brahms) were written under Marie's direct supervision. Marie Schumann moved to Interlaken, Switzerland, after the death of her mother and resided there until her own death in 1929.

Elise Schumann Sommerhoff, 1843–1928

Elise, the most independent of all the Schumann children, had the most normal adult life. Always unfavorably compared with Marie in terms of appearance, temperament, and character, Elise went her own way as early as 1863, when she left home to take a position as a governess. For many years she supported herself by working successively as governess, music teacher, and companion to wealthy or titled older women until in 1877 she met Louis Sommerhoff (1844–1911), a businessman with interests in America. They married on November 24, 1877, when she was thirty-four years old. They spent the next six years in the United States, then returned permanently to Germany. Three of Elise's four children lived to adulthood; their descendants—none of them professional musicians—live in Germany and the United States.

Unlike Marie, Elise suffered many reproaches from her mother, the worst, perhaps, when she was singled out in the letter Clara wrote to the children after their father's death:

> I can say nothing else—only later will you feel what you have lost! He was a magnificent person—may you, whom he loved so deeply, be worthy of such a father, may you, especially you, Elise, change your character, may both of you, Marie and Elise, strive to please me as much as possible, not only by your diligence, but by mild, gentle behavior, modest, friendly, noble; may you be a person such as he was. [25]

The pressure of her mother's criticism may have quickened Elise's moves toward independence, leaving Clara with ambivalent feelings about the loss of the capable, strong-minded daughter. On September 10, 1865, when Elise went to Frankfurt to begin a career as a piano teacher, Clara wrote to Ernst Rudorff and to her friend Elisabeth Werner almost identical letters in which she declared she was very unhappy to see Elise leave because she would not have her with her when she wanted her. [26] Elise developed into an adequate pianist and appeared several times in public, though after a successful performance of Robert Schumann's Andante and Variations for Two Pianos with her mother in November 1865 she declared that playing in public made her too nervous to want a career. After her marriage, she and her husband had a friendly relationship with Clara Schumann and gave her support and comfort in the last unhappy years.

Julie Schumann, Contessa Marmorito di Radicati, 1845–1872

Described by her father as "charming and graceful," Julie, always sickly and yet the prettiest of all the Schumann daughters, was frequently separated from her family (even as a two-year-old) because of her fragile health. And despite constant medical care and her mother's well-founded anxiety, this delicate young woman was not discouraged from marrying. In 1869 she married an Italian count, a widower with two children, and she bore him two sons within three years. She died of tuberculosis at the age of twenty-seven, pregnant with her third child. Julie's son Eduardo died within a few years of his mother's death; descendants of her other son, Roberto, are living in Turin.

When Robert Schumann went to Endenich, Julie was farmed out to her grandmother Bargiel in Berlin, since Clara believed she needed special attention that she could not get in a household of seven children. Thereafter she lived with a succession of wealthy friends who could provide comfortable homes, wintered in the south, and were happy to have the girl. She spent most Christmases and birthdays far from home because doctors advised

Elise Schumann (1843–1928). Robert-Schumann-Haus, Zwickau, DDR.

southern climates or medicinal spas for the fragile girl's coughs and nerves. Clara wrote in her diary in July 1867, "I yearn so much for Julie's loving, tender glances; it is so typical of Julie that she shows me her love and it does me such good. I need love as much as I need air to breathe."[27] Because she was so affectionate and tender, Julie probably suffered from her mother's incessant touring more than any of the other children. Only once, in 1861, did Julie have the opportunity to be alone with her mother; she toured with her for a few autumn months in a short respite from illness when she was sixteen. They spent some time in Hamburg while Brahms was there, and it was shortly after this that he dedicated to Julie his Variations on a Theme of Robert Schumann, op. 23. She was the only Schumann child to whom Brahms dedicated a work.

Her sisters—not her mother—kept her in contact with the other children. When Julie was confirmed in 1861, her sister Elise went to Munich to be with her, since Clara was on tour. In 1867, when Julie was too ill to come home for Christmas, Marie traveled to Divonne to see her and bring her home if possible, while Clara went to Karlsruhe to hear Hermann Levi conduct a performance of *Genoveva* before she began her winter tours. (At the time, Clara wrote to Brahms that she was very unhappy at her inability to fetch Julie herself, but explained, "I could not put such a tax on my strength in view of the exertions awaiting me.")[28]* It was Elise that visited Julie before the birth of her first child on August 31, 1870. When Julie was pregnant for the second time, Marie and Felix went to see her in Turin on an impromptu visit. Clara denied herself the pleasure of joining them, ostensibly because she thought Julie might be harmed by the excitement of seeing her under these circumstances.[29]

Clara Schumann had many qualms about Julie's marriage plans, partly because of the difference in class and religion and partly because of Julie's health. She gave her consent, she wrote in her diary in November 1868, because she believed that young true love should not—and indeed could not—be discouraged. Brahms and other close friends were informed of the engagement as soon as it was formalized. To her great surprise, she heard from Hermann Levi soon after that Brahms was in love with Julie. She confided her astonishment to her diary on July 16, 1869, and also noted in a letter to Rosalie Leser in August 1869 that Brahms had been totally changed by the unexpected news.[30] In a gesture that seemed to sum up his feelings about mother and daughter, he gave Julie a photograph of Clara as a wedding gift. When Brahms showed Clara his deeply sorrowful Alto Rhapsody a few weeks after the wedding, she was convinced that it was really a mourning piece for Julie. What Brahms's feelings were will never be known, of course, but Julie's engagement and marriage seemed to increase the tension between him and Clara.

*This comment may very well have prompted Brahms's letter of February 2, 1868, questioning her "way of life"; see p. 205.

Clara Schumann's emotional insulation from her children was shown most vividly when Julie died. On November 10, the day she was scheduled to give a concert with the contralto Amalie Joachim, Joseph's wife, in Heidelberg, she received a telegram informing her of Julie's death a day earlier in Paris. She told no one and went ahead with the concert, she wrote Rosalie Leser, because changing the date would have caused great difficulties for everyone.[31] She was astonished by her own strength and explained her feelings in a revealing letter to Levi dated November 12, 1872:

> I am calm because, since the first day I saw the dear child again in Baden [in the summer of 1872], I was convinced that she would not live much longer. Our first embrace was like a blow to my poor heart; the worry did not leave me for an instant and that may well account, alas, for my calmness now. Another reason may very well be that I fought through the loss of the beloved child three years ago [at her marriage]; it seemed to me that I had already lost her at that time.[32]

The patterns of work Clara set for herself during Schumann's illness maintained her emotionally through his death, the institutionalization of Ludwig, and the death of Julie. The death of a child was, to her misfortune, a tragedy she had known before and was to endure again.

Emil Schumann, 1846–1847

The first son and fourth child of the Schumann family suffered from poor health and was described by his father in his "Little Book of Memories" as "miserable and ailing." Emil's death at sixteen months was attributed to a "glandular" disease.[33] Though the event could not have been unexpected, Clara was depressed during the summer following his death. Emil had been left in the care of a nurse for most of his short life, and his death seemed to be a blow from which it was difficult for her to recover. When Emil died, in June 1847, Clara Schumann was already pregnant with Ludwig.

Ludwig Schumann, 1848–1899

Of all the Schumann children, Ludwig had perhaps the unhappiest fate and caused his mother the most anguish. He entered a mental hospital at the age of twenty-two and died there, having outlived her by three years.

At the age of eight, Ludwig was packed off to boarding school with Ferdinand, a year his junior. The first signs of "oddness" were not perceived until Ludwig's early adolescence. When he was thirteen his teachers' verdict that he would not be able to attend a regular school meant that he would have to be separated from Ferdinand, who was going to attend a gymnasium in Berlin to prepare for a university and eventually a profession. Clara was of course disappointed, not only because she was faced with the problem of finding a suitable career for Ludwig but because she believed it was important for the family to be together as much as possible. Yet when Ludwig was confirmed in August 1862, she did not change her vacation plans to be with him. She noted the occasion in her diary, however, with the comment "Naturally my thoughts were with him."[34] By 1863 Ludwig was deemed mature enough to go to a special school (in effect, a trade school) in Karlsruhe—still away from the family—but within two years it was clear that he would never be able to hold more than a menial job.

Clara Schumann always felt inadequate in dealing with her sons, particularly Ludwig, and continually looked to a man to guide her. Time and again she appealed to Brahms for advice about her boys, but he wisely refused to offer anything but money and perhaps a listening ear.

Everyone who knew Ludwig spoke of his upright, loving nature—perhaps to soften their comments on his "original" personality, his lack of punctuality, and his irresponsibility, which cost him his jobs. Only later were these traits recognized as symptoms of mental illness. After many sleepless nights Clara decided in 1865 to apprentice the dreamy, unrealistic seventeen-year-old to a book dealer. When he was twenty he insisted he wanted to become a musician, and so for a short time Clara, at her wits' end, devoted herself to him: she gave him music lessons, something she never would have considered doing with any of the other children at that age: "I teach him for two hours every day and he is very zealous but . . . he has neither an ear nor rhythmic feeling. . . . His composing is simply dreadful, . . . yet he exerts himself to such an extent that I am always in a state of anxiety.[35]

In 1870 Ludwig was finally sent to a clinic for observation and diagnosis. On her return from an English tour, his mother received the news that his illness was incurable and that he had a spinal disease that presumably affected his brain. A letter dated June 8 to Rosalie Leser tells the story:

> I always told you that I had no hope [for Ludwig] but the confirmation struck my poor heart like a frightful blow—it is a pain like no other. To add to it, I am tormented by the reproaches [I leveled at him]. I would like to take back every word with which I reproached the poor boy; it is true that at the time I didn't know what the situation really was but it still hurt him. And none of us were there—that is so awful for me![36]

Ludwig's tragedy had a tremendous impact on Clara; it reminded her of the troubles with her husband: "I have not felt such pains since the misfortune with Robert," she wrote in her diary in June 1870. ". . . The nights were often dreadful; for hours I would see the poor boy before me, looking at me with his good, honest eyes, which I never could resist." But as always, she marshaled her defenses by "playing industriously, wrote a good deal, and, in short, distracted myself in any way I could." For years she was

[164

Ludwig Schumann (1848–99). Robert-Schumann-Haus, Zwickau, DDR.

haunted by thoughts of Ludwig, but, as she wrote Rosalie Leser on September 16, 1871, "resolutely pushed them away."[37]

After much debate with friends and family, she committed Ludwig to a state mental hospital in Colditz, some 30 kilometers southeast of Leipzig. The buildings have been described as a "forbidding castle, used at various times as a fortress, a prison, a poorhouse, and a concentration camp."[38] Robert Schumann had visited the institution when he had been infatuated with Agnes Carus, the wife of the hospital's supervisor. (His fear of insane asylums may have stemmed from his youthful visits to Colditz.) Clara Schumann was probably unaware of the associations the place had for Ludwig's father, but she knew it was unlike the smaller, more personal sanatorium where Robert had been treated.

Julius Hübner, a painter and an old family friend in Dresden, was named Ludwig's official guardian. Clara kept in constant contact with the institution through the director and the pastor but did not visit Ludwig until 1875, some four years after he had been committed. She went only after he wrote that he wanted to see her. When she visited him, on June 3, she confided in her diary, she almost broke down:

> I finally saw my poor Ludwig again . . . I felt as though I were being torn apart. He looked well, better than before, but something in his look was disconcerting, though kindly. . . . He was extraordinarily happy to see me, embraced me convulsively and begged me to take him away with me since he was quite well. What torment to have to tell him it was not possible. . . . It was all too horrible for me. To see my child as though he were in a prison, his imploring look as I left—I will never forget it. . . .[39]

A year later she went to Colditz again in response to Ludwig's pleas to be released from the institution. She felt she had to make sure his confinement was really necessary and left convinced that he was more ill than before. In a letter to Friedrich Grössel, pastor of the institution, she wrote that she would like to visit, but that each visit left her feeling miserable for weeks.[40] As far as we know, she never saw Ludwig again.

Ferdinand Schumann, 1849–1891

Ferdinand was born two months after the May Uprising in Dresden, during which Clara had behaved so courageously; the story of his life is one of contrast between his human failings and his mother's great strength. Family talk of her heroism at that time and on later occasions may well have overwhelmed the boy. The one Schumann son who survived to a healthy adulthood also suffered a terrible fate: called up for army service in the Franco-Prussian War of 1870, he was not injured but incurred such painful rheumatism that it was treated with morphine, and he became addicted. He died of its effects at the age of forty-two. Clara assumed financial responsibility for his widow and six children.

Basically, Clara Schumann lacked faith in her children, particularly her sons, and Ferdinand undoubtedly suffered most from her attempts to control and dominate them. On April 16, 1863, she wrote to Ernst Rudorff, who had volunteered to give Ferdinand piano lessons, that she appreciated and accepted his offer but that he should give it up if it was "too dreadful." In an undated letter sent in April 1864 she thanked him again for his exertions on Ferdinand's behalf but added, "I am afraid he doesn't deserve what you have done."[41]

For a time Clara seemed proud of Ferdinand's accomplishments and choice of career: after studies in the Joachimsthaler Gymnasium, he took a position in a Berlin bank and seemed headed for a successful business career. But she disapproved of his marriage, in 1873, to Antonie Deutsch:

> I had always hoped that he would acquire more experience with other businesses, had hoped for a really good position in time and that he would continue to develop intellectually—now, with one stroke, all these hopes are in vain. . . . Yet the girl seems nice—they both believe they will love each other for all eternity—may God bless them! I could do nothing but remonstrate and finally gave them my consent.[42]

Ferdinand and his wife had seven children between 1874 and 1884; six survived. In 1884, when both parents were ill, three of his children lived with Clara in Frankfurt. When Ferdinand was still addicted to morphine at the age of thirty-eight and was unable to provide for his family, Clara agreed to take over the responsibility on condition that she be granted a decisive voice in his children's living arrangements. Ferdinand and Antonie had to agree; Ferdinand was on crutches, helpless, and moving from one institution to another in an attempt to cure his habit, and Antonie evidently had no other recourse. The determined Clara had the means, or would earn the means, to support the family, and she proceeded to arrange the lives of her grandchildren. The oldest child and only daughter, Julie, became her special care; Clara used her connections with Prussian royalty to secure a scholarship for Julie at the Luisenstift, a well-known modern girls' school in Berlin. The oldest grandson, Ferdinand, lived in Frankfurt with his grandmother and aunts, and the younger boys were sent to Clara's niece in Schneeberg. This responsibility clearly strained her financial resources. In July 1888 she wrote to Brahms, who had insisted on giving her 10,000 marks for her grandchildren:

> I cannot accept your friendly offer now; it wouldn't be right if I were to accept it without a really serious need. I still have a little sum available which I earned in England this year and last and it will suffice for this year. In addition, Elise also helps me somewhat, as she is paying for the education of one of the boys (her godchild).[43]

167]

Ferdinand Schumann (1849–91). Robert-Schumann-Haus, Zwickau, DDR.

When Brahms, ignoring her letter, sent the money anyway, Clara accepted it. In May 1890 Ferdinand, "a totally broken man" at forty-one,[44] came to see his mother about plans for his family. She did not see him again before his death a year later, on June 6. Marie went to Gera, where he had been living, to take care of the funeral arrangements. Clara resumed teaching the day after the funeral. Though her students urged her to cancel the lessons, she did not do so. "Work is always the best diversion from pain," she wrote in her diary.[45]

After Ferdinand's death, Clara's relationship with Antonie deteriorated even further. Bitter feelings were exacerbated by family alignments: Marie Wieck, Clara's half sister, made Ferdinand's children her beneficiaries. Clara could not object to the arrangement but it did not please her. In the end, Ferdinand's oldest son, who studied music with Clara and Marie Schumann, was the only grandchild who had close ties to his grandmother. He was with Clara when she died and his reminiscences of life in Frankfurt with her were later published.[46] His brothers were embittered by Clara's attitude toward their mother; the third child, Alfred Schumann, published (under a pseudonym) a scurrilous attack on his grandmother which Marie and Eugenie later unsuccessfully attempted to buy up and destroy.[47]

Eugenie Schumann, 1851–1938

Thanks to Eugenie, the youngest Schumann daughter, we have a firsthand account of life in the Schumann family. Her *Erinnerungen* (Memoirs) and *Robert Schumann: Ein Lebensbild meines Vaters* (A portrait of my father) include extensive excerpts from the marriage diary of Robert and Clara Schumann and other important material.[48]

Eugenie never knew her father and had limited contact with her mother, who was concertizing extensively during Eugenie's formative years. Raised successively by a housekeeper, then by Elisabeth Werner (a family friend who acted as governess from 1858 to 1860), and later by her older sisters, Marie and Elise, she was finally, at the age of twelve, sent off to boarding school in Rödelheim, where for almost three years she was isolated from her family and was desperately unhappy. According to Eugenie, the school combined the discomforts of a British public school with the brutal tyranny of a Prussian schoolmistress. At a smaller school near Wolfenbüttel which she subsequently attended, she had a far better experience. Despite the harshness of the years at Rödelheim, however, Eugenie had a better general education than any of her sisters.

Her musical education, too, was exceptional. In 1869 she was enrolled at the Königliche Hochschule für Musik in Berlin, directed by Joseph Joachim. Clara rarely asked for favors for her children (in fact, she bent over backward to avoid doing so) and Eugenie took the regular entrance examination, despite her family's friendship with Joachim. Her teacher there was Ernst

Rudorff, her mother's former student and though Clara trusted him as a friend and as a musician, she could not refrain from sending him advice on teaching Eugenie. Eugenie studied with Rudorff for about a year and a half and also had lessons with her mother and Brahms. (Her descriptions of their teaching are among the most vivid we have.)

From 1871 to 1891 Eugenie lived with her mother and Marie, acting as assistant hostess, companion, and teacher. In 1891, when she was forty, Eugenie decided to leave home and pursue a career on her own. Her mother did not discourage her decision, particularly because she felt that Eugenie was gifted and would be able to carry on the Schumann tradition.[49] As with Elise, however, her mother had mixed feelings. She never got along too well with Eugenie ("We unsettle each other"),[50] but she missed her companionship. The youngest daughter established herself as a piano teacher in England and achieved a modest success as a performer. Eugenie remained in England for some twenty years, returning home to Frankfurt for visits. She was with her mother when Clara died.

In her younger years, Eugenie was outgoing, spirited, and sociable; she made many friends and always attempted to lead a more independent life than Marie. After the death of her older sisters, Eugenie, who lived on into the 1930s, took on some of the stern possessiveness of Marie and fought all attempts to tarnish the image of her parents.

According to Eugenie, all of the children, with the possible exception of Marie, regarded Clara Schumann as a kind of superbeing, seen occasionally and worshiped from afar. In her memoirs she wrote, "But one thing I know for certain, that wherever she might be, we were ever conscious of her loving care, her protecting hold over us, and that to us little ones, as well as to the elder sisters and brothers, she was the greatest thing we possessed in the world."[51]

Felix Schumann, 1854–1879

Felix, the youngest and most gifted Schumann child—he had inherited his father's literary as well as musical ability—began to show symptoms of tuberculosis in adolescence and suffered for ten years before he died at the age of twenty-four. In her memoirs, Eugenie wrote that he had "brilliant gifts, a rare character, nobility, and kindness of heart, combined with a charming disposition and attractive appearance."[52] Felix's letters to his mother[53] reflect all these qualities and reveal that more than any of the other children, her youngest yearned to be with her and his older siblings, yet because of strict schoolmasters, Clara's career, and his ill health he was forced repeatedly to be separated from them.

This delicate and sensitive young man was orphaned in many senses: born after his father's hospitalization, he never knew the man he resembled, and his busy and practical mother had little sympathy for his poetic and musical

Eugenie Schumann (1851–1938). Pencil sketch by Mrs. R. Lehmann, 1871. Robert-Schumann-Haus, Zwickau, DDR.

aspirations. From birth to the age of four Felix was cared for by a house-keeper while his mother toured; then he and Eugenie lived in an apartment in Berlin with Elisabeth Werner—and later Marie—in charge; at nine he joined his older brother Ferdinand at a Berlin boarding school and saw his grandmother and sisters on Sundays. Although Felix spent some summers and vacations with his mother and siblings, he never had his mother's un-divided attention until he came home to die in 1878.

He, like all the others, was very hurt and frightened when Ludwig was institutionalized. He yearned to go home and wrote to his mother:

> I have been a great expense to you this year, and have irritated you so much with my last letter that I can only ask in fear and trembling whether you are willing to let me come home for the holidays, which are beginning on July 9? I am afraid you will say, "He does not deserve it," but please let me hear soon, so that I can get over the shock. I have been looking forward so long to the coming weeks; when I was depressed I thought of them, and mind and heart, those heavy dull things, felt refreshed.[54]

His mother, totally involved with her own problems, seemed to have no conception of the depth of his feelings. He suffered a double burden when he read such words as these from her:

> Poor Ludwig's fate is terrible; I can find no words for grief such as this—it tears my heart. I could not bear it at all if I did not feel that I owe it to you to pull myself together.
>
> . . . Oh, dear boy, never give me trouble; this one is so great that it is almost unbearable. My dearest hopes are centred in you, and I am sure you will become a useful member of society if you fight againt the faults which prevent you from doing your duty, especially your obstinacy. We can overcome much if we try, and I am sure you mean to try, if only for love of me.
>
> You know how much we too are looking forward to your holidays, and thank God I can afford to let you come; but it must be third class, dear boy! Take a cushion or rug with you.[55]

Felix was drawn to a musical career but his mother discouraged him. Still determined, he was finally forced to drop the idea because of his health and went to Heidelberg to study law. Like his father before him, he seemed to enjoy everything in Heidelberg but his legal studies. He wrote some poems that his mother, ever mistrustful of her children's talent, sent to Brahms with the request "Tell me frankly what you think of them. Don't think that I, like a weak mother, think him a genius. On the contrary, I have such fear of overrating the talent of his [Robert's] children that I probably sometimes demand too much of them."[56]

Brahms chose two of Felix's poems as texts for songs in his op. 63, "Meine

Felix Schumann (1854–79). Robert-Schumann-Haus, Zwickau, DDR.

Liebe ist grün" and "Wenn um den Holunder," and he used a third, "Es brausen der Liebe Wogen," in his op. 86. Fortunately Felix lived to hear some of his poetry in Brahms's settings. Yet in 1877 his mother asked him not to publish his poems under his own name; if his work were unsuccessful, she pointed out, a pseudonym would spare himself and his family discomfort. Though she was telling him, in effect, that she had no faith in the quality of his work, she was hurt when he answered with an "unloving" letter. She asked Brahms to visit Felix and try to set the situation straight.[57]

When Felix was dying in 1879, Clara, astounded by her own fortitude, wrote to Brahms:

> Things are going very badly with us; Felix is visibly weaker every day though he still has not taken to his bed. The poor man suffers indescribably and we suffer with him. . . . I see him only for a few minutes at a time because it excites him too much, but my heart bleeds when I see him and no matter what I am doing, whatever it is, the poor sufferer is always before my eyes so that I must summon up all my strength to keep from being overcome by the pain. . . .
>
> It was extraordinary to me that I was able to play with such freedom and strength at the concerts I gave while I was so unhappy that I could not forget my sorrow for one moment.[58]

In her diary she noted:

> On the 14th [of February] I played in the Museum concert, an engagement promised some time ago. It was frightfully difficult, alas, and I wished I had not done it. Had I known how near the end was for our sufferer I would not have done it. My heart bled as I said good night to Felix and went to the concert. The contrast was so dreadful. Throughout the entire concert I saw only him, his emaciated body, his lifeless appearance, and alas, his lack of breath—it was horrible. And yet I played quite well, without even one wrong note![59]

Most poignant of all her diary entries is the final one on Felix:

> At three o'clock during the night between Saturday and Sunday [February 15–16] our Felix died in Marie's arms; she had not called me. . . . He suffered frightfully; it was a death struggle in the fullest sense of the term. . . . Marie, the loving one, always sacrificing herself, wanted to spare me this hour. . . . So I saw him in the morning, a corpse, and oh, I must confess I felt a release for which I had to thank heaven.[60]

THE WANDERER

These tragic histories might have broken the spirit of another woman; Clara Schumann survived. As is often the case, this survivor had well-developed defenses against loss. She could not have gone on without her ability to set aside her anxiety and pain while investing all her energies in her work. Her career filled the lonely and frightening hours when she might otherwise have brooded or become unable to act; it provided a constructive outlet for her anxiety and tensions. Fortunately this means of self-preservation was accepted by society because of her position as an artist. It was generally conceded that her career—which enabled her to become the family provider—relieved her of the obligation to follow the conventional path of a middle-class German woman. During Schumann's lifetime she had accepted—with diminishing enthusiasm—the traditional role of mother. During his illness and after his death, acting as both mother and father to her children, she drew ever closer to the strongest parental model she had known: Friedrich Wieck. Like him, she set high standards of behavior and loyalty; like him, she was demanding and controlling. She was, of course, more reasonable than her father, certainly not so coarse, but she lacked the tenderness and gentleness that Robert Schumann's nature had brought to parenthood.

Clara Schumann's sorrow at the deaths and illnesses of Julie, Ludwig, Felix, and Ferdinand was deep and guilt-tinged and undoubtedly affected her own health. Yet it did not seem to occur to her that her living children also suffered losses and had as much need to mourn as she. Lacking the outlets she possessed, they suffered even more. After Julie died, Ferdinand took the long road to Vienna because he felt he had to see his mother, a natural gesture from a loving brother and son. Clara was surprised and touched, but troubled by the cost of the trip as well.

Money was, of course, a constant concern, and the fact that it was a real problem may have made it easier for her children to accept her solution. Eugenie wrote, "The thought that Mamma had to earn every penny I needed with the 'work of her hands' often troubled me when I was a mere child, and I hated to have to ask for new clothes."[61] She acknowledged that she often wished her home could be more like others.

> We knew that in our mother woman and artist were indissolubly one, so
> that we could not say this belongs to one part of her and that to another.
> We would sometimes wonder whether our mother would miss us or music
> most if one of the two were taken from her, and we could never decide.[62]

Clara knew well the value of a family life and in her own way tried to create a semblance of one. In 1857 she left her Düsseldorf apartment with all its sad memories and established a base in Berlin, which was more convenient for touring and close to her mother. Her two younger children remained there while the older children were scattered throughout Germany. The Berlin home only partially satisfied her restless spirit and she was always considering other cities for permanent settlement. A summer house in Baden-Baden (actually Lichtenthal, an outlying area of that famed Black

Forest resort) which she owned from 1863 to 1873 was the most successful in terms of family life, though even there it was rare to find everyone gathered at once. Too often her mothering was done through the mail. Restlessly Clara roamed the vacation resorts of Europe, even after she had bought the house in Baden-Baden. Inevitably she wanted to try a new spa, a new lake, a new mountain area. She needed rest from her winter tours but she also needed diversion and time with her own friends. After she sold the Baden-Baden house she established another home in Berlin, at 11 Unter den Zelten, only to move, for the last time, to Frankfurt in 1878.

THE MUSICIAN

Clara Schumann's need to make music could never be quelled. This need extended to hearing music as well as performing. In 1873 she found she had to relinquish the opportunity of hearing Hermann Levi conduct a performance of the rarely performed Schumann opera, *Genoveva*, with which she had been intimately associated. There had been few opportunities to see the work, but Marie needed her urgently in Berlin. She wrote Brahms, "I cannot describe to you how *difficult* it was for me to give this up. The children hardly suspect what a proof of my love I have given them with this renunciation. Only someone who like us is an artist—body and soul—can understand the delight we feel."[63]

There were times during and after her marriage when Clara Schumann insisted that her love for Robert was the most important consideration in her life, exceeding even her art and career. On September 20, 1840, during the second week of their marriage, she wrote in their diary, "I live only in you," and added during that same week: "I was out of sorts because Robert was not feeling well. In the evening we took a little walk and Robert spoke to me in such a friendly way that I became quite cheerful again. I am so dependent on his mood; it may not be good but I cannot help myself." On February 5, 1860, when she was thinking about growing old and having to relinquish her art, she wrote in her diary, "Only for one, for Him, could I have renounced my life as an artist; my heart would have been completely fulfilled—with the understanding of his art and his whole being."[64]

But these statements give a false impression. More characteristic, and certainly more honest and consistent with her education and personality, are the many references to her own artistic sphere found throughout her letters and diaries. Perhaps the most telling is the letter she wrote to Joachim in September 1854, after Schumann was sent to the sanatorium and she was preparing to leave home and children in order to tour:

I always pray to God to give me the strength to successfully overcome the frightful agitations that I have lived through and that still await me. My true old friend, my piano, must help me with this! Oh, dear Joachim, I always believed I knew what a splendid thing it is to be an artist, but only now, for the first time, do I really understand how all my pain and joy can be relieved only by divine music so that I often feel quite well again.[65]

If Clara Schumann felt any conflict between the roles of woman and artist, it was almost always resolved in favor of the artist. So, for example, she hesitated—but only momentarily—before deciding to participate in the August 1873 Schumann festival in Bonn which was organized to raise money for a new tombstone for Robert Schumann (and under which she, too, would eventually lie). "As a *wife*," she wrote in her diary in February, "my feelings were not [to play], but as an artist, I felt I ought not to absent myself."[66]

In a letter to Levi on May 22 she described her feelings more succinctly: "Shall I, who have been among the staunchest champions of his music all my life, be silent at this occasion in his honor? Should I relinquish to another that which is so entwined with my entire being and is, above all, my prerogative?"[67]

There were few women with whom Clara Schumann shared her feelings about art or with whom she collaborated. She had many women friends but only one or two women colleagues. She read through music with her daughters, played publicly with Julie von Asten, a Viennese pianist who had been her pupil, and Pauline García-Viardot, and worked with a few female singers, such as Amalie Joachim, Mathilde Hartmann, Livia Frege, and Marie Fillunger. Otherwise her colleagues and associates were men—Julius Stockhausen, Hermann Levi, Brahms, Joachim, and the other leading male musicians and conductors of the day. Of the female artists, only Pauline García-Viardot was regarded as an equal.

There was no question of a "weaker sex" as far as Clara Schumann's musicianship was concerned. She had been trained as a professional, she was a figure of power and authority in the musical world before she was forty, and as an artist was either extravagantly admired or fiercely criticized by both men and women. Cosima Wagner and Anton Schindler, for example, were exceedingly hostile, but not because she was a woman. She was generally regarded as unique, almost above gender.

In 1860 she wrote Joachim that she wanted to sign the militant declaration against the "new Germans" (Liszt, Wagner, and their school).[68] The document appeared prematurely and her name was not among the signatories, but it was clear that she fully expected to take a stand with Joachim, Brahms, and the two other male signers.*

Yet she turned to her men friends for advice, personal as well as professional, like any other woman of her time. In 1870, when she was invited to participate in a Beethoven festival in Vienna but did not want to participate

*The declaration is discussed further on p. 199.

in performances conducted by Liszt and Wagner, she found it difficult to face the problem squarely and asked Joachim for advice. "As a *woman*, I cannot act like you. It would seem very arrogant if I, a woman—as compared to a man—were to express my opinion openly. I must invent a lie! But what shall I say?" She went on to ask if he did not also think it right that she should refuse to play. Joachim's reply summed up what he and many others felt about her: "That you are a woman seems to me to have nothing to do with it, or perhaps it may be the very reason for you to stay away. In any case, you are, as far as art is concerned, 'man enough.' "[69]

MONEY

As a girl, Clara professed modesty about her accomplishments and was uneasy about competition from Liszt and Thalberg. As an adult, she had few reservations about her performances and could not abide the kind of false modesty that was expected of a woman of her time. She perceived herself as a professional and even during her married life took pride in the fact that she could earn money with her talent and skills, though to some extent she attempted to conceal it in deference to her husband's feelings and the tradition of male support of the family. Clara paid obeisance to this tradition but thought it was carried too far when, after her first concert in Düsseldorf, in October 1850, she was presented with nothing but a basket of flowers. Indignantly she wrote to Ferdinand Hiller, the previous music director, on whose recommendation Schumann had been engaged:

> The directors [of the Düsseldorf Municipal Concert Society] invited me to play in the first concert without asking what I wanted for an honorarium. I assumed they had learned from you—since you knew from the Dresden days—that I never play for less than 10 louis d'or (in large cities like Bremen, Hamburg, etc. I always get 20 louis d'or). Now the concert is over, and, they say, a brilliant success, and the directors send me—a basket of flowers! I was surprised at that, yet I still accepted it as a friendly gesture; now, however, they come and thank me for my courtesy and finally a light dawns. But it is simply incomprehensible that the gentlemen can think that for the first time here I will play gratis—moreover, I cannot understand the indelicacy of wanting this. Do they think we are rich people? or do they think I will play whenever they like for the salary my husband receives? Dear Herr Hiller, if I had no children or were rich, then I could play as often as the people wanted and I would be happy always to play gratis, but in my circumstances I cannot do so. . . . My playing is a separate matter, which they could not count on when they engaged my husband.[70]

After Schumann died, there was no need to tiptoe around this issue. Though friends offered money and established funds to help pay for Schumann's medical expenses, Clara was determined not to be dependent on anyone. Though she could support her family only by breaking it up, she did not hesitate. The situation was not uncommon: many widows in similar circumstances sent their children to friends or relatives or boarding schools or, if necessary, hired them out as apprentices. Clara did all of these things. She was particularly incensed at the idea of benefit concerts for her, and in 1873 she was so insulted by a "horrible" announcement in a Graz paper of a benefit concert for the Schumann family that she wrote Brahms she was "beside herself." She wanted the concert to be canceled and announced she would not accept money earned by other musicians.[71]

Her self-esteem equaled her pride; she knew her worth and demanded substantial fees. When she was negotiating for some concerts in Vienna in 1870, she asked Brahms to find out what they were thinking of paying: "They are asking me about the honorarium and I am perplexed about what to do—I don't want to ask too much, but on the other hand I don't want less than what they would give other artists."[72]

Her high fees and her great reputation led to the mistaken belief that she was wealthy. (Twice in her lifetime she was the victim of burglars who stole jewelry and valuable mementoes—gifts from wealthy admirers of her artistry.) Only her intimate friends knew how she struggled to make ends meet. In 1864 she apologized to Brahms for playing in Hamburg under Stockhausen, who had been appointed to a position that Brahms had hoped to get, because, as she put it, "In my circumstances, I cannot afford to turn down any engagement."[73]

Earlier that year, she explained to Brahms why she had to work so hard and had been unable even to spend Christmas with her children: "Last summer I had many financial worries, had to take 1,000 taler from my capital,* but had the luck to make it up through the admittedly terribly strenuous concertizing I did before Christmas."[74]

From a chatty letter from Amalie Joachim to her husband we learn of money problems again in 1872:

> I have just come from Frau Schumann. The poor dear woman made such a sad impression. That is not the worst sorrow for me—the burdensome cares are the worst—cares over her daily bread. It seems she has not yet received any money. . . . Imagine, Felix has incurred debts of 500 florins which Frau Schumann must now pay; besides that, all the money he received for the quarter was gambled away in Baden. But now she has still more grief on account of Elise, who has left her position [as a piano teacher] in Frankfurt in order to go and live as a companion to a friend. The manner in which she did this in opposition to her mother was totally horrendous. Enough—she has a lot to endure from her children. Poor Julie is doing very poorly and she awaits news of her death every day,† but

*Probably for purchase of the house in Baden-Baden.
†Frau Joachim was unaware that Julie had died the day before the letter was written.

she still wants to go to Vienna. She says she could not do otherwise and feels that art is the only thing and that, moreover, the work elevates and strengthens her. . . . The people who give money for Frau Schumann also believe she already has enough. . . . None of them know what it is like to really have sorrow and need.[75]

Until 1873, Clara Schumann toured from September to May with few stops in between and often did one-night stands, especially in England. In 1869 she gave concerts on February 4, 6, 8, 13, 15, 17, 20, 22, 23, and 27. The schedule eased in March but she continued to perform in the British Isles until April. A trip to Russia in 1864 was particularly strenuous, concluding with a forty-four-hour train trip from St. Petersburg to Berlin. Correspondence regarding the tours went on all year long but major arrangements were made in the summers, which she devoted to practicing, teaching, and writing letters, sometimes as many as fourteen a day. During the concert season she snatched a day here or a week there to see any of her children who were within reach. After 1873 she was forced to slow down somewhat; plagued by pains in her arms and other incapacitating illnesses, she found huge expenses mounting. Julie had already died but Ludwig's sanatorium, Felix's treatment for tuberculosis, Ferdinand's treatment for drug addiction and rheumatism, and her own medical bills placed a heavy burden on her. Fortunately, gifts from foundations, royalties from performances and her editions of Schumann's music, and payments from the sale of his manuscripts became available about this time;* this was money that she had no qualms about accepting. Though these funds sufficed to meet basic financial needs, any year in which she did not give at least fifty concerts was a bad year as far as she was concerned. "I get so melancholy when I cannot be active," she wrote to Brahms on June 2, 1874. "I have no talent for lazing about" ("Zum bummeln habe ich so gar kein Talent").[76]

WINDING DOWN

Among the highlights of the late years were the Bonn Music Festival of 1873 and her fiftieth and sixtieth jubilee concerts. The 1873 festival, where she played the Schumann Piano Concerto, was one of the few occasions when all the Schumann children gathered together to hear their mother perform. Close friends who attended included Jenny Lind and her husband and the Freges, and such colleagues as Brahms, Joachim, Stockhausen, Rudorff, Dietrich, Grimm, and Hiller.

*Robert Schumann had suggested (probably in the Dresden years) that his musical autographs be used to sustain the family in the future. In 1887 Clara made up her mind to sell them, and after several years of negotiations they went to the Royal Library in Berlin for DM15,000. This sum was a major source of support for the Schumann family until well into the twentieth century (Eugenie Schumann, *Robert Schumann*, 386).

A few weeks after she took a permanent teaching position at a Frankfurt conservatory in 1878, she was elated by surprise celebrations, first at the conservatory, where fellow faculty members performed an all–Clara Schumann program, and then at the Gewandhaus in Leipzig, where she had made her first solo appearance as an eleven-year-old in 1828. In her diary she wrote of the "unforgettable" day in Leipzig—October 24, 1878—on which only compositions of her husband were played. Among the listeners were old friends who had been present fifty years earlier. She described the event:

> The entire hall was decorated with green and gold wreaths and garlands of oak leaves. As I entered, the whole audience stood and a rain of flowers began, under which I was literally buried. . . . It was a long time before I could seat myself at the piano. Several times I felt as though I would be overwhelmed by the emotions I was feeling; I shook violently but I controlled myself and played the concerto with perfect calm and it succeeded magnificently.[77]

Ten years later, in 1888, she was overwhelmed by more surprise concerts and tributes, this time accompanied by addresses, letters, telegrams, flowers, poetry, and wreaths from all over the world. "I never suspected how much love was bestowed on me, and I am often quite embarrassed. . . . The celebration brought many people closer to me, and I to them, and that is really gratifying; it gives me a feeling of being at home here [in Frankfurt]—something I had not felt in this way before."[78]

Throughout her years of concertizing, Clara Schumann was often in severe physical pain. Both as a young girl and as an adult woman, she drove herself relentlessly. Despite the regimen of daily walks and outdoor exercise established by Wieck, the young Clara was not always in the best of health. The tensions between her and her father took their toll: in Paris in 1839 she had headaches, severe anxiety, pains in her fingers; in January 1840 she had several fainting spells and severe facial neuralgia just before and even during concerts in Berlin. She was in such mental and physical pain at that time that she wrote Robert she "sometimes wanted to lie down and die."[79] A few weeks following their wedding, Robert noted her "illness" in letters to friends and in his household books.[80]* Indeed, the surprisingly frequent reports of her indispositions and illnesses are intermingled with Robert Schumann's meticulously kept records of his own ill health. Her symptoms are not spelled out, but the details of her complaints given in later letters suggest that they may have been psychosomatic in origin. We know that in the 1860s and later she suffered attacks of anxiety and fits of weeping, and

*Many entries throughout the marriage diary remark on her indispositions, especially in the early months of the marriage.

Clara Schumann, age 59. Painting by Franz von Lenbach, 1878. Robert-Schumann-Haus, Zwickau, DDR.

before performances feared that she would forget her music or break down. At times she believed she could no longer play. Invariably she recovered, but the tension and fear affected her health.

When she resumed her full-time career after Schumann's illness, pains in her arms, hands, and fingers prompted visits to spas and other health resorts. Rheumatic attacks continued: on November 27, 1857, she wrote Joachim that several concerts had to be canceled; her pain was so intense that opium was prescribed, and she was forced to rest her arm in a sling for some time.[81] She was unable to perform for some eighteen months in 1874 and 1875. Over the years she tried many cures: water treatments, electric shock, "animal baths,"* massage, rest. The "rest cure," popular at that time, was the most difficult for her. She could ask her daughters to conduct her correspondence but no one could take her place at the piano. During the last decade of her life, she was plagued by arthritis in her hands, hearing difficulties, and growing infirmity. In February 1894, fearful of what the future held for her, she wrote in her diary, "What will become of me if I cannot play any more?"[82] She was desolate without her art.

By 1878, when she was fifty-nine, she found she needed a week to recuperate between concerts and recognized the necessity of cutting down on the number of engagements she accepted. In addition, she was having increasing difficulty hearing. These problems may have prompted her decision to accept the teaching position in Frankfurt. After twenty-five years of wandering, she rented—and eventually bought—a home for her family. The house, Myliusstrasse 32, which still stands in Frankfurt, was to be hers until her death. The years of wandering were over, but professional concerns did not cease.

At her last public concert, in March 1891, the seventy-two-year-old woman joined with a colleague from the conservatory to perform Brahms's arduous Variations on a Theme by Haydn for Two Pianos, and until she was felled by a stroke in 1896, she played, taught, improvised, edited, arranged, and reveled in music.

As she lay dying, she asked her grandson Ferdinand to play for her. The music, from Schumann's Intermezzi, op. 4, and the F-sharp Major Romance, op. 28, was the last she heard.

---

*An archaic treatment in which the affected limb was placed in a cavity of a recently slaughtered animal to "absorb" the bodily heat. Robert Schumann took such *Tierbäder* in 1832 in an effort to cure his hand injury.

PART II

THEMES FROM THE LIFE
OF CLARA SCHUMANN

CHAPTER 9

Clara Schumann and
Johannes Brahms

The friendship between Clara Schumann and Johannes Brahms has always been a subject of spirited speculation. The frequent published accounts that emphasize the "passionate" friendship that developed between the thirty-four-year-old pianist and the twenty-year-old composer neglect the deeper personal and artistic bonds between them.[1] Neither Clara Schumann nor Brahms ever denied the deep love they felt for each other, but a sexual liaison during the time Schumann was institutionalized would have been entirely out of character for the grieving, practical, conscientious woman. And in later years, all evidence points to a platonic relationship. The significance of their many-layered friendship, which began in 1853 and endured until her death in 1896, lay not in any sexual feelings they may have had for each other but in the musical and personal interaction between them. As she had been for Schumann, Clara was the inspiration for much of Brahms's music and the sharer of his genius.

The second child of Johann Jakob Brahms, a Hamburg musician, and his wife, Christiane, Johannes matured in an atmosphere of financial insecurity and poverty. Christiane Brahms was seventeen years older than her husband. With their children—Elise, Friedrich (Fritz), and Johannes (born in 1833)—they shared two rooms in an apartment in what is still a shabby district of Hamburg. During Johannes' childhood his parents had great hopes and ambitions for him, for he showed unusual talents. He was given the opportunity to study piano and composition with Eduard Marxsen, the best teacher in Hamburg, but until he toured as an accompanist with the Hungarian violinist Eduard Reményi beginning in April 1853, Brahms had never been away from home. Through Joseph Joachim, a countryman of Reményi, with whom the young pianist struck up an instant friendship, he met Liszt in Weimar and, a few months later, the Schumanns in Düsseldorf.

Only twenty years old when he arrived in Düsseldorf, Brahms was already an accomplished pianist and composer. At fifteen he had given his first solo concert, which, like the early programs of the young Clara Wieck, was a hodgepodge of songs and duets, solos for clarinet, violin, and cello, and several virtuoso piano pieces.[2] In his knapsack were works he had composed between the ages of seventeen and twenty: the bold, romantic sonatas for piano later labeled op. 1 and 2; the beginnings of the Sonata op. 5; the Scherzo op. 4; a violin and piano sonata, since lost; and a miscellany of songs, later published as op. 3, 6, and 7. Marxsen's prize student, the young Brahms was well schooled in the techniques of composition and knew the work of his great predecessors, including Bach and Beethoven. A performance of *The Marriage of Figaro* at the Hamburg opera house had made an indelible impression on him and begun a lifelong fascination with Mozart.[3] But he knew very little of the work of Schumann, as it was rarely played outside of Leipzig and Dresden. The Schumanns had visited Hamburg in 1850 and it is assumed that Brahms heard their programs, which included Schumann's Piano Concerto, Piano Quintet, and Variations for Two Pianos, op. 46. They did not meet on that occasion, however. Schumann had returned unopened a package of original compositions that Brahms had sent to him at his hotel. When Brahms became acquainted with Schumann's music in the summer of 1853, he felt an immediate kinship with the older composer. At the urging of Joachim and other friends, the young man shyly approached the Schumann home in Düsseldorf. But he was not timid in regard to his music. Unlike Schumann at twenty, Brahms was confident of his future; there were no doubts in his mind—or in that of anyone who knew him—that he was a supremely gifted and creative musician.

Brahms's arrival coincided with a most difficult period in the lives of the Schumann family. Robert's position as municipal music director in Düsseldorf was threatened and his mental illness was progressing. His enthusiasm for Brahms's work was so overwhelming that the younger man, a typical North German who habitually understated his feelings, may well have been embarrassed by it.

During the month Brahms spent with the Schumanns, he accepted gratefully the help they offered. Leaving Düsseldorf on November 2 with Schumann's recommendations in hand, he proceeded to Leipzig, where he met and played for influential music circles. Several Leipzig publishers, including Breitkopf & Härtel and Senff, undertook to publish some of his works. Obviously seeing the Schumanns in a parental role, he wrote to them in December 1853, when the works appeared in print, "I am taking the liberty of sending you your first foster children, who owe to you their right to exist."[4]

During October 1853, Brahms, still beardless, with softly curling blond hair, a high forehead, and a voice barely changed, had at Schumann's request been sketched by Jean-Bonaventure Laurens, a French admirer of Schumann who was visiting Düsseldorf at the time. During Schumann's

Clara Schumann, age 35, in a photo taken in 1854 or 1855, after Robert Schumann's hospitalization. Robert-Schumann-Haus, Zwickau, DDR.

Johannes Brahms, age 20, in Düsseldorf. Sketch by Jean-Joseph-Bonaventure Laurens, 1853. Schumannhaus, Bonn.

confinement at the mental hospital in Endenich, he asked for the Laurens sketch so that he might view it daily. Even in the hospital, he requested Brahms's works, played and analyzed them, and responded to them with joy and delight. He addressed Brahms now with the formal *Sie*, now with the intimate *du*. Respect and appreciation for his art are evident in all the letters Schumann wrote from Endenich.

The modern reader is inevitably troubled by such unselfish admiration. It is difficult not to assume that Schumann envied the boy who displayed his powers with a self-assurance in such marked contrast with the uncertainty of the young Schumann. It is sad to contemplate Schumann, only forty-three years old, weary and ill, already casting himself in the subordinate role of prophet. That there was an element of envy in his extravagant praise is suggested by his use of the term "demons" or "young demons" to characterize Brahms and Joachim.[5] The last few letters Schumann wrote to Joachim are fanciful, even irrational, and in retrospect are symptomatic of what was to follow in February 1854.

After Schumann's hospitalization, Clara turned for comfort and moral support to a group of young musicians (friends referred to them as "the young gentlemen")[6] who were devotees of her husband's music; the group included Albert Dietrich, Julius Otto Grimm, and Schumann's "demons," Joachim and Brahms. It must be remembered that Schumann was still virtually unknown, and Clara was deeply grateful for their advocacy. Of them all, Brahms was not only the most gifted composer, but the one most available and devoted. He sped to Düsseldorf as soon as he heard of Schumann's suicide attempt and virtually sacrificed the next two years of his life for Robert, Clara, and their seven children. On his arrival he took over the keeping of Schumann's household books. Beginning with the entries for February 1854 and continuing until December 30, 1854, he noted down all their expenses, including postage stamps, servants' wages, rent, the girls' school tuition, and income from Schumann's publishers and investments.[7] By keeping such intimate records, he became a member of the family; with these entries he stepped into the shoes of the husband—an awesome responsibility for a young man of twenty.

Unlike Joachim and Dietrich, Brahms had no regular post, and though he had begun a career as a concert pianist, he abandoned it with few regrets; his real interest lay in composing. His parents approved of his decision to aid the Schumanns, but after a few months his mother wrote:

> Schumann smoothed the way for you but you must do more. You could not live by composing alone—the greatest masters were not able to do it. Hopefully, you would have undertaken something if Schumann had not fallen ill. For the moment you did the right thing in going there. But to remain? You're losing money and time. . . . Like it or not, only the man who has money will be respected.[8]

His mother's advice was ignored. During the two years he remained in Düsseldorf, he eked out a meager living by teaching a few pupils and borrowing money from Joachim and Julius Otto Grimm, another young musician he had met in Leipzig and who came to join him in Düsseldorf. Letters from his mother continued exhorting him to seek other avenues:

> That you're giving lessons is probably good; at least it's something. But you always disliked it and it brings in very little—I mean for you, who can do so much more. Frau Schumann also gives lessons, but she prefers concertizing. Otherwise she wouldn't do it—turn her family and home over to strangers and travel about without a husband. . . . When one has been so richly endowed by God with so many gifts, it's not right to remain sitting there so calmly.[9]

Again, Brahms ignored her advice. He took lodgings near the Schumann home and settled into the family circle. When Clara resumed touring a few months after Felix's birth, he supervised the children's schooling and music lessons and assisted the housekeeper and the servants with the care of the younger children. When Clara and the children moved to a new apartment in 1855, he rented a room in the same house. He had the freedom of the Schumann apartment, used the pianos for practicing and composing, and arranged the library of books and music, a particularly grateful task for a young man who had a limited education, an avid thirst for literature, and no funds for scores or books.

After Schumann's death, Clara explained in a letter to her children what Brahms had meant to her during those two years: "Like a true friend, he came to share all my grief; he strengthened the heart that threatened to break, he uplifted my spirit; brightened my soul any way he could. He was, in short, my friend in the fullest sense of the word."[10] Brahms gave her his youth, his love for nature, consolation, passionate admiration, and above all, the opportunity to share the thinking and work of a creative genius.

The importance of this particular bond in their long relationship cannot be overestimated. As a child prodigy, Clara had been an active member of the most elite circles of Leipzig musical life; great men had rhapsodized about her artistry. Before she played Schumann's works, she was her father's right hand in the musical evenings at the Wieck home. Beginning at the age of twelve, she had introduced Schumann's works in Leipzig, Dresden, Vienna, and Paris. As an adolescent she had been honored with the friendship and respect of Mendelssohn, Liszt, and Chopin as well as Schumann. Clara's daughter Eugenie explained further:

> She once asked me if I could at all realise what it meant to have had a friend from childhood upwards who stimulated all your noblest and most artistic qualities, who in daily and hourly intercourse lavished pearls and jewels upon you; if I did not think it was natural that she felt she could not

go on living deprived of such gifts, and that she clung to friends like Brahms and Joachim who could console her in some measure for what she had lost.[11]

Just as she could understand and interpret Schumann's genius before it was generally appreciated, so she could recognize Brahms's genius; she had the musical understanding to encourage the young man who was destined to be the leading instrumental composer of his age. Her friendship with him was in keeping with a lifelong pattern of close ties with the creative figures of her time. The appreciation and support of a Clara Schumann would have overwhelmed any twenty-year-old musician, but for Brahms, whose acquaintance with educated women was limited, and who (like the young Schumann) had been stimulated by the German Romantics—E. T. A. Hoffmann, Jean Paul, Joseph von Eichendorff—it was an almost shattering experience. Many years later, Brahms referred to the time in Düsseldorf as his "Werther years."[12] Certainly there were many parallels between the young Brahms and Goethe's sensitive young hero, with his unrequited love for the beautiful, maternal Lotte, the betrothed of another man. Brahms wrote to Joachim in June 1854:

I often have to restrain myself forcibly from just quietly putting my arm around her and even—I don't know, it seems to me so natural that she could not misunderstand. I think I can no longer love an unmarried girl—at least I have quite forgotten about them. They but promise heaven while Clara shows it revealed to us.[13]

Exactly what happened in Düsseldorf will never be known, but it is clear that from the beginning their relationship was far more than a mere infatuation; meeting and loving Clara Schumann was to affect the course of Brahms's life. The young Brahms was an extraordinary phenomenon; Clara Schumann was no ordinary woman. The commonly held notion of her as a combination of artist and *"Hausmütterchen"* (little housewife) is misleading.[14] She had entered marriage as a world-famous figure and, as we have seen, maintained her career as pianist and composer in a thoroughly professional way. While bearing and raising children, she was composing serious works, arranging, editing, and teaching. She was not merely Schumann's wife and partner; she was a colleague. With Schumann's breakdowns becoming more frequent, she was forced to make the decisions, musical and personal, which in that time and place were generally left to men. At the same time, she was still a young woman, and though perhaps not beautiful in the conventional sense (solemnity and melancholy had already settled on her features), she was attractive and she had a forceful personality. Her marriage to Schumann must have been a disappointment to her by this time: he was ill and getting worse, and even if he were to recover, there seemed to be no place for him in the musical world.

Whether Brahms's love, like Werther's, was unrequited cannot be established. Clara never minimized what his presence and friendship meant to her at the time. That the two were aware of raised eyebrows and gossip is clear; all her letters to him before 1858 (the responses to his passionate letters) were later destroyed. Moreover, she evidently felt it necessary to explain their relationship to her children. Brahms, conscious that their correspondence might be compromising, urged her in May 1856 to put a note on the packet of his letters to the effect that they belonged only to the two of them.[15] He was always concerned about the safekeeping of their letters, and this question arose many times in their long correspondence.[16] Though Clara Schumann generally observed all the conventions of her time, she disregarded comments made by close friends who believed that she permitted Brahms too many liberties and deplored her acceptance of the young man as a colleague and equal. She held firmly to her decision to call him *du*, declaring that she felt like a mother to him.* Her friends were evidently skeptical, and both she and Brahms were aware of the inevitable misunderstandings. In May 1856, when she was in England, he wrote, "How I would like to come! But would it be possible? . . . If Bargiel [Clara's half brother] went, nobody could say anything, but it would be too noticeable if I, who have nothing to do there, came."[17]

After Schumann's death in July 1856, Clara invited Brahms and his sister Elise to join her and two of her sons for a month's vacation in the Rhine Valley and Switzerland. During that month, from August 14 to September 13, they may have discussed their future, perhaps even marriage, but just what was said will, of course, never be known.† It seems evident, however, that a decision was reached that they should part. By October 21 Brahms had left Düsseldorf and Clara had begun her first concert tour of the season, a wearying round of the concert halls of Europe and England to earn the money she needed to educate and raise her seven children, and eventually the six children of her son Ferdinand, who became incapacitated at the age of thirty-five. The concert circuit was to continue for thirty-five years. The correspondence between them went on, but the tone of Brahms's letters changed from impatient passion to a warm, resigned love. Though an almost desperate longing to see her still pervades the letters written between 1856 and 1860, it seems likely that they were slowly becoming reconciled to living apart and pursuing separate careers. Eugenie Schumann hints that the decision may not have been entirely mutual:

> But it was inevitable that he should recognize that the destiny he had to
> fulfill was irreconcilable with single-minded devotion to a friendship. To
> recognize this and immediately to seek a way out was the natural outcome

---

*At this time he was the only man outside her family whom she addressed in the familiar form.

†Despite persistent conjecture, I have never found any convincing evidence that they discussed marriage.

of his virile nature. That he broke away ruthlessly was perhaps also an inevitable consequence when one takes his inherent qualities and the nature of his situation into account. But without doubt he had had a hard struggle with himself before he had steered his craft in a fresh direction, and he never got over the self-reproach of having wounded my mother's feelings at the time, and felt that this could never be undone.[18]

Though Brahms had several flirtations with suitable attractive, musical young women, he avoided matrimony, and Clara Schumann never remarried. She always felt very possessive about her younger friend. In her diary Clara declared her wish to mother him, and though she expressed the conventional wish that he marry, she was unhappy when he showed an interest in younger women.[19] The thought that he might have loved Julie, the only one of her children who evoked such emotion, was so difficult for her to accept that she could not acknowledge it, even in her diary, until after Julie was engaged to someone else.[20] No matter where he was, she acted in a proprietary manner toward him. An unceasing stream of directions, admonitions, reproaches, requests flowed to him and he accepted it with patience, though not always with grace.

The special quality of their friendship was recognized by everyone who knew them. They were "best friends" to each other, with all that the term implies in respect to emotional ties, understanding, mutual interests, and background. The friendship was sustained despite jealousies, reproaches, and frequent tiffs.

Their correspondence reflects a change in Brahms's feelings toward Clara after Schumann's death. Yet though the tone of his letters became more dispassionate after she was widowed, it is clear that he loved her in his own way throughout his life. Brahms, though personally reserved (he was generally considered to be unusually secretive), had many close friends— Joachim, Grimm, Hermann Levi, the surgeon-pianist Theodor Billroth, the composer Heinrich von Herzogenberg and his wife, Elisabeth. Sooner or later, however, some disagreement always arose and the intimacy faded. His friends never doubted his integrity and genius but eventually his gruffness, lack of social skills, and blunt candor alienated many of his closest associates. The relationship with Clara, however, was unique: his letters imply a faith and trust he shared with no other person. It was one of the foundations of his life.

Brahms's interests ranged beyond music, and he forged friendships with such writers as Klaus Groth and Joseph Viktor Widmann and such artists as Anselm Feuerbach, Julius Allgeyer, and Max Klinger. Clara could not share these friendships: she was embarrassed about her lack of general education and told Brahms that she often felt uneasy in intellectual circles,[21] but she knew and respected his insatiable appetite for reading. She delighted in presenting him with books. Her first gifts to him were literary works: twelve volumes of Jean Paul at Christmas 1854, Ariosto and Dante in May 1855,

Schiller's works in June 1855, and the tragedies of Sophocles in July 1855.[22] He was encouraged, of course, to read everything in the rich Schumann library in Düsseldorf.

One of the most significant links in their friendship was their common economic situation. Both depended on their musical activities to support themselves and their families. Unlike most of their friends, neither had inherited wealth or been given the advantages of a cultivated upper-middle-class home. Friedrich Wieck had been quite as capable of boorishness as Johannes Brahms. Both as a girl and as the wife of a composer, Clara was all too familiar with financial insecurity. Though she had not endured the kind of poverty Brahms had known as a boy, money was as great a concern to her as to him, and they discussed it without embarrassment. Poverty was not an experience Brahms could share, for example, with the aristocratic Elisabeth von Herzogenberg. It would have been unthinkable for Frau von Herzogenberg to visit the humble apartment of the Brahms family in Hamburg, as Clara did.* And no other woman in Brahms's life would have invited his unsophisticated sister to join her for a vacation and offer advice about the kind of petticoats to pack.[23]

Nevertheless, their attitudes toward money differed considerably. Frau Schumann was practical and thrifty. As a child she had been rewarded with money for her efforts at the piano, and, as we have seen, probably equated it with love. The sums she earned as a child prodigy were invested by her father. Schumann's small inheritance was also carefully invested, and was the basic source of income throughout their married life, since Schumann did not earn a regular salary until 1850.

Brahms, whose family never had any money to save, knew nothing of the world of capital, investments, and interest, and alternately prized and disdained financial rewards. His ambivalence was evident in many other areas as well. Clara, who was free of such conflict, functioned as his financial consultant when he finally began to earn the money he claimed to despise, and gave him basic advice:

> Note well, tell Fritz and Elise that they should separate the coupons from the papers and secure each in different places. That is always done so that if one is stolen, one always has the other as a receipt. Also, they should write down the exact number in case of fire or theft.[24]

For many years Clara advised him on such practical matters as fees, salaries, and investments. She instructed him in the intricacies of coupon clipping, and from London she suggested when and how much he should be paying for lodgings in Baden-Baden.[25] By 1865 Brahms was receiving sizable

---

*After one visit in August 1855, Brahms asked her how she had slept crowded together with the double bass, the horns, and the fiddles (Johannes Brahms, *Johannes Brahms in seiner Familie: Der Briefwechsel*, ed. Kurt Stephenson [Hamburg: Ernst Hauswedell, 1973], 63).

royalties (he was one of the first composers to amass a small fortune from his published works) and simply sent his money to her to be banked and invested.[26] Later, when he realized the task was a burden to her, he asked his publisher, Fritz Simrock, to take it over.

In addition to discussions of music, friends, travel, money, and other mundane matters, Brahms expressed his feelings in his letters to Clara in a way he could not have done with anyone else. On March 19, 1874, after hearing of Felix's illness: "Permit my fervent love for you to be of some comfort—I love you more than myself and more than anyone or anything in the world." October 19, 1888, on the occasion of her sixtieth anniversary as a performer: "You, best of all women and artists . . ." September 13, 1892, in answer to a quarrel she had picked with him: "You, dearest to me of all persons . . ." On May 23, 1893, he wanted to send her, "foremost among my special friends," a gold medal that had been struck in his honor by the Gesellschaft der Musikfreunde.[27] In 1889 he wrote her from Vienna:

> The thought of my D Minor Sonata proceeding gently and dreamily under your fingers is so beautiful. I actually put it on my desk and gently and deliberately accompanied you through the thickets of the organ point. For me, there is no greater pleasure than to be always at your side, to sit or, as now, to promenade with you.[28]

Clara was his confidante when he suffered disappointment and offered emotional solace, particularly in the early years, when he could accept it from no one else. His successes and failures, depressions and triumphs were reported to her first. She was the first to know of his wounded feelings when he was passed over for a major position in Hamburg in 1862. (He asked her not to mention it to his parents.) For her part, Clara carried grudges on his behalf longer than he did, and turned down an engagement to play in Hamburg after he was passed over for the second time for a position in his native city. He turned to her as to a sister for comfort when he had bitter or melancholy moods, and gratefully accepted her maternal solicitude when she reminded him to take warm slippers on the trip back to Hamburg when his mother died.[29]

Brahms's frequent prickliness (of which Clara often complained) may have covered hurt feelings. He was and yet was not a family member, and his relationship with her children shows deep ambivalence. He betrayed a yearning for a place within the Schumann family as either husband or son, and his tactlessness may well have stemmed from resentment that he could be neither. It surfaced in 1892 when, soon after his sister died, they had a serious quarrel, ostensibly about music, in which, they later agreed, both had been at fault. In his letter written for her seventy-third birthday, Brahms expressed what were probably his true feelings when he termed himself an outsider:

Permit a poor outsider to tell you today that he thinks of you with the same respect he always did and from the bottom of his heart wishes you everything good, much love, and a long life to you, the dearest of all persons to him. Unfortunately, I am more of an outsider to you than to anyone else.[30]

While tensions and temporary estrangements were the unhappy aspects of their many-layered friendship, their musical association provided a supporting matrix that endured.

As Brahms himself was a pianist of concert caliber, Clara did not become the major interpreter of his works, the role she had performed for Schumann. The championship of his music by an artist of her prestige, however, was a significant aid to the young composer. She figured in both his earliest and his last piano works. Ten Brahms works were premiered by Clara Schumann, the first in Leipzig in October 1854, when she performed two movements of his Sonata in F Minor; two months later she played the entire sonata in Berlin. She also performed two movements from his Sonata op. 1, his Scherzo op. 4, and a Gavotte that year. In 1894, when she was no longer playing in public, her student Ilona Eibenschütz premiered his last works for piano, the *Klavierstücke*, op. 118 and 119, in London.

Clara propagandized incessantly for his music among friends, musicians, conductors—more than she had for the young Robert Schumann, and to greater effect because her influence had grown. Some of her efforts caused strains between her and her colleagues. Verhulst could not warm up to the Brahms *Ballades,* op. 10, and Jenny Lind warned her against performing music that had what she described as "perverse tendencies."[31] Clara was triumphant when her old friend Livia Frege was won over and became a champion of Brahms's music. In 1860 Clara agreed to play at a benefit concert in Vienna on condition that Brahms's Serenade no. 1 would be played.[32] Clara spoke and wrote to publishers on his behalf; she spoke to Simrock (toward whom she still harbored bad feelings on Robert's account) about the Harp Songs (op. 17) and recorded in her diary, "I would not do it for anyone else."[33] She reminded the Härtel brothers, Raimund and Herrmann (of Breitkopf & Härtel), of Brahms's music by speaking of it and playing it whenever they met. She continued her efforts on his behalf even after his work began to be accepted by publishers. From Paris in 1862 she wrote to the Hamburg conductor Theodor Avé-Lallemont:

> I have invited several musicians to a Brahms session here tomorrow; they should hear his Serenades and Handel Variations! Don't tell him about it; you know he doesn't take such efforts kindly. I am anxious, however, at least to inspire the musicians here to have respect for him; aside from my duty as a friend, I consider it my artistic duty.[34]

Her assistance extended to his concert work. She gave Brahms lessons during his first month in Düsseldorf, and in the early years of their friendship, when he especially needed the support of a prestigious performer, she appeared in concert with him and Joachim. The three shared the concert stage in Danzig in 1855 and in Altona (now part of Hamburg) in 1861.

As a result of her introductions to influential friends, Brahms was offered an official position at Detmold in 1857. During the 1855 Lower Rhine Music Festival, held in Düsseldorf that year, Clara saw to it that he met the leading critics of the day—Eduard Hanslick, Henry Chorley, Otto Jahn—as well as all the musical celebrities who crowded into the city for the event, which included a performance of Schumann's *Paradies und die Peri* with the universally popular Jenny Lind as the Peri.[35] He saw Liszt again (this time in the Schumann home) and renewed contact with Ferdinand David, Ferdinand Hiller, Stephen Heller, Hermann Härtel, and other eminent men of the musical world—all old friends of Clara's. She accompanied him to Cologne for his first hearing of the Beethoven *Missa Solemnis* in March 1855. In short, she left no stone unturned to expand his experiences.

In March 1860, the twenty-six-year-old Brahms and three other young musicians—Joseph Joachim, Julius Otto Grimm, and Bernhard Scholz—published a declaration in a Berlin newspaper protesting the "pernicious" influence of Liszt, Wagner, and their self-proclaimed *Zukunftsmusik* (music of the future). The Brahms-Joachim declaration was also directed against the *Neue Zeitschrift für Musik*, the journal Schumann had founded in 1834, which was now the organ of the Liszt group. Despite her former ties to the journal, Clara Schumann was prepared to align herself with the young musicians. Hasty and disorganized, they rushed the declaration to publication before she had an opportunity to sign it, as she had intended to do. Her motives were musical as well as personal. In contrast to the distaste she felt for Liszt's music and showmanship, the music of Brahms aroused her deepest sympathies. His masterful handling of form, his lyric gifts, his contrapuntal skills, his bold harmonies and rich rhythms were evidence to Clara Schumann of his genius. She and Joachim were his strongest champions in the dark days of January 1859, when his First Piano Concerto was virtually hissed off the stage in Leipzig.

Both publicly and privately, Brahms acknowledged his indebtedness for her support, advice, criticism, and friendship. Even as a young man, Brahms, who had little patience with lesser musicians, recognized and appreciated her unique qualities. It was far more than friendly admiration and adoration for an older woman: he valued her professionalism and respected her work as both performer and composer.

Brahms the pianist is often forgotten in the general admiration of the composer. Yet he earned his living as a pianist until fees from his compositions became a major part of his income. (In his later years he practiced little, and Clara frequently complained about his sloppy playing.) He honored her by programming several of her works in the 1850s: he played her Trio op. 17 on December 17, 1854, in Hamburg; he accompanied Livia Frege in a private Leipzig performance of Clara's unpublished "Volkslied" in January 1856; and he played her *Romanze* op. 21, no. 1, in Cologne on May 29, 1856, soon after it was published. In his Variations op. 9, "on a theme by Him and dedicated to Her," he wove a theme from her *Romance variée* into one of the variations, symbolizing, as Schumann so often had done, the personal and musical relationship between them.

In two other works of his youth—the early version of the Trio in B Major and the Piano Quartet op. 60—Brahms paid homage to Clara Schumann.* Both of these works were initially conceived during 1854–56, the years of his most passionate letters to Clara. As early as December 1854 the young Brahms wrote, in a style reminiscent of the young Schumann years before, "I often visualize you as if you were here in person; for example, in the trills of the closing passages of the Andante of the C Major Symphony, in the organ point of the Great Fugue, where you suddenly appear to me like the holy St. Cecilia."[36]

Brahms knew Clara as an artist who never stopped growing. Her repertoire expanded throughout her life, her appetite for new music was never sated, and, most telling of all, her own responses to music never ceased to be immediate and total. In February 1861 he advised her to listen to two Mozart piano concertos previously unknown to her. After she heard and played them she wrote to him:

> . . . if I could only pour out my whole heart to you, face to face, you would have to listen for a long time, even though I would only be saying what you yourself already know very well. I think you can guess that I am speaking of the Mozart concertos, both of which I played with indescribable delight. My first reaction was to embrace you in thankfulness for providing me with this pleasure. What music this is—these adagios! I could not restrain tears as I played them both. The Adagio of the C Major was particularly affecting—heavenly bliss streams through one in that work. The first movement—how splendid; the last one in A major—doesn't it seem as though sparks were flying out of the instruments—how everything weaves and breathes together. But enough—I thought I could not stop talking about it and yet this is only a weak expression of what I feel.[37]

Her comments on the music of Brahms are reminiscent of the terms in which she spoke of Schumann's creations: she perceived them as gifts for her. Her modesty prevented her from telling him what she confided to her diary: "I know that nobody else plays it [the Trio] as I do."[38] While regretting her inability to express in words how she felt about his music, she repeatedly wrote that the music "filled" her (the German *erfüllt* also implies fulfillment). The effect of his music on her was described in such phrases as

---

*Eric Sams carries this idea further by pointing out the use of "Clara themes" in these and other Brahms works ("Brahms and His Clara Themes," *MT*, 112 [1971], 432–34).

"the pleasures you create," "the blissful hours," "treasures I am gathering," "my most beautiful hour," "the sunshine you have bestowed on me."[39] She described his Trio in C Major as "invigorating, charming, magnificent"[40] and the Third Symphony as "such a wonderful creation," and though she claimed she could find no words for it, she rhapsodized about it for a page and a half.[41]

She felt that Brahms's music, like her husband's, was written for her, and that only she could truly feel and understand it: "Every tone in your Serenade [op. 11] has become part of me, just as everything you create is deeply and totally absorbed [by me]."[42] When, after an illness, she was finally able to play his Trio op. 101, she wrote, "If only your things were not so often beyond my physical strength. It is so painful for me because I know that I understand and feel them better than so many others do, and yet I must resign myself."[43]

Of the Violin and Piano Sonata op. 78 she wrote:

After the first delicate enchanting movement, and then the second, you can imagine my delight when, in the third movement, I found my beloved melody again. . . . I say *"mine"* because I don't believe there is another person who can experience this melody as [both] blissful and melancholy as I do.[44]

And a few days later, after she had played it again, she wrote, "Many others could perhaps understand and speak about it better but no one could feel it more than I do—the deepest and most tender strings of the soul vibrate to such music."[45]

The sonatas for violin and piano and the Trio in C Minor, op. 101, were special favorites. When she first played through the A Major Sonata, she wrote in her diary, "It was a joy that removed all my miseries for that evening." (She was plagued at the time by illness—her own and that of her son Ferdinand.) When, in 1887, she played through the "wonderfully gripping" Trio, she wrote in her diary, "No other work of Johannes' has transported me so completely. . . . How happy I was tonight, how long it has been!" Of the last movement of his *Regenlied* Sonata (op. 78) she wrote, "This last movement is what I would wish to accompany me on my journey to the other world." When, in 1894 (she was seventy-five years old), she played Brahms's Third Violin Sonata with Joachim, she told Brahms, "It was a pure delight—something one is rarely given. In the surging of harmonies in the first movement, I always have the feeling that I am soaring in the clouds. I love this sonata indescribably—each movement of it!" Earlier, after a performance she gave of this sonata, she wrote, "Again I felt sheer rapture and thought of you with a thankful heart. How magnificent this sonata is and how my pulse still throbs for something truly beautiful!"[46]

Such encomiums were not merely romantic or sentimental enthusiasms couched in extravagant phrases. Clara was forthright, and if something did not please her, she was quick to point out weaknesses. In his early years, Brahms found her ecstatic reactions embarrassing, and more than once asked her to tone them down.[47] She believed in him more than he believed in himself: "You are a man of genius and you know it well!"[48] As he gained self-confidence he was better able to accept her faith in his work, although he had self-doubts to the end of his life. When he wrote her about a new piece he had written in 1888, at the peak of his immensely successful career, he confided, "You may not believe why I did not send it to you first. The truth is I never have any faith that a new piece could please anyone."[49]

The close musical bonds continued to the end. In 1893 he referred to his op. 119 as "your and my little pieces."[50] In 1891, when Clara was preparing an edition of her cadenzas, she was suddenly overwhelmed by guilt when she realized that the cadenzas to the Mozart D Minor Piano Concerto which she had been playing as her own had been borrowed largely from Brahms. She wrote to ask if she shouldn't put his name on it too. Brahms answered, "By rights, I should have to inscribe all my best melodies, 'Really by Clara Schumann.' If I just think of myself, nothing clever or beautiful occurs to me. I have you to thank for more melodies than all the passages and such things you might take from me."[51]*

Soon after their parting in 1856, Brahms began to send her his manuscripts for comments, suggestions, advice, and criticism. Of his 122 compositions later published with opus numbers, he had asked for her advice, reactions, and comments on at least 82. Other pieces were dispatched to her immediately after publication. Op. 2 and op. 9 were officially dedicated to her, and the autograph of op. 24, the Handel Variations (presented as a birthday gift in 1861), bears the inscription "For a beloved friend." Several works without opus number were also dedicated to her: Theme and Variations in D Minor, an arrangement of Gluck's Gavotte, and two Preludes and Fugues. Countless other works, though not expressly dedicated to her, were written for her birthday or as Christmas presents or simply with her in mind.

After 1882 Brahms was less punctilious about sending manuscripts to her, and she knew that some works went to other friends first. She did not hesitate to reproach him: "Do you want to slight your old friend entirely? Why are you not sending her anything?"[52] By this time Clara was sixty-seven and finding it increasingly difficult to play through his manuscript scores and send them back as promptly as he liked. (She complained that she could not sight-read through his full scores, especially since he persisted in using the old clefs, a source of difficulty for more than one later musician.) As she grew older, Brahms showed more consideration and awareness of her

---

*The autograph of Brahms's cadenza for the first movement of Mozart's Concerto in D Minor, K. 466, now in the Library of Congress, bears a note from Clara Schumann in which she identified the passages she used. Her own cadenzas for this concerto are also in the Library of Congress.

need for his music. During the last years of her life, when she was suffering from hearing problems, rheumatism, and stomach afflictions (all carefully reported to him), he wrote tenderly and solicitously, rushed published scores to her, and arranged for her to hear performances of his works in comfortable surroundings. After 1893 he visited Frankfurt often, particularly eager for her to hear his late chamber works with clarinet, the Trio, Quintet, and sonatas, played in her own home by Richard Mühlfeld, the clarinetist for whom he had written them.

Unlike Schumann, Brahms kept her informed of what he was writing and planning, and this may have been a trust she cherished above all others. Though he did not care to discuss works in progress, she was usually the first to know about a new project when he was ready to divulge his thoughts. Though she realized she might learn more if she did not ask too many questions, she could not always restrain herself; she came to feel it was her right to know and was indignant if word of his creations or performances reached her from other sources.[53] For the most part, Brahms respected, even welcomed, her interest. He sent her his manuscripts with such requests as "Write me in as much detail as you can; that is most agreeable and also most important to me. What do you say about the 'Wechsellied' [from op. 31]? Is it any good?" When he began work on the Requiem, he sent her the magnificent "How lovely is thy dwelling place, O Lord," along with several songs and piano works, and wrote, "Perhaps you will have a free hour to strum through these things and perhaps another to write me just a word as to whether there is any sense or purpose in my having two volumes of the Variations [op. 35] published. Please, just a word on that." And again, in 1865, in reference to the Requiem, "Please don't show Joachim the choral piece yet—it is probably the weakest. . . ." In the same letter he wrote out some of the texts he was using in his great masterpiece and ventured, "I hope that such a German text can please you as much as the customary Latin one."[54]

In June 1878 he sent her "a few duets that I intend to publish together with 'Edward.' Write me what you think of the idea, and also how you like the duets and also the songs. . . . If you wish it—and write good reviews— I'll send more."[55] A year earlier he had written:

> I would like to publish my Lieder [op. 69–72] and want very much for you
> to play through them once beforehand and write me a word about them. I
> would rather sit down beside you—but I could not get to Düsseldorf, and
> Berlin too has its difficulties. . . . The songs are numbered. . . . Write me
> which of them pleased you—and if others perhaps didn't please you at
> all. . . . Write, where possible, a brief word about each.

In his usual self-deprecatory manner he added, "You can just write the opus or number and mark it like this: op. X, 5, bad; 6, dreadful; 7, ridiculous, etc."[56]

Clara would have preferred to be his only critic but she accepted the fact that she was one of several, though admittedly it was a very elite group. Brahms customarily asked all of his intimate friends to comment on his works before publication. A continuous round robin of new works went from one friend to another and then often directly to the publisher. The circle included Joachim, Grimm, Dietrich, and Clara Schumann in the early years, Joachim, Levi, and Clara from about 1865 to 1875. It was enlarged to include Billroth and the Herzogenbergs a few years later. In the last eight years of his life, from 1888 to 1896, the inner circle included Hanslick, Joachim, Clara, and Eusebius Mandyczewski, the archivist of the Gesellschaft der Musikfreunde and later co-editor of Brahms's complete works. From time to time Brahms consulted Julius Stockhausen and George Henschel on vocal music, and from 1890 on he played over new works from manuscript with Ignaz Brüll, a Viennese pianist. None of his friends could resist Brahms's requests for criticism of his music, least of all Clara. When she heard of a work she had not seen or learned it had been sent to another friend first, she complained bitterly. Brahms sent the Third Violin Sonata, op. 108, to Elisabeth von Herzogenberg before Clara had seen it, and when she kept it longer than he expected, he wrote in alarm that it was to be sent to Frau Schumann *immediately*. Elisabeth von Herzogenberg commented, "Frau Schumann must be jealous of our having had the pleasure first." Brahms had no doubts about that. "You know Frau Schumann is very touchy," he wrote on another occasion.[57]

For the most part, Brahms disregarded his friends' advice. Works that Clara praised were not necessarily published; others that she criticized as "ordinary" were retained. Although he always insisted he was shy about his work and lacked self-confidence, Brahms was always his own master, and his friends understood that he sought their comments in order to strengthen or confirm his own thoughts. (However, Brahms readily accepted recommendations from such conductors and instrumentalists as Joachim, to whom he sent almost all the chamber works, the Violin Concerto, and the Double Concerto, and he generally followed suggestions on range and transposition made by Stockhausen, Amalie Joachim, Henschel, and other singers.) Final decisions were his alone, and the works were often published in the form in which they were first cast.

Whether or not her advice was taken, Clara relished the opportunity to have her say. In answer to his request for her opinion on op. 69–72, she carefully went through each song and made detailed comments on each. Despite her advice ("Only about half should be published; the others are not worthy of your name, etc.") all the songs were published. She described a motif from op. 25 as "too ordinary for Johannes Brahms," but he retained it. On the other hand, he agreed with her perception of his "Brautgesang" as "ordinary" (he had, in fact, used the same term earlier in a letter to Grimm about the work), and it was never published.[58] It would not be entirely accurate to describe Clara Schumann as Brahms's musical adviser, but it is clear that she remained longest as a member of that special circle of musicians and trusted intimates on whom he depended throughout his life.

Brahms was, in turn, Clara's "best friend." (This was a phrase they both used.) Besides deriving joy and solace from his music throughout her tragedy-ridden life, she turned to him for personal advice and became increasingly dependent on him. His opinion of her playing was crucial; compliments meant more from him than from any other musician.[59] Every decision, no matter how trivial, which had to be made about editions of Schumann's music or correspondence, letters from journalists and would-be biographers, moves to other cities, offers of teaching positions—all were discussed with Brahms.

As the years went on, Clara attempted to use him as a surrogate father, asking for his help particularly with decisions involving her sons. He generally refused to cooperate, though he evidently did help out with one difficult situation with Felix.[60]* He gave piano lessons to Eugenie for a short time, and never begrudged any effort or time when musical decisions were involved.

Though Brahms may have been reluctant to give advice about the education or rearing of her children, he was deeply concerned about her mental and physical health and well-being. This interest may have been responsible for their first major quarrel, in 1861. He tried to persuade her to cut down on her work. "You certainly have enough money," he wrote. "It would be far more reasonable and better if you cared for your health and your beautiful self."[61] Though the letter was couched in flattering terms, she found it offensive. She pointed out that her responsibilities included seven children whom she hoped to educate and for whom she wanted to provide a normal family life, and that she was, moreover, obliged to provide for her own future. She added a phrase that could well stand for her life's motto: "My health may well be better preserved if I exert myself less, but in the end doesn't each person give his life for his calling?" To the implied criticism of her playing, which certainly hurt most, she answered, "I am not doing too much for I feel no less freshness and warmth than I did twenty years ago. On the contrary, I feel younger and believe that a quieter life would leave me too much time to brood on my sorrows."[62]

The next time he chastised her for her "unsettled way of living," in 1868, she was puzzled and angry at what she took to be more criticism of her playing and the implication that it might be time to retire gracefully. She answered from London, where she was giving her usual season to warm applause and sold-out halls: "You actually seem to imagine that I really have enough money and travel merely for my own pleasure. . . . This is hardly

*Among his songs are three with texts by Felix; see chap. 8.

the point at which I should retire from public appearances, as you advise."[63] The exchange of letters over the next few months skirted a possible break. There was talk of "hatred" and a wall that had grown up between them. Finally, in a letter of October 15, 1868, she revealed the full extent of her dissatisfaction with Brahms: he was rude and boorish, inconsiderate of her feelings and of those of her children. "One cannot have a friendly relationship with the mother which does not carry over to the children."[64]

Unfortunately, his hints that it was time to slow down had come at the worst possible time. In 1868 she was facing multiple catastrophes and feeling very much alone. None of her friends, not even Brahms, could help her shoulder the responsibilities facing her: the possibility that Felix's illness might be fatal, the continued ill health of Julie, and the mental symptoms that were to bring Ludwig to the institution where he was confined for the remainder of his life. Brahms was often brusque (she once begged him not to write when he was in an angry mood), and all his friends suffered from his tactlessness sooner or later. This time Brahms apologized, the breach was healed, and the correspondence continued (until the next quarrel), but with some resentment on Clara's part. Clara Schumann's letters had none of the delightful charm of those of Elisabeth von Herzogenberg. In her serious, solemn way, Clara could never respond adequately to his dry wit and humor; in fact, she was embarrassed by the realization that her letters were often nothing but recitals of family problems and illnesses. Brahms, however, never failed to be moved by her troubles, listened sympathetically, and responded with sympathy. He did not reject her trust so long as he could make his own decisions.

Clara was easily offended and never forgot slights, real or imagined. She did not conceal her feelings from Brahms. Fully aware of the contrast between herself and the childless, beautiful, wealthy, young, talented aristocrat to whom Brahms began sending manuscripts in 1877, Clara reminded him why she could not always return manuscripts as quickly as he would like: "I am not master of my time and energies so that I can burrow in a work for days, as Frau von H. does."[65] In her diary she wrote, "They have all the time in the world while I have lessons to give in the morning, am entirely exhausted in the afternoon, and continually have a piano loaded with proofs for Härtel, which also demands strength."[66]

The subject of money arose in almost every letter between Clara and Brahms. She reported to him how much she earned, how much she lost if a concert had to be canceled, how she lived from season to season, and never hesitated to ask frankly about his fees. By 1888 Brahms was financially secure, making more money than he could spend—his tastes remained simple—and, knowing that she had accepted additional responsibilities for Ferdinand's children when he was ill, insisted on sending her a considerable sum of money. She had refused similar offers from other friends many times before, partly from a fear of losing her independence and partly because she was proud that she possessed the skills to support her family. Brahms's offer was made so discreetly and tactfully, however, that she could not refuse.[67] She felt comfortable enough with her old friend to accept, and, ever prudent, invested her money for her grandchildren.

After a tender exchange of letters on this subject, however, she was just as touchy as ever. He held his breath when he wrote to her, asked for forgiveness, and avoided the unthinkable. Their last argument (in 1891–92, over the publication of the original version of Schumann's D Minor Symphony and her omission of some of Brahms's editions of Schumann music from the *Collected Works*), to which he reacted with unwonted bitterness,[68] was resolved when they both realized that it was caused by extraneous considerations: her great age and forgetfulness were partly to blame, and his tactlessness was probably the result of unhappiness over his sister's illness and death. After that incident, Brahms's letters were unfailingly tender and solicitous. When Clara suffered a series of strokes in 1895, he realized that the woman he had always loved could not live forever. As her death approached, he wrote to her daughter Marie: "When you believe that the worst may be expected, be so kind as to send word to me so that I can come and still see those dear eyes—those eyes that, when they finally close, will close so much for me."[69]

His deepest feelings about her are revealed in his last great songs, the *Vier ernste Gesänge,* written in May, 1896, as she lay dying in Frankfurt. Officially dedicated to the artist Max Klinger, the songs were first played to a group of close friends in a private gathering immediately after Clara's funeral.[70] After publication in July, a copy was sent to Marie Schumann with the words:

> I wrote them during the first week of May. . . . Deep inside us all there is something that speaks to us or drives us, almost unconsciously, and that may emerge at times sounding as poetry or music. You will not be able to play through these songs just now because the words would be too affecting. But I beg you to regard them . . . as a true memorial to your beloved mother.[71]

Clara's death came on May 20, 1896. Brahms died eleven months later.

CHAPTER 10

Other Friends and
Contemporaries

Clara Schumann needed to have people around her and she cultivated friends and acquaintances assiduously. Her friendships sustained her musically and emotionally; her children could not fulfill this need. She explained to sixteen-year-old Felix when he questioned the need for her enormous correspondence,* a daily task that he seemed to believe deprived him of her presence and care:

> You have to consider how many people I get to know on my tours and how fond I become of them, how they always shower me with love and kindness, and all I can give them in return is constancy. . . . I do not like to offend people who have been close to me; there are so many now that even if I keep in contact with just some of them, my correspondence is still very large. Above all, however, it is naturally my deepest desire to communicate as regularly as possible with all of you—those dearest in the world to me.[1]

With her friends she played many roles: to such younger male associates as Brahms, Rudorff, Grimm, Joachim, and Stockhausen, musicians with whom she toured and performed, she was a comrade; to male musicians of her own age or older, such as Mendelssohn, Chopin, and Hiller, she was a professional colleague above gender; to Amalie Joachim, Clara Stockhausen, and the other wives of her colleagues she was a mother figure. And despite the devotion of her daughters, the adoring public, and her male colleagues, she also needed the friendship, sympathy, and understanding of women. Her mother became a good friend, and after her death, her daughter Marie took on this role. There were many other women with whom she had lifelong

---

*She spent several hours almost every day of her adult life writing letters. She often received more than a hundred letters on her birthday and on New Year's Day. Each was answered personally and usually at some length.

contact, among them Emilie List, Lida Frege, Pauline García-Viardot, Rosalie Leser, Livia Bendemann, and Laura von Beckerath. With these friends she could express her feelings about her husband, her children, and her life. Though all of these women were musicians or intensely interested in music, only Pauline García-Viardot was both friend and colleague.

Clara Schumann was a public figure and her professional relationships with the great musicians of her time were well known. One intimate relationship, however, was kept from public notice: in the 1860s she had a very discreet liaison with Theodor Kirchner, a composer of the Schumann circle.* Kirchner, one of the first students at the Leipzig Conservatory, was a composer and organist active in Winterthur and Zurich at the time of their relationship. His compositions were very much in the Schumann style and he was said to have physically resembled Robert Schumann. The intimacy with Kirchner was of short duration. Whether she had other such affairs during her life is not known.

FRANZ LISZT, 1811–1886

Clara Schumann's deteriorating relationship with Franz Liszt tells us more about her than it does about the great virtuoso, who treated her with consistent courtesy and respect. Though she could acknowledge his generosity, even at the very beginning of their acquaintance Clara was jealous of his technical prowess and felt uneasy about his personal and musical style. By 1854, the year in which he sent her his B Minor Sonata, dedicated to her husband, she could barely disguise her hostility.

Liszt, like Chopin and Mendelssohn, had been in Paris in 1832, the year of Clara's first big concert tour, but he did not take cognizance of her until 1838, when the glamorous young man, eight years her senior, was at the height of his performing career. Chopin had spoken highly of Clara's playing and Liszt was eager to meet her. In a letter to Friedrich Hofmeister, the Leipzig publisher, he expressed his hope of hearing soon the young woman who played with "energy, intelligence, and accuracy," declaring that such a pianist was "an exceedingly rare phenomenon in any country."[2]

In Liszt, showmanship and genius were combined with generosity. He heard Clara in Vienna in April 1838 and wrote glowingly about her in a letter that appeared in the Parisian *Revue et Gazette musicale* and was republished in the *Neue Zeitschrift*. To the Comtesse d'Agoult, the mother of his three children, he reported:

> Just one word about Clara Wieck—distintissimo [most distinguished]— (but not a man, of course). We are living in the same hotel, Zur Stadt

*Conversation June 6, 1984, with the well-known Brahms bibliographer Kurt Hofmann, Hamburg, who has a number of letters written by Clara Schumann to Theodor Kirchner.

Frankfurt, and after dinner we make as much music as possible. She is a very simple person, cultivated . . . totally absorbed in her art but with nobility and without childishness. She was astounded when she heard me play. Her compositions are really very remarkable, especially for a woman. There is a hundred times more ingenuity and true sentiment in them than in all the fantasies, past and present, of Thalberg.[3]

He showed his interest in many ways: Liszt's Paganini Etudes are dedicated to Clara; his many letters are models of affectionate esteem; three of her songs figured in his famed song transcriptions. His article about her performances in Weimar in 1854 was published in the *Neue Zeitschrift für Musik* of December 1, 1854, and translated in *Dwight's Journal of Music,* a Boston music periodical that followed the careers of Clara Schumann, Joachim, Brahms, and others of that circle with great interest. In *Dwight's* translation, Liszt's comment "The lovely playmate of the Muses has become a consecrated, faithfully devoted, severe priestess" was often quoted.[4]

In 1838, at the end of Clara's Viennese tour, Liszt and the Wiecks spent ten whirlwind days together. His playing overwhelmed her and she wrote in her diary:

We heard Liszt. He cannot be compared to any other player—he is absolutely unique. He arouses fear and astonishment and yet is a very kind artist. His appearance at the piano is indescribable—he is an original— totally involved with the piano. . . . His passion knows no bounds; he often injures one's sense of beauty by tearing the melodies apart and using the pedal too much so that his compositions must become even more incomprehensible, if not to the connoisseur, then certainly to the layman. He has a great soul; one may say of him, "His art is his life."[5]

During the time they spent together, the two artists played with and for each other. She described his effect on her in a letter to Robert: "I receive as much applause as ever yet my playing seems so dull and I don't understand it, but I have almost lost the desire to continue to travel. Since I have seen and heard Liszt's bravura, it seems to me that I am only a schoolgirl."[6]

Wieck, of course, took a different view. He admitted that "the musical powers of this Liszt truly border on the incredible," but believed that he was hampered by lack of "proper training" and inability to "tame and control himself and his energy." After Wieck heard Liszt's big solo concert of April 18, 1838, however, he raved about him; "It was the most remarkable concert of our life—and will not be without influence on Clara, but the old school-master is worried about her getting used to his bad habits and mannerisms."[7] His description of those "bad habits and mannerisms" makes clear the reason for his anxiety:

The gravity of the concert and his artistic appearance, combined with the greatest, most unbelievable mastery of every possible mechanical problem, aroused the stormiest applause. Who could describe his appearance as a concert artist? After he had destroyed Thalberg's Erhard [Erard piano] in the first piece, he played the Fantasie on a Conrad Graff [Graf], broke two middle strings, went and fetched the second Graff from the corner, and played his Etude. After he broke two strings again, he played it once more, but not before he had loudly proclaimed to the audience that he had not succeeded, and would play it again. When he first appeared, he vehemently threw his gloves and handkerchief on the floor in front of the piano.[8]

Despite his showmanship, bordering at times on the eccentric, Franz Liszt was a great and genuine musician and proved to be a loyal friend to both Clara and Robert. The chill that descended later was not initiated by Liszt. As early as 1837, well before the two men met, Robert's spirits were lifted by Liszt's long article about Schumann's keyboard music in the *Revue et Gazette musicale*. And after Clara had played privately for Liszt in Vienna, he wrote to Robert, "Your *Carnaval* and *Fantasiestücke* have interested me greatly. I play them with delight and God knows I cannot say that of most other things. To speak frankly and freely, only Chopin's compositions and yours have a strong interest for me." He then asked Robert to write some trios, quintets, or septets, since, as he put it, "it seems to me that you could do it admirably and nothing really interesting has been published in this genre for a long time. If you ever decide to do this, please let me know at once. I would like to have the honor of introducing it to the public."[9]

Less than a year later he reiterated his feelings about the German composer: "My friends . . . have often heard me say that Chopin and Schumann are the colleagues for whom I have always had the highest esteem, the greatest sympathy."[10] The correspondence between Liszt and Schumann continued for several years. Schumann's *Fantasie* op. 17 was dedicated to Liszt, and he acknowledged it with thanks on June 5, 1839: "The Fantasie that you have dedicated to me is a work of the highest rank. I am truly proud of the honor you have done me in dedicating so grand a composition to me. I intend to work at it and learn to know it thoroughly so as to make the utmost possible effect with it." He noted that the work would be "difficult for the public to digest," and added a tactful paragraph that must have pleased Schumann during the difficult months of Clara's stay in Paris:

> What you tell me of your private life has interested me and touched me deeply. If I could, I know not how, be agreeable or useful to you in the slightest way in these circumstances, I am completely at your service. Whatever happens, you can count on my absolute discretion and sincere devotion. If I am not asking too much, tell me if it is Clara of whom you speak. But if this question seems misplaced, do not answer it.[11]

The two young men finally met in Leipzig in March 1840. At that time Clara was in Berlin with her mother, awaiting the outcome of the court hearings, practicing, performing, and studying French and English. Though Liszt arrived at a time when Robert was extremely busy, Schumann welcomed him: this was an event to which he had been looking forward for many years. On March 18 he wrote to Clara:

> Yesterday he said to me, "I feel as if I had known you for twenty years," and I feel the same. . . . And how extraordinarily he plays, daringly and madly, and then again tenderly and sweetly—I have heard it all. But Clärchen, this world, I mean his, is no longer mine. Art, as you practice it, and as I often do at the piano when composing—this beautiful intimacy [*Gemütlichkeit*] I would not give up for all his magnificence—and there is also some tinsel with it all—too much. No more today, you already know what I mean. 12

But Liszt's wonderful good nature and extraordinary musicality triumphed over the "tinsel" and turned all heads, Mendelssohn's included. Robert's letters sang such praises of Liszt that on March 24, 1840, Clara lamented from her "isolation" in Berlin:

> Ah, unfortunate me, I am sitting here now and cannot partake in the tiniest part in all the pleasures you are giving each other! What would I not have given to have been in Leipzig yesterday, how happy I would have been; how I sighed! I was in the theater, but my thoughts were totally with you. I saw you in musical raptures and wanted so much to be at your side. For some time, I actually intended to come with Mother, but then I thought I would just disturb you in your companionship with Liszt and wouldn't be as welcome as I would have liked. I believe it is better that we didn't come. . . . Does Liszt still yearn for the aristocratic Vienna, for the countesses, etc.? I should think that he would not have time to think of such things with you. The Bach concerto, was it in D minor?* Oh, God, I could cry! I think it is a nice thought that Liszt seems to you to become more and more powerful—sometimes one would think it was a supernatural being sitting there at the piano. 13

Even before Robert received this letter, however, he had urged her to come to Leipzig to hear Liszt play. She did go, with her mother. She confided her reaction to her diary on March 30, 1840:

> One could hear and see that he felt most comfortable in the *Hexameron* [his own work]. He didn't play the first things [of Mendelssohn and Hiller] as freely and it was disturbing to see him continually looking at the music. He did not play *Carnaval* to my satisfaction and altogether did not make the same impression on me that he had made in Vienna. I believe it was my own fault; my expectations were too high.

*This was the work that Clara, Mendelssohn, and Louis Rakemann had premiered in Leipzig in 1835. She was to play it several more times in Leipzig.

She also noted, with great disapproval, that he had performed a Mendelssohn concerto that he had learned that same day at rehearsal. A day later she wrote:

> This morning Liszt spent several hours with us and endeared himself to us even more by his refined and artistic personality. His conversation is full of life and spirit; he is also quite a flirt, but one can easily forget this. . . . He played his "Erlkönig," "Ave Maria," his own Etudes, etc. I had to play some things for him but did it with real anguish. Otherwise I didn't feel the slightest bit intimidated in his presence, as I had feared; he acts so naturally that everyone in his company has to feel at ease. But I could not be around him for long: this agitation, this restlessness, this enormous vivacity, these are all a great strain.

In the diary entry of April 4, a few days after Liszt had departed, Clara inadvertently contrasted the two composers:

> I went to Connewitz with Robert. I never feel so well, so comfortable, as when I am with him. He doesn't have to talk at all. I like it so much when he is just thinking and would like to be able to listen to each thought. And when he gently presses my hand, I am totally happy. Then I feel so sure that I am his best beloved.

In the autumn of 1841, the Schumanns, now married, met Liszt in Weimar at their hotel, "where the champagne flowed like water,"[14] and he proposed joint concerts in Leipzig in December. He played as assisting artist at her December 6 concert and she did the same for him at his December 13 concert. Although the *Neue Zeitschrift* reported that the usual applause was replaced by a "transport of fanaticism" at the first concert, Clara wrote in her diary in December 1841 that she was unhappy about the concert: Robert's works had not been performed well and he had been dissatisfied with her playing.

Though their unhappiness was not specifically with Liszt, it was certainly associated with the great virtuoso. In the excitement over Liszt's presence, Schumann's works were all too easily overlooked. Moreover, Schumann himself was not satisfied with his D Minor Symphony, which, unlike his first, the *Spring* Symphony, was coolly received. He revised it several times before he had a second version published in 1853. In addition, he may have felt some discomfort at seeing his wife and Liszt on the stage together.

The Schumanns had several more encounters with Liszt. At each Clara's esteem for him fell, and she made no attempt to conceal her feelings. The reasons are, as always, complex, and both personal and musical. Though Clara admired Liszt's playing and said so publicly and privately, some uneasy competitiveness was always mixed with her deference. Her competetiveness was no doubt fueled by an essay that had appeared in the *Neue Zeitschrift* in April 1838, in which she was favorably compared with three other pianists of the first rank: Liszt, Thalberg, and Adolph von Henselt. Thus from the beginning of their relationship she was publicly given a place in the constellation of the great performers of her time and greeted as an equal. A tribute at this level could only have intensified the inner tensions of the young woman who was struggling with divided loyalties to her father and Schumann. As we have seen, her letters to Schumann in 1839–40 reveal much self-doubt, and she was continually questioning whether she could sustain her position, whether she was intelligent enough to study fugue, if she could (and should) compose. She knew she could play as well as any woman but had recurring doubts that she could compete with men. Her confidence was shaken when she read Schumann's words of enthusiasm about other pianists, and she suffered severe pangs of jealousy over his reaction to Liszt. Moreover, Clara always felt proprietary about Robert's works and would have preferred to be their sole interpreter. Realistically, of course, she knew this was not possible, and that for Schumann's sake it was important to have such a performer as Liszt as a champion, since there was no doubt that his performances would have more impact than hers. Yet she was hurt when Schumann was ecstatic about Liszt's playing of his *Novelletten, Fantasie,* and Sonata—"her" pieces.[15]

There were deeper reasons for her dislike of Liszt, some beyond her awareness. But she knew in December 1841 that her respect for him had been shaken. "Liszt likes to play the way he wants. It is always clever even though tasteless at times, and that is especially true of his compositions. I can only call them horrible." She found his compositions, she wrote in the marriage diary in December 1841:

> a chaos of the worst dissonances with an endless murmuring in the deepest bass and the highest treble at the same time, boring introductions, etc. I could almost hate him as a composer. As a performer, however, his concert on the 13th absolutely astounded me, especially in his *Don Juan* Fantasy, which he played overpoweringly—his performance of the Champagne Aria will remain unforgettable—the bravado, the pleasure with which he played was unique! One saw Don Juan with the popping champagne corks, in his wantonness, as only Mozart could have possibly imagined him. After the concert we all had supper together. . . . Of Liszt there was not much to be seen, since two women had attached themselves to him. I am convinced that the reason Liszt displays such arrogance at times is really the fault of the women, because they pay court to him everywhere in a way that is intolerable to me and that I also find highly improper. I venerate him too, but even veneration must have a limit. On the 16th, Liszt played for the last time and performed Beethoven's E-flat Major Concerto masterfully, but then he played Robert's *Fantasie* in dreadful taste, and after that, the *Galopp*. He seemed tired, which is not surprising, considering the way he lives—he had come early that day from Halle, where he had a wild night, and still had three rehearsals in the morning. Liszt came to the

soiree [at the Schumann house], as always, late. He seems to enjoy making people wait for him, which is something I don't like. He strikes me as a spoiled child, good-natured, tyrannical, amiable, arrogant, noble, and generous, often hard on others—a strange mix of characters. Yet we have become very fond of him and he has always treated us in the friendliest way.

Yet Clara reciprocated this friendliness with coldness and eventually with outright hostility. Why? First, she was genuinely offended by his attitude toward the music he performed. From Wieck she had learned that her duty as an interpreter was to play in a manner as close as possible to the spirit and intention of the composer. This attitude was reinforced, of course, when she married Schumann. Liszt, on the other hand, though a composer himself, had no compunctions about embellishing the music he played, his own and that of others, adding trills and cadenzas, doubling octaves, exaggerating tempo changes, rolling arpeggios, "as he wanted," as Clara put it. Moreover, the serious young Leipziger probably resented his careless ease: he played in public without rehearsal, caroused half the night before a performance, canceled concerts at will—all without noticeable effect on his playing. In a sense, he dishonored her high musical ideals, and the conscientious Clara Schumann found such an attitude unforgivable.

Clara herself gave a clue to her antagonism when she described Liszt's verve, his zest for life and excitement, and what she sensed as his capacity for happiness. These characteristics were unnerving to the sober young pianist who still retained the "inclination to melancholy" that had struck observers of the adolescent Clara. All the sufferings and strains of the years of courtship took their toll, and the marriage brought its own problems. The portraits of the years 1840–50 show a sad, solemn woman. She was still slender and had the soulful eyes that were so remarkable in the child's face, but the responsibilities of marriage, motherhood, and career weighed heavily upon her. The continuing hostility between the Schumanns and Wieck was also an emotional burden. It must be remembered that Clara had never known the gaiety, flirtations, lightheartedness, spontaneous laughter—the excitement and carefree fun most girls experience in their teens. She always took herself seriously and carried out her duties and responsibilities gravely, even grimly as she grew older. Furthermore, she believed she was not pretty, found it difficult to understand that a man could find her attractive, was even overcome at times by doubts that she could keep Robert's love. The vivid, outgoing personality of the womanizing Liszt was profoundly disturbing to her—perhaps doubly so because he never paid court to her. While she scrupulously deplored his flirtations, she may have unconsciously resented his lack of attention.

The later contacts between the Schumann household and Liszt widened the gulf between them. When Liszt visited the Schumanns in Dresden in

1848, he outraged Clara by appearing two hours late for a dinner party, insulted Robert by pronouncing his Quintet "Leipzigerish," praised Meyerbeer at Mendelssohn's expense, and horrified both Schumanns by his "dreadful" playing. There was an outburst from Schumann and Liszt is reported to have said to Clara, "Tell your husband that there is only one person in the world from whom I would take such words calmly."[16]

Despite this scene, Liszt generously presented Schumann's works in Weimar, attended premieres of his works in Leipzig, visited him in Düsseldorf in 1851 and Clara in 1855, invited Clara to play in Weimar in 1854, and dedicated his great Sonata in B Minor to Schumann. This act, too, annoyed Clara, who described the Sonata in her diary on May 25, 1854, as "merely a blind noise—no healthy ideas anymore, everything confused, one cannot find one clear harmonic progression—and yet I must now thank him for it. It is really too awful."[17]

When Liszt came to Düsseldorf on September 1, 1851, with Princess Wittgenstein (supposedly soon to be his wife, Clara added in her diary), she noted, "He played, as always, with a truly demonic bravura and possessed the piano really like a devil (I cannot express it in any other way) . . . but oh, his compositions, that was really too horrible!" When she met and played with him in Leipzig in 1852, she raged, "Liszt at his piano . . . no longer music, but like demonic boozing and bluster"; and after her performances in Weimar, to which she had come at his gracious invitation, she wrote, "His playing sounded like infernal, devilish music."[18]

Her remarks must finally have reached his ears, for they saw each other infrequently after 1856.

RICHARD WAGNER, 1813–1883

As a young student, Richard Wagner lived and studied in Leipzig. During these years he had contact with both Clara Wieck and Robert Schumann. Wagner borrowed music and books from Wieck's lending library, studied theory with Christian Weinlig at about the same time as Clara, and was acquainted with Schumann. The acquaintance was renewed when the Schumanns moved to Dresden in 1844. There Wagner, an assistant director at the opera, saw Schumann more frequently: they enjoyed visits, walks, and talks together, discussed opera, libretti, and aesthetics. It is doubtful that Clara was present at these meetings. Though Wagner is rarely mentioned in her diary, the few notes she did make about him make it clear that she not only disliked his music, but even in 1843 found the man offensive. (On February 12, 1843, she described him in the marriage diary as talking endlessly and displaying great arrogance.)

After her husband's death, she saw Wagner now and again, but remarked in her diary after seeing him in Zurich in December 1857: "I can't say very much about him. He is certainly friendly to me and that makes me feel even worse because I cannot bring myself to feel the least spark of sympathy for him."[19]

Her comments on Wagner and his music became increasingly corrosive:

> I decided to go to see *Rheingold*. I felt as if I were wading in a swamp the whole evening. The one good thing about the opera is that one is not deafened by the brass as one is in his other operas. . . . The boredom that one must endure, however, is dreadful. In every scene the actors on stage are in a cataleptic trance in which they remain fixed for such a long time that one cannot look at them any more. The women have just a few measures to sing in the entire opera and just stand around forever; in general they are all nothing but tattered, villainous gods.[20]

Her reaction to *Die Walküre* was no kinder:

> There was much that was interesting in *Walküre*, but boredom was the dominating feature. . . . The gods don't interest me in the slightest, they are all such scoundrels; that Wotan is the dumbest fellow. . . . Musicians are always talking about the interesting orchestration—I will try to hear the opera once more and pay special attention to that. . . .[21]

A few days later she went to hear *Das Rheingold* and *Die Walküre* again and did admit to hearing some sections that sounded quite beautiful, but also, she wrote, many harmonies that reminded her of Mendelssohn, Schumann, and Heinrich Marschner.[22] Her reaction to *Tristan und Isolde* is as revealing about herself as about its composer. In September 1875 she wrote in her diary:

> In the evening we went to see *Tristan und Isolde*. That was the most disgusting thing I have ever seen or heard in my life. To be forced to see and hear such crazy lovemaking the whole evening, in which every feeling of decency is violated and by which not just the public but even musicians seem to be enchanted—that is the saddest thing I have experienced in my entire artistic life. I remained to the end since I wanted to hear the whole thing. During the entire second act the two of them sleep and sing; through the entire last act—for fully forty minutes—Tristan dies. They call that dramatic!!![23]

Wagner's music as well as his personality was the antithesis of everything Clara held sacred. Unlike Liszt, whose generosity of spirit Clara could acknowledge (however grudgingly), Wagner was supremely selfish and self-serving. She refused to play in Vienna in 1870 under Wagner and wrote Brahms that she could not play under the direction of a man who shamelessly spoke of Robert, Mendelssohn, and Brahms in such a scornful manner.[24] Her friendship with Hermann Levi was marred by Levi's Wagner worship, which she tried in vain to overlook. Levi, strangely enough, was able to forgive Wagner his violent anti-Semitism; Clara obviously could not.

Richard and Cosima Wagner spoke of both Schumanns and the Schumann circle with crude contempt, and though Clara Schumann could not have been aware of the kind of spiteful gossip that seemed to be the daily talk in the Wagner home,[25] she had ample reason to despise the man and enough sense of history to fear his influence. She described his death as simply "an event."[26]

FELIX MENDELSSOHN BARTHOLDY, 1809–1847

The elegant and worldly Felix Mendelssohn Bartholdy, already illustrious at twenty-five, arrived in Leipzig on the last day of August 1835 to take over the leadership of the Gewandhaus orchestra. The new conductor, one year older than Robert Schumann, was aware of Clara Wieck's talent. He had already visited her the year before, in October 1834, and had heard her play Schumann's Toccata, some Chopin works, and her own *Concertsatz*. Impressed by the girl's abilities, he told Wieck that he would have to return because he had not heard enough of Clara's art.[27] Soon after his arrival in 1835, he visited the Wiecks again and heard more of Robert's works and some of Clara's own compositions.[28] He seemed to be more impressed by Clara's accomplishments than by those of her friend Robert Schumann. Schumann's position as editor and littérateur meant little or nothing to the brilliant pianist, conductor, and composer, who had little patience with critics and other writers about music. Clara, on the other hand, was a respected colleague. Though they had met in Paris years before, there is little evidence that Felix had paid much attention to the awkward, serious child she then was. In 1835, however, the presence in Leipzig of the graceful and accomplished young pianist aroused the conductor's interest. At her sixteenth birthday celebration they played together and for each other: she performed a Bach fugue and, at his special request, the scherzo from Schumann's unpublished sonata. He, in turn, played for her and gave her an autograph of his *Capriccio*, op. 5.[29]

Within a few weeks, Mendelssohn, conducting the Gewandhaus Orchestra, accompanied Clara in the premiere of her Concerto for Piano and Orchestra. On the same program she played with Mendelssohn and Rakemann the Bach Concerto for Three Claviers in D Minor, the first performance of this work at the Gewandhaus. Clara Wieck performed under Mendelssohn's direction and played with him frequently, both in public and in private.[30] Over the years Mendelssohn depended on her, asked her to substitute for him when he was unable to play, and obviously considered her to be a musician of the first rank.* In answer to a letter from Clara asking if he

---

*Mendelssohn conducted at twenty-one of her concerts (*Grove*, 12:139).

would like to play with her, he wrote on November 24, 1845, "You know I am *always* ready to do this and am *always* thinking of playing something with you whenever you want to give me that pleasure."[31] In August 1844 she joined the faculty of the Leipzig Conservatory, which he had established, but Schumann's illness and the subsequent move to Dresden prevented her from continuing that association.

Despite several misunderstandings, Schumann loved and admired Mendelssohn. And for all his extraordinary and numerous activities, Mendelssohn, generally known to be reserved and rather cool, proved himself a true friend when he came forward to testify for Schumann during Wieck's suit. Mendelssohn's death in 1847, at the age of thirty-eight, was a severe blow to both Schumanns. In his uncompleted memoirs of Mendelssohn, Schumann noted his many courtesies to Clara. Mendelssohn gave her small but cherished gifts and praised her playing both publicly and privately. Schumann took pride in Mendelssohn's high regard for Clara, though he may very well have had mixed feelings about it. "He always thought highly of her," he wrote "and said, 'She really understands how to play the piano.' It always gave him great pleasure to take really lively tempos with her in the four-hand works they played together, especially when they were sight-reading."[32]

Clara idolized Mendelssohn as pianist, composer, and conductor. She felt his playing of Bach was beyond compare. On December 30, 1838, after hearing Thalberg, Liszt's rival, she wrote in her diary, "As a player, he has a place among the greats, but towering above all others—stands Mendelssohn." In 1840 she described his performance of his Trio in D Minor and Mozart's G Minor Piano Quartet as so masterful and fiery that she was brought to tears. "Aside from the pleasure, I believe that I learn a great deal when I hear him."[33]

As conductor of the Gewandhaus Orchestra, Felix Mendelssohn was the leader of musical life in Leipzig, and both Clara and Robert were in awe of his talents, proud of his interest in their affairs, and also a bit jealous of his lofty position.* Schumann valued Mendelssohn's opinions not only because of his powerful position but because he respected the experience and judgment of this creative genius who seemed to have everything in his favor—wealth, the best education, early experience, social and administrative talents, unflagging industry, and self-discipline. Clara, whom her husband described as "glowing for hours after a nice word from Mendelssohn,"[34] approached the director for help and advice several times without Robert's knowledge. In November 1843, for example, when Schumann was unable to make a decision about a trip to Russia—a journey on which she had long set her heart—she went to Mendelssohn for counsel. On December 9, 1843, she wrote to him:

*Though Schumann and Mendelssohn were about the same age, they were not on *du* terms, as Schumann was with Ferdinand David and Ferdinand Hiller, for example.

> My husband is now talking seriously about the trip. I am very happy about this but I also know whom to thank. When I think of the morning when I came to you in such despair, I am embarrassed and realize that I must have seemed really childish to you, but I will never forget how kindly and patiently you listened to me, and how you met all my wishes with such sympathy.[35]

Apparently Clara was not troubled by the fact that she had gone behind her husband's back to a male friend, only by the fear that she might have appeared childish.

She maintained her close ties with Mendelssohn until his death, and with other members of his family afterward. When Schumann was hospitalized, Mendelssohn's brother Paul offered help so tactfully that Clara accepted it though she had refused aid from others. Clara visited Mendelssohn's mother when she was in Berlin and was greatly taken with Fanny Mendelssohn Hensel, Felix's sister. She was not particularly impressed by Fanny's compositions, but found her so congenial that she noted in the marriage diary that the presence of such an accomplished woman who could be a real friend was a lure that made the thought of settling in Berlin an attractive prospect.[36] Fanny Hensel's death in May 1847, six months before her brother's, was a blow to Clara.

The youngest child of Clara and Robert Schumann was named in memory of their friend, the "unforgettable one," as Schumann wrote from the hospital.[37]

JOSEPH JOACHIM, 1831–1907

As a concert performer Clara Schumann was most closely associated with two artists, the violinist Joseph Joachim and the singer Julius Stockhausen, both considerably younger than she. They reached positions of eminence early in life and were regarded by Clara and the public alike as her equals in stature, rank, and musicianship.

Her long-lived relationship with Joachim was particularly close. She first met the violinist when he came to Leipzig as a boy of twelve to study with Ferdinand David, concertmaster of the Gewandhaus Orchestra. In May 1853 Joachim came to Düsseldorf, at Schumann's urging, to perform the Beethoven Violin Concerto at the Lower Rhine Music Festival, in which Schumann, as Düsseldorf's municipal music director, played an important role. Joachim's dazzling performance and sympathetic artistry impressed the Schumanns,[38] and he visited Düsseldorf frequently in the following months. In August of that year he and Clara played chamber music together, and he returned for another public concert on October 27, at which he premiered Schumann's new *Fantasie*, op. 131, which was dedicated to him.[39]

When Robert fell ill, Joachim and Brahms were the two friends on whom Clara most depended. She was never on *du* terms with Joachim, but in July 1854, soon after her husband went to Endenich, she wrote in her diary:

> He is as dear a friend as Brahms, and in him, too, I have the utmost confidence. He has such spirit and delicate perception that he understands my slightest and most subtle feelings immediately. These two, Brahms and Joachim, seem made to be Robert's friends, but he does not know them yet as I do. One learns to know one's friends in adversity.[40]

Her first concerts after Schumann's hospitalization were with Joachim. They never missed an opportunity to make music together, at home or on the concert stage. She admired his playing and musicianship more than those of any other performer of her time. The two were particularly noted for their playing of Beethoven's sonatas for violin and piano. Clara Schumann and Joachim saw eye to eye musically and the collaboration gave them—and their audiences—unending joy. (She also toured extensively with his wife, Amalie, a mezzo-soprano. Frau Joachim was one of the few singers—Stockhausen was another—for whom she played accompaniments. Amalie Joachim and Julius Stockhausen, she felt, were colleagues, not assisting artists.) She played with Joseph Joachim in England as well as on the Continent from 1854 until the 1880s.

Clara Schumann was so fond of Joachim that she mentioned to him several times that she wished they could live in the same town. In January 1858 she wrote that she needed to live near him so that he "could stand by me with counsel and help, uplift me through your music, and through praise and criticism inspire me to self-study."[41] Failing that, they corresponded for forty years.* Since they were both basically performers, their letters centered on such common problems as conductors, orchestras, the scheduling of engagements, and touring, on musical questions dealing with tempi and interpretation, and on the physical afflictions that troubled many performing artists. She also turned to Joachim for advice about her career, as one artist to another. Like Brahms, Joachim responded sympathetically; the most trivial questions were answered with respect for her feelings and with affirmation of his admiration for her artistry.

The separation of Joseph and Amalie Joachim in the early 1880s and their subsequent divorce caused Clara much anguish. The impending divorce may have brought back memories of the breakup of her own family so many years earlier, and she wrote with great emotion to a mutual friend that she hesitated to come to Berlin, even to perform, because she was so troubled by the Joachim situation.[42] Unlike Brahms, however, she did not take sides in

---

*Many of the several hundred letters appeared in *Briefe von und an Joseph Joachim*, published in English as *Letters from and to Joseph Joachim*, trans. Nora Bickley (London: Macmillan, 1914).

the controversy and maintained her friendship with both Joseph and Amalie as long as she could.

As director of the Königliche Hochschule für Musik in Berlin, Joachim endeavored year after year to lure her to a faculty position at the school. Finally, however, he gave up: her conditions were always too demanding (one suspects she did not want to be tied down to a regular job) and he was never able to procure the necessary funds from the trustees. Though Joachim had the greatest respect for Clara Schumann, it seems that even her luster could not compete with prevailing attitudes toward women, and he may not have tried very hard to persuade his board to hire her. As he wrote to Ernst Rudorff, his assistant and head of the Piano Department, she could teach only girls, and as it was chiefly the men that needed a teacher at the time, he had given up trying to get a position for her. Rudorff, himself a Schumann student, agreed.[43] Joachim was hurt when in 1878 she accepted a professorship in Frankfurt—where she taught both men and women—but the friendship continued nevertheless.

Among her last joys was Joachim's playing. In May 1890 she wrote to him that when he played, she forgot all her physical pains.[44] A few months before her death, Joachim visited her. At that time she wrote of the friend of her youth: "He brought his violin with him, but this time I wanted the man, the friend, rather than the violinist."[45]

JULIUS STOCKHAUSEN, 1826–1906

Clara Schumann met Julius Stockhausen during the first summer of her husband's hospitalization and after one hearing proclaimed him a "star in the artistic heavens." She dubbed him *Herrlicher Sänger* (magnificent singer),[46] and he was referred to in the Schumann circle by that term ever after. Stockhausen, an Alsatian-born baritone trained in Paris, was one of the first great lieder singers of the nineteenth century. He gave the first complete performances of Schubert and Schumann song cycles: Schubert's *Schöne Müllerin* in 1854, Schumann's *Dichterliebe* with Brahms in 1861 and with Clara Schumann in 1862. Later he premiered complete performances of Robert Schumann's *Frauenliebe und Leben, Liederkreis,* and the *Spanisches Liederspiel.*[47] One of Stockhausen's great achievements was his championship of Schumann's *Faust* Scenes. Ferdinand Hiller, the conductor in Cologne, wanted to present only excerpts, but Stockhausen telegraphed him, "All or nothing," and Hiller capitulated. Stockhausen gave the first complete performance of this little-known work in Cologne in 1861.[48] In April 1855, knowing that Stockhausen's singing would give her husband great pleasure, Clara attempted to arrange a private concert at Endenich, but the plan did not work out and Schumann never heard the young man sing.[49]

Her delight with Stockhausen's voice and musicianship was equaled by his admiration for her. "Madame Schumann is one of those rare persons for whom I would go to the ends of the earth. . . . What an artist!" he wrote to his father in 1856.[50] After he met her, his circle of musical associates enlarged to include Brahms, Joachim, and later, in London—where he toured with Clara Schumann in 1859—her old friends Jenny Lind, Pauline García-Viardot, and Ferdinand Hiller.

Stockhausen's appointment in 1862 as music director in Hamburg was a blow to Brahms and to Clara Schumann as well, but the friendship and musical collaboration among the three of them survived. Soon after Clara Schumann moved to Frankfurt to teach at the Hoch Conservatory, Stockhausen followed to become the principal voice teacher. His years in Frankfurt were marked by great battles with Joachim Raff, the director, and he left for a time, but returned to the conservatory after Raff's death. Later he established his own voice school in Frankfurt. He and Clara Schumann remained friends and colleagues to the end.

PAULINE GARCÍA-VIARDOT, 1821–1910

Clara Schumann first met Pauline García—actress, singer, pianist, composer, teacher, and talented painter—in Leipzig in June 1838 and recognized her genius instantly. She believed that Pauline was an exception among singers: "She has a lively interest in music," Clara wrote in her diary on June 25, 1838, "and is the most musical singer who exists." The two girls—Clara almost nineteen, Pauline almost seventeen—became fast friends; indeed, fifty-four years later Pauline described them as "the two oldest friends of this century."[51] When they first met, Clara, overwhelmed by the singer's mastery, intellectual skills (she read and understood Schiller and Goethe), and talents, was envious and on the verge of losing her self-confidence. She was relieved by her father's reassurances and by Pauline's generous and unfailing admiration. Clara was captivated by Pauline's vivaciousness, temperament, and seemingly carefree way of life. The earnest Clara alternated between envy and disbelief at the way in which Pauline, the daughter of the famed Spanish singer and impresario Manuel García, enjoyed life.

Despite the vast differences in personality, the two artists respected each other and relished the few opportunities they had to meet. After three hearings of a group of operettas that Pauline Viardot had composed, orchestrated, and produced, Clara Schumann wrote to Brahms, "Once more I have confirmation of what I have always said: she is the most gifted woman I have ever met."[52]

Over the years their paths crossed now and again: in Paris in 1839 Clara saw Pauline almost daily; in 1843 they appeared together in a concert with Mendelssohn in Leipzig; they met in London in 1856, in Pest in 1858, in Paris in 1862. With Pauline's encouragement, Clara bought her cottage in Baden-Baden; they were neighbors there for the ten summers Clara Schumann owned the house.

The Schumanns arrived in Russia in 1844 just as Pauline García-Viardot was completing a triumphal tour. In her farewell press interview the singer announced, "I am leaving you Clara Schumann. Her singing on the piano is better than mine."[53]

CHAPTER **11**

Clara Schumann as

Composer and Editor

Clara Wieck Schumann's achievements as a composer and editor of her husband's music are not so well known as her accomplishments on the concert stage. Apparently she had many conflicts about the value of her creative work and she left few records of her efforts in this sphere. There is no doubt that she was a great interpreter and a uniquely skilled and talented musician. Despite alternating feelings of despair and exhilaration about her creative powers, she persevered and continued to compose as long as her husband was alive. A number of her compositions rise above the ordinary. On the whole, however, her work was not that of a major composer.

Perhaps the greatest significance of her creative work lies in what it tells us about the musical and personal interdependence between Clara Wieck Schumann and Robert Schumann. In 1832 Robert Schumann already depended on the twelve-year-old girl to perform his music for him. By 1833 their correspondence was filled with musical games, riddles, and secret messages referring to the music they both were creating. In 1834 Clara turned to Robert for help with her concerto. In the years before 1840 they shared musical themes and quoted from each other's works. Beginning in 1839, they exchanged information about texts that could serve as song settings. In that year Robert wrote to their old teacher Heinrich Dorn that Clara had been the inspiration for all of his greatest piano works. He often declared that he could feel her very presence as he composed. Each criticized, advised, and dedicated important works to the other. After their marriage Robert entrusted her with the piano arrangements for several of his major works. He continually urged her to compose and to catalogue, organize, and preserve her manuscripts. He corresponded with publishers about her compositions, a task she might not have undertaken on her own. Husband and wife studied and worked together on projects ranging from the study of Bach fugues to the reading of orchestral scores and the chamber

225]

music of Haydn, Mozart, and Beethoven. They encouraged, supported, and inspired each other before and during their marriage.

From her very first days at the piano, creative activities were integrated into Clara Wieck's daily routine at the piano. As a consequence of her father's innovative approach to the instrument, the five-year-old Clara could play—even before she could read notes—cadential progressions in all the major and minor keys, transpose little pieces that she learned by ear, and improvise on her own or given themes. Years later, in her seventies, she still began her daily practice sessions with improvisatory preludes. In 1895, a few months before her death, her daughters urged her to write them down and she did so, but reluctantly. In her diary she wrote, "I would like to write the preludes that I always play before scales but it is difficult since I always do it differently—just the way it strikes me as I sit at the piano." The act of fixing them on paper was probably antithetical to her purpose—to allow her imagination to roam freely and to maintain her inspiration at the keyboard. She was persuaded, however, and the preludes survive, though they have not been published.[1]

Formal harmony, counterpoint, and composition lessons began when Clara was barely ten, and her own compositions appeared on her earliest programs, as was customary in the 1830s. For Friedrich Wieck, concerts had two purposes: to impress audiences with his own and his daughter's talents and to fill the coffers by presenting what the public was accustomed to hear. An improvisation or an original work was included in almost every concert Clara gave between 1830 and 1838. Many of these works for voice and for piano, with and without orchestra, have disappeared; we know of them only through mention in the diaries, in her authorized biography, or in the programs of her concerts.* If the extant works are a reliable guide, we may assume that the first piano pieces were popular crowd-pleasers, technically showy, in the style of the works she performed by Henri Herz and Friedrich Kalkbrenner. Within a few years, however—and while she was still under Wieck's aegis—a new style began to emerge.

In 1837, when Clara and her father were on their way to Vienna, a Prague newspaper, presumably with Wieck's consent, published an article describing her as a "member of the romantic school," thus linking her with such composers as Chopin, Mendelssohn, and Schumann.[2] Most descriptions of her work, both then and later, refer to her compositions as "Chopinesque" or "Schumannesque," or note a resemblance to Mendelssohn. (Even Brahms is cited, though she could not have known any of his music until well after she had composed most of her own.) Although she was ten years younger than these men, she was aware of the musical currents of her time. She heard and played all the music, old and new, which was performed or published in Leipzig in the 1830s. Moreover, the music of Chopin,† Men-

---

*See Appendix.

†Frédéric Chopin visited Clara in Leipzig on September 27, 1835, and again on September 12, 1836.

delssohn, and Schumann was played to her by the composers themselves, and she, in turn, played her own works for them.

Like Chopin, she heard and was inspired by the Italian opera composers Vincenzo Bellini, Gaetano Donizetti, and Gioacchino Rossini. Like Liszt, she was swept off her feet by the dazzling brilliance of Nicolò Paganini. Through the efforts of Mendelssohn, she was acquainted with the music of Bach. Through Schumann, she surely must have heard the *Symphonie Fantastique* of the "radical" French composer Hector Berlioz, a work that Schumann analyzed in a remarkable essay in the *Neue Zeitschrift* in the summer of 1835. The music she wrote in her girlhood reflected all these influences.

Wieck was receptive to the new music and included himself, and hence his daughter, among the avant-garde. His identity confusion is evident in such diary entries as "I am readying the *Valses Romantiques* . . . and the first movement [of the Concerto] for publication"; "I played my concerto; the first movement was just finished"; "My concerto op. 7 has just been published."[3] Such entries and the canon that women were unable to compose may have contributed to a widespread assumption that Wieck wrote Clara's compositions. That he did not write for her is certain. His own published works have neither the charm nor the skill of even her earliest attempts. Her continued growth as a composer and Wieck's own expressions of joyous surprise at her talent[4] give the lie to assertions that he composed her works. He must be credited, of course, for the creative music education and ambiance he provided, but her compositions were her own.

By the time Clara was twelve years old, many features of the new romanticism could be heard in her compositions: the bravura technique; the lyrical aria-like middle sections; the miniature forms with extramusical associations; the loosening of regular phrase structure; the experiments with rhythm and meter and the use of such dance rhythms as the polonaise and mazurka. Admittedly Clara Wieck did not have the imagination, power, or creative gifts of the leaders of the "new romantic" school, but she was accepted as one of them.

By 1840, the year of her marriage, concert practices had changed; it was no longer essential for a concert artist to feature his or her own music or to improvise. Moreover, Clara Schumann, who never exhibited much pride in her own work, was now eager to introduce and play the music of her husband. Her own compositions, however, were not totally neglected: the programs of many of her concerts after 1840 list at least one work by Clara Schumann, usually a song or short piano piece, and the reviews indicate that they were well received.

After her marriage, her composing efforts followed closely the patterns set by her husband. Her first works after her marriage were songs—like Robert's—with texts by Friedrich Rückert, Emanuel Geibel, Heinrich Heine, and Robert Burns (in translation). Both produced music that reflected their joint studies of contrapuntal techniques and the classical masters. Clara's op. 16 consisted of three preludes and fugues, and her Trio for Piano, Violin, and Cello, op. 17, by far her most outstanding work, was structured in the classical tradition but filled with romantic tenderness and lyricism.

Though her husband encouraged and praised her original efforts and exerted his influence to have them published, he had some questions regarding the time she spent on creative work. An entry in the marriage diary dated February 17, 1843, reveals his feelings:

> Clara has written a number of small pieces that show a musical and tender invention that she has never attained before. But to have children and a husband who is always living in the realms of imagination do not go together with composing. She cannot work at it regularly and I am often disturbed to think how many profound ideas are lost because she cannot work them out. But Clara herself knows her main occupation is as a mother and I believe she is happy in the circumstances and would not want them changed.

Clara herself was always ambivalent about her creative work. There is no doubt that composing brought a glow of satisfaction. "Nothing surpasses creative activity, even if only for those hours of self-forgetfulness in which one breathes solely in the world of sound," she wrote after completing the six songs of op. 23 in 1853. After she composed the Trio, she wrote in her diary, "There is no greater joy than composing something oneself and then listening to it." But her conflicts are exposed when we read on: "There are some nice passages in the Trio and I believe it is also fairly successful as far as form is concerned, but naturally it is still women's work, which always lacks force and occasionally invention." Her insecurity about her creative capabilities was reiterated a year later; "I received the printed copies of my trio today, but after Robert's [D Minor] I did not especially like it. It sounded quite effeminate and sentimental."[5]

Other musicians enjoyed playing the work and were unaware of her conflicts. On March 13, 1860, for example, Joachim wrote her, "I would rather have heard your trio [than music by Moritz Hauptmann]. I recollect a fugato in the last movement and remember that Mendelssohn once had a big laugh because I would not believe that a woman could have composed something so sound and serious."[6] Even praise from such an esteemed colleague, however, could not convince her of the Trio's worth. She played her husband's trios far more often than her own and never gave any special care to the autographs of her works, while the autographs of Robert's music were treasured and carefully preserved.

The contradictory feelings about her creative work appeared well before her marriage. On November 26, 1839, she confided to her diary:

> I once believed that I had creative talent, but I have given up this idea; a woman must not wish to compose—there never was one able to do it. Am

I intended to be the one? It would be arrogant to believe that. That was something with which only my father tempted me in former days. But I soon gave up believing this. May Robert always create; that must always make me happy.

Yet shortly before, she had written to Robert, "It is really sinful that I have not composed anything for such a long time. Father is beside himself and I too am often unhappy about it and in general more dissatisfied with myself than I can say."[7]

The correspondence with Robert regarding her *Trois Romances* further illustrates her ambivalence. On April 18, 1839, Clara wrote from Paris, "Yesterday evening I was very happy. I had a pretty idea for a little Romanze, but today I am already dissatisfied with it." A few days later she wrote, "I have written a tiny little piece but I don't know what to call it. I have a peculiar fear of showing you anything I have composed; I am always so ashamed."[8] Yet she was offended when Robert asked to see the third Romance and then returned it with alterations and suggestions.

> I have received the Idylle [Romance no. 3] and thank you for it, my dearest, but you will surely forgive me if I tell you that there are some things in it I do not like. You have completely altered the ending, which was always my favorite part and precisely the one that made the biggest impression on everyone I played it to. . . . You are not angry with me, are you?[9]

Clara evidently felt safe in derogating her own work but resented any criticism from others.

Though it is tempting to cite societal influences for her contradictory attitudes and her discomfort about her creative efforts, her own letters and diary provide much evidence that creativity did not come easily to her. She rarely composed of her own volition but simply because she was expected to do so—by the public, by her father, later by her husband. She envied and admired those who could create but believed her primary field of competence was as a performer; she thought of herself as an interpretive rather than a creative artist.[10] Whether she would have composed more or felt less insecure about her creative ability if she had married someone who was not a composer is doubtful. She composed because all professional performers of her time did so; she had been trained to compose and dutifully fulfilled the expectations of her father and the concert public.

When her relationship with her father weakened and he no longer urged her to compose, she found that her husband—to whose life composing was essential—raised similar expectations. In May 1840, when Robert Schumann was in the midst of a feverishly exalted creative period and working on his greatest songs, he urged, "Write to me again of what you see and hear and compose. Try to compose a song; you'll see how well it will turn out."[11]

A few months after their marriage, in January 1841, we find this plea from husband to wife in the marriage diary: "From Monday to Friday, the 11th, I completed the nine songs from Rückert's *Liebesfrühling*. I think I've found the special tone [they require]. Now Klara should also compose a few from *Liebesfrühling*. Oh, do it, Klärchen."

Composing was never simple for Clara, however, and her household responsibilities added to the burden. After her marriage, her compositions were almost always written for Christmas or birthdays or at her husband's special request. She found marriage to a creative genius intimidating and frequently expressed fears that she might embarrass herself and him. Her moods fluctuated wildly. In the marriage diary in May 1841 she wailed, "I can't compose any more. All poetry has abandoned me." Yet on June 8 she presented four songs to Schumann on his birthday, and was pleased, she wrote in the marriage diary, that he treated them with "indulgence" and "wanted to publish them with several of his own." In September, when the songs were published jointly as his op. 37 and her op. 12,* she referred to her efforts as "several of my weak products."

In December 1840, three months after their marriage, she noted in the marriage diary:

> Whenever Robert went out of the house, I spent my time in attempts to compose a song (something he always wanted), and finally I succeeded in completing *three*, which I will present to him at Christmas. If they are really of little value, merely a *very weak attempt*, I am counting on Robert's forbearance and [hope] that he will understand that it was done with the best will in the world in order to fulfill this wish of his—just as I fulfill all his wishes. Be kind, my friend, and have indulgence for this weak gift, which is bestowed with so much love.

Her gifts to him—presentation copies written out on paper with decorative borders and nicely tied with a ribbon—were invariably accompanied by self-deprecatory notes. In 1841 she worked on a sonatina and completed two movements for Christmas. The work was inscribed: "Accept this with love, my good husband, and have forbearance for your Clara." Her op. 20, written more than ten years later, was inscribed, "To my beloved husband on June 8, 1853, this weak attempt once more from your old Clara."[12] Her contradictory dependence on his approval and pride in her own work are embodied in a letter to her sister Marie, August 16, 1853: "To my great joy, all the pieces were so well done that there was nothing that Robert wanted to change. So you see, as one gets older there are also many pleasures that only a more mature mind and feelings can bring."[13]

And although her husband obviously felt that the role of wife and mother was primary, he pressed her to treat her own work with care and respect: he urged her to make and keep fair copies of her songs; with his obsession for

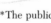

*The publication date was planned by Robert as a surprise for her birthday.

systematic order, he wrote out the title pages and tables of contents of her manuscript collections; he arranged for the publication of many of her works. Yet the conflicts seen in her letters and diaries continued to the very end of her composing career, which, not unexpectedly, closed when her husband died. After 1856 she wrote only one work, a march to commemorate the wedding anniversary of some friends.[14] Any time that was available after family duties and concert responsibilities was devoted to her self-imposed task as editor of her husband's complete works.

From our vantage point, it seems safe to say that Clara Schumann was a gifted and creative person, that the men she knew best encouraged her to compose, that social pressures may have disheartened but did not discourage her. Her music, admittedly not in the same class as that of her husband, nonetheless repays study; by mirroring an age of great ferment, it sheds light on the musical life and thought of the early decades of the nineteenth century and the music of the "new romantic" composers. It delineates more clearly than words the uncommon unity between Clara and Robert Schumann.

No complete authoritative collection of her compositions has ever been published, nor has a serious study of her complete oeuvre and its implications for Robert Schumann research been attempted.[15] The *Pianofortewerk* issued by Breitkopf & Härtel in 1878 is not complete. The discussion here of the genesis and publication history of each work and the information given in the Appendix must fill the gap until such time as a complete edition is available.[16]

WORKS FOR PIANO

Only half of Clara Schumann's piano works were included in the 1878 *Pianofortewerk*. Omitted were op. 1 through 9 and op. 11, all composed by the young Clara Wieck between 1831 and 1839. The Scherzo op. 10, composed before her marriage, was evidently considered worthy of inclusion in this collection.

Despite the publisher's (and the composer's) disregard of the early works, they have considerable musical as well as historical interest. And beginning with her op. 2, an extraordinary sharing and flow of ideas between Robert Schumann and Clara Wieck is recognizable.

During the years 1830 to 1836, the two young musicians were working and playing in such close proximity that it is often difficult to determine the origin of many musical ideas they shared. Schumann often used music and words that symbolized Clara for him, incorporating her into his work, as it were.[17]

The many ways in which she appeared in his music include direct quotations from her works. The best known of "her" themes, titled "Quasi Vari-

Example 1.   Robert Schumann, Sonata in F Minor, op. 14, third movement, "Quasi Variazioni. Andantino de Clara Wieck."

azioni, Andantino de Clara Wieck" (Example 1), used in the slow movement of Schumann's Sonata in F Minor op. 14, cannot be found as such in any of the autographs that survive. It strongly suggests, however, a motif outlining a descending fifth which is found in many of her works and which Schumann used more than once. In describing the theme as a melody by Clara Wieck, Schumann proclaimed the name of the sixteen-year-old girl to the world. The theme not only appears in the variation movement; it plays a major role throughout the sonata, beginning with the bold octaves in the opening measure of the first movement (Example 2). Almost always Schumann modified

Example 2.   Robert Schumann, Sonata in F Minor, op. 14, first movement, "Allegro."

Clara Wieck's motifs, but in using them he seems to be taking pleasure in revealing the special relationship between Clara Wieck and Robert Schumann.

Op. 1, *Quatre Polonaises pour le pianoforte*

The first of Clara's works that Friedrich Wieck deemed worthy of an opus number and publication were four polonaises composed when she was eleven. The review in *Iris*, a Berlin musical journal, found portions to praise but was in essence an indictment of her father:

> From a woman? No; this time from a little girl who is yet to become a woman. As far as we know, the young composer is just ten or eleven years old and already a very accomplished pianist. Early accomplishments are no barrier to future performance; in fact, it is certain that those who are early achievers generally accomplish later on as well. The polonaises that lie before us are quite artful; at times the harmonies are a bit forced, often too dissonant, yet not without talent and with a good rhythm. Small details are very likable. Yet there remains a question of how much of it was the child's own work and how much contributed by another. In any case, we would have considered it better if this publication had not appeared. Not on

account of the compositions—these are no better and no worse than many other modern piano pieces—but for the child's own sake. What reasonable person wants to have school exercises printed, even if they turn out well? But that is the sorry fate of our time—not to take heed of art or the needs of the public, but only to pay allegiance to the purse or homage to vanity.[18]

Wieck paid no attention, of course, and Clara's op. 2 was published the following year.

Op. 2, *Caprices en forme de valse pour le piano*

After hearing the twelve-year-old Clara play her newly composed Caprices in May 1832,* Schumann (whose *Papillons,* op. 2, had appeared a month earlier) was critical. In his diary he commented, "She played the new Caprices, it seemed to me, like a hussar." And the next day he wrote: "She is playing like a cavalryman. The Caprices are not caprices but rather impromptus or Wieckian moments musicales." The comment is apt: the little dances are not particularly capricious. But Robert Schumann, who already felt he was a special friend of Clara's, also noted a few days later that Clara wanted to dedicate the Caprices to him, and despite his deprecatory remarks, it is clear that he would have been pleased by the compliment.[19] Wieck, however, apparently found it more expedient to dedicate the work to another Leipziger, a Madame Foerster,† rather than the aspiring young composer.

As Schumann was living in the Wieck home while he was working on his *Papillons,* Clara must have heard the work in progress and her Caprices (begun before the trip to Paris) were undoubtedly influenced by it. The works share a similar structure: each is a series of loosely related short works with a dance character, probably influenced by the waltzes of Schubert and Weber. And in the opening measures of her Caprice no. 1 and in Caprices 3, 5, and 6 Clara used the ascending figure associated with Florestan in *Papillons* and *Carnaval.*[20]

Op. 3, *Romance variée pour le piano*

The *Romance variée* was the first of Clara's works to be dedicated to Robert Schumann, and in the complex story of the origin of the theme (Example 3) there is further confirmation of the musical interaction between

Example 3. Clara Wieck, *Romance variée,* op. 3, "Romanza."

*The Caprices were published in Paris just before the Wiecks left (Diary, May 10, 1832). They were printed again in Leipzig by Friedrich Hofmeister in August 1832.

†Henriette Weicke Foerster was one of the two girls with whom Clara had begun piano lessons in 1825.

Clara, thirteen years old when she composed this work, and the twenty-three-year-old Robert Schumann. This work also reveals indications of the three-sided relationship of Clara, Robert, and Friedrich Wieck. And the mature Clara Schumann recalled this childhood work when she skillfully wove the theme from her op. 3 into the coda of her op. 20, the Variations on a Theme by Robert Schumann (Example 4). A version of her theme also

Example 4. Clara Schumann, Variations on a Theme by Robert Schumann, op. 20, Coda, measures 9–12.

appeared in Brahms's variations on the same theme by Robert Schumann (Example 5).

Example 5. Johannes Brahms, Variations on a Theme by Robert Schumann, op. 9, Variation 10, measures 30–32.

The Romance has always been of special interest to Schumann scholars because Robert Schumann's *Impromptus sur une romance de Clara Wieck,* op. 5, dedicated to Friedrich Wieck, was supposedly based on the theme in Clara's Romance (Example 6). In 1850 Schumann revised op. 5, used a

Example 6. Robert Schumann, Impromptus on a Romance by Clara Wieck, op. 5 (1833 version), "Romanza."

slightly different version of the theme (Example 7), changed "Romance" to

Example 7. Robert Schumann, Impromptus on a Theme by Clara Wieck, op. 5 (1850 version), "Thema."

"Theme," and dropped the dedication to Wieck. Both the *Romance variée* and Schumann's Impromptus were published in the summer of 1833, but the tangled history of the theme goes back to 1830, possibly even earlier.

It has always been assumed that the theme was Clara's own: Schumann himself labeled it hers, Berthold Litzmann reported that she played op. 3 in 1831, and in May 1833, just before Schumann began work on the Impromptus, he wrote to Clara, asking her to send him all her variations.[21] However, two scholars, working independently, have traced the first appearance of the theme to an entry in Schumann's diary for September 28/29, 1830 (Example 8), thus identifying it as Robert's rather than Clara's.[22] Again,

Example 8. Robert Schumann, theme from *Tagebuch* (1830).

as with op. 2, the two young musicians shared ideas and inspiration. We can speculate that Clara heard Schumann improvising on his melody and then incorporated it in her own daily improvisations and later in her op. 3. Schumann, on hearing her play it, may have forgotten the source and assumed it was her musical idea.

Although Schumann's op. 5 paid tribute to the young girl, Clara's *Romance variée* is scarcely in a style of which he approved. The variations are replete with the musical clichés of the day, and it is precisely the kind of shallow work Robert Schumann was to hold up to ridicule in the *Neue Zeitschrift.*[23]

Op. 4, *Valses romantiques pour le pianoforte*

Clara Wieck's fourth opus is similar to op. 2 but lacks the joyous vivacity and structural sturdiness of the earlier group of dances. Clara and Robert shared a musical idea that in all likelihood first appeared in her op. 4: the descending figure in measures 7–10 (Example 9) is repeated almost exactly

Example 9.   Clara Wieck, *Valses romantiques*, op. 4, measures 7–10.

in the "Valse allemande" of Schumann's *Carnaval* (Example 10).

Example 10.   Robert Schumann, *Carnaval*, op. 9, "Valse allemand," measures 9–12.

Op. 5, *Quatre Pièces caractéristiques . . . pour le pianoforte*

The works that make up op. 5, typical of the "new romantic" school, were composed over a period of years and have borne varying titles. They were much admired by contemporary composers: one of the miniatures was played for Spohr in June 1836 and all of op. 5 and selections from op. 6 were performed for Chopin in September 1836. According to Wieck's entry in the diary, the young Polish composer, impressed and enthusiastic, took a manuscript copy of the work with him.[24]

No. 1, Impromptu, Le Sabbat

The tempo (allegro furioso), wide leaps, reiterated chromatic appoggiaturas that provide sharp dissonances, accents on weak beats, chromatically ascending bass passages in the middle section—all typical nineteenth-century "demonic" touches—contribute to the supernatural effect of "Le Sabbat," a reference to the rite of the witches' sabbath, a theme that intrigued many romantic composers.

The Impromptu began to appear on Clara's programs in November 1834 and, as *Hexentanz* was published separately in Vienna in 1838, after Clara's debut there. She played it for the royal family and Prince Esterhazy in

Vienna and in her public concert there on January 7, 1838. It enjoyed enormous popularity in that city.

No. 2, Caprice à la Boléro

The opening section of the Caprice has a repeated rhythmic pattern suggesting an instrumental accompaniment to the dance. But the composer soon introduces duple meter within the triple meter and syncopations that offer welcome rhythmic contrast. The middle section (from measure 110) is flowing and lyrical; the sustained melody and shifting metric patterns suggest the rhythmic inventiveness so evident in Robert Schumann's *Davidsbündlertänze* (1837).

No. 3, Romance

There has been considerable confusion over the wistful, melancholy Romance in B Major, marked "Andante con sentimento." An autograph copy in the Gesellschaft der Musikfreunde inscribed "Wien, 1838," led two modern editors to believe it was a newly discovered work of Clara Schumann, and it was published, by one editor in 1977 and by the other in 1979, as "Andante con sentimento."[25] Evidently neither knew of the existence of op. 5, no. 3, published well before 1838.

No. 4, Scène fantastique: Le Ballet des revenants

Because motifs from this piece figure in the first movement of Robert Schumann's great F-sharp Minor Sonata, dedicated to Clara, it is perhaps the best-known piece in op. 5. The "Scène fantastique" opens with a rocking motif using diminished fifths (Example 11). Schumann used this motif

Example 11. Clara Wieck, *Quatre Pièces caractéristiques*, op. 5, no. 4, "Scène fantastique."

throughout the first movement of his sonata but altered it to perfect fifths. Although the second motif in Clara's "Scène fantastique" (Example 12) bears

Example 12. Clara Wieck, *Quatre Pièces caractéristiques*, op. 5, no. 4, "Scène fantastique," measures 44–47.

a great resemblance to a fandango theme in Schumann's sonata, this motif seems clearly to have originated with Robert Schumann.[26] There is no question, however, that in combining the two figures (Example 13), Schumann

Example 13. Robert Schumann, Sonata in F-sharp Minor, op. 11, first movement, "Allegro vivace."

was complimenting the young composer he loved. In a letter to Clara, Schumann wrote that the sonata "was a cry from my heart to yours in which your theme appears in every possible form."[27]

Op. 6, *Soirées musicales contenant toccatina, ballade,*
nocturne, polonaise, et deux mazurkas pour le pianoforte

Like op. 5, with which it is often grouped, op. 6 consists of character pieces in the "new romantic" tradition. Five of the miniatures in op. 6—a ballade, nocturne, polonaise, and two mazurkas—are reminiscent of Chopin and the musicians who influenced his work, John Field and Johann Hummel. Another influence, rarely mentioned, may have been the Polish composer Marie Szymanowska (1790–1832), whose polonaises and mazurkas were published in Leipzig and who performed in that city in 1823.

In a poetic and enthusiastic review in the *Neue Zeitschrift* on September 12, 1837, Schumann described Clara's op. 6 as "like the buds before the wings of color are exploded into open splendor, captivating and significant to view, like all things that contain the future within themselves."[28] Two musical ideas from this work were incorporated into his oeuvre. The first, a melody hinted at in the Toccatina, appears in the Notturno and resembles the melody in Schumann's *Novellette* no. 8, labeled "Stimme aus der Ferne" (Voice from Afar) (Examples 14–15). The second, the buoyant, surging

Example 14. Clara Wieck, *Soirées musicales,* op. 6, no. 2, "Notturno," measures 3–10.

Example 15. Robert Schumann, *Novelletten,* op. 21, no. 8, "Stimme aus der Ferne."

theme of the Mazurka in G Major (Example 16), is the "Motto von C. W."

Example 16. Clara Wieck, *Soirées musicales,* op. 6, no. 5, "Mazurka."

(motto by Clara Wieck) that begins Schumann's *Davidsbündlertänze* (Example 17).

Example 17. Robert Schumann, *Davidsbündlertänze,* op. 6.

Op. 7, *Premier Concerto pour le pianoforte avec accompagnement d'orchestre (ou de quintuor)*

The concerto that Clara began in January 1833, when she was fourteen years old, was first conceived as a *Concertsatz,* a one-movement work for piano and orchestra. This work eventually became the third movement, Allegro non troppo, of the concerto. Schumann scholars have not been aware of Robert Schumann's close involvement with this work. Clara's diary and a score in Schumann's hand in the Deutsche Staatsbibliothek, East Berlin, tell the story: On November 22, 1833, Clara noted in her diary, "I have finished my concerto and Schumann will orchestrate it now so that I can play it at my concert." And on the first page of the extant score is written, in Schumann's hand, "Concertsatz by Clara, my instrumentation."* The manuscript contains many erasures and alterations, but the major ideas for the instrumentation have been retained. Whether Schumann orchestrated the other movements is not known; no other manuscripts or references to his participation have been found.

Entries in the diaries and surviving concert programs reveal that Clara performed the *Concertsatz* in Leipzig on May 5, 1834. The complete concerto was premiered at the Gewandhaus under Mendelssohn's direction on November 9, 1835.[29]

The Concerto is a remarkable achievement for a fourteen-year-old. Many of its stylistic features are typical of the concertos of such contemporaries as Kalkbrenner and Herz, those fashionable composers whose efforts Schumann so cleverly derided in his journal.[30] But Clara also offers some innovative ideas, perhaps inspired by Mendelssohn's G Minor Concerto, written a few years earlier and performed in Leipzig by the composer on October 29, 1835. Clara's concerto, like Mendelssohn's has no pauses between movements or cadenzas in the traditional classical style. Unlike Mendelssohn, however, Clara was not greatly concerned about the conventional inner structure of the first movement: the development section leads directly to a coda that serves as a transition to the second movement.

In the second movement, a simple "Romanze" with a graceful, tender melody, a solo cello is featured in a duet with the piano, a touch foreshadowing prominent cello parts in the Intermezzo movement of Robert Schumann's Piano Concerto (1845) and later, interestingly enough, a solo cello in the Andante of Brahms's Second Piano Concerto (1882).

In the first two movements of Clara's concerto, the orchestra functions mainly as a support; there is little interplay between the soloist and the instrumental groups. In the third movement, however, the orchestra plays a more significant part: tympani rolls beginning in the closing measures of the second movement are repeated just before the brass fanfares that open the third movement. They herald the piano, which enters with a lively rhythmic figure; later in the movement, dialogues develop between the lower and upper instrumental groups and between piano and woodwinds.

Up until the Concerto, Clara had written only miniatures. Though continuous growth can be observed throughout her oeuvre from op. 1 on, the boldness and maturity of this work are unexpected; the listener is taken aback by the sweep of Clara Wieck's conception in this concerto and the skillful manner in which she now handles material on a large scale. The

---

*The score of the last movement (Bds Mus. Aut. 20427) is dated 1836 in Schumann's hand. This date is obviously incorrect; it may have been the year in which he wrote the inscription. That the first movement was written *after* the third is clear from the diary entry of November 9, 1835, which records: "my concerto, whose first movement was just completed."

discovery of Robert Schumann's contribution does not lessen the importance of Clara's op. 7.

Op. 8, *Variations de concert pour
le pianoforte sur la "Cavatine du Pirate" de Bellini*

Staples of the repertory for the pianist-composers of Clara's day were works based on themes from operas by Bellini, Rossini, Donizetti, and other popular Italian composers, variously titled "Impromptu," "Fantasia," "Variations," "Reminiscences." Their function was clear and their impact predictable.[31] Clara's op. 8 was a piano work in this category. Dedicated to Adolph von Henselt, the composer-pianist whose popular works were often featured on Clara's concert tours, the Variations on Bellini's *Il Pirata* (an opera Clara saw in 1832) were played frequently on Clara's 1837 tour to northern Germany and in Vienna during 1837–38. Her op. 8 was published by the Viennese firm of Haslinger after her triumphant Viennese season.

The Variations were written during the months of Schumann's diatribes against the virtuosos and their "bungling, mediocre" variations on "vulgar" and "hackneyed" Italian themes, in contradistinction, Schumann wrote, to "good, boring German tunes."[32] Like Clara's *Romance variée*, this work contains many clichés: a grandiose introduction, diminished seventh chords, spectacular keyboard leaps, recurring thirds, sixths, and octaves, and a coda in which one brilliant coup succeeds another—running scale passages in sixteenth notes, ascending arpeggios, thundering bass rolls, and a spectacular closing section marked "Fortissimo" and "Presto."

Gasparo Spontini, the popular Italian composer and kapellmeister in Berlin in 1837, is reported by Wieck to have praised Clara's Variations as a grand and beautiful bravura work.[33]

Op. 9, *Souvenir de Vienne; Impromptu
pour le pianoforte*

Clara played the *Souvenir* for the first time on April 30, 1838, in Graz, where, Wieck wrote in her diary, it created a "furor." The work was published shortly thereafter by the Viennese publisher Diabelli.

In the same tradition as Clara's op. 8, the *Souvenir* is a bravura work based on a good (but presumably not boring) German tune, Haydn's "Emperor" hymn. The work, in a free variation style, opens with an Adagio quasi fantasia, moves to an embellished presentation of Haydn's theme, and then proceeds to an exhibitionistic display à la Thalberg. The Impromptu, a tribute to the Vienna that had taken Clara up so warmly, was a showcase for the accomplished young pianist, who had just been named Royal and Imperial Virtuosa to the court of the Austrian emperor.

Op. 10, *Scherzo pour le pianoforte*

The independent spirit with which Clara, defying her father, prepared to go to Paris without him is evident in the Scherzo. It remains a display piece but without the showy, ostentatious features of op. 8 and 9.

The Scherzo is an extended work with two contrasting trios. It was a great success in Paris. Writing about the piece to Robert, Clara expressed surprise that it was so popular: "everyone likes my Scherzo so much; I always have to repeat it."* This remark may have been meant as a mild rebuke to Robert; it was followed immediately by a request that he compose something brilliant.[34] The work was published by Breitkopf & Härtel in 1838 and was reprinted many times.

Op. 11, *Trois Romances pour le piano*

The Romances were composed in Paris in 1839 and occasioned some excited correspondence between there and Vienna, where Robert was living. Schumann probably arranged for its publication by Mechetti in Vienna, where it appeared in the fall of 1839. The second Romance was published separately, in a supplement to the *Neue Zeitschrift* in September 1839, where it appeared as "Andante und Allegro"; it was reprinted in the 1860s by Schuberth & Co. in Leipzig.

The three miniatures, each in ternary form, are in E-flat minor, G minor, and A-flat major. The first, though probably written last, functions as a prelude to the other two. It is a slight work with much piano figuration. The second Romance found complete favor in Schumann's eyes. Clara described this piece as "the little melancholy romance," and she added, "I was thinking of you continually throughout its creation." She sent it to him on July 2 with the admonition: "You must play it very freely—at times passionately and then again in a melancholy way. I like it very much; please return it right away and don't be afraid to find fault with it. That can only be useful to me."[35]

Schumann could find nothing to criticize and answered on July 10:

> In your Romance I can hear again that we are destined to be man and wife. You complete me as a composer just as I do you. Each of your thoughts comes from my very soul; indeed, it is you I have to thank for all my music. There is nothing to change in the Romance; it must remain exactly as it is.[36]

One scholar has speculated that the opening of Clara's Romance inspired the "innere Stimme" (inner voice) in Schumann's *Humoreske*. Others have pointed to the similarities between measures 53–54 of the Romance and

---

* "Everyone," that is, but Berlioz; see p. 90. The review of the music which appeared in *Iris*, 10 (October 4, 1839), 159, was not altogether favorable either.

measures 667–68 of *Humoreske*.[37] The exact points of identification are less significant than Schumann's reaction. His emotional response to her Romance confirms, as Hans Joachim Köhler puts it, "Schumann's struggle toward an inner identity with Clara."[38]

Op. 14, *Deuxième Scherzo pour le pianoforte*

The second Scherzo for Piano was probably composed sometime in 1844. On January 9, 1845, Robert Schumann wrote to Breitkopf & Härtel informing them that his wife had just completed writing a scherzo, four short pieces (op. 15), and an impromptu.* He evidently hoped that an inquiry from the publisher about her new works would spur his wife on to completion. The ruse was effective. The Scherzo was published soon after the letter was written.

The Scherzo begins with a stormy figured passage in C minor, resembling the piano accompaniment to "Er ist gekommen," a song Clara composed in 1840. The material is developed into a glittering display piece. The chordal middle section, marked "un poco più tranquillo," has a brief reference to Schumann's song "Aus alten Märchen" from *Dichterliebe*, 1840.

Op. 15, *Quatre Pièces fugitives pour le pianoforte*

The Four Short Pieces for Piano, published at the same time as op. 14, are unrelated works composed over a period of several years, almost certainly all after Clara's marriage. Op. 15 is dedicated to her half sister, Marie Wieck, then about thirteen years old and beginning a concert career. The first three *Pièces fugitives* are character pieces in a style similar to that of the Romances op. 11. The extant autograph of the fourth piece, an elfin-like Scherzo, shows that it is identical with the scherzo movement of an unpublished sonatina presented to Robert Schumann for Christmas 1841.[39]

Op. 16, *Drei Praeludien und Fugen für das pianoforte*

In January 1845 Robert Schumann noted in his household book that he and Clara were moving ahead industriously with their fugue studies. As usual, Clara saw her work as subordinate to her husband's. In her diary she wrote:

> Today we began contrapuntal studies that gave me much pleasure, despite all the trouble, because I soon saw what I had not believed possible—I wrote a fugue and then several more since we are continuing the studies on a daily basis. I cannot thank Robert enough for his patience with me and am doubly happy when something is successful since he can view it as his work as well. He himself is in the midst of a fugue passion.[40]†

---

*See Jansen, 440.
†Schumann himself referred to his *Fugenpassion* (*Hb*, 381).

Schumann's "fugue passion" led to his canonic studies and fugues, op. 56, 60, and 72. Clara's interest in fugue never became a "passion" but she did continue her studies up to March 10, the day before the birth of Julie. There was a temporary cessation after the birth, but on April 7, the day before Julie's christening, mother and father resumed their studies.[41] Fair copies of several dated autographs of Clara's preludes and fugues are in the archives of Robert-Schumann-Haus.[42] The dates are testimony to the diligence of the young mother soon to give birth to her third child. She composed three four-voiced fugues based on Bach subjects on February 11, 17, and 22, 1845, and three more based on subjects by Robert Schumann on March 1 and 2, a week before Julie's birth. Without Clara's knowledge, Robert chose the last three fugues for publication and wrote to Breitkopf & Härtel on August 17:

> I would like to surprise my wife with the Preludes and Fugues for her birthday on September 13. Would it be possible to complete the volume for that occasion? If it is indeed possible, then I beg you not to send the last final proofs directly to me, but to send them to my father-in-law, so that my wife will not learn of it.[43]

Schumann took great pride in Clara's preludes and fugues. In an earlier letter to C. F. Peters, he pointed out that this may have been the first time a woman artist attempted this "difficult genre."[44] It is possible that Schumann chose to have them published as a gesture of respect and encouragement to his wife, and indeed, within a few months she began her greatest work, the Trio for Piano, Violin, and Cello.

Op. 17, *Trio für Pianoforte, Violine, und Violoncello*

The Trio was composed in Dresden during a difficult period in Clara's life. She began work on it in May 1846 and completed it on the eve of her birthday, in September 1846. Though chamber music was a genre familiar to her, she had never before attempted to compose for any combination other than voice and piano. Soon after her marriage, she and her husband had studied together the chamber music of Haydn, Mozart, and Beethoven. She had often played the chamber music of the classical masters. As early as November 1834 she had performed the Beethoven Trio op. 97—at the time, a startling choice for a young pianist.[45] Robert Schumann's Quintet, dedicated to her, became the cornerstone of her repertoire almost immediately after its composition in 1842. Schumann had composed other works for chamber groups—string quartets (1842) and the Piano Quartet (1842)—but when she set out to write her Trio for Piano, Violin, and Cello, Schumann had not yet published a full-fledged work for that particular combination. Some months after Clara completed her Trio, Schumann noted in his household book, "Thoughts about a trio."[46] Entries on the days following show that he worked on his first trio (op. 63, in D minor) at his usual frenzied pace and had it performed on September 13, 1847, just at the time her work appeared in print. The expertise and quality of his D Minor Trio shook Clara's confidence in her own work, yet Schumann—and many other musicians—respected and admired it. It was often paired with Schumann's first trio in concerts during his lifetime and was the Clara Schumann work most frequently performed during the nineteenth century.

The Trio is Clara Schumann's only published work in four-movement sonata form. The movements are (1) Allegro moderato, (2) Scherzo (Tempo di menuetto), (3) Andante, and (4) Allegretto. The fugato that so impressed Mendelssohn is heard in the development section of the final movement.

Never before and never again did Clara Schumann attempt to carry out her musical ideas on such a large scale. Especially impressive is the fact that she was able to rise to these creative heights a few months after the birth of her fourth child, Emil, and during a period when both she and her husband were ill and depressed. The Trio was completed during the hectic summer when the Schumanns traveled to Norderney in an effort to divert and cure Robert and Clara suffered a miscarriage. It is possible that the creative activity served as a welcome outlet and relief during this period of extraordinary tension and pressure.

That the Trio was her own work (some critics have expressed doubt that she could have produced such a skilled work and assume her husband had a hand in it) is indisputable. Robert's household books document all of his activities during this period in obsessive detail. We know also that Clara had the talent, education, and experience to write this work; her individual mark is heard in every movement. Moreover, the one surviving autograph, a draft with alterations, reinstrumentation, crossouts, and other emendations, shows Clara at work.[47] Robert's participation is seen on the carefully written title page and in some penciled notes and directions that indicate that he may have made suggestions. These, however, seem to be his only contribution.

Though Clara Schumann, with her characteristic self-abnegation, described her trio as "effeminate and sentimental," the work does not belong in that category. In a forthright and vigorous musical statement, the composer laid out her plans, carried them out with skill and ingenuity, and produced an eminently playable and delightful work.

In the list of Clara Schumann's compositions published in Berthold Litzmann's biography there is a gap between op. 17 and op. 20. Litzmann speculates that op. 18 may have been meant for the "Andante und Allegro" published by Schuberth in the 1860s and op. 19 for the song "Am Strande" (also printed as "Am Strand") published by Schuberth about the same time. Litzmann may not have known of the relationship between op. 11 and the Schuberth publications. As noted above, the "Andante und Allegro" is actually the second Romance, op. 11, no. 2, published by Mechetti, reprinted by Schumann in the *Neue Zeitschrift*, and after Schumann's death published as an independent piece by Schuberth. While it is conceivable that the song—which has no opus number—was meant to be op. 19, it is more likely that Clara was holding these opus numbers open for more extended works, such as her unfinished sonata (1840), her unfinished concerto (1847), or three unpublished choral works on texts by Emanuel Geibel (see Appendix).

Op. 20, *Variationen für das Pianoforte über ein Thema von Robert Schumann*

Op. 20 is one of the works written in May and June 1853, Clara Schumann's final creative period. She presented the autograph to her husband on the last birthday he was to spend with his family. The Variations for Piano on a Theme by Robert Schumann, dedicated to Robert ("to HIM"), were not published until the fall of 1854, when Schumann was in Endenich.

By the time arrangements had been made for publication with Breitkopf & Härtel, Brahms had arrived in Düsseldorf and, undoubtedly inspired by Clara's example, begun *his* variations on the same Schumann theme. His work, conceived as a tribute to both Schumanns, was sent to Clara shortly after the birth of Felix, on June 11, 1854. In a graceful play on her dedication, Brahms wrote on his manuscript that his op. 9 was on "a theme by HIM" and "dedicated to HER."[48]

Both Clara Schumann and Johannes Brahms wove into their Schumann Variations the theme from Clara's childhood Romance, op. 3. (Clara may have followed Brahms's lead, adding her version of the op. 3 theme after she heard Brahms's op. 9.)* For Clara, the quotation may have recalled the glowing days of her childhood; for Brahms, it was a musical tribute to the two Schumanns. On September 25, 1854, Brahms wrote to Breitkopf & Härtel, who had accepted his work, requesting that his variations appear simultaneously with those of Frau Schumann. The proofs of her work were enclosed with his letter.[49]

Op. 21, *Drei Romanzen für das Pianoforte*

In June 1853 Clara Schumann composed four romances for piano. She presented the first, in A minor, to her husband, on his birthday, June 8;[50] manuscripts of the second, in F major, and the third, in G minor, are dated June 25 and 27. The autograph of a fourth romance, in A minor, now in the Deutsche Staatsbibliothek, Berlin, composed on June 23 for her blind friend, Rosalie Leser, remains unpublished.[51]† By the time negotiations for

*Janina Klassen (August 15, 1984) has pointed out that neither the Zwickau autograph, dated June 1853, nor the Vienna autograph, dated July 1854, includes the musical reference to Clara's op. 3. It seems likely that Clara added it just before the manuscript went to the publisher.

†The Romance presented in Clara Schumann, *Drei kleine Klavierstücke*, ed. Rosario Marciano (Vienna: Doblinger, 1979), was not written in 1855, as Marciano asserts, but is in fact op. 21, no. 1.

the publication of the Three Romances were completed, Brahms had become a close and trusted friend and the works were dedicated to him.[52]

Op. 22, *Drei Romanzen für Pianoforte und Violine*

The Three Romances for Piano and Violin, Clara Schumann's only works for this combination, were composed in July 1853, the last music of her final creative period. Conceived for and dedicated to Joseph Joachim, these lyrical character pieces were presented to the young violinist who was to become a devoted friend in October 1853.[53] Published about the same time as her op. 21, they quickly won favor with the audiences of the day. A few years later, Joachim, then engaged at the Hannover court, reported to Clara that the king was in total "ecstasy" over the Romances and could "hardly wait" to enjoy such "marvelous, heavenly pleasure again."[54]

Songs

Fifteen songs by Clara Schumann have been published and autographs of some ten other unpublished works in this genre are extant in Robert-Schumann-Haus, Zwickau, and in the Deutsche Staatsbibliothek, East Berlin. The first group of published songs was composed in 1841 and the last in 1853. Again, as in the instrumental works, we are struck by the continuing personal cooperation and interchange of musical ideas between husband and wife.

The poets of Clara Schumann's published songs are Heinrich Heine, Friedrich Rückert, Emanuel Geibel (all poets whose texts were favorites of Robert Schumann), and one relatively unknown poet, Hermann Rollet. Both Clara and Robert read poetry with an eye toward possible settings, and each brought poems to the attention of the other. We know that Robert enlisted Clara's aid in finding song materials for him. In May 1840, for example, at the height of his "song fever," he requested, "Write to me often. And bring me poems to set to music."[55]

A notebook in the Zwickau archives labeled, in Clara's hand, "Abschriften verschiedener Gedichten zur Composition" (Copies of various poems for composition), includes poetry written out by both husband and wife.[56] That Clara was involved in this activity even before her marriage is clear from the section of the book labeled "Gesammelt von Robert und Clara Schumann vom Jahre 1839 an" (Collected by Robert and Clara Schumann from 1839 on). Many of the texts she herself used can be found in this notebook; some were copied by Robert Schumann, and conversely, many of the texts he used are in her hand. Others, not copied into this collection, were evidently in the Schumann family library.

Sometime in 1843, Clara made fair copies of all the songs she had written since her marriage and assembled them in a music manuscript notebook that is in the Deutsche Staatsbibliothek today.[57] Robert, a great believer in systematic organization, wrote in their diary on June 28, 1843, "Clara is now setting her songs and several piano pieces in order." Clara copied and dated the songs and noted the poets, but her husband wrote the title page, "Lieder mit Begleitung des Pianofortes [Songs with piano accompaniment] von Klara Schumann, 1842," and listed the contents. She evidently planned to include only songs written between 1840 and 1843, but others were added, and the notebook eventually included all the songs she composed between 1840 and 1853. Thus an authoritative record of the songs she thought worthy of preserving survives.

Clara Schumann, the wife of one of the greatest song writers of all time, was a distinguished musician but not a gifted melodist. This weakness is evident in the instrumental works as well, but here skillful handling of other elements—rhythm, structure, and idiomatic writing for the piano—compensates for the lack of memorable melodies. In the songs, however, this is a major shortcoming. The songs of op. 12 and 13 are often sentimentalized by chromatic passing notes in voice and piano. Yet several of her songs rise above these problems; the best of them—"Er ist gekommen," "Sie liebten sich beide," "Die stille Lotosblume"—are moving. "Am Strande," first performed at the concert of March 31, 1841, when Schumann's *Spring* Symphony was premiered, is another unforgettable song.

Her piano accompaniments are elaborate, as one might expect from a pianist, but do not overpower the voice. In "Er ist gekommen" and "Geheimes Flüstern," for example, the piano parts are particularly effective: by creating a setting and mood or delineating a character or emotion, they work with voice and text to produce a memorable experience. Three of Clara Schumann's songs, "Warum willst du and're fragen," "Ich hab' in deinem Auge," and "Geheimes Flüstern," were transcribed for piano by Franz Liszt. (In view of her feelings about Liszt, the compliment may not have pleased her.)[58]

Unlike her husband, Clara never set ballads, epic poetry, or folk verses to music; she chose poems of two to three stanzas on such subjects as love, rejection, springtime, and nature and set them in a strophic or modified strophic form.

Op. 12, *Zwölf Gedichte aus F. Rückert's "Liebesfrühling"* *für Gesang und Pianoforte von Robert und Clara Schumann*

The three songs by Clara Schumann published with nine by Robert Schumann as Schumann's op. 37 were not the first Clara had written, as we know. Clara's Christmas gift to her husband in 1840 was three songs, "Am Strand," "Ich stand in dunkeln Träumen," and "Volkslied." In April he wrote to Friedrich Kistner, the music publisher, "My wife has composed some very interesting songs, which have inspired me to compose a few more from Rückert's *Liebesfrühling*. Together they form a very nice whole, which we should like to publish in *one* book." (The suggestion was premature. Clara had not yet actually composed the songs that eventually went into this group.) The letter continued, "As I should like to give my wife a surprise, I should prefer to keep the matter private for the present."[59]

Clara presented four songs to Robert on his thirty-first birthday, and they chose three for the joint publication. The songs were sold to Breitkopf & Härtel (not Kistner), and Clara received the first printed copy on her birthday in 1841, just thirteen days after the birth of her first child. The title page of the collection, which lists them as op. 37/12, gives no inkling as to the authorship of each song, and reviewers were confused—probably to Schumann's amusement. He identified Clara's songs on the flyleaf of his copy of the first edition, and the extant autograph manuscripts in Zwickau and Berlin confirm her authorship of no. 2, "Er ist gekommen"; no. 4, "Liebst du um Schönheit?" and no. 11, "Warum willst du and're fragen?" in Schumann's op. 37.

Op. 13, *Sechs Lieder mit Begleitung des Pianoforte*

Op. 13 was an independent publication, but it is clear that the composer's husband urged and encouraged her in this effort, as in all her others. The songs set to texts by Emanuel Geibel, Heinrich Heine, and Friedrich Rückert and composed for various occasions between Christmas 1840 and the summer of 1843, were gathered together and published in 1843 by Breitkopf & Härtel. The dedication to Denmark's queen Caroline Amalie probably reflected the composer's appreciation of the warm hospitality extended to her on her visit to Copenhagen in 1842. Of the six songs, "Die stille Lotosblume," with its rhythmic irregularities, poignant melody, and unresolved ending, is most memorable.

Op. 23, *Sechs Lieder aus "Jucunde" von Hermann Rollet*

The six songs in op. 23, dedicated to Clara's old friend Livia Frege, are set to texts by Hermann Rollet, a little-known Austrian poet, whose *Jucunde* Robert Schumann was reading in January 1853. His comment that the verses were "very musical"[60] may have aroused her interest; in any event, she chose six of them for song settings.* Op. 23 is not a song cycle in any sense of the word; the songs are grouped together because they were composed at the same time and set to the work of one poet.

---

*One of the last letters Schumann wrote before his hospitalization was to Rollet, who evidently believed that it was Robert Schumann that had set his poems to music. Schumann assured him that it was his wife that had composed the six songs from *Jucunde* and added that they were songs "that I would like very much even if they were not by my wife" (Robert Schumann to Hermann Rollet, February 7, 1854, Schumannhaus, Bonn).

Though the texts are simple and rather sentimental, the settings are not. The piano and vocal lines in op. 23 show greater independence and the accompaniments have greater rhythmic variety and flexibility than those of the earlier songs. Several songs, notably "Was weinst du, Blümlein" and "Das ist ein Tag," display a playfulness, even a joyousness, rarely found in the music of Clara Schumann. These songs should be better known.

MISCELLANEOUS WORKS

Several of Clara Schumann's works without opus numbers, some published, some not, have survived. Her cadenzas for Beethoven's Piano Concertos no. 1 and no. 4 are well known; the cadenzas for Mozart's D Minor Concerto, K. 466, have been discussed in connection with Brahms.*

A sonatine for piano, her Christmas present to Robert Schumann in 1841;[61] three works for mixed chorus on texts by Geibel, written for Robert's birthday in 1848 and rehearsed and sung by the chorus he was directing in Dresden at the time;[62] an incomplete concerto movement, her birthday gift to her husband in 1847,[63] and a number of songs all await publication.

A Romanze in B Minor, part of the Brahms legacy in the Gesellschaft der Musikfreunde in Vienna and not published until the 1970s,[64] may have been the Romanze she wrote for Brahms's birthday in 1855 (although it is inscribed "Christmas 1855"). In her diary she noted that she had composed a work for Brahms on April 2, 1855, when he was visiting her husband in Endenich. She described it as having a sad mood and added, "I was so sad when I wrote it."[65]

The appearance in 1885 of a solo piano work, an *Impromptu*, in a French collection, *Album du Gaulois*, was evidently a pleasant surprise for the composer.[66] The *Impromptu* was composed many years earlier. It may have been the work mentioned by Robert Schumann in the January 1845 letter to Breitkopf & Härtel.

EDITED WORKS

On June 6, 1851, Robert Schumann wrote a document that clearly set forth his wishes regarding his unpublished works:

> Since we are all of us mortal, I would like to direct that decisions about my remaining publications be made by Gade or—if he is unable to do so—by J. Rietz;† this should be done, naturally, with the agreement and understanding of my dear Clara, and after the most severe critical examination.[67]

---

*See p. 202.

†Niels Gade, a Danish composer, succeeded Mendelssohn as conductor at the Gewandhaus: Julius Rietz, a cellist, composer, and conductor active in Düsseldorf, Leipzig, and Dresden, edited Mendelssohn's collected works and works by Bach, Mozart, and Beethoven.

Despite the clearly written request, Clara turned neither to Gade nor to Rietz after Schumann's death. In regard to those unpublished works that survived, she consulted with Brahms and Joachim, the two young musicians to whom her husband was closest at the time he was hospitalized. And although she discussed every detail with them ("There is no one in whom I have the confidence that I have in you [two]," she wrote in 1860),[68] she ultimately assumed full responsibility for all decisions about Schumann editions.

After she died, and despite all efforts by her daughters, her wishes were ignored by zealous editors who vied with each other to publish any available works by Schumann. While she was able, however, she made decisions about publication of such late Schumann works as the 1853 piano accompaniments for the Bach cello sonatas (never published), the Mass (published in 1862), and the Requiem (published in 1864). Just as she had feared, many of the works whose publication she had opposed appeared in the twentieth century: the two Schumann movements of the *FAE* Sonata,* for example, were published in 1935, and the variations for the theme he wrote in February 1854 appeared in 1941. The Violin Concerto remained unpublished until 1937, and was issued against the expressed desire of Eugenie Schumann, the sole surviving Schumann child. In an article in which she protested its publication, she wrote:

> Never shall I forget the moment in our home at Frankfurt am Main when my mother came in to see us and said with deep but suppressed emotion visible on her face, "I have just settled with Joachim and Johannes that the Concerto is not to be published, now or at any other time. We are quite agreed on the subject."[69]

Clara Schumann was always uneasy about the works of Schumann's last years, fearing that the music was weaker and showed signs of the mental confusion he suffered.†

On January 27, 1860, she wrote to Julius Schuberth about her decision not to publish the piano accompaniments for the Paganini Caprices which Schumann had written in 1853: "My husband is too dear to me to permit me to have something of his published which is trivial."[70] And from the household books we learn that she kept five romances composed in November 1853 out of sight and destroyed them in 1893 because she feared they might be published after her death.[71]

Brahms and Joachim were aware of her anxiety over the late works; indeed, they shared it. She asked them to look at the unpublished Requiem

---

*A sonata written in 1853 by Schumann, Brahms, and Albert Dietrich for Joachim, whose motto was "*Frei aber einsam*" (free but lonely).

†She remained sensitive about his last illness. In 1877 she wrote to Brahms that she was alarmed because Edward Hanslick, who had requested copies of Schumann's letters from Endenich, seemed to be interested in writing only about Schumann's "sick years" (*Schumann: Brahms Briefe,* 2:90–91).

and Mass and advise her about publication. In August 1860 Brahms responded that since these two works had been composed in 1852 and prepared for publication by Schumann himself, he and Joachim believed they had no right to withhold them even if they did not meet the standard set by earlier works. Some eleven months after receiving Brahms's letter, Clara went to Aachen to hear the Mass conducted by Franz Wüllner and was struck by the beauty of the work. She wrote Brahms that she no longer had any hesitation about its publication.[72] The work appeared in 1862.

All the decisions she made regarding Schumann's work—including the great critical *Werke* (Collected Works)—were made in conjunction with Brahms and other friends. The one Schumann edition that can truly be said to be hers was the so-called Instructive Edition, published in 1887.

Why did the widow not go to Gade or Rietz, as Schumann had requested? Why did she turn to the two "young demons"? In 1851, the year Schumann wrote the testament regarding his works, he had not yet met Brahms; Joachim he knew only as a young violinist, the student of their old Leipzig friend Ferdinand David. But the friendship, almost a kinship, which developed as soon as these musicians met was immediate. The younger men loved and respected Schumann, referring to him in such terms as "honored master," "respected friend," "sir," and "Mynheer Dominie." The two young men who stood at Clara's side in the worst days of the troubled autumn in Düsseldorf and throughout the Endenich years were not only loyal friends; they were certainly the most gifted musicians of their generation. There were other men to whom she could have turned—Hiller, Dietrich, Reinecke, Woldemar Bargiel, all musicians who admired Schumann and in whom she had confidence—but none, as she well knew, of the caliber of Joachim and Brahms.

The Collected Works of Robert Schumann, 1879–1893

In May 1877 Clara Schumann asked Brahms for his opinion about an offer she had received from Breitkopf & Härtel to edit a critical edition of all the Schumann works.[73] She was in a potentially embarrassing position, since she was on the verge of signing a contract with the English firm of Novello for an edition of the piano works. By this time, Brahms, no longer a shy and inexperienced composer, was able to suggest a graceful way out of the situation. She decided to go ahead with the *Collected Works*, however, only after she was assured of Brahms's active assistance with the project. On his advice and with his backing, she signed with Breitkopf & Härtel on favorable terms.

The letter in which she asked for his counsel was the first of hundreds they exchanged about the edition, and although Clara Schumann is officially listed as the editor of the thirty-one-part series,* it is clear it could not have

*The thirty-one parts are usually bound in fourteen volumes.

been completed without the patient, guiding hand of Johannes Brahms. Clara turned to him with questions ranging from the petty and trivial to the most significant; she made no move without him and sent him proofs of every work she edited. She begged him to take over the editing of the orchestral, choral, and ensemble works, as she did not feel confident about them and needed his help. She urged him to take half the money offered by Breitkopf & Härtel, but he refused, although he did eventually (and reluctantly) assume full responsibility for the supplementary volume (1893), in which his name and a brief preface appeared.[74]

A reading of the published Schumann-Brahms correspondence gives only a partial idea of Brahms's involvement, as Berthold Litzmann, the volume's editor, omitted many details, partly because of considerations of length and partly because of pressures from the Schumann family. But despite the precautions taken by Litzmann (and by Marie, who supervised his work), the correspondence does reveal the enormous tensions engendered by the edition. Several times, especially in 1891 and 1892, the long friendship almost foundered because of bitter disagreements over editions and versions of Schumann's works. On close examination, however, many of the arguments seem to be not necessarily products of musical disagreement but deflections of other anxieties. By 1892, Clara Schumann, old, forgetful, and weary, begged him to take over the supplementary volume, writing, "Please tell me I can count on your old friendship."[75]

From the beginning Brahms had urged her to consult with other friends (as he did in regard to his own works), and sooner or later she solicited advice from all the Schumannians in Germany: Joachim, Heinrich von Herzogenberg, Philipp Spitta, Hermann Levi, Julius Otto Grimm, Ernst Rudorff, Franz Wüllner. Other musicians were paid for their efforts but neither their names nor their contributions were mentioned in the pages of the edition. She made no secret of the participation of such young musicians as Ernst Franck, Woldemar Bargiel, and Alfred Volckland. It must have seemed clear to her, her friends, and her publishers that *The Collected Works of Robert Schumann* would have most authority if hers were the sole name to appear, and Breitkopf acted accordingly.

Frau Schumann's willingness to embark on such a great responsibility when she was already burdened with so many duties is hard to understand until one realizes her motivations. The money was no doubt alluring to this woman with a large family to support, but the greater attraction was what she perceived as her duty to her husband. Annoyed by the proliferation of new Schumann editions—particularly in England—which she felt had no validity, convinced (and rightly so) that no one knew Schumann and his music as she did, determined to protect him (as she had done in his lifetime) and put the stamp of authenticity on what she perceived as a project for at least a century, she set to work. Having spent so many years in the service of his music, she saw the edition as a logical extension of her life's work.

Clara Schumann's efforts on the *Collected Works* have been severely criticized by many modern scholars who consider them to be incomplete and inaccurate.[76] But her work must be seen in the context of her time and the special circumstances in which the edition was prepared. Standards of editing differed considerably from those of today. True, many of the critical editions published by Breitkopf & Härtel (the collected works of Beethoven, Mozart, Chopin, Schubert, Mendelssohn, Liszt, Wagner, and others) were edited by committees of musical scholars and included textual commentary, identification of sources, indexes, and other features of scholarly apparatus which confer credibility. But evidently Breitkopf & Härtel believed that the authority of Clara Schumann would be sufficient for the Robert Schumann edition (and a good selling point). As far as is known, she was never asked for, nor did she suggest, a critical commentary that might have given information on her sources or explained the rationale for her choices.

Clara Schumann chose to begin the *Collected Works* with the piano compositions. Conscientious and concerned, she followed the example of Schumann and the advice of Brahms,[77] requesting manuscripts that were no longer in her possession, examining carefully those autographs and proofs she retained, and consulting the first and second editions published during Schumann's lifetime.

She was well aware of Schumann's passion for good editions and studied the collection of his first editions which he had had bound and in which he had entered comments and alterations. There is no doubt that she knew of the letter he had written to Härtel on January 31, 1845, in which he proposed a "really good edition" of Bach's *Well-Tempered Clavier:* "My object is to obtain as *correct an edition as possible, based on the original manuscript and the oldest editions, and quoting the various readings. . . .*"[78]

She searched her memory for comments Schumann had made about her performances and interpretations of his works.* Particularly sensitive to charges that her tempos were too fast, she made a special effort to determine exactly what the tempos should be. She wrote Brahms that she labored for months, timing her own performances with the second hand of a watch and attempting to take an average, although Brahms had warned her that such painstaking work would not be appreciated. She finally gave it up, admitting he was right and declaring that the work was "torture."[79]

The changes Clara Schumann made in metronome markings have occasioned more discussion and indignation than other aspects of her edition.[80] (These alterations were actually not so significant as many others she made.) Apparently she was convinced that Schumann's metronome was faulty: as early as 1855, an announcement appeared in the *Neue Berliner Musik-*

---

*Some scholars have made much of the disagreements between husband and wife about interpretation and tempos. The Schumanns had their differences of opinion over the years, often expressed openly in the marriage diary, but the fact remains that Robert Schumann regarded his wife as the foremost interpreter of his music (see chap. 12).

zeitung informing the public, on Frau Schumann's authority, that Schumann's metronome was incorrect and that many of the indicated tempos were faster than he meant them to be.[81] In 1863 she wrote Julius Stockhausen that she found that metronomes varied greatly and he should not be too concerned about the markings, since "a musician like you will not blunder."[82] Brahms expressed similar thoughts more than once.[83] Although she had advanced the "faulty metronome" theory in 1855 and subsequently vacillated on the question of the importance of metronome markings, she retained—contrary to popular belief—most of Schumann's metronome markings in the *Collected Works*.*

The Instructive Edition, 1887

In the Instructive Edition,[84] often confused with the *Collected Works*, there is no question that Clara Schumann frankly expressed her own views. Many twentieth-century musicians view her decisions as arbitrary, but her contemporaries—and her publishers—expressed no indignation at the liberties she took. Indeed, she was encouraged on all sides to take on this task, and the edition, of course, sold widely in its original form and in the numerous revisions and editions based on it.

Breitkopf & Härtel proposed an instructive edition of Schumann's piano works in May 1882, while Clara was still laboring on the *Collected Works*. This was the age of annotated editions of the classics, complete with analyses. Hans von Bülow was preparing volume after volume of works by Bach, Beethoven, Scarlatti, Mendelssohn, Schubert, Chopin, and Cramer (150,000 copies of this minor master's work alone were sold, according to one publisher, Universal of Vienna). These heavily annotated, didactic editions, "as played by von Bülow in his concerts," directed the pianist's attention to every detail of performance: fingering, phrasing, tempos, accents, pedaling, embellishments, dynamics, voicing, emphasis. Bülow left nothing to the imagination of the performer; he altered the text freely, usually without acknowledgment. Clara Schumann disliked Bülow's editions,[85] and fearing that he or someone else might attempt something similar with Schumann's piano works, she agreed—after consultation with Brahms—to edit an instructive edition for Breitkopf & Härtel. She wrote in her diary, "It is clear to me that I must do it, so that at least one correct edition will be available for students."[86]

And so once more, and during the same year she and Brahms were correcting the last proofs of the *Complete Works*, she undertook a major edi-

---

*Dietrich Kämper compared 32 Schumann first editions with the same works in the *Gesamtausgabe* and concluded that in the overwhelming majority of cases, Clara had remained true to the original metronome markings ("Zur Frage der Metronombezeichnungen Robert Schumanns," *AfMw*, 21 [1964], 145). Brian Schlotel came to the same conclusion ("Schumann and the Metronome," in *Robert Schumann: The Man and His Music*, ed. Alan Walker [London: Barrie & Jenkins, 1972], 111).

torial task. For the Instructive Edition she relied on the help of Marie, who had always acted as her assistant, and engaged in less frantic correspondence with Brahms and other friends. As a result, she left fewer records of how she arrived at her decisions.

The Instructive Edition differs from the *Collected Works*—and Schumann's early editions—in many ways: alterations in metronome markings and tempos (some faster, some slower);* the addition of tempo and expressive markings (grazioso, tranquillo, a tempo, ritenuto, etc.), fingerings, additional dynamic indications (sometimes in parentheses to distinguish them from Schumann's), and a particularly large number of additional pedal markings; deletion of Schumann's dedications—in the first printings only—in the *Fantasie* op. 17 (to Liszt), the *Fantasiestücke*, op. 12 (to Robena Laidlaw), and the G Minor Sonata, op. 22 (to Henriette Voigt).† In later printings the dedications were restored, but other changes and errors made then reappear to this day.‡ In 1901 Marie Schumann asked the publisher to indicate which changes had been made by her mother, but by this time the scores had been so thoroughly amended that Breitkopf & Härtel could not distinguish between those made by Clara Schumann and those made by Carl Reinecke, who had been given the responsibility for the edition after Clara's death. [87]

There is no doubt that users of the Instructive Edition would have found a brief critical commentary useful, but like Bülow and other nineteenth-century editors of student editions, Clara Schumann chose not to explain her decisions, choices, or sources or to discuss Schumann's sometimes cryptic titles and mottos, all of which would have been particularly appropriate and helpful.

Other Editions and Editorial Work

Among the other editing responsibilities that Clara Schumann accepted were Czerny's *School of Fingering*, a manual she used throughout her teaching career. Although the book was issued under her name, it was actually prepared by Marie Schumann with the help of Brahms. Both Marie and Brahms were intrigued by the project; in August 1880, well before a contract

---

*Kämper, 148, points out that 59 percent of the metronome markings in the Instructive Edition agree with Schumann's own first editions and 41 percent depart from the original scores.

†Alan Walker, in "Schumann, Liszt, and the C Major Fantasie, Op. 17: A Declining Relationship," *ML*, April 1979, 156–65, states: "When the Fantasie was prepared for re-publication, Clara had no hesitation in striking out the dedication to Liszt and substituting her own name instead." The dedication to Liszt was omitted in the first printing of the Instructive Edition only and was later restored. I have not found Clara Schumann's name substituted for Liszt's in any of the printings I have examined, including the first printing in RSH.

‡Some riddles (perhaps merely misprints or misunderstandings) in the Instructive Edition remain puzzling: the dedication of op. 58 to Comtesse Abegg (pointed out to me by Edwin M. Good), for example, and discrepancies in dates of composition.

was signed, Clara Schumann reported to Brahms that Marie could not wait to get started and was already working on it.[88]

Other published arrangements, transcriptions, and editions by Clara Schumann include a four-hand arrangement of Schumann's Quintet, the piano-vocal score of *Genoveva*, thirty songs by Robert Schumann transcribed for piano, and—at the age of seventy-six—an arrangement for piano of some of the studies from Schumann's op. 56 and 58.[89]

As early as 1874, when an arm injury gave her the time to reread her husband's correspondence, she began to consider an edition of his letters.[90] It was not until May 1885, however, that she began to read, select, and edit the letters of Schumann's youth. With the help of Marie Schumann and their friend Heinrich von Herzogenberg, the task was completed within a few months. Unlike her editions of Schumann's music, the book included a preface (signed by Clara Schumann but actually written by Herzogenberg) which informed readers about omissions, deletions, changes, and sources.[91] Few composers had written with the imagination and grace of the young Schumann; the very popular *Jugendbriefe* appeared in four German printings and was translated almost immediately into English as *Early Letters*.[92] This project brought both sorrow and joy to its editor as she looked back on her own early years and the happiness for which the two young artists had hoped.

Many of the piano arrangements of Robert Schumann's music were prepared by Clara Schumann and published during his lifetime with his full approval. In undertaking the publication of his *Collected Works*, the Instructive Edition, and the *Jugendbriefe*, his wife and "creative partner" performed a heroic service and preserved Schumann's work in the best way possible at the time.

CHAPTER 12

The Concert Artist

Clara Schumann's life as a concert artist parallels the history of concert life in the nineteenth century. A study of her long and illustrious career, beginning with her debut at the Leipzig Gewandhaus in 1830 and closing with her last public performance in Frankfurt in 1891, gives us an intimate knowledge of programming traditions, repertoire, concert arrangements, customs in various cities, the child prodigy phenomenon, women in concert life, and changes in musical standards and taste. In each of these spheres Clara Schumann had a decisive influence.

Her lengthy career on the concert stage—over sixty years—may be divided into three parts: 1828 to 1840, the years in which she concertized as Clara Wieck, first as a local prodigy and then as an international celebrity; 1840 to 1854, the years of her marriage and childbearing, during which her concertizing was somewhat curtailed, but not nearly to the extent that popular literature would have us believe; and 1854 to 1891, the years after Robert Schumann's hospitalization and death, when she toured the British Isles and the Continent, hailed as one of the top pianists of the world while supporting and supervising a household and seven children. Her perseverance and stamina throughout the trials of these years are legendary. That she was able to study and premiere works and maintain her position and popularity despite many tragedies was due to her talent, determination, and discipline, and in no small part to her father's genius as a teacher and his obsession with her career; this debt she always acknowledged.

Her first program, arranged by her father, was typical of those given in the 1830s by virtuoso pianists in all the major cities of Europe. Inherited from the late eighteenth century was a tradition of a diversified concert that would appeal to the new middle-class audiences that paid for an evening of musical entertainment. Whether the concert was arranged by the soloist or an organization such as the Gewandhaus board of directors, the soloist shared the program and alternated with a group of "supporting" artists—singers, instrumentalists, perhaps a small ensemble. Occasionally a monologist or a theatrical troupe varied the fare. The soloist made all arrangements, received the proceeds of the ticket sales, and was responsible for hiring and paying the supporting artists.

In small cities, such programs were truly a hodgepodge of events, musical and nonmusical. In Altenburg, for example, on May 18, 1831, Clara Wieck shared a program with a Dr. Langenschwarz, an "improviser." Members of the audience submitted topics—historical, philosophical, epic—on which the doctor would speak. His share of the evening included an improvisation in honor of the ladies of Altenburg and closed with a recitation in comic Austrian dialect. Between Langenschwarz's numbers, Clara played a concerto by Pixis and her own Variations on a Theme by Bellini.

On her first appearance in Hamburg, March 28, 1835, she performed Moscheles' Concerto in E-flat Major and Herz's *Bravour* Variations between two comedies, *Der Secretair und der Koch* and *Richards Wanderleben*.[1] And as late as February 13, 1864, in such smaller towns as Mitau, her performance was flanked by two theatrical works.

The tradition of playing with assisting artists is said to have ended officially when Liszt gave what is now considered to be the first solo "recital," in London in 1840. Soon after, Clara Schumann began to experiment with this concept. She decided to dispense with the assistance of an orchestra and supporting artists on her Russian trip of 1844 simply because it was so difficult to arrange. She wrote to her father, "I gave all my concerts alone, without any supporting artists, something I shall always do from now on; it is the best way."[2] She was not able to break entirely with the tradition, however, because audiences expected to hear a variety of performers, and Clara, like her father, always kept the demands of the public in mind.

By the 1870s, her reputation was secure enough, particularly in England, to ensure the success of solo recitals. She continued to work with other artists, however, choosing ranking musicians who were friends and colleagues rather than "supporting" artists. This decision may have been dictated by considerations of health and increasing family needs. For Clara's responsibilities, unlike those of most other working women, did not lessen as her children grew up; their deaths and illnesses and her assumption of responsibility for Ferdinand's children took their toll of her health and stamina. She probably accepted the fact that sharing a program was the only way she could continue to concertize. And so she appeared regularly with such congenial colleagues as Joseph and Amalie Joachim, Brahms, and Julius Stockhausen. The performers alternated solo and ensemble works and closed the program by playing together; interestingly enough, they sometimes shared the platform throughout the concert. A critic for *Dwight's Journal* described Clara and Joachim chatting between numbers and listening attentively to each other.[3]

Almost to the end of the century, audiences demanded singers at every

259]

concert. Arias and lieder alternated with instrumental numbers. Schumann often resented the presence of singers, but because of public pressure for the "glamorous" vocalists, she was forced to continue the tradition. More than once (in Vienna in 1847, Hamburg in 1850, Ems in 1855) Jenny Lind, the universally admired "Swedish Nightingale," a loyal old friend, rescued her from financial failure when she programmed concerts of unpopular instrumental music.

Clara must have been taken aback by William Sterndale Bennett's warning in a letter dated January 26, 1855: "In England, they must always have so many expensive singers at concerts that they will not always give Pianistes as much as they deserve."[4] In her early years Clara accompanied all the singers herself; as her prestige grew, she was able to choose the singers (and the repertoire) to appear on her programs, and after 1860 she accompanied only vocalists of the stature of Julius Stockhausen and Amalie Joachim. Together with these singers, she gave some of the early performances of complete song cycles: Schubert's *Winterreise* and *Schöne Müllerin*, and Schumann's *Dichterliebe* and *Frauenliebe und Leben*. But even such works were interspersed with instrumental selections, a custom unthinkable today. On February 22, 1862, in Zurich, for example, three pieces from Schumann's *Kreisleriana* were performed between parts 1 and 2 of *Dichterliebe*. And in Hamburg on November 27, 1862, at a concert with Stockhausen in which, perhaps for the first time, *Die Winterreise* was performed in its entirety, the program was arranged as follows: I. Schumann, Piano Quintet; II. *Winterreise*, parts 1–4; III. Selections by Bach and Scarlatti; IV. *Winterreise*, parts 5–9; V. Mendelssohn, *Lieder ohne Worte*; VI. *Winterreise*, parts 10–13.

The tradition of using assisting artists in the early nineteenth century resulted in programs that were mixtures of many genres. A sonata or movements from one, variations on a theme (with applause after each variation), songs, a symphony, arias, declamations, instrumental and vocal duos were all thrown together like a musical variety show. By the middle of the century, Clara Schumann's programs show more integration. There was still a mixture of works on the orchestral programs in which she was an invited artist, but on her own programs of the 1850s and 1860s, works are grouped by composer and fewer genres were presented. By 1880, Schumann's programs were not only shorter—allowing for greater concentration on each work—but more homogeneous.

REPERTOIRE

Until 1839, when Clara went to Paris alone, her father was responsible for all her concert arrangements and repertoire. Her debut program in 1830, an *Extra-Concert* for which the Gewandhaus directorate presumably had to give special permission, included Kalkbrenner's *Rondo Brillant*, op. 101;

Kleiner Saal des Saalbaues zu Frankfurt a. M.

Donnerstag, den 12. März 1891, Abends 7 Uhr:

Dritter Kammermusik-Abend

des Frankfurter Trio's

(die Herren **James Kwast**, **Fritz Bassermann** u **Hugo Becker**)
unter freundlicher Mitwirkung der Frau **Clara Schumann** und
des Herrn **E. Welcker**.

PROGRAMM.

1. **Quartett** (G-moll) für Pianoforte, Violine,
   Viola und Violoncell. . . . . . . *W. A. Mozart.*
   a) Allegro.
   b) Andante.
   c) Rondo (Allegro).

2. **Variationen** für zwei Pianoforte über ein
   Thema v. J. Haydn, Op. 56, No. 6 (B-dur) *Joh. Brahms.*
   (Das Werk wurde ursprünglich für 2 Pianoforte
   componirt, und erst später instrumentirt.)

3. **Trio** für Pianoforte, Violine und Violoncell,
   Op. 70, No. 2 (Es-dur). . . . . . *L. v. Beethoven.*
   a) Poco sostenuto. — Allegro ma non troppo.
   b) Allegretto.
   c) Allegretto ma non troppo.
   d) Finale (Allegro).

Die Instrumente (von **Steinweg** und **Schiedmayer**) sind aus dem
Pianofortelager der Herren **L. Lichtenstein & Co.**, Zeil 69, Hier.

Einzelbillets à 3 Mark
den Musikalien-Handlungen der Herren C. A. André, B. Firnberg,
Schillerstr. 10, Th. Henkel und Steyl & Thomas, bei Herrn Richard Koch,
Gutleutstrasse 103, sowie Abends an der Kasse.

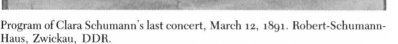

Program of Clara Schumann's last concert, March 12, 1891. Robert-Schumann-Haus, Zwickau, DDR.

Herz's *Variations Brillantes*, op. 23; a *Quatuor Concertant* for four pianos, op. 230, by Czerny; and Clara's own Variations on an Original Theme. Clara had her own supporting artists: Henriette Grabau, a regular singer at the Gewandhaus, and Heinrich Hammermeister, a court singer. The three Leipzig pianists who played with her in the Czerny quartet—all of them ten to twelve years older than she—were Heinrich Dorn, composer and director of the Leipzig opera; Julius Knorr, a writer and piano teacher; and Emil Wendler, a medical student and ardent musical amateur.

The Paris concerts of 1832 featured two overtures by Weber arranged for six pianos—four hands at each—and singers, guitarists, and a cellist. These concerts lasted three to four hours. At private soirees the twelve-year-old girl waited her turn in an anteroom while all the "acts" went on, sometimes until one or two o'clock in the morning.

None of the works played were pieces that we would hear today, nor, as we shall see, were they works that Clara was likely to play even ten or fifteen years later. The choices reflected not her father's taste but what he deemed to be the popular taste of the 1830s. Wieck would not jeopardize her career by programming too much Bach or Beethoven or music of the "new romantic" composers (Mendelssohn, Chopin, Schumann).

In Paris at age nineteen, Clara planned her own programs. She found musical life in the French capital to be "frivolous and superficial." She discovered that she could not play anything serious (or anything she truly loved) at the aristocratic soirees unless it were perhaps at 2 A.M., when most of the guests had left and the real connoisseurs remained to hear her play Schumann, Chopin, and Scarlatti. She recognized that her own Scherzo op. 10, which was so well received, was flashy enough to please the Parisian public. And though Robert Schumann was crusading against superficiality and "philistinism" in the columns of his *Neue Zeitschrift*, she did not hesitate to write and make a request:

> Listen, Robert, won't you compose something brilliant and easy to under-
> stand for once, something that has no titles or headings, but hangs to-
> gether as a whole, not too long and not too short? I want so much to have
> something of yours to play in public, something that suits the audience. It
> is indeed humiliating for a genius, but policy demands it for once.[5]

This hardheaded practicality was probably anathema to her fiancé; in any case, he ignored her request.

Clara soon realized to her dismay that fashion and coquetry played leading roles in Paris. Compared to the dazzle of such players as Liszt and the coquettish ways of Camilla Pleyel, the serious German girl must have seemed dull to Parisian audiences. She reported that she had considered playing with Alexander Batta, a highly regarded cellist, but deplored the way in which he flirted with the ladies, "who adored it," while he played.

"He plays delicately," she wrote, "but has an affected French soul." She abandoned the idea of playing with him after he treated her rudely at a rehearsal. The famous soirees at the home of Pierre Zimmermann, professor of piano at the Conservatoire, were attended by "150 ladies so closely packed together in a tiny room that they could not move, and then there is music until late at night, but what music! Nothing but badly sung arias, one after the other. . . ."[6]

But Clara wanted success in Paris, and though she could not afford to dress stylishly or bring herself to flirt with her audiences as Pleyel did, she valued the drawing power of a brilliant supporting artist. She was fortunate enough to secure the services of the violinist Charles de Bériot (brother-in-law of Pauline García-Viardot), and programmed works in which they could play together as well as works in which her splendid technique could be displayed. With Bériot she played a duet on themes from Bellini's *Sonnambula* and alone she played Liszt's transcriptions of Schubert's *Erlkönig* and *Ständchen*, a Chopin Etude, a Thalberg Caprice, and her own Scherzo. She chose wisely: the hall, Erard's Salon, was packed, and she wrote to Schumann, "Mein renommé ist gemacht."[7]

The preferences of the Paris audiences reflected the great rage for vocal music; entire recitals consisted solely of arrangements and transcriptions of works derived from other genres, principally opera and song. Original works or improvisations by the performer were also basic fare. Thus every program of Clara's up to the time of her marriage included at least one composition of her own and at least one work derived from an opera. Robert Schumann's piano pieces were unknown in Paris, and though Clara had braved her father's wrath when she packed them with her other music, she did not attempt them in public. In Paris, as in Vienna, she played Schumann's works at small private soirees and only for those connoisseurs who would appreciate them.

On her return to Germany, however, she offered programs more in keeping with her own sentiments, with Schumann's ideals, and with a presumably more serious German public. In Berlin on January 25, 1840, for example, she played Beethoven's Trio op. 70, no. 2; solos by Henselt, Liszt, Mendelssohn, and Scarlatti; and her own Variations on a Theme by Bellini. A few days later she gave a concert that included a Schubert trio (she wrote Robert that the audience understood it so little that they didn't know when to applaud) and his Second Sonata, op. 22, in G minor—the first performance of a Schumann work in Berlin.

The change in her programming became decisive after her marriage.[8] The display pieces by Herz, Pixis, and Bellini all but disappeared from her programs; fewer arrangements and variations show up; the dominating works are those written for the keyboard by Bach, Beethoven, Chopin, Mendelssohn, Mozart, Schubert, and Schumann.

The influence of her husband was, of course, an important factor, but there were other reasons for the change. As a child prodigy and a girl, Clara Wieck could not afford the role of crusader or educator. Her aim—and her father's—was to build and sustain a career. But she loved and believed in Schumann's music, and once they were married, she felt her primary mission was to present these works to the public, particularly inasmuch as Robert himself could not do so. This partnership was implicit in their marriage. Moreover, her sphere of knowledge was enlarged through their common studies of Bach's *Well-Tempered Clavier,* Beethoven's symphonies, and the chamber works of Mozart and Haydn. In August 1841, after one year of marriage, she wrote in the joint marriage diary:

> I pity the musician who has no understanding of this magnificent art [Beethoven's sonatas]. The less I play in public now, the more I hate the whole mechanical world of virtuoso showpieces; concert pieces like Henselt's Etudes, Thalberg's Fantasies, Liszt, etc. have become quite repugnant to me. . . . I will play them only if I need to for a concert tour.

Despite her protestations, she did play Liszt's *Hexameron* in December of that year and his *Lucia* Fantasy in Berlin in 1847, but this kind of work rarely appeared on her programs after 1850.

The friendship and close ties with Mendelssohn also stimulated changes in her repertoire. Mendelssohn's perfectionism had raised standards of playing and programming, and his revivals of the music of Johann Sebastian Bach prompted study and performances of the old Leipzig cantor. With Mendelssohn, Clara—as the young Clara Wieck and later as Madame Schumann—played several Bach works that had not been heard before at the Gewandhaus.[9]

By 1840, Schumann's editorials and reviews in the *Neue Zeitschrift* were affecting the thinking and taste of a large number of music lovers, particularly in northern Germany, and audiences were thus better prepared for a new repertoire.

THE INFLUENCE OF THE PRIESTESS

Clara Schumann was frequently described metaphorically as a "priestess" by Schumann, Brahms, Hanslick, Liszt, and many others—undoubtedly because of her devotion and quiet dignity. Her evolving repertoire may have contributed to the saintly aura. As she grew older and her reputation more secure, she programmed what she loved and her adoring audiences generally respected her choices, though as late as 1856 there was some head-shaking in Budapest about her "serious" programming: Beethoven's *Waldstein* Sonata, a Chopin Nocturne and Impromptu, Mendelssohn's *Variations sérieuses* and a *Lied ohne Worte,* and two pieces from Schumann's *Fantasiestücke.*[10]

Because of her great prestige and longevity on the concert stage, Clara had considerable influence on repertoire and programming throughout the nineteenth century. Though she was not the first pianist to play Bach fugues and Beethoven sonatas in public concerts, she was certainly one of the first to program such works consistently after 1840. The pattern still followed by recitalists today—a work by Bach or Scarlatti, a major opus such as a Beethoven sonata followed by groups of shorter pieces by Schumann, Chopin, Mendelssohn—was pioneered by Clara Schumann. The works she performed were generally new to audiences accustomed to opera transcriptions and flashy variations. Liszt, it is true, had a wide and varied repertoire that included ten Beethoven sonatas, the *Diabelli* Variations, concertos by Bach, Beethoven, Chopin, and Mendelssohn, and some Schumann works.[11] But it must be remembered that the great Hungarian pianist stopped concertizing in 1848. Thalberg, the other great rival of Clara's youth, rarely played Beethoven and certainly did not attempt Schumann; as late as 1849 (he died in 1853) he was still giving programs consisting solely of opera fantasies and overtures. Mendelssohn and Chopin, two great composer-pianists whose musical ideals were similar to hers, died in 1847 and 1849. Thus of all her generation, she alone held sway on the concert stage to the end of the century.

In the 1850s a new generation of pianists—Carl Tausig, Hans von Bülow, Anton Rubinstein—emerged; their programs and repertoire were modeled after those that Clara had popularized in the 1840s. Meanwhile, in London, a young German immigrant who had changed his name from Karl Halle to Charles Hallé began to give all-Beethoven recitals in the 1850s. By the end of the century, the tradition of the assisting artist, the improvisations and fantasies, and the vaudeville aspects had all but disappeared from the programs of the leading European pianists, and at least one Beethoven sonata was obligatory. Following the example set by Clara Schumann, concerts were shorter and less varied, permitting greater concentration on each work.

CLARA SCHUMANN AND THE MUSIC OF ROBERT SCHUMANN

One of Clara Schumann's great achievements was to bring the work of Robert Schumann to the attention of European concert audiences. There is no doubt that without her crusading performances it would have been many more years before his music was played and accepted. A recent study of piano programs in the nineteenth century makes it clear that Schumann's works began to appear regularly on programs of the leading pianists a few years after Clara first performed them.[12] Among the great pianists who were undoubtedly stimulated by Clara Schumann's performances were Bülow, Tausig, and especially Anton Rubinstein. Though Liszt included the *Fantasie*, selections from *Carnaval*, and the F-sharp Minor Sonata in his reper-

Musikalischen Unterhaltung

Sonntag den 13. Januar 1833

Vormittags präsis 9½ Uhr

w i r d   e r g e b e n s t   e i n g e l a d e n

von

Friedrich Wieck.

(Reichsstrasse № 579.)

Erster Theil.

1.) *La belle Union*, Rondo à 4/m von **Moscheles.**
2.) Vier *Mazurkas* von Chopin, H. 1., für Pianoforte solo.
3.) Drittes *Trio* für Pianoforte, Violine & Violoncello
von **Pixis.**
4.) *Romanze* für Physharmonica & Pianoforte.
5.) *Caprices en forme de Valse* von **Clara.**
6.) *Gesang.*
7.) Zwei *Studien* für die Violine von **Paganini,** für
das Pianoforte bearbeitet von **R. Schumann.**

===

Zweiter Theil.

8.) Sechstes *Trio* von **Reissiger.**
9.) Vier *Mazurkas* von Chopin, H. 2.
10.) *Gesang.*
11.) *Notturno* von **Chopin,** für Pianoforte solo.
12.) Viertes *Trio* von **Pixis.**

Program of Clara Schumann's concert of January 13, 1833, when she gave the first
public performance of a work by Robert Schumann. Robert-Schumann-Haus,
Zwickau, DDR.

toire list of 1850, he told Wilhelm von Wasielewski that he had played Schumann's works in private circles but "they did not suit the public taste and most pianists did not understand them," and so, regretfully, he had given up the attempt.[13] Clara, on the other hand, played almost every piano work Schumann had written, though she, too, sometimes waited for years until she considered the public ready for them. She premiered almost every one of Schumann's chamber and orchestral works that had a piano part. (The only works she did not premiere were op. 63, 73, and 94; she did, however, perform them frequently.) And most significant, his symphonies and many orchestral works were first presented at concerts in which Clara was the soloist and leading attraction.* (There was one exception: at the premiere of his Third Symphony, in Düsseldorf in 1851, three of her students played in her stead, performing Bach's Concerto for Three Claviers.) Almost every program she played after her marriage included at least one Schumann work—often three or four—for piano alone, orchestra, chamber combinations, or voice.

She considered it not only her sacred duty to play his music but her sacred right, and was jealous if his music was played by any other pianist, anywhere. "Robert wrote a very nice letter to Wilhelmine Claus in Paris today," she wrote in her diary on April 9, 1853, "but I was sad that she had to be the one to give the first performances of his works in Paris and London, when I am certainly the one who has the right to do this before anyone else."[14]

There are misunderstandings and some controversies about when and just how much of Schumann's music was performed by Clara. Table 1 gives the dates on which Schumann's works were first played publicly by Clara. These occasions were not necessarily premieres; a few works were performed by other pianists before Clara played them. But she and her public always believed that her performances were definitive.

Clara was performing Robert's works even during the years when her father was planning her programs. Friedrich Wieck was an advocate of the music of the "new romantic school" and billed Clara as a representative of that style. She introduced many new Chopin works; his op. 2, as we have noted, became one of the staples of her repertoire. Mendelssohn's *Lieder ohne Worte* and Schumann's Toccata appeared on her programs even during the height of Wieck's fury at the young suitor. Wieck limited his daughter's performances of the music of Schumann, Chopin, and Mendelssohn primarily because of box-office considerations, not necessarily because of his feud with Schumann. He permitted her to play Schumann's music privately in Vienna and even at home when they returned to Leipzig.

The first Schumann works Clara played in public—the *Paganini* Etudes and the Toccata—were virtuoso pieces, not too different from the popular works of Clara's girlhood. Before her marriage she occasionally played sections of his *Novelletten*, *Fantasiestücke*, and *Etudes symphoniques*. The next

---

*One movement of an early incomplete symphony (first published in 1972) was performed at Clara's Gewandhaus concert of April 29, 1833.

Table 1. Piano works of Robert Schumann and years of first public performances by Clara Wieck Schumann

Opus no.	Title	Year	Comments
1	*Abegg* (Variations)		No public performance known
2	*Papillons*	1871	Place and date of concert unknown; played in Wieck home, 1832
3	(Paganini) *Etudes*	1833	Leipzig, Jan. 13; 2 selections played in Wieck home
4	*Intermezzi*		No public performance known
5	*Impromptus*	1866	Vienna, March 11; performed privately beginning 1833
6	*Davidsbündlertänze*	1860	Vienna, March 27; 10 selections only at first performance
7	*Toccata*	1834	Leipzig, Sept. 11
8	*Allegro*	1841	Leipzig, March 31; frequent performances in Russia, 1844
9	*Carnaval*	1856	Vienna, Feb. 7; many private performances beginning 1837
10	(Paganini) *Etudes*	1844	Place and date of concert unknown
11	*Sonate 1* (in F-sharp Minor)	1884	London, March 17; many private performances beginning 1835
12	*Fantasiestücke*	1838	3 played in Wieck home, August 12
13	*Etudes Symphoniques*	1837	3 selections played in Leipzig, Aug. 13; first complete performance, Holland, Dec. 10, 1853
14	*Concert sans orchestre* (Sonata no. 3, in F Minor)		No performance listed in program collection
15	*Kinderscenen*	1868	London March 19; performed privately beginning 1840
16	*Kreisleriana*	1859	Vienna, Jan. 2, selections only; performed privately beginning 1840
17	*Fantasie*	1866	Leipzig, Dec. 15; performed privately beginning 1839
18	*Arabeske*	1867	London, Feb. 18
19	*Blumenstück*	1871	Place and date of concert unknown
20	*Humoreske*	1866	Vienna, Feb. 9
21	*Novelletten*	1839	Stettin, Nov. 7, probably no. 2 only; others played later
22	*Sonate 2* (in G Minor)	1840	Berlin, Feb. 1
23	*Nachtstücke*	1865	London, June 13; single pieces played 1854, 1861
26	*Faschingsschwank aus Wien*	1860	Vienna, March 15; selections only?
28	*Drei Romanzen*	1846	Norderney, August 18; selection only
32	*Scherzo, Gigue, Romanze und Fughette*	1856	London, June 30; Romanze (?) only
44	*Quintett*	1843	Leipzig, Jan. 8
46	*Andante und Variationen*	1843	Leipzig, Aug. 19
47	(Piano) *Quartett*	1844	Leipzig, Dec. 8
54	*Concert* (Piano Concerto)	1845	Dresden, Dec. 4
56	*Studien für den Pedal-Flügel*	1846	Vienna, Dec. 10
58	*Skizzen für den Pedal-Flügel*	1863	Paris, March?
60	*Sechs Fugen* (Bach)	1849	Place and date of concert unknown
63	*Trio 1* (in D Minor)	1849	Leipzig, Jan. 20
66	*Bilder aus Osten*	1850	Leipzig, February
68	*Album für die Jugend*	1849	Dresden, Feb. 7; 6 selections only

Table 1. *(Continued)*

Opus no.	Title	Year	Comments
70	*Adagio und Allegro*	1850	Dresden, Jan. 26
72	*Vier Fugen*	1845	Leipzig, Oct. 5; 1 selection only
73	*Fantasiestücke*	1853	Bonn, Feb. 24
76	*Vier Marsche*		No performance known
80	*Trio 2* (in F Major)	1850	Leipzig, Feb. 22
82	*Waldscenen*	1869	London, March 18; selections played beginning 1854
85	*Vier-Händige Clavierstücke*	1851	Düsseldorf, March 13; 2 selections only
88	*Phantasiestücke*	1866	Vienna, March 1
92	*Introduction und Allegro appasionato*	1850	Leipzig, Feb. 14
94	*Drei Romanzen*	1867	London, Feb. 4
99	*Bunte Blätter*	1862	Selections only
102	*Fünf Stücke im Volkston*	1855	Berlin, Nov. 11; 3 selections only
105	*Sonate 1* (for Piano and Violin, in A Minor)	1852	Leipzig, March 21
109	*Ball-Scenen*		No public performance known
110	*Trio 3* (in G Minor)	1852	Leipzig, March 21
111	*Drei Fantasiestücke*	1857	Elberfeld, March 28; one selection only
113	*Märchen-Bilder*	1853	Bonn, Nov. 12
118	*Drei Clavier-Sonaten*		No public performance known
121	*Sonate 2* (for Piano and Violin, in D Minor)	1853	Düsseldorf, October 29
124	*Albumblätter*	1862	Rostock, Dec. 12; "Schlummerlied" played beginning 1854
126	*Sieben Clavierstücke*		No public performance known
130	*Kinderball*		No public performance known
132	*Märchenerzählungen*	1876	Leipzig, Jan. 9
133	*Gesänge der Frühe*		No public performance known
134	*Concert Allegro mit Introduction*	1853	The Hague, Nov. 30

Sources: Litzmann; Program Collection, reviews, and diaries, RSH; *Hb*; Alfred Dörffel, ed., *Geschichte der Gewandhausconcerte zu Leipzig vom 25. November 1781 bis 25. November 1881* (Leipzig, 1884).

group of Schumann works that she programmed consistently was made up of chamber and orchestral works in which the piano was prominently featured. Between 1840 and 1854 Clara premiered or performed the Piano Concerto, Quintet, Piano Quartet, trios, and sonatas for piano and other instruments. The great piano cycles of his youth, however, were almost totally neglected in public concerts. Schumann himself never heard his piano cycles performed in concert.[15]

Only after 1854, when Schumann was already hospitalized, did single pieces from the *Fantasiestücke, Novelletten,* and *Waldscenen* begin to appear regularly on Clara's programs. And finally, between 1864 and 1870, such works as *Kreisleriana, Davidsbündlertänze, Humoreske,* and *Arabeske* took their places in her concerts. Even a work as significant as *Kreisleriana,* however, was not performed in its entirety when she first played it. After some urging, she performed excerpts in Vienna in 1859 but wrote Brahms that she did so reluctantly because she did not feel the work was "suitable for a concert."[16]

Audiences had to wait until 1866 for the great *Fantasie*. She did not perform *Papillons* in public until 1871. Once played, however, these works remained in her programs. Between 1864 and 1879, for example, she played the Concerto eighteen times, *Carnaval* fifteen times, the Symphonic Etudes twelve times. She performed the Quintet so regularly that it could almost be said to have been her signature piece.

Table 1 raises an important question. Clara Schumann, who repeatedly declared that her mission was to bring her husband's work to the attention of the public, did not, in fact, perform many of his works until years after his death; indeed, some of them she never played publicly at all. There may have been several reasons for this seeming paradox.

In terms of financial success, Clara Schumann reached the top early, and she was quite determined to stay there. She may have felt it her duty to the living—to herself and the children and grandchildren dependent on her—to do so. But for many years she must have felt as though she were treading a narrow line between conflicting goals: to make her husband's music known and to sustain her own popularity on the concert stage. Schumann himself agreed that his early works were particularly controversial; both he and Clara were aware that the public was not ready for these imaginative piano cycles with their autobiographical and esoteric literary allusions, innovative rhythms and harmonies, and experimental sounds (though we now see them as having a natural place in a particular German musical tradition). In his day Schumann was not generally perceived as a solid composer, and for many years his music was ignored outside of a small circle of enthusiasts. The correspondent for *Dwight's Musical Journal*, for example, wrote on March 24, 1855, "Some pillars of the musical world here [Berlin] seem to think that Joachim is injuring himself by the amount of study he bestows upon the works of Schumann and the school to which he belongs." Schumann's music was neither showy nor virtuosic; his variations were based on original melodies or motifs rather than on arias or popular tunes of the day; the very idea of the piano cycles was strange and unfamiliar; and the imaginative titles and title pages confused, even irritated the public.

Clara loved, indeed reveled in his compositions. As we know, she had grown with them and played them since she was twelve. Since Schumann was not a pianist of concert caliber, he depended on Clara to try out and perform his works for friends and other musicians. In Paris in 1839, Friedrich Kalkbrenner told her that he had heard that no one played Schumann's compositions as she did.[17] With appropriate girlish modesty, she demurred, but there is no doubt that she agreed completely. When she was sixteen, she played Schumann's First Sonata to Mendelssohn, Chopin, Ignaz Moscheles, and Ferdinand David in Leipzig, to Ernst Becker in Dresden, to Joseph Fischhof and Aloys Fuchs in Vienna, and to other friends and composers in Breslau and Paris. She played it again at home after their marriage, yet she delayed public performance of this difficult sonata until 1884, almost fifty years after it had been written. At that time Clara, now a widow of sixty-five, restudied the sonata and presented it to an enthusiastic British audience, an audience carefully educated, as it were, by her playing of carefully selected Schumann works over the years.* It is interesting to note that this was one of the few piano works she did not premiere. Anton Rubinstein played it on October 30, 1883, in Frankfurt, then her home. It is possible that her first performance was given in an attempt to show audiences, as she wrote in her diary, the right way to play it, as she believed Rubenstein could not do it justice.[18]

Even *Carnaval,* today one of Schumann's best-known piano works, was carefully eased onto her concert programs. Clara had introduced it to Liszt in Vienna in 1838, and the great virtuoso chose to play ten of its movements at his Leipzig concert of 1839, an act of honor and respect for the hometown composer and editor. Clara played it for friends in Paris and Hamburg but did not perform it in public until 1856, after Schumann was ill. At that time, and for some thirty years thereafter, a statement headed *"Zum besseren Verständnis"* (For better understanding) was distributed with the program to familiarize the audience with the characters portrayed in this unknown piano cycle.

Clara and Robert engaged in much serious discussion about her playing of his works. He gave her many suggestions about what and when to play to best effect, emphasizing the importance of making the right choices. On December 1, 1839, he wrote:

> I am totally opposed to your doing the Novellette in A [for a Berlin concert in January 1840]—that works only as part of the whole cycle and by itself is over too quickly. . . . You would certainly make the biggest effect with the second, in D. That has a beginning and an end, spins itself out nicely so that the public can follow it, and the Trio also has a good melody. Don't be angry at me because I always find fault with something, but *it is not unimportant.* I am not yet so well known or recognized that one could expect the public to accept *everything* just because it is mine. Therefore, to play the most beautiful, the most clever work is not always suitable for the masses; instead, give them those things that are more charming and brilliant. . . . Just for a test, play the one in E, for my sake, and the one in D later, and see which will have more effect. If you don't want to play either, then it would be best to play the Sonata in G Minor (but *without* the Scherzo), because it develops a character that is comprehensible. Think about it, because, as I said, I do not consider it unimportant to have

---

*In 1871 she noted in her diary that a piece must be played frequently so that the audience can hear it and get used to it. "The right moment to introduce a whole new work must be carefully calculated" (Litzmann, 3:255).

my music played by you in a city like Berlin. If it is not effective, I will be the one taken to account, no matter how well you play, and that does not make me unhappy, yet it does not make me happy either.[19]

In February 1838 he suggested that she might play "Traumeswirren" with "Des Abends" (from op. 12) but advised that "In der Nacht" was perhaps too long.[20] From Leipzig he wrote that she should not expect applause for the Symphonic Etudes. "It's impossible for them to suit the public taste." He repeated the thought a month later: "You were right not to play my pieces—they are not suitable for the public."[21] In September 1839, on her return from Paris, she noted in her diary:

I am often pained that Robert's compositions are not recognized as they deserve to be. I would play them gladly, but the public doesn't understand them. I'm so afraid that someday Robert will have to witness the fact that his compositions arouse little interest in comparison with other works that are dull and insipid. I think this will be dreadful for him. He has much too deep an intellect for the world and because of this must be misunderstood. I believe that the best thing is for him to compose for orchestra; his fantasy is limited by the piano. The piano doesn't have enough scope; his pieces are all in orchestral style, and I think that is why they are so inaccessible to the public: the melodies and figures cross so much that it takes a great deal to discover all their beauties. I myself always find new beauties each time I play one of his works (I'm finding this to be the case with the *Novelletten* now). The *Novelletten* are really beautiful works. Intellect, soul, humor, the greatest tenderness, everything is united in it—there is no end to the most delicate features. One must know them as I do, and then his entire personality will be found in his compositions. If Beethoven and Mozart were alive today, he would be the third in that trinity. The time will come when the world will recognize the third one, but it will come late. His improvisations hold such a wealth of fantasy that one can only be continually amazed. My greatest wish is that he compose for orchestra—that is his realm. If I could only succeed in persuading him!

These words have been criticized as a demonstration of Clara's ignorance and insensitivity.[22] They can also be viewed, however, as a rare statement of understanding from a young musician. Schumann himself was eager to write for orchestra and, as his 1839 letter indicates, was aware of the problems his music posed; he was quite resigned to wait for the judgment of posterity.*

---

*This is not to imply that Schumann was passive about promoting his works; he made every effort to have them performed but was realistic about the difficulties he might encounter. In 1843 he explained to Carl Kossmaly, composer, conductor, and writer on music, that his piano works (especially op. 12, 16, 21, and 28) were not too well known because "1. There are difficulties in form and content; 2. I am not a virtuoso who could perform them publicly; 3. I am the editor of my journal, in which I cannot mention them; 4. Fink is the editor of the other journal and does not want to mention them" (Boetticher, ed., *Robert Schumann in seinen Schriften und Briefen*, 391).

Schumann rarely consulted Clara about his compositions, but he respected her judgment as a seasoned performer, and when he did turn to her with a question, he generally took her advice. She wrote from Vienna in 1838:

> I am enormously excited with the idea of your Second [G Minor] Sonata; it reminds me of so many happy as well as painful hours. I love it, as I do you. Your whole being is so clearly expressed in it, and besides, it's not too obscure. Only one thing. Do you want to leave the last movement as it was before? Better to change it and make it a bit easier because it is much too difficult. I understand it and can play it all right, but people, the public, even the connoisseurs for whom one actually writes, don't understand it. You won't take this badly, will you?[23]

There were times when Schumann reacted angrily, as when she questioned his ability to write a string quartet, but he seemed to have no qualms about accepting her suggestions for the G Minor Sonata.[24] On December 28, 1838, he wrote that he had composed another, simpler final movement, thought it went well with the first movement, and was sending it to the publisher.[25]

It has been suggested that Clara did not understand his titles and objected to them because of her own lack of sensitivity, but Schumann himself knew that his fanciful title pages and headings might be a deterrent to audiences unaccustomed to fantasy and imagination. In January 1840 he asked Clara what she thought of the proposed titles for *Nachtstücke*, his op. 23: "1. Trauerzug [Funeral procession] 2. Kuriose Gesellschaft [Peculiar company] 3. Nächtliches Gelager [Nocturnal revels] 4. Rundgesang mit Solos [Round with solo voices]."[26] The young lady answered in her confident, practical way, ". . . the public will not know what you mean . . . and will just take offense at it. I think you should leave the general title, *Nachtstücke*. . . ."[27] Here, too, he took her advice.

In 1838 he suggested to Friedrich Kistner, the publisher of his first sonata, which had originally appeared under the pseudonym "Florestan and Eusebius": "Wouldn't it be better for you and for me if you had a *new* title page prepared with my real name without the romantic appendage?"[28] The second, *"nouvelle"* edition was published under his name. On January 24, 1839, he asked Clara's advice about writing to Heinrich Probst to discuss reprinting a number of works, including *Davidsbündlertänze* and *Kreisleriana*— "the latter," he wrote, "perhaps *with different titles.*"[29] And a few years later, on November 5, 1842, he offered the *Davidsbündlertänze* to Friedrich Hofmeister and proposed that instead of, or perhaps in addition to, the "mystic" title, the explanatory phrase *"12 Charakterstücke"* (12 character pieces) should appear.[30] (Hofmeister rejected the offer and a second, revised edition was published as *Davidsbündlertänze, 16 Charakterstücke* in 1850/51 by Schuberth in Leipzig.)

Schumann's response to Clara's playing is revealed in these words, written in 1838:

> I have heard you play only twice in two years. . . . It seemed to me, however, as though it were the most perfect playing one could imagine; I will not forget how you played my [Symphonic] Etudes [August 1837]. The way you portrayed them, they were absolute masterpieces—the public cannot possibly understand how to value them—but there was one person sitting in the audience—and though his heart was pounding with other feelings, at that moment his whole being paid homage to you as an artist.[31]

Occasionally Schumann reproached her, but mildly. When he chastised her for not wanting to play his works in Paris in 1839, she answered that it was too painful for her to play for people who did not understand him.[32] Difficult as this judgment was for a composer, Schumann could accept it.

From their inception, Schumann's concerted and chamber works were less problematical than the early piano cycles. The Quintet, the trios, the sonatas, the Concerto were played frequently during Schumann's lifetime. Critical reception of Clara's playing of these works was almost invariably enthusiastic; the same, however, could not be said for his music. As far as we know, Schumann did not begrudge her the praise. He more than merely approved: he admired and loved her performances. For the most part, he delighted in her interpretations and rarely criticized her playing. (She found *any* criticism from him hard to take, and could barely tolerate his praise of any other pianist, male or female.)

Thus his criticism of her playing in 1854 was particularly devastating.* Though she must have recognized that he was not himself, this world-famous artist still trembled at any criticism from her husband. She may have found some belated comfort in the praise he sent from Endenich. On September 14, 1854, he wrote, "Oh, how I would love to hear your glorious playing just once." And on October 12, after receiving her published variations (op. 20) on his theme, he wrote, "Now I must tell you how your variations enchant me more and more and remind me of your magnificent playing of this and of my work."[33]

Table 1 makes it clear that the first Schumann works that Clara played in public were those that could not fail to appeal to audiences. As Martin Schoppe has pointed out, the excerpts from op. 12 and 13—carefully chosen, brief, simple works—prepared the audiences for such larger works as *Carnaval* and *Humoreske*.[34] This strategy was clearly pursued with Schumann's approval. It is interesting to note, however, that sections of certain works were always excluded. Clara never played *Carnaval* or *Waldscenen*, for example in its entirety. She always omitted "Estrella" (supposedly a portrait of Ernestine von Fricken), "Florestan," and "Eusebius"

*See chap. 7.

from *Carnaval* and "Verrufene Stelle" (with its accompanying macabre poem) from *Waldscenen*. Perhaps they evoked painful memories; perhaps they were too surrealistic, too fanciful, too extravagant for this practical, down-to-earth woman.

RECEPTION IN FOREIGN COUNTRIES

The nineteenth-century virtuosos with international reputations achieved their stature by dint of tireless traveling. This circumstance may explain the large number of divorces among women artists and the fact that many dropped out of the competition after they married and had children. Clara apparently never even thought of doing so. Table 2 shows the concert tours she made before, during, and after the years with Schumann.

From her first trip, it was obvious that Clara found touring exhilarating. Thus in Moscow in 1844, while Robert, ill and depressed, retired to their hotel room, Clara trotted round to play, made calls, visited institutions, and enjoyed her fame. All in all, Clara Schumann made thirty-eight journeys outside of Germany. In each foreign land she made a point of performing her husband's music and was often surprised and delighted by its reception. Writing to her young friend Ernst Rudorff from Paris on March 19, 1862, she reported on an altogether new attitude among French audiences:

> I received such pressing invitations to come here and they wanted so much to hear me, especially to hear my husband's works, which are becoming widely known here, that I decided to come, partly because I regarded it as a duty to my husband. I wouldn't have thought of coming for that reason alone—to popularize his music among the French—because I never would have believed that such a thoroughly German nature as his could become so greatly appreciated in another country. I still don't believe it, but considering the heartfelt reception that I've had for his works here, it would have been wrong to say no.

In Paris she played Schumann's Quintet and a Bach fugue. "You really would have enjoyed seeing the enthusiasm with which they were received by the public," she told Rudorff. "It's peculiar; in one's heart one thinks little of the public, yet in the concert hall their interest is really needed. It stimulates one and, for the moment, heightens the performance."[35]

Her Paris reception in 1862 contrasted greatly with the difficult experiences of 1832 and 1839. This time Madame Erard, of the Erard piano manufacturing family, provided Clara and her daughter Marie with an escort and made housing arrangements for them; the leading French artists came to pay their respects; she was invited to play at the Conservatoire (a signal honor) and was overwhelmed by the enthusiasm her playing provoked. Her opinion of the French public softened, though she remained critical of the "cold

275]

Table 2. Countries where Clara Schumann performed on foreign tours, 1832–1888

Year	Country
1832	France
1837–38	Austria, Hungary
1839	France
1842	Denmark
1844	Russia
1846–47	Austria
1853	Holland
1854	Belgium
1855	Holland
1856	Austria, Hungary, England, Denmark
1857	England, Switzerland
1858	Switzerland, Austria, Hungary
1859	Austria, England
1860	Holland, Austria
1861	Belgium
1862	Switzerland, France, Belgium
1863	Holland, France, Belgium
1864	Russia
1865	Bohemia, England
1866	Austria, Hungary
1867	England
1868	Belgium, England, Austria, Hungary
1869	Holland, England, Austria
1870	England
1871	Holland, England
1872	England, Austria, Hungary
1873	Belgium, England
1876	Holland, England
1877	Holland, England, Switzerland
1879	Switzerland
1880	Switzerland
1881	England
1882	England
1883	Holland
1884	England
1886	England
1887	England, Switzerland
1888	England

Source: Gerd Nauhaus, RSH.

perfectionism" of the Conservatoire orchestra, with which she played Beethoven's E-flat Piano Concerto. Practical and cautious as always, she charged Brahms not to repeat her words to anyone because the Conservatoire was a "musical shrine" to the French, and if word of her criticism were to get out, it would be most damaging to her.[36]

Clara Schumann is also credited with influencing the taste and standards of music in Russia. Before her 1844 tour, the music of Robert Schumann and her standards of programming and playing were unknown in that country. Commenting on that trip, Daniel Wladimirowitsch Shitomirski wrote, "Clara's successful appearances ensured significant success for a serious rep-

ertoire and a deeper, concentrated interpretation."[37] In 1844 her playing in
Moscow inspired the following remarks:

> We have had an abundance of famous pianists here, but what have we
> heard? Frightful noise, cannon salvos, difficult things that merely as-
> tounded; and what touched the heart? In point of fact, very little . . . we
> soon forgot that they had ever visited Moscow and not one of us remem-
> bers their playing. Can we say the same of Clara Schumann? Absolutely
> not! The "Spring Song" of Mendelssohn, the nocturnes of Field, a presto
> by Scarlatti, fantasies by Liszt and Thalberg, fugues by Bach, masterpieces
> by Beethoven—these works have been so vividly impressed in our hearts
> and memory that henceforth they will hold us captive with their sweet
> fetters.[38]

Another Russian critic described the effect of her playing thus:

> Who would have thought this possible ten years ago? Who would have
> believed that this music [Scarlatti and Bach] would have made such an
> extraordinary impression and that Frau Schumann would have had to
> repeat works several times? This is a noteworthy lesson for every artist
> who believed, up to now, that one could please the public only by perfor-
> mances of variations on the one and only Bellini motif.[39]

Once the critics had been won over, she cautiously introduced a few of
Robert Schumann works in her public concerts in Russia and played more of
them at private parties. These performances turned the tide for Schumann
in tsarist Russia. Prominent Russian composers, among them Anton Rubinstein (who premiered several Schumann works) and Tchaikovsky, became
great adherents of Schumann's music then and later. On her second and last
Russian tour, in 1864, Clara Schumann was again greeted with wild enthusiasm. César Cui pointed out in a review of her concerts, "During the first
sojourn of Clara Schumann with her husband in Petersburg, people said,
"'Monsieur Schumann, the husband of Clara Schumann'; now people say,
'Madame Schumann, the wife of Robert Schumann.'"[40]

Clara Schumann crossed the English Channel nineteen times to play in
the British Isles, an adventure not always to be undertaken lightly.* The
impetus to visit England the first time came from William Sterndale Bennett, Robert's old friend, who for years had been issuing invitations to the
Schumanns. In January 1856, much to the consternation of Brahms and
other friends, she resumed correspondence with Bennett, which led to her
first concert with the Philharmonic Society on April 14, 1856. This premiere

---

*Karl Geiringer speculates that Brahms never visited the British Isles because he feared
seasickness while crossing the narrow waterway between Europe and England. (*Brahms: His
Life and Work*, 2d ed. [New York: Doubleday/Anchor, 1961], 115).

tour set the pattern for those that followed, though her association with Bennett was of short duration. Concert arrangements in England were generally made by professionals (often a music publisher, such as William Chappell) and thus were not burdensome, so that the pleasures of touring were considerably enhanced. On most trips, she and her traveling companion—usually one of her daughters—lived with wealthy English friends, such as Arthur Burnand, who delighted in providing warm hospitality. After some initial difficulties, she became immensely popular in England and was gratified not only by the money she earned but also by the unanticipated warmth she experienced in the traditionally chilly British Isles. On March 3, 1884, she wrote in her diary that news of political events in England had led her to fear an explosion, but instead she had received a *"Blumenexplosion"*: flowers had rained down on her from the balconies and galleries of the concert hall.[41]

She always gave lessons in England, and her reputation drew many English students to work with her in Germany.* In 1888, after she had almost ceased concertizing on the Continent because of her health, she was persuaded to come once more to the British Isles. After her final concert, she wrote in her diary: "The last 'Popular.' I was very nervous again but made a brilliant closing with *Carnaval.* I believe I never played it as I did today and yet I have decided that this shall be the finale for England and was sadder than I can say."[42]

Her reputation spread across the Atlantic, and invitations came from the New World several times. Although Jenny Lind, Thalberg, and other friends had made brilliant and lucrative tours in the Western Hemisphere, she declined the offers. It was not only fear of the voyage or reluctance to leave her children that accounted for her rejection; rather she felt the tours might not be financially feasible for an artist with expenses as great as hers. American interest in her playing grew, however, stimulated by glowing reviews in such journals as the Boston-based *Dwight's Journal of Music,* which mentioned her name in almost every issue, and many ambitious young American pianists traveled to Frankfurt to study with her.

THE PRESS AND PUBLIC OPINION

Long before her marriage Clara's relationship with the press was well established. Because German nouns have genders, the perennial phrase *die erste Pianistin,* for example, is ambiguous; it is never clear whether she is being called first among all pianists or first among women pianists. But there is no mistaking her status when she is ranked with Liszt, Thalberg, and Henselt, or when "Clara Schumann" is listed, in a review of a Thalberg

*See chap. 13.

concert in 1847, along with "Liszt, Doehler, Litolff, . . . Dreischock," among the "most distinguished names of the day."[43]

In 1841 she joined the glamorous Liszt in two concerts in Leipzig. The *Allgemeine Musikalische Zeitung* concluded:

> We have already spoken about his exaggerations and also about *Hexameron*, which Frau Dr. Clara Schumann performed with Herr Liszt for the second time. We do not like to compare . . . but we must admit that the quiet, beautiful, correct, and refined playing of Frau Dr. Schumann was more effective than the stormy extravagances of Herr Liszt.[44]

It is difficult to locate outright hostility in reviews of Clara Schumann's performances. Of some 200 reviews examined, 10 were unfavorable. Anton Schindler was one of the few critics who detested her performances, calling her "infinitely overrated" and complaining that she had "sorely maltreated" Beethoven.[45] Occasionally she was faulted for poor programming, but the major complaint related to fast or erratic tempos—comments about which she was very sensitive.

Like most artists, she was not fond of critics, and she kept her distance even from Eduard Hanslick, who was her great admirer. But she never lost a sense of proportion about her playing and was her own severest critic. In a remarkable letter to the critic Selmar Bagge she wrote on March 29, 1856:

> But, dear friend, why do you wish to deny that I have occasionally taken tempos that are somewhat too fast? . . . I believe that now and then this reproach may have been justified. You know that I rarely play without inspiration—it just seems to happen of itself—but it is so easy to allow oneself to be carried away so that one loses one's sense of judgment as to whether it was too fast or not. This does happen to me, particularly with the very pieces that I love so much that I lose myself in them and forget myself completely. Of course, that should not happen—the artist should always be master of his feelings, just as a calm and composed person is in ordinary life. Well, now—I will strive to do better and the reproach will certainly be useful to me.[46]

On the whole, press reports ranged from approbation to raving enthusiasm. In later years there were grumbles that she always played the same pieces,[47] but neither her interpretation nor her artistry was ever questioned. Terms commonly used to describe her performances were "elegant, solid playing," "clarity and solidity," "extraordinary accomplishment," "incomparable," "clear," "pure," "deeply artistic nature." After a Gewandhaus concert on January 1, 1842, in which Clara, now married and the mother of one child, played Mendelssohn's G Minor Concerto and Thalberg's *Moses* Fantasy, a local journal (not Robert's) reported: "Again we come to the conclusion that there is scarcely a virtuoso living today who might stand

beside her in terms of virtuosity as well as in genuine artistic development."[48]

In October of that year the same journal reported:

> In general, Clara Schumann is more remarkable in the performance of
> compositions in which, from the intellectual point of view, there is some-
> thing worth working out than she is in the execution of purely one-sided
> virtuoso pieces . . . although one cannot deny that Frau Dr. Schumann
> can also achieve recognition as a pure virtuoso.[49]

And in 1865, in a review of a concert with Julius Stockhausen, a critic
wrote, "There are many virtuosos who are not inferior to her in technique or
general interpretation, but she distinguishes herself from all the rest through
her high level of musicality, which gives her performances the stamp of a
divine summons."[50]

In her late forties, as family problems and physical ailments multiplied,
she became very anxious about performing and fearful of forgetting the
music. Clara Wieck had been one of the first pianists to play from memory.
When she played in Berlin in 1837, Bettina von Arnim is reputed to have
remarked, "How pretentiously she seats herself at the piano, and without
notes, too. How modest, on the other hand, is Doehler, who placed the
music in front of him."[51] Under Wieck's thorough tutelage, Clara had
learned to memorize as a child, and she never found it to be a problem.
Reviewers commented on this feat when she was only thirteen, an indication
of how exceptional this practice was.[52] But with age and heavy responsibilities she found playing from memory increasingly difficult.*

In 1871 she wrote to Brahms from London:

> God knows how I can begin to control the anxiety that is attacking me. . . .
> Though I am often so nervous from one piece to the next, I cannot make
> the decision to play without notes; it always seems to me that it is almost as
> though my wings were clipped—and yet they still retain some buoyancy—
> more for art than for life, which never ceases to bring me new trials.[53]

She played without music as long as possible, despite the anxiety that assailed her as she mounted the platform.

What did she sound like? Several of her contemporaries—Joachim, for
example—recorded performances on cylinders to be played on the recently
invented phonograph, but Clara never did so. We have only some unreliable
recordings by her students—Fanny Davies, Adelina de Lara, Ilona
Eibenschütz, and Nathalie Janotha, for example—and descriptions of her
playing by contemporaries. In German discussions of her artistry, the term

---

*As early as October 1850 she commented that only the young had the confidence to play
from memory (Litzmann, 3:229).

werktreu (true to the text) was invariably used. Because of her personal severity, her loyalty to Schumann, and her reputation for integrity, it is natural to assume that she never tampered with the music, as so many other respected nineteenth-century pianists did. Yet even the "priestess" was known to play too fast, double an octave, or add an occasional embellishment. Unlike Liszt, however, she was never guilty of adding effects to gain attention. Reviewers universally remarked on her masterful technique and her deep respect for and understanding of the music; particularly striking was the quality of her beautiful, full, "singing" tone, an aspect of her art carefully cultivated by her father.

CONCERT MANAGEMENT

When Clara Wieck toured with her father, he attended to the hundreds of details of concert giving: he rented the halls and instruments, hired the supporting musicians, had the tickets printed and distributed, arranged for refreshments to lure the reluctant, peddled Clara's picture, set up advertisements in the papers and on the streets, collected and counted the money. All these tasks became Clara's from 1839 to the close of her performing career. Though she advised her students to hire professional managers (not available in Germany until the 1880s), she herself did not do so. She had developed a network of friends throughout Europe, and in letters filled with requests and directives she enlisted their help. Proud to assist the great artist, they never failed her. But her greatest aid came from her daughters, who were pressed into service as soon as they were old enough to help. One daughter saw to her clothes, another made arrangements for the shipping of her instruments and music, a third arranged for transportation and housing for the artist and her traveling companion or helped with the selling and distribution of tickets. Each daughter took her turn as traveling companion, but in the end it was Marie that became her constant attendant.

In the early part of the century, few halls existed for the sole purpose of concerts, and most cities had no box offices. Tickets were bought from local music dealers or directly from the artist. In these days of international contracts prepared five years in advance, it is astonishing to read of the speed with which concerts were announced and arranged. Cities were smaller, music lovers were known to each other, and interested parties could easily be reached through the reliable mail service. Concerts were announced in the newspapers, on placards posted around the city, and by word of mouth only two or three days before they took place.

Clara insisted on making all her own arrangements, necessarily a tedious and thankless job, and over the years wrote thousands of letters regarding details that she would not entrust to her daughters, associates, or friends. In their obsessive and meticulous attention to minutiae, the letters resemble those written by her father to Clementine Wieck.[54]

Much thought and energy went into the planning of Madame Schumann's concerts. Often ten or more letters were exchanged before final agreement could be reached on ticket prices, hall, and program. She always kept in mind the works that she and other artists had performed in a particular city and the size and interests of the potential audience; she juggled rehearsals so they would not interfere with the busy lives of her fellow artists and her own schedule of teaching, mothering, and traveling. A letter sent to Wilhelm Joseph Wasielewski when she was arranging a concert in Bonn in November 1853 indicates the style of her management:

> I am sending you 200 tickets as well as 20 free tickets. I will bring tickets for the box office with me. The program remains as described earlier: I. Quartet no. 1 [Schumann, op. 47], II. Vocal works, III. Beethoven C Major [*Waldstein*] Sonata. Second half: IV. Three *Märchenbilder* with you [Schumann, op. 113], V. Vocal works, VI. Etude in C Major and B Major Nocturne by Chopin, *Lied ohne Worte* by Mendelssohn. We leave here [Düsseldorf] tomorrow, Friday afternoon, at 3 and will arrive, I believe, in Bonn at 6 or 7. Would you reserve a room in the Stern for us, but please, not the same one where my poor husband was sick. I saw some very nice rooms on the other side facing the court; we do not like to face the street— it is too noisy. On account of the tickets, I am sending this letter separately so there will be no extra delay. Also I am sending this unfranked, it is safer, also because of the tickets. Add it up with the concert costs.[55]

WUNDERKINDER

One of the unforgettable comments about Clara Wieck was Hanslick's "kein Wunderkind—und doch noch ein Kind und schon ein Wunder."

Wunderkinder were not uncommon in eighteenth-century Europe. Vienna had its share well before Clara appeared on the scene; Wolfgang Amadeus Mozart made a dazzling impression when he played there in 1762, at the age of six. As early as 1736 the Hamburg and Frankfurt papers published reports of child performers; a 1756 advertisement read: "A child of six years, of the female sex . . . will perform publicly on the violin."[56] So popular were the wunderkinder that in 1792 it was said that over half the concert artists in Vienna were under fourteen. Though Hanslick claimed that this was an exaggeration, he admitted that Vienna was an important marketplace for wunderkinder, who were "by no means all Mozarts."[57]

There is general agreement that the young Mozart received a valuable musical education on his concert tours: the varied musical styles and techniques that he heard were integrated into and enriched his music. This was not his father's primary concern, however; Leopold Mozart was hoping for money, fame, and eventually a secure position for his son at a prestigious court. In the late eighteenth century, a virtuoso without a city or court appointment was dependent on private appearances at courts or homes of music-loving noblemen; the elder Mozart bowed, scraped, and petitioned, courting connections and the goodwill of influential aristocrats and wealthy music-loving merchants who might arrange a concert for a larger audience.

Fifty years later, Friedrich Wieck faced a different situation. From the beginning of her career, his daughter gave public concerts to which admission was charged, and he could and did pocket the profits. He did, however, have to act as his own manager and accept all the attendant commitments and anxieties.

The glamour of presenting a wunderkind proved irresistible. Wieck, usually honest about Clara's achievements and genuinely concerned about her welfare, followed the example of other stage fathers and deducted a year or two from her age when he could. Schumann noted in his diary in July 1831 that Wieck swore that Clara was ten and half when she was almost twelve.[58]

Yet Wieck was convinced (and on the concert trips his opinion was confirmed by Louis Spohr and others) that Clara was no mere wunderkind. Knowing that the general opinion of child prodigies was not high, he wrote his wife that the combination of Clara's age and skills presented an obstacle: "Most have had a few pieces crammed into them and they're not musical— nothing can come of them and nothing will." He worried about the response to his daughter's genuine talent. "Where are the cognoscenti and the pianists who will recognize Clara's extraordinary training and know how to examine it without prejudice?"[59] Wieck's own prejudices aside, it was generally agreed that Clara's playing was extraordinary. Her name became a byword for child prodigies, just as Mozart's had been before her. In 1839 Hector Berlioz, in his role as music reviewer, wrote about a Mlle Emilie Poussèze, "a nice child of eleven years who plays the piano in a way that raises hopes of a new Clara Wieck."[60]

WOMEN ARTISTS

At eighteen, Clara Wieck ranked with the principal artists of the day. When she resumed active concert life at the age of thirty-five she was hailed once again as one of the two or three leading pianists of Europe. She plunged into public concerts with such difficult and unfamiliar works as Beethoven's *Hammerclavier* Sonata and C Minor Variations, neither of which she had performed before. No other woman achieved the eminence she did on the concert stage, nor did any other pianist, male or female, maintain a like position for so long a time. She was not a feminist and it is doubtful that she sympathized with the views of those few women who were just beginning the struggle for equal rights in nineteenth-century Germany. On the contrary, she assumed her position as a premiere pianist without self-consciousness. From her birth it had been understood that she would be an artist, and she never doubted her success. Several times in her life she wrote that she regretted not having learned any "feminine skills," such as cooking and household management, but these moments were rare. Such tasks were left to servants—as was the custom even in lower-middle-class families—or to her daughter Marie, who from the age of twenty supervised the Schumann household and did the cooking when servants were unavailable.

In planning a concert career for his young daughter, then, Wieck was not treading an unknown path. When Clara was a child, there were no stage mothers, only stage fathers. In almost every case of a young musician in the eighteenth and early nineteenth centuries, it was the father—usually a musician himself—that stood behind the artist. Many ambitious fathers had attempted to carve careers for their daughters, and indeed, there were almost as many female as male wunderkinder touring Europe, among them pianists, violinists, singers, and harpists. The music journals reviewed a surprisingly large number of concerts given by women artists and compositions by female composers, often without comment on the gender of the musician. Those who continued past the child prodigy stage generally concertized until marriage and then settled down to court appointments (in the eighteenth century) or teaching (in the nineteenth), situations that did not require travel and were more compatible with family life.

In any discussion of women musicians of the early nineteenth century, a distinction must be made between professional musicians who, like Clara Wieck, performed in order to earn money and those highly proficient performers of the upper classes and aristocracy who, like Elisabeth von Herzogenberg, Henrietta Voigt, and Fanny Mendelssohn, had received professional training but never performed for a fee. Such artists as Livia Frege, who married into the upper middle class, were forced by convention or their husbands to discontinue their professional activities. These women carried on significant musical lives from their own homes, building music rooms large enough for audiences of a hundred or more connoisseurs in the tradition of the great music-loving aristocrats of the eighteenth century. They did not simply run salons, nor did they necessarily serve as the proverbial feminine inspiration for composers. They sang, played, made suggestions, and performed a valued service, providing a stage, even a forum for such composers as Beethoven, Mendelssohn, Brahms, and the young Schumann. But these gifted amateurs did not perform in public and so did not undergo the scrutiny of reviewers or have to battle for the attention and money of the public. As a professional, Clara Schumann competed with men on an equal footing.

When Clara Wieck first made her entrance into the concert world, she was favorably compared with other young women pianists of her generation, notably Leopoldine Blahetka and Anna de Belleville.* Another name to be

---

*Leopoldine Blahetka (1811–87) studied with Friedrich Kalkbrenner and Ignaz Moscheles, toured successfully, and was very popular in Vienna in the 1820s. She composed an opera and many works for piano. Anna de Belleville (1808–80) studied with Carl Czerny in Vienna before she settled in London and married James Oury, a violinist with whom she toured. Clara met her in Paris in 1839 and reported her to be disagreeable and vain.

reckoned with was Maria Moke, later Marie Pleyel but better known as
Camilla Pleyel (1811–75). Like Clara, these women were all survivors of the
child prodigy experience. Of the three women rivals, Marie Pleyel had the
longest career and the only one that rivaled Clara's in any way. Born in Paris
in 1811, she was eight years older than Clara. A student of Henri Herz,
Ignaz Moscheles, and Friedrich Kalkbrenner, she created a European sensation when she began to concertize at the age of fifteen. Berlioz was madly in
love with the very beautiful Marie, but she spurned him and in 1831 married
Camille Pleyel, of the Paris piano manufacturing family. The French were
very proud of Marie Pleyel, and François-Joseph Fétis, the reigning Parisian
music critic, declared that among the many famous pianists he had heard,
"no other gave the feeling of perfection that her playing created."[61]

Pleyel played in Leipzig in 1839. Clara, then living in Berlin, suffered
needless torment at the thought of Pleyel in *Leipzig*. Pleyel, whose marriage
lasted only four years, concertized until 1848 and then retired to a life of
teaching in the Brussels Conservatory. Clara met her for the first time in
1854 but never heard her play.

From time to time Clara acknowledged jealousy of another female pianist
in her diary, but in each case it was clearly based on the rival's youth or
beauty or on attentions bestowed by Wieck, Robert, or Brahms. In 1841, for
example, she wanted to be present during Robert's lessons with Amalie
Rieffel, ostensibly to learn from Robert's teaching but more likely because
she feared her husband might prefer the girl's playing to hers.[62] She feared
Camilla Pleyel not because of her playing but because of her flirtatious
manner and the attention she received from Wieck at a time when Clara was
estranged from him. She had no doubts that her own playing was superior to
Pleyel's: in 1838, just before her trip to Paris, she heard Thalberg play and
wrote Robert, "If I were not a woman, I would have said farewell to the life
of a virtuoso long since, but I can calm myself a little—I can surely cope with
the ladies."[63]

As her career advanced, younger women took their places on the concert
stage—Wilhelmina Clauss-Szarvady (1834–1907); Arabella Goddard (1836–
1922), an Englishwoman; Sophie Menter (1846–1918), a Liszt protégée;
Annette Essipof (1851–1914); and eventually her own students—but there
was unanimous agreement that she was more than a match for them. No
other pianist, male or female, appeared at the Gewandhaus as a soloist more
frequently than she (see Table 3).

The goals, desires, and needs of the woman artist in the nineteenth century differed in no substantial way from those that confront women in every
era. Clara Schumann knew well the stresses and strains of the life of a
concert artist, yet again and again she confessed that her music brought her
fulfillment that she could not live without. In 1853, for example, when she
finally had her own room and could practice without disturbing her husband,
she wrote in her diary:

Table 3. Number of performances given at Gewandhaus, Leipzig, by male and female piano soloists, 1794–1881

Men	Number of performances	Years	Number of performances	Women	Years
Felix Mendelssohn	47	1835–45	74	Clara Schumann	1828–81
Carl Reinecke	46	1843–81	17	Elisabeth Catharina Müller	1794–1810
Ignaz Moscheles	20	1816–61	12	Louise Hauffe	1854–70
Friedrich Schneider	16	1809–23	7	Marie Wieck	1845–56
Hans von Bülow	15	1857–80	7	Charlotte Fink	1835–38
			6	Wilhelmine Clauss-Szárvady	1850–60
Alexander Dreyschock	12	1838–61	5	Emilie Reichold	1826–29
Anton Rubinstein	10	1842–79	3	Anna de Belleville	1830–31

Note: Of the 261 pianists who appeared at the Gewandhaus in these years, 84 were women.
Source: Alfred Dörffel, ed., *Geschichte der Gewandhausconcerte zu Leipzig vom 25. November 1781 bis 25. November 1881* (Leipzig, 1884).

When I am able to practice regularly, then I really feel totally in my element; it is as though an entirely different mood comes over me, lighter, freer, and everything seems happier and more gratifying. Music is, after all, a goodly portion of my life, and when it is missing, it seems to me that all my physical and spiritual elasticity is gone.[64]

In a notable exchange with Brahms, who had urged her to give up her strenuous life as a performer, she wrote: "You regard it *only* as a way to earn money. I do not. I feel a calling to reproduce great works, above all, also those of Robert, as long as I have the strength to do so. . . . The practice of art is, after all, a great part of my inner self. To me, it is the very air I breathe."[65]

Clara Schumann as
Student and Teacher

As pianist and as teacher, Clara Schumann followed the precepts taught her by Friedrich Wieck. She retained the greatest respect and admiration for his guidance and instruction despite his irrational intrusions into her personal life. Friedrich Wieck had many successful students and took great pride in them, but his daughter Clara was by far the most outstanding pianist he ever produced. In typical Wieck fashion, he dismissed any influence other musicians might have had on his daughter. This proscription included Robert Schumann, of course.

How did Wieck teach? Frederick Niecks, who spoke with many students of Wieck, including Clara Schumann herself, reported:

> In spite of much inquiry, I have never yet succeeded in meeting a fairly adequate presentation of Wieck's method by himself, by his pupils, or by his critics. . . . I am quite sure that when I questioned Madame Schumann—the most carefully, patiently, lovingly and perfectly trained pupil that ever went through his hands—about her father's method she was taken aback and really puzzled. She said her brother Alwin Wieck's Materialen (finger exercises) gave an idea of it. Of course they do nothing of the kind. Then, trying as it were to seize the main features of the method, Madame Schumann remarked (conversation at Frankfurt on June 12, 1889): "He aimed especially at equality of touch, and the cultivation of right feeling for the use of the soft pedal."[1]

Both Marie and Alwin Wieck edited versions of their father's work; each purported to give the pianist the key to the method of this remarkable teacher and each claimed that these were the studies from which Clara Schumann had learned.

In the preface of her edition of her father's works, Marie Wieck wrote:

[288

These have been published because I have never met with this kind of rhythmic exercise, united with the first rudiments of theory, in any pianoforte method. These exercises, taught and played in the manner my father intended, are designed to produce a fine touch, to encourage playing from memory and transposing, and to cultivate a taste for the more refined style of piano playing.*

Wieck's method is difficult to describe, not because it is complicated but because he did not use a uniform approach; he attempted to give each student what was needed for individual growth and development. His philosophy is one we would characterize today as "progressive." He used the best of several systems, notably that of Johann Bernhard Logier, a music teacher born in Germany but trained in England.

The major elements of Logier's teaching consisted of (1) the use of a "chiroplast," a device placed over the keyboard to aid (actually to enforce) the development of correct finger, hand, and wrist positions (Wieck never used one); (2) group instruction of pupils of various levels of proficiency simultaneously: he arranged works so that beginners, for example, could play a basic theme while at the same time more advanced students played variations on it; and (3) incorporation of music theory and harmony in basic piano instruction, with the aim of fostering knowledgeable musicianship. This method, enthusiastically endorsed by such influential musicians as Louis Spohr, who saw Logier in action in England, became very popular in Germany, and though this approach was not used universally, aspects of Logier's method, such as group instruction and the combining of theory with piano lessons, are used in music instruction today and are still considered innovative.

Though many features of his method were sensible and effective, Logier acquired a reputation as a charlatan, probably because he instituted a successful public relations campaign and earned a great deal of money. (Spohr reported that he was charging 100 guineas a lesson to impart his "secrets" to London teachers.)[2]

Wieck was teaching piano before Logier's method was well known in Germany but he admitted that he learned a great deal from him. Clara's instruction actually began before she left for Plauen with her mother in the spring of 1824, but Wieck began to teach her (and two other girls) by the

*In the preface, dated Summer 1875, Marie Wieck also wrote: "These are the celebrated studies used by the composer in teaching his two daughters, Madame Clara Schumann and Marie Wieck" (Friedrich Wieck, *Pianoforte Studien*, ed. Marie Wieck [Leipzig: C. F. Peters, 1875).] The title page of Alwin Wieck's edition, titled *Materialen zu Friedrich Wieck's Pianoforte Methodik* (Berlin: Simrock, 1875), states: "Friedrich Wieck instructed his daughter, Frau Clara Schumann, née Wieck, according to this method." Clara, who had a more cordial relationship with her brother than with Marie Wieck, helped contact a publisher for his edition and supported it to the best of her ability. Both editions are undoubtedly authentic representations of Wieck's work.

Logier method in September, when she returned to his home. By Easter he was giving her lessons privately, according to his own system.

There is no doubt that this harsh, opinionated, and often crude man had immense gifts as a teacher. Even without Clara and her signal success— which he admitted to his wife surprised him as much as it did the rest of the world—he would have enjoyed a reputation as an outstanding piano teacher. His philosophy was expressed in an inimitable style in his 130-page treatise, *Clavier und Gesang* (Piano and Song). Most of the chapters are written as dialogues in which Wieck appears as "DAS" (*Der alte Schulmeister:* the old schoolmaster); others are in the form of letters or lectures—one might even call them harangues.

Wieck insisted that the accomplishments of Clara and her half sister Marie were the best proof of the superiority of his system. Despite the five-year-old Clara's supposed deafness, she was taught to play dance tunes and accompaniments to them by ear. She developed an extraordinary memory for musical phrases and could play a short piece after a single hearing. All of Wieck's students were taught to play first by ear so that they could concentrate on producing a good, full tone. All understood tempo and meter, and all played scales and cadential progressions of I, IV, and V chords in every key before they could read music. They were expected to find and practice triads and dominant seventh chords with inversions in all keys, and then to use what they had learned in new ways by improvising and composing their own little pieces.[3] Wieck wrote individual exercises for each student in a sequential order of difficulty; thus each could reach his or her potential in a natural way.

The title of his book indicates his concern with the art of singing—the basis, he believed, of beautiful, refined piano playing. All of his students were required to study voice; recall that Clara studied voice with Johann Aloys Miksch (the teacher of the famous soprano Wilhelmine Schröder-Devrient and the man with whom Wieck himself later studied).

Wieck's approach was inherently musical and demonstrates the kind of understanding of the learning process outlined by many twentieth-century music psychologists. As early as 1853 we find him writing:

> As a psychologist, thinker, man, and teacher, I have striven to work for all-around musical development, never making excess demands and always attempting to maintain the student's interest. I never stood still, learned daily as I taught, and always sought to improve. When possible, my direction was determined by the mood of the students at the time. With each child and with each lesson, I was always new and different and in a cheerful and happy state of mind. Moreover, I was never one to follow patterns; I never behaved like a pedant, sticking to fixed ideas and opinions.[4]

Wieck did not believe in overpracticing: he expected his students to practice every day, but only when they were fresh. Even ten minutes of practice could be effective, he believed, if the student practiced frequently and made the most of each minute. Piano instruction should begin, he felt, at about age six, and to maintain correct habits three lessons a week with a cheerful, devoted, energetic teacher were optimal. Two cornerstones of his method were his beliefs that musical education was nourished by listening to good music and that outdoor exercise was essential for health. As we know, Wieck could be sarcastic, insensitive, even cruel, but he brought an abundance of humor and common sense to his teaching.

When Clara's father left Leipzig to settle in Dresden, he set out to learn as much as possible about singing and then took up the teaching of singing, though he continued to teach piano as well. Some pupils came to study both. Amy Fay described an evening in the Wieck household in Dresden in 1872. After Marie Wieck had played,

> the old Herr then said, "Now we'll have something else," and got up and went to the piano, and called the young girls. He made three of them sing, one after the other, and they sang very charmingly indeed. One of them he made improvise a cadenza, and a second sang the alto to it without accompaniment. He was very proud of that. He exercises his pupils in all sorts of ways, trains them to sing any given tone, and "to skip up and down the ladder," as they call the scale.[5]

Wieck believed that every virtuoso should know how to teach. In his letter of August 9, 1830, to Robert Schumann's mother, he made a special point of the fact that he was educating his eleven-year-old daughter to be a teacher even though, he claimed, she was already the best female pianist in the world.[6] At twelve Clara began to teach her brother Alwin (Friedrich paid her several groschen for her work), and she continued to teach throughout her life.

The experience she gained by teaching her brother under Wieck's guidance served her well. When Clara went off to Paris alone at nineteen, she paid her way by giving lessons to aspiring pianists in every city in which she performed. Indeed, Henriette Reichmann, the young woman she met in Stuttgart who accompanied her to Paris, was both companion and student. In the French capital Clara taught wealthy French and English women who were eager to study with the young virtuosa.

Clara Schumann appreciated her father's talents and his total devotion to her career. Many years after Wieck's death she wrote to an Englishman who had studied with her, Dr. Richard Wilkinson, a letter that tells us much about the relationship between daughter and father, student and teacher. She was worried, she wrote, about the health of one of her students:

> She does not have—as I did—the good fortune to have a wise father at her side, a father who guarded her health, took care that she took walks, that when she practiced she took breaks, and that in the afternoon before an

evening concert she did nothing but rest; in short, a father who stood guard. Indeed, people would call him a tyrant, a term my father had to accept—but I still thank him daily; the freshness I have retained even at my great age (at least as far as art goes)—for that I have him to thank! It was also a blessing for me that he was extremely strict, rebuked me when I deserved it and thus prevented the praises from making me insolent. Sometimes the rebuke was bitter, yet it was good![7]

Though the daughter lacked her father's humor and instincts as a teacher, she had the advantage of years on the concert stage. Moreover, she displayed warmth toward her students, a quality that Wieck lacked (and that was not always apparent in her relationships with her own children). She followed each student's career with great interest, was saddened by poor reviews, rejoiced at triumphs. Like all great teachers, she became a parental figure to her students, and young women and men flocked to study with her wherever she was—in Berlin, Frankfurt, Baden-Baden, and on summer vacations in Austria and Switzerland.

When Clara Schumann accepted a position as principal teacher in the Hoch Conservatory* in Frankfurt at the age of fifty-nine, she had never before committed herself to a full-time teaching position. In Frankfurt, Frau Kammervirtuosin Schumann, as she was named in the first annual report of the Conservatory, taught in her own home and was permitted much free time for touring. She was the only woman on the faculty when the school opened in 1878 and was accorded this privilege because of her unique position in the German musical world. Once again her talents and reputation placed her above considerations of gender. In 1879 Joachim Raff, the first director, wrote to another woman who was seeking a position: "With the exception of Madame Schumann there is no woman and there will not be any women employed in the Conservatory. As for Madame Schumann, I count her as a man."[8]†

Raff knew Madame Schumann would draw students; her presence in Frankfurt was an asset to the Conservatory and to the musical life of the city. She taught at the Hoch Conservatory until the end of the school year of 1892, when she was almost seventy-three. The roster of students she attracted included pianists from Chicago, New York, Florence, Edinburg, London (she had an unusually large group of students from Great Britain), Vienna, and every city in Germany.††

---

*In German, the Hoch'sche Conservatorium. The school, founded by a wealthy Frankfurt music lover, was headed first by Joachim Raff, then from his death in 1882 until 1908 by Bernhard Scholz. It is now part of the Staatliche Hochschule für Musik in Frankfurt.

†Raff soon changed his mind: by 1880 two other women had joined the school's faculty. And from that year on, Raff established composition classes for women, probably the first of their kind in Germany.

††During the first school year, 1878–79, the class included Edward MacDowell of New York. See Peter Cahn, *Das Hoch'sche Konservatorium in Frankfurt am Main (1878–1978)* (Frankfurt am Main: Waldemar Kramer, 1979).

As Raff was a prominent Lisztian, Clara Schumann had many qualms about him. Her doubts were stilled by Brahms, who encouraged her to take the position and helped her time and again to unravel the intricacies of academic politics. Madame Schumann was treated royally by the director and governing board, and in return was the model of a conscientious teacher. She pondered questions of curriculum, standards, auditions, scheduling, examinations, and similar educational issues—some petty, some serious— with interest and concern.*

Reports by many of her former students indicate that although Clara Schumann based her technique on Wieck's principles, she developed her own style of teaching. As a working artist, she was forced to limit her teaching time, and accepted only advanced students who had mastered basic piano technique and had already studied theory. She taught mainly by example, though she did not expect her students to follow slavishly. Her daughters Marie and Eugenie (and later her students Nathalie Janotha, Lazzaro Uzielli, and others) acted as assistant teachers and coached less advanced pupils who sought admittance to her classes. Some never achieved this distinction. One young English student, Clement Harris, noted his triumph when he was accepted by Clara Schumann in 1889: "At home I was overwhelmed by congratulations. . . . Telegraphed London, 'It is done; I finally made it. Hurrah. Long live seven hours of daily practice.'" A few days later he wrote: "I am proud to be a Schumann scholar now. I would never have dreamed how difficult it would be to be accepted in her class. Everyone in my generation is trying for it. I believe that fortune really favored me, but I also certainly worked hard enough to earn it."9

Her carefully chosen students took their lessons, usually two a week, in the presence of other students so that they benefited doubly. Less advanced students listened in from other rooms. All of her students were invited to musicales at her home to hear her play with Brahms, Joachim, Stockhausen, and other artists. They were expected to attend opera, orchestral, and chamber music performances, and generally to participate in the musical life of Frankfurt.

Even as a young girl Clara Schumann took her teaching responsibilities seriously. In Frankfurt her loyalty to her students was legendary. Mathilde Verne, one of her students at the Conservatory, wrote, "To her each pupil represented a sacred trust, not only in music, but as a character, and she influenced us for good in every way."10

Audiences and admirers always expressed interest in her teaching techniques, and many of her English students described their lessons with Clara Schumann in English-language newspapers and journals. In an article in the *Musical Times*, Marie Fromm, a Hoch Conservatory student, reported,

*Her correspondence with Raff concerning Conservatory matters is preserved in the Bayerische Staatsbibliothek, Munich.

"The very foundation of her training was that the arm must be absolutely loose, not a single muscle in upper or lower arm or wrist strained or forced, the fingers kept loose in the knuckle-joints, all power and quality coming from the back muscles."[11]

Though she did not insist, as her father had done, that her students study voice in order to learn the essence of the bel canto legato style, she did teach her students to "caress" or press the keys in order to produce the "singing" tone for which she was noted. Franklin Taylor told Sir George Grove that "nothing ever sounded harsh or ugly in her hands" and that "the peculiarly beautiful quality of the tone she produced, which was rather vigorous without the slightest harshness, was obtained, even in the loudest passages, by pressure with the fingers rather than by percussion." He went on to say, "Indeed, her playing was particularly free from violent movement of any kind; in passages, the fingers were kept close to the keys and squeezed instead of striking them, while chords were grasped from the wrist, rather than struck from the elbow."[12]

Other students also recorded their reactions to her emphasis on a loose wrist; Eugenie Schumann writes of her first lesson with her mother:

> She played the first eight bars [of a Czerny étude] from the wrist with all the notes of equal strength, forte, yet exquisitely mellow in tone, never stiffening the wrist for an instant, and knitting the chords rhythmically together so that the simple piece suddenly took on life and character. It was a revelation to me; my feeling for beauty of touch and rhythm was stirred into life from that moment.[13]

Though her own position at the piano was often characterized as "hunched over," her students remember that she insisted on an air of seeming relaxation at the keyboard. She taught that the arms should fall easily from the shoulders, Carl Friedberg reminisced, but never pressed against the sides of the body.[14] The greatest pressure came from the fingers; this may have contributed to the control of tone and expressivity which was the hallmark of her playing and of that of many of her pupils.

In her typical conscientious fashion, she meticulously observed every note and marking and, according to Eugenie, never allowed "the smallest inexactitude to pass."[15] Adelina de Lara also noted her patience with details. "Her vigilance never relaxed in matters of tone-quality, rhythm and phrasing; in short, she treated the pianoforte as an orchestra and required her pupils to consider every minute phrase and to express it as though it were given to a separate instrument."[16]

No one dared question Clara Schumann's authority; indeed, she was perceived as having a direct link not only to Schumann, Mendelssohn, Chopin, and Brahms, but to Bach and Beethoven as well. "Do you think Beethoven would have taken the trouble to write all this notation, dots, ties, crotchets here, quavers there, if he had meant it to be otherwise?" she asked Eugenie.[17] Fanny Davies, another English student, wrote, "Clara Schumann summed up the essentials in these words, 'Play what is written; play it *as* it is written. It all stands there.'"[18] At the same time, however, she was never loath to correct an edition if she believed it to be faulty. And because of her firsthand experience with early editions of Bach, Beethoven, and the early romantic masters, she never doubted that she was in the right.

All of her students knew that she deplored ostentation in any form: no exaggeration of dynamics, of tempo or change of tempo, or of pedaling, no tricks that might detract from the purity of the interpretation was permitted. De Lara's description of Clara Schumann's admonition to students delineates her position vis-à-vis technical prowess: "'Keine Passagen' [No passages], she would cry out in despair if one tried to rattle through any rapid figuration with mere empty virtuosity . . . she would tolerate nothing that was done for mere brilliance and pace."[19]

Her feeling that technique should serve the composer was characteristic of the "priestess," and was reflected in the music she chose to play and to teach. Though she had a magnificent technique at her disposal, she selected her repertoire for its intrinsic beauty, style, and musical qualities and not necessarily because its difficulty might impress audiences. She expected her students to adhere to the standards of technique and repertoire she set for herself. Scales, arpeggios, and exercises by Clementi, Cramer, and Czerny (in her edition) were included in every lesson, along with piano works by such composers as Bach, Beethoven, Brahms, Chopin, Haydn, Heller, Mendelssohn, Mozart, Schubert, Schumann, and Weber. A collection of music belonging to Emma Schmidt, a Schumann pupil, includes a few pieces by little-known contemporaries—Nicolai von Wilm, Eduard Strauss (brother of Johann)—but no showpieces by Liszt or Thalberg.[20]

In many letters and diary entries Clara Schumann expressed (with some envy) her conviction that only a composer—a creator—could achieve immortality; the interpretive artist would soon be forgotten. As a performer she was only too well aware of the younger stars waiting to take their places in the spotlight and of the evanescence of an interpreter's career, no matter how brilliant. As a teacher, however, she did achieve some degree of immortality: her influence extends to this day. Many of her pupils concertized; others became prominent teachers and thus passed on her philosophy. The Schumann tradition colored the playing of such pianists as Fanny Davies, Leonard Borwick (her favorite student), Nathalie Janotha, Adelina de Lara, and Mary Wurm. Mathilde Verne (sister of Mary Wurm), though not a well-known performer, was the teacher of Harold Samuel and Cutner Solomon, eminent English pianists; Carl Friedberg brought the tradition to the United States, where during his many years at the Institute of Musical Art (later the

Juilliard School) he taught such artists as Malcolm Frager, William Masselos, Bruce Hungerford, and Yaltah Menuhin.*

As a teacher Clara Schumann demonstrated the same qualities that made her a great artist. Her teaching style, infused by her resolute and determined spirit, combined her high ideals and scrupulous attention to details, her emphasis on expressivity and tone, her insistence that technique be cultivated to serve the music, and her demand that the performer honor, above all, the composer—the creator. This was her legacy to the future.

---

*Julia Smith in *Master Pianist: The Career and Teaching of Carl Friedberg* (New York: Philosophical Library, 1963), 160–66, lists many of Friedberg's students.

Catalogue of Works

Titles are given as they appear on the title pages of the first editions.

Op. 1. QUATRE POLONOISES pour le Pianoforte
Composed: 1830.
Published: Leipzig: Hofmeister, February 1831. Plate no. 1590.
Dedication: None.
Location of autograph: Unknown.

Op. 2. CAPRICES en forme de Valse Pour le Piano
Composed: 1831–32.
Published: Paris: Stoepel; Leipzig: Hofmeister, 1832. Plate no. 1675.
Dedication: Madame Henriette Foerster, née Weicke.
Location of autograph: Caprices 3 and 6, Bds, Mus. Ms. Autogr. C. Schumann 3; locations of others unknown.

Op. 3. ROMANCE varié Pour le Piano
Composed: 1833.
Published: Leipzig: Hofmeister; Paris: Richault, Summer 1833. Plate no. 1897.
Dedication: MONSIEUR ROBERT SCHUMANN.
Location of autograph: Unknown.

Op. 4. VALSES ROMANTIQUES pour le Piano
Composed: 1835.
Published: Leipzig: Whistling, 1835. Plates sold to Hofmeister (Leipzig), 1838; subsequent editions bearing plate no. 2307 issued by Hofmeister.
Dedication: Madame Emma Eggers née Garlichs.
Location of autograph: Unknown.
Comments: The Valses were orchestrated but none of the instrumental parts survive.

Op. 5. QUATRE Pièces caractéristiques. No. 1, Le Sabbat   No. 2, Caprice à la Boléro   No. 3, Romance   No. 4, Ballet des Revenants
Composed: 1835.

Published: Leipzig: Whistling, 1835 or 1836. Reissued, with op. 6, as *Soirées musicales. 10 PIÈCES CARACTÉRISTIQUES* (Leipzig: Hofmeister, 1838). Plate nos. 2148, 2308.

Dedication: Mademoiselle Sophie Kaskel.

Location of autograph: "Romance" (given as "Romanze für Klavier" and inscribed "Leipzig, Im Juni 1836") in Bds, Mus. Ms. Autogr. C. Schumann 1 (Aloys Fuchs Collection). An autograph of the Romance, titled "Andante con sentimento" and inscribed "zu Wien im April 1838," is in Wgm. Location of autographs of other movements unknown.

Comments: No. 1, titled "Hexentanz," was published separately by Haslinger in Vienna, in April 1838 (Plate no. 7548). No. 3, "Romance" (in B major), renamed "Andante con sentimento," was published as a "work composed in 1838" in Clara Schumann, *Romantische Klaviermusik*, ed. Franzpeter Goebels, vol. 2 (Heidelberg: Willy Müller, 1977), and in Clara Schumann, *Drei kleine Klavierstücke*, ed. Rosario Marciano, Diletto Musicale no. 812 (Vienna: Doblinger, 1979).

Op. 6. Soirées Musicales contenant Toccatina, Ballade, Nocturne, Polonaise et deux Mazurkas

Composed: 1836.

Published: Leipzig: Hofmeister; Paris: Richault, October 1836. Plate no. 2148. (See op. 5 on publication of op. 5 and 6.)

Dedication: Madame Henriette Voigt.

Location of autograph: Unknown.

Op. 7. Premier CONCERT pour le Piano-Forte avec accompagnement d'Orchestre (ou de Quintour)

Composed: 1833–35.

Published: Leipzig: Hofmeister; Paris: Richault; Hamburg: A. Cranz, 1837. Plate no. 2169.

Dedication: Monsieur Louis Spohr.

Location of autograph: A draft of the last movement, orchestrated by Robert Schumann and in Schumann's hand, is in Bds, Mus. Ms. 20427. What appears to be a fragment of the Concerto, piano part only, is in Bds, Mus. Ms. Autogr. C. Schumann 1, verso.

Op. 8. VARIATIONS de Concert pour le PIANO-FORTE, sur la Cavatine du Pirate, de Bellini

Composed: 1837.

Published: Vienna: Haslinger, October 1837. Plate no. 7368.

Dedication: Monsieur Adolph Henselt.

Location of autograph: Unknown.

Op. 9. Souvenir de Vienne. Impromptu.

Composed: 1838.

Published: Vienna: Diabelli, [1838]. Plate no. 6530.

Dedication: None.

Location of autograph: Unknown.

Comments: An engraver's copy with many penciled corrections, erasures, and crossouts is in Bds, Mus. Ms. Autogr. C. Schumann 2.

Op. 10. SCHERZO pour le Pianoforte

Composed: Probably 1838.

Published: Leipzig: Breitkopf & Härtel; Paris: Schonenberger, c. 1838. Plate no. 5987.
Dedication: None.
Location of autograph: Unknown.

Op. 11. Trois ROMANCES pour le PIANO
Composed: 1839.
Published: Vienna: Mechetti; Paris: Richault, 1840. Plate no. 3391.
Dedication: Monsieur Robert Schumann.
Location of autograph: Unknown.
Comments: The Romance no. 2 was published separately, as "Andante und Allegro," in the supplement to the *Neue Zeitschrift für Musik* in September 1839 and was later reprinted under that title by Schuberth, Leipzig, in 1866 or 1867 (Plate no. 4106).

Op. 12. ZWÖLF GEDICHTE aus F. Rückert's Liebesfrühling für Gesang und Pianoforte von ROBERT UND CLARA SCHUMANN
Three songs by Clara Schumann: no. 2, "Er ist gekommen"; no. 4, "Liebst du um Schönheit"; no. 11, "Warum willst du And're fragen?"
Composed: June 8, 1841.
Published (in two parts, as op. 37/12): Leipzig: Breitkopf & Härtel, 1841. Plate nos. 6596, 6597.
Dedication: None.
Location of autograph: RSH, 5985-A1; Bds, Mus. Ms. Autogr. C. Schumann 5.

Op. 13. SECHS LIEDER mit Begleitung des Pianoforte
Composed:
No. 1, "Ich stand in dunkeln Träumen" (text by Heinrich Heine), Christmas 1840.
No. 2, "Sie liebten sich Beide" (text by Heinrich Heine), June 8, 1842.
No. 3, "Liebeszauber" ("Die Liebe sass als Nachtigall," text by Emanuel Geibel), June 8, 1842.
No. 4. "Der Mond kommt still gegangen" (text by Emanuel Geibel), July 1842.
No. 5, "Ich hab' in deinem Auge" (text by Friedrich Rückert), June 1843.
No. 6, "Die stille Lotosblume" (text by Emanuel Geibel), July 1842.
Published: Leipzig: Breitkopf & Härtel, c. 1843. Plate no. 6996.
Dedication: Queen Caroline Amalie of Denmark.
Location of autographs: All in Bds, Mus. Ms. Autogr. C. Schumann 5, and in RSH: no. 1, 5984-A1; no. 2, 4473-A1 and 7311-A1; no. 3, 7311-A1; no. 5, 5987-A1 and 10346-A1.

Op. 14. Deuxième SCHERZO pour le Pianoforte
Composed: After 1840.
Published: Leipzig: Breitkopf & Härtel, 1845. Plate no. 7214.
Dedication: Madame Tutein née Siboni.
Location of autograph: Unknown.

Op. 15. Quatre PIÈCES FUGITIVES pour le Pianoforte
Composed: Probably 1840–44.
Published: Leipzig: Breitkopf & Härtel, 1845. Plate no. 7215.
Dedication: Marie Wieck.
Location of autograph: Unknown except for Scherzo, RSH, 5986-A1, originally composed for unpublished Sonatine (see below, "Works For Piano," under "Unpublished Works").

Op. 16. III Praeludien und Fugen für das Pianoforte
Composed: 1845.
Published: Leipzig: Breitkopf & Härtel, 1845. Plate no. 7334.
Dedication: None.
Location of autograph: All but Praeludium 2, RSH, 5982-A1.

Op. 17. TRIO für Pianoforte, Violine und Violoncello
Composed: 1846.
Published: Leipzig: Breitkopf & Härtel, 1847. Plate no. 7562.
Dedication: None.
Location of autograph: RSH, 12886-A1 (draft).
Comments: Some emendations on autograph seem to be by Robert Schumann.

Op. 20. VARIATIONEN für das Pianoforte über ein Thema von Robert Schumann
Composed: June 1853.
Published: Leipzig: Breitkopf & Härtel, 1854. Plate no. 8944.
Dedication: Robert Schumann.
Location of autograph: RSH, 5989-A1; Brahms legacy, Wgm.

Op. 21. DREI ROMANZEN für Pianoforte
Composed: 1853.
Published: Leipzig: Breitkopf & Härtel, 1855 or 1856. Plate no. 9200.
Dedication: Johannes Brahms.
Location of autograph: RSH, 5990-A1 (no. 1); Bds, Mus. Ms. Autogr. C. Schumann 10 (nos. 2 and 3, not entirely in composer's hand).
Comments: The autograph in RSH is inscribed to Robert Schumann: "Dem geliebten Mann am 8ten Juni 1853" (To my beloved husband on June 8, 1853). No. 1 in Wgm is inscribed: "Meinem lieben Freunde Johannes, componirt den 2. April 1855" (To my dear friend Johannes, composed April 2, 1855). The discrepancy in dates remains a puzzle. Nos. 2 and 3 in Bds are dated "June 25, 1853," and "End June 1853."

Op. 22. DREI ROMANZEN für Pianoforte und Violine
Composed: 1853.
Published: Leipzig: Breitkopf & Härtel, 1855 or 1856. Plate no. 9201.
Dedication: Joseph Joachim.
Location of autograph: Bds, Mus. Ms. Autogr. C. Schumann 4 (presentation copy) and 10 (working copy).
Comments: The inscription on the presentation copy reads: "Dem erhabenen Musikern und Freund Joseph Joachim" (To the illustrious musician and friend Joseph Joachim).

Op. 23. SECHS LIEDER aus Jucunde von Hermann Rollet
Composed:
No. 1, "Was weinst du, Blümlein?" June 9, 1853.
No. 2, "An einem lichten Morgen," June 13, 1853.
No. 3, "Geheimes Flüstern," June 10, 1853.
No. 4, "Auf einem grünen Hügel," June 16, 1853.
No. 5, "Das ist ein Tag," June 21, 1853.
No. 6, "O Lust, O lust," June 19, 1853.
Published: Leipzig: Breitkopf & Härtel, 1855 or 1856. Plate no. 9202.
Dedication: Livia Frege.
Location of autographs: Bds, Mus. Ms. Aut. C. Schumann 5.

PUBLISHED WORKS WITHOUT OPUS NUMBERS

Walzer für Gesang und Klavier. Text by Johann Peter Lyser.
  Composed: 1834?
  Published: In *Lyser's Liedersammlung* (1834).
  Dedication: None.
  Location of autograph: Unknown.
  Comments: Engraver's copy of song in RSH, 10935-A3; copy of entire song collec-
    tion in Bds Ds544. According to Paula Rehberg and Walter Rehberg, *Robert
    Schumann: Sein Leben und sein Werk,* 2d ed. (Zurich: Artemis, 1969), 666, an
    autograph of the work can be found in a Dresden song album published in 1846.
    The song and its inclusion in the Lyser collection is noted in Clara Schumann's
    diary, December 4, 1833.

Am Strande (also published as "Am Strand"). Text by Robert Burns.
  Composed: Christmas 1840.
  Published: *Neue Zeitung für Musik,* 14 (July 1841), suppl.; Leipzig: Schuberth,
    1867 or 1868. Plate no. 4268.
  Location of autograph: Bds, Mus. Ms. Autogr. C. Schumann 5; RSH, 5984-A1.

Mein Stern ("O du mein Stern"). Text by Friederike Serre.
  Composed: June 1846.
  Published (as "O Thou My Star"): London: Wessell, 1848. Plate no. 6945.
  Location of autograph: RSH, 7261-A1; Bds, Mus. Ms. Autogr. C. Schumann 5;
    Heinrich-Heine-Institut, Düsseldorf, 53.78.
  Comments: "O Thou My Star" was translated by Leopold Wray.

Impromptu
  Composed: ca. 1844.
  Published: in *Album du Gaulois* (Paris, 1885) (anthology of piano works by eminent
    composers published by the journal *Le Gaulois*).

Romanze für Clavier
  Composed: April 2, 1855?
  Published: In Clara Schumann, *Romantische Klaviermusik,* ed. Franzpeter
    Goebels, vol. 2 (Heidelberg: Willy Müller, 1977); Clara Schumann, *Drei kleine
    Klavierstücke,* ed. Rosario Marciano, Diletto Musicale no. 812 (Vienna:
    Doblinger, 1979).
  Location of autograph: Wgm.
  Comments: The Vienna autograph, a presentation copy, is dated Christmas 1856;
    the words "Liebendes Gedenken! [Loving thoughts] Clara" are inscribed at the
    end of the piece. It may have been presented to Brahms at Christmas 1856.

Cadenzas

Cadenzas (2) for Beethoven Piano Concerto in G Major, op. 58
  Composed: 1846.
  Published: Leipzig: Rieter-Biedermann, c. 1870. Plate no. 636.
  Location of autograph: Unknown.

Autograph of the first page of Clara Schumann's Song "Am Strande." Musikabteilung, Deutsche Staatsbibliothek, Berlin/DDR.

Cadenza for Beethoven Piano Concerto in C Minor, op. 37
Composed: 1868.
Published: Leipzig: Rieter-Biedermann, c. 1870. Plate no. 636.
Location of autograph: Unknown.

Cadenzas (2) for Mozart Piano Concerto in D Minor (K. 466)
Composed: Unknown. (See discussion on p. 202)
Published: Leipzig: Rieter-Biedermann, c. 1891. Plate no. 1770.
Location of autograph: Library of Congress, Washington, D.C.

UNPUBLISHED WORKS

Songs for Voice and Piano

Das Abendstern. Text by?
Composed: ?
Location of autograph: RSH 11-A1.
Comments: The autograph, in Clara Schumann's hand, is written on presentation paper but has neither inscription nor date. It is not among the songs in the music notebook of songs in Bds.

Volkslied ("Es fiel ein Reif in der Frühlingsnacht"). Text by Heinrich Heine.
Composed: Christmas 1840.
Location of autograph: RSH, 5984-A1; Bds, Mus. Ms. Autogr. C. Schumann 5.
Comments: The same text was set for voice and piano by Robert Schumann, op. 64, no. 3b.

Die gute Nacht. Text by Friedrich Rückert.
Composed: June 8, 1841.
Location of autograph: RSH, 5985-A1; Bds, Mus. Ms. Autogr. C. Schumann 5.
Comments: This text was set for four voices by Robert Schumann, op. 59, no. 4.

Loreley ("Ich weiss' nicht was soll es bedeuten"). Text by Heinrich Heine.
Composed: June 8, 1843.
Location of autograph: RSH, 5987-A1; Bds, Mus. Ms. Autogr. C. Schumann 5.

O weh des Scheidens. Text by Friedrich Rückert.
Composed: June 1843.
Location of autograph: RSH, 5987-A1; Bds, Mus. Ms. Autogr. C. Schumann 5.

Beim Abschied (Letzten Abschied). Text by Friederike Serre.
Composed: June 1846.
Location of autograph: RSH, 7261-A1; Bds, C.S. Aut. 5.
Comments: The RSH autograph, "Beym Abschied," is a presentation copy inscribed to Friederike Serre. The Berlin autograph is titled "Letzten Abschied." In the table of contents of the Berlin collection, Robert Schumann lists it as "Zum Abschied."

Drei gemischte Chöre: "Abendfeyer in Venedig," "Vorwärts," "Goldoliera." Text by Emanuel Geibel.
Composed: 1848.

Location of autograph: RSH, 10427-A1.

Comments: Written for four voices. The autographs, only partially in the composer's hand, bear the stamp of the Dresden Chorgesang Verein and some emendations and additional measures in the hand of Robert Schumann. They were rehearsed with that choral group in July, August, and September 1848.

Das Veilchen ("Ein Veilchen auf der Wiese stand"). Text by Johann von Goethe.

Composed: July 7, 1853.

Location of autograph: Bds, Mus. Ms. Autogr. C. Schumann 5.

Works for Piano

Etude

Composed: Presumably early 1830s.

Location of autograph: Bds, Mus. Ms. Autogr. C. Schumann 3.

Comments: Bound together with op. 2, nos. 3 and 6.

Sonatine: Allegro, Scherzo, Adagio, Rondo

Composed: First two movements, 1841; last two movements, probably January 1842.

Location of autograph: RSH, 5986-A1.

Comments: When the Sonatine was presented to Robert Schumann as a Christmas gift in 1841, it was accompanied by the message: "The last movement and perhaps a small Andante will follow later, I think. In the meantime, I beg your kindness for these two movements." When the last two movements were added, the Scherzo was shifted to become the third movement. This scherzo was used as the last number of Clara Schumann's op. 15.

Concerto (one incomplete movement only)

Composed: 1847.

Location of autograph: RSH, 5988-A1.

Comments: The autograph is inscribed: "Meinem geliebten Robert zum 8ten Juni 1847 von seiner Clara" (To my beloved Robert on June 8, 1847, from his Clara.)

Romanze (A minor)

Composed: July 1853.

Location of autograph: Bds, Mus. Ms. Autogr. C. Schumann 7 (presentation copy) and 10.

Comments: The inscription on the cover page of Aut. 7 reads, "Composed for my faithful Rosalie [Leser] . . . Clara Schumann. Düsseldorf, July 1853." Aut. 10, a working copy, is dated July 23, 1853.

Marsch

Composed: 1879.

Location of autograph: RSH, 5993-A1.

Comments: The autograph is inscribed: "Composed for the golden wedding anniversary of Julius and Pauline Hübner, May 21, 1879." An arrangement of the march for four hands, RSH 5994-A1, is in a copyist's hand but signed by the composer and dated December 1891. The orchestration by Julius Otto Grimm, dated March 2, 1888, is in RSH, 5995-A1.

Vorspiele
  Composed: Improvisations written out probably in 1895.
  Location of autograph: Manuscript in copyist's hand (17 pages), RSH, 11514-A1.

Präludium and Präludien für Schüler
  Composed: Improvisations written out probably in 1895.
  Location of autograph: Bds, Mus. Ms. Autogr. C. Schumann 8 and 9. The Präludium may have been written by another hand. The Präludien für Schüler are in her hand.
  Comments: Autograph 9 was given to the Berlin library by Marie Schumann in 1929.

LOST WORKS

Songs

Alte Heimath. Text by Justinius Kerner.
  Composed: 1831.
  Comments: A performance on December 13, 1831, is mentioned in Clara Schumann's diary.

Der Traum. Text by Christoph August Tiedge
  Composed: 1831.
  Comments: The song is noted in Clara Schumann's diary, December 13, 1831. Her father describes a performance in Frankfurt on January 27, 1832 (Friedrich Wieck, *Briefe aus den Jahren 1830–1838*, ed. Käthe Walch-Schumann [Cologne: Arno Volk-Verlag, 1968], 40).

Der Wanderer. Text by Justinius Kerner.
  Composed: 1831.
  Comments: A performance on December 13, 1831, is mentioned in Clara Schumann's diary.

Works for Piano

Variationen über ein Originalthema
  Composed: 1830.
  Comments: A performance on November 8, 1830, of a work with this title is noted in Clara Schumann's diary. Litzmann includes it in the Repertoire List for 1830, and Alfred Dörffel lists a performance on November 8, 1830 (*Geschichte der Gewandhausconcerte zu Leipzig vom 25. November 1781 bis 25. November 1881* [Leipzig, 1884]).

Variationen über ein Tyrolerlied
  Composed: 1830.
  Comments: A performance of a work called simply "Variationen für Clavier" on October 9, 1831, is noted in Clara Schumann's diary. Litzmann includes it in the Repertoire List for 1830.

Phantasie-Variationen über ein Wieck Romanze
   Composed: 1831.
   Comments: A performance of this work on October 26, 1831, is noted in Clara
   Schumann's diary. The "Wieck Romanze" was probably the work for "physhar-
   monica" which was featured on several of her programs between 1830 and 1832.

An Alexis
   Composed: 1832.
   Comments: In a letter of January 27, 1832, Wieck wrote that Clara was composing
   variations "An Alexis" for performance in Paris (Wieck, *Briefe*, 41). The work is
   also mentioned by Litzmann, 1:57, as one of a group of smaller works for piano
   on which she worked in the summer of 1833.

Rondo in H Moll
   Composed: 1833.
   Comments: The completion of a rondo on a theme by Carl Reissiger is mentioned
   in Clara Schumann's diary on June 6, 1833.

Work for Orchestra

Scherzo für Orchester
   Composed: c. 1830–31.
   Comments: A performance of this work on May 18, 1831, is noted in Clara
   Schumann's diary.

Note: Several other works are mentioned briefly in the diary in the years 1828–38.
Because they are cited in such general terms as "a waltz," "a scherzo," "lieder," it
has not been possible to identify them.

Notes

Chapter 1. *Prelude: The Wiecks of Leipzig*

1. Clara Schumann always treasured the autograph of the poem (RSH 5973-A3). The German text can be found in Litzmann, 1:170–71. A creditable translation is in Litzmann, *Clara Schumann: An Artist's Life, Based on Material Found in Diaries and Letters,* trans. Grace E. Hadow, 2 vols. (London: Macmillan, 1913), 1:136.

2. *AmZ,* 40 (1838), 164–65.

3. Diary, March 1838.

4. Eduard Hanslick, *Geschichte des Concertwesens in Wien* (Vienna: Wilhelm Braumüller, 1869), 332.

5. Diary, March 8, March 21, 1838.

6. For information on Wieck I have relied on three biographies: Anna von Meichsner, *Friedrich Wieck und seine beiden Töchter, Clara Schumann, geb. Wieck, und Marie Wieck* (Leipzig: Heinrich Matthes, 1875); Adolph Kohut, *Friedrich Wieck: Ein Lebens- und Künstlerbild* (Dresden: Pierson's, 1888); Victor Joss, *Der Musikpädagoge Friedrich Wieck und seine Familie* (Dresden: Oscar Damm, 1902). The Schumann family papers, RSH 2174-A3 and A3b, have also been consulted.

7. See Hans Eberhardt, *Die ersten deutschen Musikfeste in Frankenhausen am Kyffhäuser und Erfurt, 1810, 1811, 1812 und 1815* (Jena: Frommann, 1934).

8. Meichsner, 15–21. Weber's letter is dated August 13, 1815.

9. *AmZ,* 17 (1815), 673.

10. Joss, 7.

11. Carl Ramshorn, *Leipzig und seine Umgebungen* (Braunschweig: George Westermann, 1841), 146.

12. Hajo Holborn, *A History of Modern Germany, 1648–1840* (New York: Knopf, 1964), 309.

13. Diary, June 24, 1840.

14. Excerpts from a letter Wieck wrote after meeting Beethoven in 1826 were published in Dresden in 1873 and have been translated in Oscar Sonneck, ed., *Beethoven: Impressions of Contemporaries* (New York: G. Schirmer, 1926), 207–9.

15. See Fritz Demmler, "Johann George Tromlitz (1725–1805): Ein Beitrag zur Entwicklung der Flöte und des Flötenspiels," dissertation, Freie Universität, Berlin, 1961.

16. *AmZ,* 19 (1817), 158, 355, 357.

17. Meichsner, 14.

18. *AmZ*, 26 (1824), 489.

19. Rudolf Huebner, *A History of Germanic Private Law*, trans. Francis S. Philbrick (Boston: Little, Brown, 1918), 664. Further to confound the modern reader, the diary entry of May 12, 1824, written by Wieck as if Clara herself were writing, states: "Das Recht mich vom 5ten Jahre an zu besitzen stand ihm zu" (He had the right to take possession of me beginning in my fifth year).

20. Joss, 13–15.

21. Wieck correspondence, RSH 5967-A2; also Litzmann, 1:4n.

22. Diary, 1825 and 1826.

23. Diary, June 1827; Litzmann, 1:1–2. See also Meichsner, 34.

24. See Friedrich Wieck, *Clavier und Gesang* (Leipzig: F. Whistling, 1853), iv, in which he refers to his "caustic brevity and bluntness."

25. Robert Schumann, *Tagebücher (1827–1838)*, ed. Georg Eismann (Leipzig: Deutscher Verlag für Musik, 1971), 1:364.

26. Diary, November 12, 1839.

27. Diary, June 1827.

28. Diary, July 3, 1828.

Chapter 2. *Clara's Career Begins*

1. Litzmann, 3:194.

2. Friedrich Wieck, *Briefe aus den Jahren 1830–1838*, ed. Käthe Walch-Schumann (Cologne: Arno Volk-Verlag, 1968), 34.

3. Wieck, *Clavier und Gesang*, 60.

4. Ibid., 23.

5. Diary, November 16, 1828.

6. Quoted in Meichsner, 69.

7. Quellenwerk, 1:100.

8. *AmZ*, 30 (1828), 805–6.

9. Wieck, *Briefe*, 24.

10. Ibid., 27.

11. *AmZ*, 32 (1830), 752–53.

12. Diary, October 11, 1831.

13. *AmZ*, 34 (1832), 196–97.

14. Wieck's article appeared in *Caecilia* (Mainz), 14 (1832), 219–23. The review is followed by a testimonial by Gottfried Weber, the editor, on Clara's brilliant playing of the Chopin work and Wieck's role in developing her artistry.

15. *AmZ*, 33 (1831), 805–8. See also the discussion in Leon B. Plantinga, *Schumann as Critic* (New Haven: Yale University Press, 1967), 34–35.

16. Diary, November 14, 1831. Clara copied Wieck's long letter to Fechner into the diary.

17. Wieck, *Briefe*, 36, 38.

18. *Chopin's Letters*, ed. Henryk Opieński, trans. E. L. Voynich (New York: Knopf, 1931), 155–56.

19. Eugenie Schumann, *Robert Schumann: Ein Lebensbild meines Vaters* (Leipzig: Koehler & Ameling, 1931), 225.

20. *Caecilia*, 1 (1833), 253–58. This journal is not to be confused with that referred to in n. 14, above. In the diary, January 1833, Wieck wrote, "There is a singular article about me and my special qualities in Lyser's Caecilia which may have been taken from a letter by Heine."

21. Litzmann, 1:44.

22. Wieck, *Briefe*, 44.
23. Ibid., 45–46.
24. See "Musical Life in Paris 1817–1848: A Chapter from the Memoirs of Sophie Augustine Leo," trans. Oliver Strunk, *MQ*, 17 (1931), 259–71, 389–403.
25. Eda Sagarra, *A Social History of Germany* (New York: Holmes & Meier, 1977), 406.
26. Litzmann, 1:358.
27. *Hb*, 2:710n233. See also Litzmann, 2:9.
28. Robert Schumann, *Tagebücher*, 1:364.
29. Ibid., 362, 402.
30. Wieck, *Briefe*, 51.
31. Ibid., 48–49.

Chapter 3. *Robert Schumann and the Wiecks*

1. Schumann, *Tagebücher*, 1:382.
2. *Jugendbriefe*, 117.
3. Wilhelm Joseph von Wasielewski, *Robert Schumann: Eine Biographie*, 3d ed. (Leipzig: Breitkopf & Härtel, 1880), 60–61.
4. Litzmann, 1:21–24.
5. Eugenie Schumann, *Robert Schumann*, 223–24.
6. *Quellenwerk*, 1:44.
7. Robert Schumann, *Tagebücher*, 1:334.
8. *Jugendbriefe*, 138.
9. Robert Schumann, *Tagebücher*, 1:371, 364, 389.
10. *Quellenwerk*, 1:66.
11. *Jugendbriefe*, 1:161–62, 181.
12. *Briefwechsel*, 1:64.
13. *Jugendbriefe*, 134.
14. See Peter Ostwald, "Florestan, Eusebius, Clara, and Schumann's Right Hand," *Nineteenth-Century Music*, 4 (Summer 1980), 17–31.
15. *Jugendbriefe*, 149, 151.
16. Robert Schumann, *Tagebücher*, 1:358, 371; *Quellenwerk*, 1:75–76.
17. Robert Schumann, *Tagebücher*, 1:398.
18. *Jugendbriefe*, 295.
19. Robert Schumann, *Tagebücher*, 1:419.
20. Ibid., 419
21. See Plantinga, chaps. 1–3.
22. *Jugendbriefe*, 243.
23. *Briefwechsel*, 1:12.
24. Robert Schumann, *Tagebücher*, 1:420.
25. *Briefwechsel*, 1:111.
26. Frederick Niecks, *Robert Schumann* (London: J. M. Dent, 1925), 144.
27. Eugenie Schumann, *Robert Schumann*, 227.
28. *Briefwechsel*, 1:9–10.
29. Ibid., 1:4–5.
30. Eugenie Schumann, *Robert Schumann*, 233–35.
31. Robert Schumann, *Tagebücher*, 1:421.
32. Litzmann, 1:92.
33. *Briefwechsel*, 1:148.
34. Diary, February 14 to April 1836.
35. Leopold Hirschberg, "Robert Schumann und der Davidsbündler Fritz

Friedrich: Mit einer Auswahl bisher unveröffentlicher Briefe J. P. Lyser's an Schumann," *Velhagen & Klasings Monatshefte*, 24 (1909–10), 90.

36. Wasielewski, 342, 349.
37. Diary, February 8, 1837.
38. Diary, March 21, 1837.
39. All quotations on pp. 73–74 are from Wieck, *Briefe*, 58–69.
40. Wasielewski, 348–49.
41. *Briefwechsel*, 1:67–68.
42. Robert Schumann, *Tagebücher*, 1:422.
43. *Briefwechsel*, 1:21.
44. Robert Schumann, *Tagebücher*, 1:422.
45. Litzmann, 1:123–26.
46. Wolfgang Boetticher, ed., *Briefe und Gedichte aus dem Album Robert und Clara Schumanns* (Leipzig: Deutscher Verlag für Musik, 1979), 28–29.
47. *Briefwechsel*, 1:24.
48. Ibid., 1:26.

Chapter 4. *The Break with Wieck*

1. Diary, October 9, 1831.
2. This and all subsequent references to the Viennese tour are from Wieck, *Briefe*, 75–97.
3. *Briefwechsel*, 1:88.
4. The autograph of "Erlkönig" which she received is now in the Pierpont Morgan Library, New York. See the facsimile, *Erlkönig*, with introduction by Rigbie Turner (New York: Pierpont Morgan Library, 1978). According to the Diary, December 22, 1837, Antonio Diabelli published Schubert's Duo in C Major for Four Hands (D. 812, old op. 140), the so-called Grand Duo, dedicated it to Clara Wieck, and presented her with the autograph.
5. *Briefwechsel*, 1:164.
6. Ibid., 1:58–59.
7. Ibid., 1:37, 61.
8. Ibid., 1:46. The remainder of this line was crossed out and is illegible.
9. Ibid., 1:48.
10. Ibid., 1:108, 110.
11. Ibid., 1:118, 121.
12. Ibid., 1:134.
13. Ibid., 1:177.
14. Ibid., 1:179.
15. Ibid., 1:140, 168.
16. Litzmann, 1:214–15.
17. Ibid., 1:215.
18. Ibid., 1:216.
19. Ibid., 1:218.
20. *Briefwechsel*, 1:197.
21. Ibid., 1:215, 223.
22. Ibid., 1:184.
23. Ibid., 195–96.
24. Litzmann, 1:230. A translation of the poem follows:
From heaven comes an angel child,
Sits at the piano and ponders on songs,

And as she strikes the keys
In the magic circle above float
Shapes and forms
Images and pictures
The old Erlkönig
And gentle Mignon
And defiant knights
Arrayed in armour
And a kneeling nun
In blissful prayer
Those who heard, they went wild
As if it were a singer, highly praised,
But the angel child, dismayed,
Slipped away, and
Back to her home returned.

25. Litzmann, 1:229–30.
26. See "Nachwort" in Schumann, *Humoreske*, ed. Hans Joachim Köhler (Leipzig: Peters, 1981), 41.
27. Litzmann, 1:233n.
28. *Briefwechsel*, 1:250.
29. Ibid., 1:272.
30. Ibid., 1:301.
31. Ibid., 1:230.
32. Diary, January 8, 1839.
33. Litzmann, 1:295. Berlioz took another view of the opera. In a letter to Liszt dated January 22, 1839, he wrote, "The revival of *Benvenuto* was a great success" (*Hector Berlioz: A Selection from His Letters*, ed. and trans. Humphrey Searle [New York: Vienna House, 1973], 75).
34. Litzmann, 1:285–86.
35. Ibid., 1:300.
36. Ibid., 1:299.
37. Wolfgang Boetticher, ed., *Robert Schumann in seinen Schriften und Briefen* (Berlin: Hahnefeld, 1942), 250.
38. Ibid., 257.
39. Litzmann, 1:315–16.
40. Ibid., 1:321.
41. Ibid., 1:322–26.
42. Ibid., 1:328.
43. Ibid., 1:331.
44. Ibid., 1:340.
45. Ibid., 1:342.
46. Ibid.
47. *Hb*, 1:72.
48. Diary, October 18, 1839.
49. Litzmann, 1:367.
50. Ibid., 1:368.
51. Ibid., 1:378.
52. *Hb*, 1:116, 2:700n129.
53. Diary, October 13, November 11, 12, 1839; April 2, 1840.
54. Diary, November 12, 1839.
55. Litzmann, 1:413; Diary, March 11, 1840.
56. Diary, September 26, 1839, and March 3, 1840.

57. Litzmann, 1:399.
58. Ibid., 1:395.
59. Ibid., 1:408, 410–11.
60. Ibid., 1:254.
61. See, for example, his letter of August 29, 1840, in Boetticher, ed., *Robert Schumann in seinen Schriften und Briefen*, 344.

Chapter 5. *The Marriage*

1. Md, September 13, 1840.
2. Ibid., April 11–25, 1841. (Dates of entries in the diary were usually given in terms of the week of marriage [e.g., "Twenty-fourth week"] or the time period, and only occasionally for a specific day.) See also *Hb*, 2:700n129.
3. *Hb*, 1:175.
4. Siegfried Kross, ed. *Briefe und Notizen Robert und Clara Schumanns* (Bonn: Bouvier, 1978), 59.
5. In the Diary, November 12, 1839, Clara wrote that he had already resettled in Dresden. See also Marie Wieck, *Aus dem Kreise Schumann-Wieck*, 2d enl. ed. (Dresden: Zahn & Jaensch, 1914), 231–34, 244.
6. Although Litzmann, 2:9, refers to this letter, Gerd Nauhaus (*Hb*, 1:193 and 2:713n263) reports that it seems to have disappeared.
7. See Schumann's letter to Clara, p. 115.
8. Md, July 17, 1841; May 10–22, 1841.
9. Ibid., May 19, 1842.
10. Joss, 79–80. See also *Hb*, 2:725n351.
11. Litzmann, 2:10–11.
12. *Hb*, 1:237.
13. Md, February 14, 1843; February 1843.
14. Friedrich Wieck to Robert Schumann, RSH 6940-A2.
15. Schumannhaus, Bonn.
16. *Briefwechsel*, 1:108.
17. Md, February 14–21, 1841.
18. Md, March 29–April 4, 1841.
19. Litzmann, 2:29n.
20. Ibid., 2:40.
21. Md, February 2, 1842. Also see, for example, *Hb*, 1:206–7, 362.
22. Boetticher, ed., *Robert Schumann in seinen Schriften und Briefen*, 359.
23. Litzmann, 2:42–43.
24. *Hb*, 209–12.
25. Excerpts from all letters from March 13 to April 22 are from Boetticher, ed., *Robert Schumann in seinen Schriften und Briefen*, 364–69.
26. Joan Bulman, *Jenny Lind* (London: James Barrie, 1956), 226.
27. Boetticher, ed., *Robert Schumann in seinen Schriften und Briefen*, 364.
28. See also *Hb*, 1:239–40 (March 8, 9, 13, 1843).
29. Niecks, 211.
30. Litzmann, 2:57, 58.
31. Boetticher, ed., *Robert Schumann in seinen Schriften und Briefen*, 392–93.
32. Ibid., 395–96.
33. Ibid., 396–97, 399.
34. Litzmann, 2:85.
35. Md, November 6, 1840. Clara had received similar advice in 1839 when she contemplated a trip to Russia.

36. *Quellenwerk,* 1:142–43.
37. Litzmann, 2:62.
38. Md, February 1844.
39. *Hb,* 1:268.
40. *Quellenwerk,* 1:138.
41. Ibid., 1:144.
42. The comment was written after their return to Germany but entered under the date of January 31, 1844.
43. Litzmann, 2:76.

Chapter 6. *The Dresden Years*

1. Litzmann, 1:416.
2. Henry F. Chorley, *Music and Manners in France and Germany,* 3 vols. (London: Longman, Brown, Green & Longmans, 1844), 3:86.
3. Gustave F. Jansen, ed., *Robert Schumanns Briefe: Neue Folge* (Leipzig: Breitkopf & Härtel, 1904), 244.
4. Ibid., 519.
5. Ibid., 246.
6. Litzmann, 2:125; Jansen, 247.
7. Jansen, 249.
8. Ibid., 322–23.
9. Ibid., 302.
10. *Hb,* 1:284, 285.
11. Ibid., 1:418, 419.
12. Ibid., 2:676.
13. Litzmann, 2:174.
14. Jansen, 251.
15. Boetticher, ed., *Robert Schumann in seinen Schriften und Briefen,* 412.
16. Ibid., 413.
17. Karl Laux, "Dresden ist doch gar zu schön," in *Robert Schumann,* ed. Hans Joachim Moser and Eberhard Rebling (Leipzig: Breitkopf & Härtel, 1956), 32, 33.
18. Wilhelm Löhner, ed., "Clara Schumann: Unbekannte Briefe an Emilie Steffens," *Zeitschrift für Musik,* 97 (1930), 177–79.
19. Quoted in Litzmann, 2:145–46.
20. Jansen, 311–12.
21. Litzmann, 2:219, 220.
22. Ibid., 2:97.
23. Jansen, 256, 273.
24. Ibid., 251, 242, 249.
25. Ibid., 318.
26. Litzmann, 2:164.

Chapter 7. *Düsseldorf and the Death of Robert Schumann*

1. Paul Kast, ed., *Schumanns rheinische Jahre* (Düsseldorf: Droste, 1981), 29.
2. Clara Schumann to Pauline Schumann, April 10, 1851 (private collection).
3. Clara Schumann to Pauline Schumann, January 7, 1851 (private collection).
4. Renate Federhofer-Königs, *Wilhelm Joseph von Wasielewski im Spiegel seiner Korrespondenz* (Tutzing: Schneider, 1975), 39–40.
5. Niecks, 302.

6. Litzmann, 2:241.

7. Ibid., 2:245.

8. Jansen, 302.

9. Quoted in Niecks, 274.

10. Litzmann, 2:242.

11. Wasielewski, 284.

12. Ibid., 285–86.

13. Litzmann, 2:253.

14. Niecks, 270–71.

15. Litzmann, 2:254–55.

16. Ibid., 2:264–66.

17. Ibid., 2:265.

18. Ibid., 2:277.

19. Ibid., 2:279.

20. Hb, 2:637.

21. Quoted in Eugenie Schumann, *Robert Schumann*, 357.

22. Joseph Joachim, *Briefe von und an Joseph Joachim*, ed. Johannes Joachim and Andreas Moser, 3 vols. (Berlin: Julius Bard, 1911–13), 1:84.

23. *NZfM*, 39 (1853), 185–86.

24. Hb, 2:639.

25. See excerpts in Kast, 130.

26. Ibid., 129, 130.

27. Litzmann, 2:291.

28. *Quellenwerk*, 1:190–91.

29. Litzmann, 2:299–300.

30. Quoted in Eugenie Schumann, *Robert Schumann*, 391–92.

31. *Schumann-Brahms Briefe*, 1:13.

32. The letters were published in Eduard Hanslick, *Am Ende des Jahrhunderts 1895–1899 (Die Moderne Oper. Part 8)*, 2d ed. (Berlin: Allgemeiner Verein für deutsche Literatur, 1899), 317–42, and in Jansen, 397–409. Note that the letters did not appear during Clara's lifetime.

33. Clara Schumann to Bettina von Arnim, April 13 and May 25, 1855, Biblioteka Jagiellońska, Kraków. See also Joachim's appraisal of the situation after Bettina's visit in Johannes Brahms and Joseph Joachim, *Johannes Brahms in Briefwechsel mit Joseph Joachim*, ed. Andreas Moser, 2 vols. (Berlin: Deutsche Brahms-Gesellschaft, 1908), 1:105–8.

34. See Kast, 161, 164; Brigitte Berenbruch and Helmut Helberg, *Robert Schumann und Bonn* (Bonn: Stadt Bonn, 1980), 8.

35. The thought was repeated, "Completely away from here!" in a letter to Brahms dated March 11, 1855. See Jansen, 406, and Hanslick, 339, for Brahms's letter; Hanslick, 333, describes the letter to Joachim.

36. Johannes Brahms, *Johannes Brahms in seiner Familie: Der Briefwechsel*, ed. Kurt Stephenson (Hamburg: Ernst Hauswedell, 1973), 63, 68.

37. Max Kalbeck, *Johannes Brahms*, 4th ed. (Berlin: Deutsche Brahms-Gesellschaft, 1921), 1:271–72.

38. Joachim, *Briefe*, 1:165.

39. Federhofer-Königs, *Wasielewski im Spiegel seiner Korrespondenz*, 69–70.

40. Kalbeck, 1:168–69.

41. Federhofer-Königs, *Wasielewski im Spiegel seiner Korrespondenz*, 72.

42. Compiled from diaries, letters, reviews, and Program Collection, RSH.

43. Litzmann, 2:387.

44. Clara Schumann to Pauline Schumann, March 23, 1856 (private collection).

45. *Schumann-Brahms Briefe*, 1:96.

46. Litzmann, 2:309.

47. Ibid., 2:308, 336.

48. Ibid., 2:415.

49. Ibid.

50. See Peter Ostwald, *Robert Schumann: The Inner Voices of a Musical Genius* (Boston: Northeastern University Press, 1985), 303–7.

Chapter 8. *The Later Years*

1. Litzmann, 1:189.

2. Ibid., 2:48n.

3. Diary, December 1839.

4. Sir George Henschel, *Musings and Memories of a Musician* (New York: Macmillan, 1919), 41.

5. Amy Fay, *Music Study in Germany*, 18th ed. (New York: Macmillan, 1903), 26.

6. *Dwight's,* 7 (April 1855), 9.

7. Quoted in Gordon S. Haight, *George Eliot: A Biography* (New York: Oxford University Press, 1968), 156–57.

8. Litzmann, 3:230.

9. Ibid., 3:231.

10. *Dwight's,* 8 (December 1855), 77.

11. *Memoirs,* 93.

12. Litzmann, 3:285.

13. See April Fitzlyon, *The Price of Genius: A Life of Pauline Viardot* (New York: Appleton-Century-Crofts, 1964), 11.

14. *Hb,* 1:192.

15. Litzmann, 2:125.

16. Ibid., 2:180.

17. *Hb,* 1:284–85; see also Ostwald, *Robert Schumann,* 208.

18. Jansen, 250, 294, 321.

19. Published in *Memoirs,* 206–18.

20. Litzmann, 3:15.

21. Ibid., 3:81.

22. Clara Schumann to Ernst Rudorff, September 4, 1866, Rudorff-Archiv: Privatarchiv v. Gottberg, Salzhemmendorf.

23. Litzmann, 3:240, 220.

24. See chap. 2, p. 42n.

25. Martin Schoppe and Gerd Nauhaus, *Das Robert-Schumann-Haus in Zwickau* (Zwickau: Robert-Schumann-Haus, 1973), 55.

26. Clara Schumann to Ernst Rudorff, September 10, 1865, Rudorff-Archiv; Clara Schumann to Elisabeth Werner, September 10, 1865, in Litzmann, 3:183.

27. Litzmann, 3:206.

28. *Schumann-Brahms Briefe,* 1:573.

29. Ibid., 1:644.

30. Litzmann, 3:230n.

31. Ibid., 3:278n.

32. Ibid., 3:279.

33. Ibid., 2:125n.

34. Ibid., 3:125.

35. Ibid., 3:228n.

36. Ibid., 3:238.

37. Ibid., 3:238, 263.

38. Ostwald, *Robert Schumann*, 29.

39. Litzmann, 3:322.

40. Clara Schumann to Pastor Friedrich Grössel, May 5, 1877, Stadtarchiv und Wissenschaftliche Stadtbibliothek, Bonn.

41. Rudorff-Archiv.

42. Clara Schumann to Ernst Rudorff, February 1, 1873, Rudorff-Archiv.

43. *Schumann-Brahms Briefe*, 2:355.

44. Litzmann, 3:528n.

45. Ibid., 3:537.

46. Ferdinand Schumann, "Brahms and Clara Schumann," *MQ*, 2 (1916), 507–15, based on "Erinnerungen an Johannes Brahms," *NZfM* 82 (1915), 225–28, 233–36, 241–43; *Reminiscences of Clara Schumann: From the Diary of Her Grandson Ferdinand Schumann*, ed. J. Dickinson, 2d ed. (New York: Musical Scope, 1973), a translation (with many errors) of "Erinnerungen an Clara Schumann," *NZfM*, 84 (1917), 69–72, 77–80, 85–88, 93–96, 101–4.

47. The title page reads: "*Johannes Brahms, der Vater von Felix Schumann: Das Mysterium einer Liebe. Eine sehr ernste Parodie auf die Erinnerungen von Eugenie Schumann* [Johannes Brahms, the Father of Felix Schumann: The Mystery of a Love. A Very Serious Parody on the Memoirs of Eugenie Schumann]. By Titus Frazeni" (Bielefeld: Manfred, 1926).

48. *Erinnerungen* (Stuttgart: Engelhorn, 1925) has been translated into English by Marie Busch and published as *The Memoirs of Eugenie Schumann* (London: William Heinemann, 1927) and as *The Schumanns and Johannes Brahms: The Memoirs of Eugenie Schumann* (New York: Dial, 1927). Citations here are to the New York edition. *Robert Schumann: Ein Lebensbild meines Vaters* has not been translated.

49. Litzmann, 3:424.

50. *Schumann-Brahms Briefe*, 2:474.

51. *Memoirs*, 9.

52. Ibid., 72.

53. See ibid., 74–86.

54. Ibid., 83.

55. Ibid., 84.

56. *Schumann-Brahms Briefe*, 2:25–26.

57. Ibid., 2:109–10.

58. Ibid., 2:165–66.

59. Litzmann, 3:396.

60. Ibid.

61. *Memoirs*, 47.

62. Ibid., 152.

63. *Schumann-Brahms Briefe*, 2:30.

64. Litzmann, 3:70.

65. Joachim, *Briefe*, 1:211.

66. Litzmann, 3:286.

67. Ibid., 291.

68. Joachim, *Briefe*, 2:85–86.

69. Ibid., 3:42–43.

70. Ferdinand Hiller, *Aus Ferdinand Hillers Briefwechsel (1826–1861)*, ed. Reinhold Sietz (Cologne: Arno Volk-Verlag, 1958), 1:85–86.

71. *Schumann-Brahms Briefe*, 2:20.

72. Ibid., 1:623.

73. Ibid., 1:458.

74. Ibid., 1:436.

75. Amalie Joachim to Joseph Joachim, November 11, 1872, transcription, Newberry Library, Chicago.

76. *Schumann-Brahms Briefe*, 2:52.

77. Litzmann, 3:389.

78. Ibid., 3:509–10.

79. Ibid., 1:391.

80. *Hb*, 1:165.

81. Joachim, *Briefe*, 1:463–64.

82. Litzmann, 3:578.

Chapter 9. *Clara Schumann and Johannes Brahms*

1. See, for example, Alfred Schumann, *Johannes Brahms, der Vater von Felix Schumann*. Though Marie and Eugenie Schumann attempted to suppress this malicious document written by a son of Ferdinand Schumann under the ill-concealed pseudonym Titus Frazeni, it was published and circulated. It is, of course, totally specious. Other writings, not so vicious but equally free of documentary proof, have appeared in the popular press.

2. Kalbeck, 1:44.

3. Florence May, *The Life of Johannes Brahms*, 2d ed., 2 vols. (London: William Reeves, 1905), 1:83.

4. *Schumann-Brahms Briefe*, 1:3.

5. Joachim, *Briefe*, 1:154.

6. Eugenie Schumann, *Robert Schumann*, 358.

7. *Hb*, 2:649–55, 683–84.

8. Brahms, *Johannes Brahms in seiner Familie*, 56.

9. Ibid., 60–61.

10. Litzmann, 2:337.

11. *Memoirs*, 152.

12. Kalbeck, 1:231–32.

13. Artur Holde, "Suppressed Passages in the Joachim–Brahms Correspondence, Published for the First Time," *MQ* 45 (1959), 314.

14. See Kalbeck, 1:115.

15. *Schumann-Brahms Briefe*, 1:187.

16. See ibid., 2:300–301 (May 14, 1886), 315–16 (May 1887), 321 (August 1887).

17. Ibid., 1:186.

18. *Memoirs*, 154.

19. Litzmann, 2:354; *Schumann-Brahms Briefe*, 1:613.

20. Litzmann, 3:230.

21. In 1890 Clara commented to Brahms, "I always feel shy in relation to clever people" (*Schumann-Brahms Briefe*, 2:411). See also Litzmann, 3:455.

22. See Karl Geiringer, "Schumanniana in der Bibliothek von Johannes Brahms," in *Convivium Musicorum: Festschrift Wolfgang Boetticher*, ed. Heinrich Hüschen and Dietz-Rüdiger Moser (Berlin: Merseburger, 1974), 79–82. See also Kurt Hofmann, *Die Bibliothek von Johannes Brahms* (Hamburg: Wagner, 1974).

23. Karl Geiringer, *Brahms: His Life and Work*, 2d ed. (New York: Anchor Books, 1961), 45.

24. *Schumann-Brahms Briefe*, 1:339.

25. Ibid., 1:506.

26. See, for example, ibid., 1:337.

27. Ibid., 2:45, 362, 476, 510.

28. Ibid., 2:396.

29. Ibid., 1:413–14, 560, 217, 493.

30. Ibid., 2:476.

31. Litzmann, 2:365–66, 381.

32. Ibid., 3:53, 72.

33. Ibid., 3:88.

34. Ibid., 3:120.

35. See Kalbeck, 1:241–47.

36. *Schumann-Brahms Briefe*, 1:50.

37. Ibid., 1:353–54.

38. Litzmann, 3:498.

39. *Schumann-Brahms Briefe*, 2:128; Litzmann, 3:498; *Schumann-Brahms Briefe*, 2:526, 530, 516.

40. *Schumann-Brahms Briefe*, 2:258.

41. Ibid., 2:273.

42. Ibid., 1:300.

43. Ibid., 2:317.

44. Ibid., 2:177.

45. Ibid., 2:179.

46. Litzmann, 3:490; *Schumann-Brahms Briefe*, 2:415, 541–42, 395.

47. See, for example, her letter to him of July 1, 1858, in *Schumann-Brahms Briefe*, 1:223, in which she defends her enthusiasm.

48. Ibid., 1:226.

49. Ibid., 2:363.

50. Ibid., 2:517.

51. Ibid., 2:463.

52. Ibid., 2:308.

53. Ibid., 1:560.

54. Ibid., 1:323, 504–6.

55. Ibid., 2:144.

56. Ibid., 2:94–96.

57. Brahms, Heinrich von Herzogenberg, and Elisabeth von Herzogenberg, *Johannes Brahms im Briefwechsel mit Heinrich und Elisabet von Herzogenberg*, ed. Max Kalbeck (Berlin: Deutsche Brahms-Gesellschaft, 1907), 2:217, 221, 220.

58. *Schumann-Brahms Briefe*, 2:96–98; 1:370, 234; Brahms and Julius Otto Grimm, *Johannes Brahms im Briefwechsel mit Julius Otto Grimm*, ed. Richard Barth (Berlin: Deutsche Brahms-Gesellschaft, 1907), 78.

59. Litzmann, 3:367.

60. *Schumann-Brahms Briefe*, 2:109–10.

61. Ibid., 1:356.

62. Ibid., 1:357.

63. Ibid., 1:576, 579.

64. Ibid., 1:598–99.

65. Ibid., 2:307.

66. Litzmann, 3:481.

67. *Schumann-Brahms Briefe*, 2:353–56.

68. Ibid., 2:464–70.

69. Ibid., 2:617.

70. May, *Life of Johannes Brahms*, 2:658–59.

71. *Schumann-Brahms Briefe*, 2:623. Though Kalbeck (4:443) insists that the songs were not written for Clara, Brahms's letter to Marie indicates otherwise.

Chapter 10. *Other Friends and Contemporaries*

1. Litzmann, 3:247–48.
2. Ibid., 1:198.
3. Franz Liszt, *Correspondance de Liszt et de Madame d'Agoult,* ed. Daniel Ollivier, 2 vols. (Paris: Grasset, 1933), 1:217 (April 13, 1838).
4. *Dwight's,* 7 (1855), 9.
5. Litzmann, 1:199.
6. *Briefwechsel,* 1:159.
7. Wieck, *Briefe,* 93, 94.
8. Ibid., 93–94.
9. Boetticher, ed., *Briefe und Gedichte,* 109–10.
10. Ibid., 111 (March 1, 1839).
11. Franz Liszt, *Franz Liszts Briefe,* ed. La Mara, 8 vols. (Leipzig: Breitkopf & Härtel, 1893), 1:26–28.
12. Litzmann, 1:413.
13. Ibid., 1:417–18. She expressed similar emotions in her diary on March 23, 1840.
14. Md, November 14–December 1, 1841.
15. Litzmann, 1:414.
16. Ibid., 2:122.
17. Ibid., 2:317.
18. Ibid., 2:263, 268, 351.
19. Ibid., 3:29.
20. Ibid., 3:425–26.
21. Ibid., 3:426.
22. Ibid., 3:427.
23. Ibid., 3:326.
24. *Schumann-Brahms Briefe,* 1:622.
25. See, for example, Cosima Wagner, *Cosima Wagner's Diaries,* ed. Martin Gregor-Dellin and Dietrich Mack, trans. Gregory Skelton (New York: Harcourt Brace Jovanovich, 1978, 1980), 1:170, 555, 763, 824, 838–39; 2:110, 203, 317, 355, 441, 609, 812.
26. Litzmann, 3:443.
27. Diary, October 2, 1834.
28. Diary, September 12, 1835.
29. Diary, September 16, 1835.
30. See the many entries in *Hb,* beginning on p. 77.
31. Felix Mendelssohn Bartholdy to Clara Schumann, November 24, 1845, Staatsbibliothek, Preussischer Kulturbesitz, Musikabteilung, Berlin (West).
32. Robert Schumann, *Erinnerungen an Felix Mendelssohn Bartholdy: Nachgelassene Aufzeichnungen,* ed. Georg Eismann (Zwickau: Predella, 1947), 70.
33. Litzmann, 1:423.
34. Md, October 11–18, 1840.
35. Litzmann, 2:85.
36. Ibid., 2:161–62.
37. Jansen, 398.
38. Litzmann, 2:278.
39. *Hb,* 2:809n916.
40. Litzmann, 2:321.
41. Joachim, *Briefe,* 2:4–5.
42. Clara Schumann to Ernst Rudorff, January 17, 1882, Rudorff-Archiv.

43. Joachim, *Briefe*, 3:24.
44. Ibid., 3:370.
45. Litzmann, 3:590.
46. Ibid., 2:326.
47. See Julia Stockhausen Wirth, ed., *Julius Stockhausen, der Sänger des deutschen Liedes: Nach Dokumenten seiner Zeit* (Frankfurt am Main: Englert & Schlosser, 1927), 489–98.
48. Litzmann, 3:114.
49. Wirth, 150.
50. Ibid., 155.
51. Litzmann, 3:556.
52. *Schumann-Brahms Briefe*, 1:565.
53. Fitzlyon, 166.

Chapter 11. *Clara Schumann as Composer and Editor*

1. Litzmann, 3:601. The *Vorspiele* are in RSH, 11514-A1. Other preludes are in Bds, Mus. Ms. Autogr. C. Schumann 8 and 9.
2. Litzmann, 1:139.
3. Diary, August 26, 1835; November 9, 1835; January 27, 1837.
4. Wieck, *Briefe*, 27.
5. Litzmann, 2:274, 139–40.
6. Joachim, *Briefe*, 2:79.
7. Litzmann, 1:355–56.
8. Ibid., 1:353, 352.
9. Ibid., 1:353–54.
10. See, for example, Joachim, *Briefe*, 2:86: "Bin ich auch nicht producierend, so doch reproducierend" (Even if I am not a creative artist, still I am re-creating).
11. Boetticher, ed., *Robert Schumann in seinen Schriften und Briefen*, 338.
12. RSH, 5986-A1, 5989-A1.
13. Marie Wieck, *Aus dem Kreise Wieck-Schumann*, 38.
14. A two-hand version of this march is in RSH, 5993-A1. A four-hand version, 5994-A1, and an orchestration by Julius Otto Grimm, 5995-A1, are also extant. See Litzmann, 3:400.
15. The major discussions of her creative work are the following: a brief review of her works in Paula Rehberg and Walter Rehberg, *Robert Schumann: Sein Leben und Sein Werk*, 2d ed. (Zurich: Artemis, 1969), 662–71; an incomplete survey by Richard Hohenemser (who was unable even to find prints of most of her works), "Clara Wieck-Schumann als Komponistin," in *Die Musik* 20 (1905), 113–26, and 21 (1906), 166–73; and two works by Pamela Susskind: "Clara Wieck Schumann as Pianist and Composer: A Study of Her Life and Works," Ph.D. dissertation, University of California, Berkeley, 1977, and Introduction to the reprint *Selected Piano Music of Clara Schumann* (New York: Da Capo). In "Life and Works" Susskind presents a survey and harmonic analysis of selected compositions; the Introduction gives an overview of Schumann's compositional efforts and a works catalogue based on the Zwickau sources. Janina Klassen, University of Kiel, is currently working on a study of all the compositions.
16. Sources for the discussion here are entries from the published and unpublished diaries, letters, and inscriptions on the manuscripts and first editions in RSH and Bds.
17. The literature on this aspect of Robert Schumann's work is extensive. See, for example, Wolfgang Boetticher, "Zur Zitatpraxis in R. Schumanns frühen Klavier-

werken," in *Speculum Musicae Artis*, ed. Heinz Becker and Reinhard Gerlach (Munich: Wilhelm Fink, 1970), especially 69–72; Roger Fiske, "A Schumann Mystery," *MT*, 105 (1964), 574–78; Gregory Harwood, "Robert Schumann's Sonata in F♯ Minor: A Study of Creative Process and Romantic Inspiration," *Current Musicology*, 29 (1980), 17–30; Eric Sams, "Schumann and the Tonal Analogue," in *Robert Schumann: The Man and His Music*, ed. Alan Walker (London: Barrie & Jenkins, 1972), especially 398–405.

18. *Iris*, 2 (June 17, 1831), 96.

19. Robert Schumann, *Tagebücher*, 1:383, 384, 388.

20. Boetticher, "Zur Zitat," points out several other striking resemblances between the *Caprices* and *Papillons*.

21. Litzmann, 3:617, 1:61.

22. See Claudia Stevens Becker, "A New Look at Schumann's Impromptus," *MQ*, 67 (October 1981), 568–86, and Robert Schumann, [Klavierwerke] *Op. 5*, ed. Hans Joachim Köhler, 27–31. Both refer to an entry in Schumann's *Tagebücher*, 1:321.

23. See Plantinga, chap. 10.

24. Diary, June 24, 1836; September 12, 1836.

25. Clara Schumann, *Romantische Klaviermusik*, ed. Franzpeter Goebels (Heidelberg: Willy Müller, Süddeutscher Musikverlag, 1977), vol. 2, Preface, and Clara Schumann, *Drei kleine Klavierstücke*, Diletto Musicale no. 812, ed. Rosario Marciano (Vienna: Doblinger, 1979), Preface.

26. See the discussion in Robert Schumann, [Klavierwerke] *Sonata in F♯ Moll*, ed. Köhler, 78–79.

27. Litzmann, 1:109.

28. Robert Schumann, *Gesammelte Schriften*, 3d ed., 2 vols. (Leipzig: Wigand, 1875), 1:251.

29. Alfred Dörffel, ed. *Geschichte der Gewandhausconcerte zu Leipzig vom 25. November 1781 bis 25. November 1881* (Leipzig, 1884), pt. 2, "Statistik," 77, gives the following dates for performances of Clara Wieck works: *Concertsatz für Piano*, May 5, 1834; *Concert für Pianoforte*, November 9, 1835, and October 8, 1837. Clara also performed the *Concertsatz* at a benefit concert in Leipzig on September 11, 1834.

30. Plantinga, 203.

31. See Charles Suttoni, "Piano and Opera: A Study of the Piano Fantasies Written on Opera Themes in the Romantic Era," Ph.D. dissertation, New York University, 1973.

32. Plantinga, 197.

33. Wieck, *Briefe*, 68.

34. Litzmann, 1:311.

35. Ibid., 1:354–55.

36. Ibid., 1:355.

37. Robert Schumann, [Klavierwerke] *Humoreske*, ed. Köhler, 40–43; Joan Chissell, *Clara Schumann: A Dedicated Spirit* (London: Hamish Hamilton, 1983), 67.

38. Robert Schumann, [Klavierwerke] *Humoreske*, ed. Köhler, 44.

39. RSH, 5986-A1.

40. Litzmann, 2:131.

41. According to *Hb*, 1:385 and 2:749, the text they used was Cherubini's *Theorie des Contrapunktes und der Fuge*.

42. RSH, 5982-A1.

43. Jansen, 444.

44. A facsimile of this letter appears in *Erst- und Frühdrucke von Robert Schumann in der Musikbibliothek Leipzig* (Leipzig, 1960), 47.

45. Concert in Magdeburg, November 25, 1834 (Program Collection, RSH).

46. *Hb,* 2:429.

47. RSH, 12886-A1.

48. *Schumann-Brahms Briefe,* 1:6n2.

49. Kalbeck, 1:176–77. Brahms obviously treasured Clara Schumann's Variations. He owned two copies: one was the inscribed autograph she gave him in July 1854 and the other a printed copy that he received in November 1854. Both are part of his legacy to Wgm.

50. RSH, 5990-A1.

51. Romances 2 and 3 and the unpublished romance, in a copyist's hand, are in Bds, Mus. Ms. Autogr. C. Schumann 10. A presentation copy of the unpublished romance for Rosalie Leser can be found in Bds, Mus. Ms. Autogr. C. Schumann 7.

52. In the Brahms library in Wgm are a copy of the first edition and a presentation copy of the autograph of no. 1. The inscription on the autograph, "Meinem lieben Freund Johannes componirt den 2. April 1855" (To my dear friend Johannes, composed on April 2, 1855), is puzzling since the autograph of the same work in RSH is dated 1853 and, according to the inscription, was presented to Robert Schumann on his birthday in that year.

53. Two autographs, a fair copy (Mus. Ms. Autogr. C. Schumann 10) and the presentation copy (Mus. Ms. Autogr. C. Schumann 4), are in Bds.

54. Joachim, *Briefe,* 1:380.

55. Boetticher, ed. *Robert Schumann in seinen Schriften und Briefen,* 339.

56. RSH, 4871/VIII, 4-5977-A3. Many thanks to Rufus Hallmark for bringing this notebook to my attention and kindly permitting me to use his notes on the collection. See Rufus Hallmark, *The Genesis of Schumann's "Dichterliebe": A Source Study* (Ann Arbor, Mich.: UMI Research Press, 1979), 21.

57. Mus. Ms. Autogr. C. Schumann 5.

58. Franz Liszt, *Lieder von Robert und Clara Schumann* (Leipzig: Breitkopf & Härtel, 1872).

59. Jansen, 430–31.

60. *Hb,* 2:802.

61. RSH, 5986-A1.

62. The titles are "Abendfeyer in Venedig," "Vorwärts," and "Gondoliera" (RSH, 10427-A1).

63. RSH, 5988-A1.

64. See Clara Schumann, *Romantische Klaviermusik* and *Drei kleine Klavierstücke,* n. 25 above.

65. Litzmann, 2:370.

66. Impromptu, no. 17 in *Album du Gaulois* (Paris, 1885). The album consists of a collection of 61 piano pieces by 61 composers. The genesis of the Impromptu is unknown, but that the composer knew of its publication is clear. The collection of letters to Clara Schumann, in the Staatsbibliothek, Preussischer Kulturbesitz, Berlin (West), Musikabteilung, vol. 5, no. 25, contains a letter written on September 22, 1866, from Arthur Meyer, the director of *Le Gaulois,* about the work and its inclusion in the collection.

67. Schoppe and Nauhaus, 52.

68. *Schumann-Brahms Briefe,* 1:315.

69. Eugenie Schumann, "Über das letzte Werk ihres Vaters Robert Schumann," *Schweizerische Musikzeitung,* 78 (January 1, 1938), 9. The Concerto was published by Schott, Mainz; the movements of the *FAE* Sonata were issued by Heinrichshofen, Magdeburg; and the Variations were published by Hinrichsen, London. See Robert Schumann, *Robert Schumann: Thematisches Verzeichnis Sämtlicher . . . ,* ed. Kurt Hofmann and Siegmar Keil (Hamburg: J. Schuberth, 1982).

70. Heinrich-Heine-Institut, Düsseldorf. The Caprices were published by C. F. Peters of Leipzig, 1941.

71. *Hb*, 2:641, 809.

72. *Schumann-Brahms Briefe*, 1:318, 372.

73. Ibid., 2:100–101.

74. Ibid., 2:209, 119, 121, 480–88.

75. Ibid., 2:484.

76. See, for example, Wolfgang Boetticher, "Neue textkritische Forschungen an R. Schumanns Klavierwerk," *AfMw*, 25 (1968), 46–76; Edward A. Lippman, "Robert Schumann," *MGG*, 12:320; and William Newman, *The Sonata since Beethoven*, 2d ed. (New York: W. W. Norton, 1972), 264.

77. See, for example, *Schumann-Brahms Briefe*, 2:135, 169.

78. Jansen, 440.

79. *Schumann-Brahms Briefe*, 1:359–69, 2:142.

80. Two scholars have dealt with the question of Schumann's metronome markings and Clara Schumann's editions. See Dietrich Kämper, "Zur Frage der Metronombezeichnungen Robert Schumanns," *AfMw*, 21 (1964), 141–55; Brian Schlotel, "Schumann and the Metronome," in *Robert Schumann: The Man and His Music*, ed. Alan Walker (London: Barrie & Jenkins, 1972), 109–19.

81. *NBMz*, 9 (December 19, 1855), 407.

82. Wirth, 253. Her letter was a reply to one in which Stockhausen had written that he found the metronome markings for Schumann's Third Symphony "frighteningly" fast and wondered if Schumann's metronome was correct.

83. See, for example, Sir George Henschel, *Personal Recollections of Johannes Brahms* (Boston: R. G. Badger, 1907), 78–79.

84. Titled in German *Klavierwerke von Robert Schumann. Erste mit Fingersatz und Vortragsbezeichnung versehene Instructive Ausgabe. Nach den Handschriften und persönlicher Überlieferung.* After Clara's death it was revised by Carl Reinecke but continued to carry her name on the title page for many years. The Instructive Edition is best known to English-reading pianists as Robert Schumann, *The Complete Works for Piano Solo, Edited According to Manuscripts and from her Personal Recollections by Clara Schumann.* A number of prints and revisions of the Instructive Edition have appeared in English, French, and German, some as recently as the 1960s.

85. *Schumann-Brahms Briefe*, 2:252.

86. Litzmann, 3:442.

87. Breitkopf & Härtel to Marie Schumann, January 26, 1901, RSH.

88. *Fingerübungen und Studien aus Carl Czerny's grosser Pianoforte Schule, Op. 500*, ed. Clara Schumann (Hamburg: Cranz, [1880]). See also *Schumann-Brahms Briefe*, 2:219–20. According to a footnote to the correspondence, p. 217, this work was evidently the inspiration for Brahms's own *51 Übungen für das Pianoforte* (1893).

89. Robert Schumann, *Quintett, Op. 44, für Klavier vier-händig* (Leipzig: Breitkopf & Härtel, [1845]); *Genoveva, Oper in Vier Acten nach Tieck und F. Hebbel . . . Clavierauszug von Clara Schumann, geb. Wieck* (Leipzig: C. F. Peters, 1850); *30 Mélodies de Robert Schumann, transcrites pour piano* (Paris: Durand & Schonewerk, 1873); and *Studies for the Pedal Piano from Op. 56 and 58, Arranged for Pianoforte Solo by Clara Schumann* (London: Novello, Ewer, 1896).

90. In a letter to Philipp Spitta dated September 1874, Brahms inquired, on Clara Schumann's behalf, whether Spitta could offer any advice on the subject (Johannes Brahms and Philipp Spitta, *Johannes Brahms im Briefwechsel mit Philipp Spitta*, ed. Carl Krebs [Berlin: Deutsche Brahms-Gesellschaft, 1920], 61).

91. Litzmann, 3:467.

92. *Jugendbriefe von Robert Schumann, nach den originalen mitgeteilt* (Leipzig:

323]

Breitkopf & Härtel, 1885). The English edition, *Early Letters* (London: George Bell, 1888), was translated by May Herbert.

Chapter 12. *The Concert Artist*

1. Frank Munte, "Robert und Clara Schumann in Hamburg," in *Brahms Studien*, vol. 2, ed. Helmut Wirth (Hamburg: Wagner, 1977), 9–10.
2. Litzmann, 2:62.
3. *Dwight's*, 6 (March 24, 1855), 196.
4. Staatsbibliothek, Preussischer Kulturbesitz, Musiktabteilung, Berlin (West).
5. Litzmann, 1:311.
6. Ibid., 1:301.
7. Ibid., 1:315. This is the concert reviewed by Berlioz. See chap. 4.
8. See Pamela Susskind Pettler, "Clara Schumann's Recitals, 1832–1850," *Nineteenth-Century Music* 4 (1980), 70–76.
9. For example, she played Bach's Concerto in D Minor for Three Claviers with Mendelssohn and Rakemann on September 11, 1835, and again with Mendelssohn and Hiller on October 30, 1843. On December 19, 1861, she premiered, with Moscheles and Reinecke, Bach's Concerto in C Major for Three Claviers.
10. Litzmann, 2:401.
11. See Humphrey Searle, "Franz Liszt," *Grove*, 11:33, for "Programme général des morceaux exécutés par F. Liszt à ses concerts de 1838 à 1848," compiled by A. Conradi and Franz Liszt.
12. See George Kehler, ed., *The Piano in Concert* (Metuchen, N.J.: Scarecrow Press, 1982).
13. Wasielewski, 318.
14. Litzmann, 2:273.
15. Martin Schoppe, "Schumann-Interpretation Clara Schumanns (Tageskritik und Konzertbericht)," in *3. Schumann-Tage des Bezirkes Karl-Marx-Stadt, 1978* (Zwickau: Robert-Schumann-Gesellschaft, 1978), 20.
16. *Schumann-Brahms Briefe*, 1:237, 246.
17. Litzmann, 1:293.
18. Ibid., 3:448.
19. Boetticher, ed., *Robert Schumann in seinen Schriften und Briefen*, 302–3.
20. *Briefwechsel*, 1:105.
21. Ibid., 1:93, 126.
22. Robert Haven Schauffler, *Florestan: The Life and Work of Robert Schumann* (New York: Henry Holt, 1945), 147. Schauffler knew only the abridged version of her words in Litzmann, 1:372–73; Litzmann omitted the three sentences beginning "If Beethoven and Mozart were alive today . . ."
23. Litzmann, 1:186.
24. *Briefwechsel*, 1:126.
25. Boetticher, ed., *Robert Schumann in seinen Schriften und Briefen*, 221. The original last movement was published in the supplement (vol. 14) of the *Collected Works*.
26. Robert Schumann, *Jugendbriefe*, 309.
27. Boetticher, ed., *Robert Schumann in seinen Schriften und Briefen*, 320.
28. Jansen, 422–23.
29. Boetticher, ed., *Robert Schumann in seinen Schriften und Briefen*, 228.
30. Jansen, 434.
31. Litzmann, 1:180–81.
32. Ibid., 1:294.

33. Jansen, 397, 401.

34. Schoppe, 17, 20.

35. Rudorff-Archiv.

36. *Schumann-Brahms Briefe*, 1:395.

37. Daniel Wladimirowitsch Shitomirski, "Schumann in Russland," in *Sammelbände der Robert-Schumann-Gesellschaft* (Zwickau, 1961), 21.

38. Cited in ibid., 22.

39. Cited in ibid., 22.

40. Cited in ibid., 28.

41. Litzmann, 3:452.

42. Ibid., 3:500.

43. Ibid., 1:202; *NmZfB*, 1 (April 21, 1847), 141.

44. *AmZ*, 44 (1842), 16–18.

45. Anton Schindler, *Beethoven as I Knew Him*, ed. Donald W. MacCardle, trans. Constance S. Jolly (New York: W. W. Norton, 1966), 434, 433.

46. Martin Kreisig, "Einige Briefe Clara Schumanns," *Neue Musik-Zeitung*, 41 (1919), 35–36.

47. Budapest, 1872. Personal communication from Marie Párkai-Eckhardt.

48. *Iris*, 11 (February 27, 1840), 24; *NmZfB*, 24 (March 24, 1847), 165; *AmZ*, 44 (1842), 80–81.

49. *AmZ*, 44 (1842), 804–5.

50. *NZfM*, 61 (1865), 57.

51. Litzmann, 1:107.

52. *AmZ*, 34 (1832), 532.

53. *Schumann-Brahms Briefe*, 1:636.

54. See, for example, the letters to Emilie Steffens written in 1850 (chap. 6), which are surprisingly similar to the Wieck letters cited in chaps. 2 and 4.

55. Federhofer-Königs, *Wasielewski im Spiegel seiner Korrespondenz*, 67. Excerpts from other letters to Wasielewski are in chap. 7 above.

56. Arthur Loesser, *Men, Women, and Pianos: A Social History* (New York: Simon & Schuster, 1954), 93.

57. Hanslick, *Geschichte des Concertwesens in Wien*, 224.

58. Robert Schumann, *Tagebücher*, 1:337–38.

59. Wieck, *Briefe*, 39.

60. *Journal des Débats*, March 22, 1839.

61. Rita Benton, "Pleyel," in *Grove*, 15:11.

62. Md, September 20–27, 1840, and August 8–22, 1841.

63. *Briefwechsel*, 1:328.

64. Litzmann, 2:273.

65. *Schumann-Brahms Briefe*, 1:599.

Chapter 13. *Clara Schumann as Student and Teacher*

1. Niecks, 71–72.

2. Louis Spohr, *Lebenserinnerungen*, ed. Folker Göthel (Tutzing: Schneider, 1968), 2:88. Reginald Gerig, *Famous Pianists and Their Techniques*, 2d ed. (Washington, D.C.: R. B. Luce, 1974), has a good discussion of Logier and Wieck.

3. Litzmann, 1:4–6.

4. Wieck, *Clavier und Gesang*, 7.

5. Fay, 166.

6. Litzmann, 1:23.

7. Ibid., 3:585.

8. See Peter Cahn, *Das Hoch'sche Konservatorium in Frankfurt am Main (1878–1978)* (Frankfurt am Main: Waldemar Kramer, 1979), 51.

9. Quoted in Claus Victor Bock, "Pente Pigadia und die Tagebücher des Clement Harris," *Castrum Peregrini*, 50 (1961), 15. I am indebted to Peter Cahn for bringing this article to my attention.

10. Mathilde Verne, *Chords of Remembrance* (London: Hutchinson, 1936), 55.

11. Marie Fromm, "Some Reminiscences of My Music Studies with Clara Schumann," *MT*, 73 (1932), 615.

12. Quoted in Sir George Grove, "Clara Schumann," in *Grove's Dictionary of Music and Musicians*, ed. H. C. Colles, 3d ed. (New York: Macmillan, 1935), 4:647.

13. *Memoirs*, 97.

14. Julia Smith, *Master Pianist: The Career and Teaching of Carl Friedberg* (New York: Philosophical Library, 1963), 58.

15. *Memoirs*, 98.

16. Adelina de Lara, "Clara Schumann's Teaching," *ML*, 26 (1945), 145.

17. *Memoirs*, 98.

18. Fanny Davies, "On Schumann—and Reading between the Lines," *ML*, 6 (1925), 215.

19. Lara, p. 146.

20. See Siu-Wan Chair Fang, "Clara Schumann as Teacher," DMA thesis, University of Illinois, 1978. This dissertation, a study and analysis of the Schmidt Collection, now housed at Butler University, Indianapolis, confirms what many Schumann students have written. The editions used by Emma Schmidt still bear Schumann's decisive notes and comments on fingering, phrasing, articulation, pedaling, accents, and other aspects of piano performance.

Bibliography

UNPUBLISHED SOURCES

Major Collections of Letters*

Bayerische Staatsbibliothek, Munich, Handschriftenabteilung.
   Clara Schumann Correspondence. Letters to various correspondents, including a
      group to Hermann Levi (in Leviana) and Joachim Raff (Raffiana).
Heinrich-Heine-Institut, Düsseldorf.
   Clara Schumann Correspondence. More than 300 letters from Clara Schumann to
      friends, relatives, and officials, 1834–96. (Additional letters have recently been
      added to this basic collection.)
Robert-Schumann-Haus, Zwickau.
   Wieck family letters; Schumann family letters, including 2,278 letters from Clara
      Schumann to friends, children, and other relatives.
Rudorff-Archive: Privatarchiv v. Gottberg, D-3216 Salzhemmendorf 2, West Ger-
   many.
   Clara Schumann–Ernst Rudorff correspondence. Some 221 letters from Clara
      Schumann to Rudorff, 1858–96.
Staatsbibliothek Preussischer Kulturbesitz, Musikabteilung, Berlin (West).
   Clara Schumann–Johannes Brahms correspondence. Letters of Brahms only.† I,
      1854–77, 160 letters; II, 1878–96, 170 letters.
   Clara Schumann–Robert Schumann correspondence. In three parts: I, 1832–38,
      106 letters; II, 1839, 191 letters; III, 1840–51, 214 letters.
   Letters to Clara Schumann. In six volumes: I, 1838–59, 281 letters; II, 1860–69,
      289 letters; III, 1870–79, 413 letters; IV, 1880–85, 363 letters; V, 1886–89, 286
      letters; VI, 1890–96, 322 letters.
   Letters from Clara Schumann. Some 170 letters to various correspondents and
      related materials, 1837–96.
Stadtarchiv und Wissenschaftliche Stadtbibliothek, Bonn.
   Schumann family correspondence. Some 2,000 letters from various members of

---

*Fifty or more Clara Schumann letters.
†Thirty-four letters from Clara Schumann to Johannes Brahms, all published in Litzmann,
are in RSH.

327]

the Schumann family, including correspondence between Clara Schumann and her children and grandchildren.

Stadt- und Universitätsbibliothek, Frankfurt am Main, Musik- und Theaterabteilung.

   Clara Schumann Papers. Programs, newspaper clippings, and letters from Clara Schumann to various correspondents, including 55 letters to Julius Stockhausen, 1855–95,* and 47 to Mary Fiedler.

Universitätsbibliothek, Leipzig, Handschriftenabteilung.

   Clara Schumann correspondence. Includes 53 letters to Eduard and Lida Bendemann, 1859–95, and letters to other friends.

Other Unpublished Sources

Deutsche Staatsbibliothek, Berlin/DDR, Musikabteilung.

   Music autographs of Clara Schumann. Titles and catalogue numbers may be found in the Appendix.

Robert-Schumann-Haus, Zwickau.

   Diaries (*Tagebücher*) of Clara Wieck, catalogue no. 4877-A3, 1–4, and transcription by Martin Schoppe. Seven notebooks bound into four volumes: I, pts. 1 and 2, pp. 1–247, June 7, 1827–December 16, 1832; II, pts. 3 and 4, pp. 1–181, January 1, 1833–December 26, 1835; III, pts. 5 and 6, pp. 1–207, January 1, 1836–April 20, 1838; IV, pt. 7, pp. 1–217, April 23, 1838–September 13, 1840.

   Family papers (*Familien-Urkunde*), catalogue nos. 2174-A3 and A3b. Birth, baptismal, marriage, and death certificates of the Wieck, Tromlitz, and Schumann families.

   Legal papers (*Prozessakten*), catalogue no. 5725-A3c, and transcriptions by Georg Eismann. Copies of originals in Staatsarchiv Dresden, Bestand Landgericht Leipzig, Nr. 1.

   Marriage diaries (*Ehetagebücher*) of Robert and Clara Schumann, catalogue no. 7087-1/2-A3, and transcription by Gerd Nauhaus. Three parts bound into two volumes: I, September 12, 1840, to July 8, 1841; II, pt. 1, July 9, 1841–February 18, 1842; pt. 2, September 20, 1842–January 25, 1844. The marriage diaries are currently in press and will constitute *Tagebücher* 12, 13, and 15 in Robert Schumann, *Tagebücher*, vol. 2, ed. Gerd Nauhaus (Leipzig: Deutscher Verlag für Musik).

   Music autographs of Clara Schumann. Titles and catalogue numbers may be found in the Appendix.

   Program collection (*Programm Sammlung*) of Clara Schumann, catalogue no. 10463. The 1,299 programs, numbered and with the city in which the performance took place noted on each, are bound into five volumes: I, nos. 1–320, 1828–53; II, nos. 321–484, 1853–1858; III, nos. 485–709, 1858–64; IV, nos. 710–1188, 1864–80; V, nos. 1189–1299, 1881–91.

PUBLISHED SOURCES

Abraham, Gerald, ed. *Schumann: A Symposium.* London: Oxford University Press, 1952.

Bary, Helene de. *Museum: Geschichte der Museumsgesellschaft zu Frankfurt am Main.* Frankfurt: Brönners, 1937.

---

*Most published in *Julius Stockhausen, der Sänger des deutschen Liedes: Nach Dokumenten seiner Zeit*, ed. Julia Stockhausen-Wirth (Frankfurt am Main: Englert & Schlosser, 1927).

Barzun, Jacques. *Berlioz and the Romantic Century*. 2 vols. Boston: Little, Brown, 1950.

Becker, Claudia Stevens. "A New Look at Schumann's Impromptus." *Musical Quarterly*, 67 (1981), 568–86.

Benton, Rita. "Pleyel." In *The New Grove Dictionary of Music and Musicians*, ed. Stanley Sadie, 20 vols., 15:10–11. London: Macmillan, 1980.

Berenbruch, Brigitte, and Helmut Hellberg. *Robert Schumann und Bonn*. Bonn: Stadt Bonn, 1980.

Berlioz, Hector. *Hector Berlioz: A Selection from His Letters*. Ed. and trans. Humphrey Searle. New York: Vienna House, 1973.

Beschreibung von Leipzig für Fremde und Reisende. Leipzig: Baumgärtnersche Buchhandlung, 1816.

Bock, Claus Victor. "Pente Pigadia und die Tagebücher des Clement Harris." *Castrum Peregrini*, 50 (1961), 5–31.

Boetticher, Wolfgang. "Neue textkritische Forschungen an Robert Schumanns Klavierwerk." *Archiv für Musikwissenschaft*, 25 (1968), 46–76.

———. *Robert Schumanns Klavierwerke: Neue biographische und textkritische Untersuchungen*. Pt. 1, op. 1–6. Wilhelmshaven: Heinrichshofen, 1976.

———. "Robert Schumann und seine Verleger." In *Musik und Verlag: Karl Vötterle zum 65. Geburtstag am 12. April 1968*, ed. Richard Baum und Wolfgang Rehm, 168–74. Kassel: Bärenreiter, 1968.

———. "Zur Zitatpraxis in R. Schumanns frühen Klavierwerken." In *Speculum Musicae Artis: Heinrich Husmann zum 60. Geburtstag*, ed. Heinz Becker and Reinhard Gerlach, pp. 63–73. Munich: Wilhelm Fink, 1970.

———, ed. *Briefe und Gedichte aus dem Album Robert und Clara Schumanns*. Leipzig: Deutscher Verlag für Musik, 1979.

———, ed. *Robert Schumann in seinen Schriften und Briefen*. Berlin: Hahnefeld, 1942.

Brahms, Johannes. *Johannes Brahms in seiner Familie: Der Briefwechsel*. Ed. Kurt Stephenson. Hamburg: Ernst Hauswedell, 1973.

——— and Theodor Billroth. *Letters from a Musical Friendship*. Trans. and ed. Hans Barkan. Norman: University of Oklahoma Press, 1957.

——— and Julius Otto Grimm. *Johannes Brahms im Briefwechsel mit Julius Otto Grimm*. Ed. Richard Barth. Berlin: Deutsche Brahms-Gesellschaft, 1907.

———, Heinrich von Herzogenberg, and Elisabeth von Herzogenberg. *Johannes Brahms im Briefwechsel mit Heinrich und Elisabet von Herzogenberg*. Ed. Max Kalbeck. Berlin: Deutsche Brahms-Gesellschaft, 1907. Published in English as *The Herzogenberg Correspondence*. Ed. Max Kalbeck. Trans. Hannah Bryant. London: John Murray, 1909.

——— and Joseph Joachim. *Johannes Brahms im Briefwechsel mit Joseph Joachim*. Ed. Andreas Moser. 2 vols. Berlin: Deutsche Brahms-Gesellschaft, 1908.

——— and Philipp Spitta. *Johannes Brahms im Briefwechsel mit Philipp Spitta*. Ed. Carl Krebs. Berlin: Deutsche Brahms-Gesellschaft, 1920.

Brody, Elaine. "Schumann's Legacy in France." *Studies in Romanticism*, 13 (1974), 189–212.

Bulman, Joan. *Jenny Lind*. London: James Barrie, 1956.

Burk, John. *Clara Schumann: A Romantic Biography*. New York: Random House, 1940.

Cahn, Peter. *Das Hoch'sche Konservatorium in Frankfurt am Main (1878–1978)*. Frankfurt am Main: Waldemar Kramer, 1979.

Callomon, F. T. "Unbekannte Briefe Robert und Clara Schumanns." *Neue Zeitschrift für Musik*, 118 (1956), 396–400.

Chissell, Joan. *Clara Schumann: A Dedicated Spirit*. London: Hamish Hamilton, 1983.

Chopin, Frédéric. *Chopin's Letters*. Ed. Henryk Opieński. Trans. E. L. Voynich. New York: Knopf, 1931.

Chorley, Henry F. *Music and Manners in France and Germany: A Series of Travelling Sketches of Art and Society*. 3 vols. London: Longman, Brown, Green & Longmans, 1844.

Davies, Fanny. "On Schumann—and Reading between the Lines." *Music and Letters*, 6 (1925), 214–23.

Demmler, Fritz. "Johann George Tromlitz (1752–1805): Ein Beitrag zur Entwicklung der Flöte und des Flötenspiels." Dissertation, Freie Universität, Berlin, 1961.

Deutsch, Otto Erich. *Mozart: A Documentary Biography*. 2d ed. London: Adam & Charles Black, 1966.

Dörffel, Alfred, ed. *Geschichte der Gewandhausconcerte zu Leipzig vom 25. November 1781 bis 25. November 1881*. Leipzig, 1884. The second section of this book, "Statistik," pp. 1–100, is not found in every copy.

Eberhardt, Hans. *Die ersten deutschen Musikfeste in Frankenhausen am Kyffhäuser und Erfurt, 1810, 1811, 1812 und 1815*. Jena: Frommann, 1934.

Eismann, Georg. "Robert Schumanns Ehetagebücher entsiegelt," *Musik und Gesellschaft*, 9 (1951), 279–84; 10 (1952), 7–9.

————, ed. *Robert Schumann: Ein Quellenwerk über sein Leben und Schaffen*. 2 vols. Leipzig: Breitkopf & Härtel, 1956.

Erst- und Frühdrucke von Robert Schumann in der Musikbibliothek Leipzig. Ed. Ferdinand Hirsch and Ellen Roeser. Leipzig: Bibliographische Veröffentlichungen der Musikbibliothek der Stadt Leipzig, 1960.

Fang, Siu-Wan Chair. "Clara Schumann as Teacher." DMA thesis, University of Illinois, 1978.

Fay, Amy. *Music Study in Germany*. 18th ed. New York: Macmillan, 1903. First published 1880.

Federhofer-Königs, Renate. "Der Briefwechsel von Wilhelm Joseph von Wasielewski (1822–1896) in seiner Bedeutung für die Schumann-Forschung." In *Convivium Musicorum: Festschrift Wolfgang Boetticher,* ed. Heinrich Hüschen and Dietz-Rüdiger Moser, pp. 52–67. Berlin: Merseburger, 1974.

————. *Wilhelm Joseph von Wasielewski im Spiegel seiner Korrespondenz*. Tutzing: Schneider, 1975.

Fellinger, Imogen. "Clara Schumann." In *Die Musik in Geschichte und Gegenwart*, ed. Friedrich Blume, 12:261–69. Kassel: Bärenreiter, 1965.

Fiske, Roger. "A Schumann Mystery." *Musical Times*, 105 (1964), 574–78.

Fitzlyon, April. *The Price of Genius: A Life of Pauline Viardot*. New York: Appleton-Century-Crofts, 1964.

Frager, Malcolm. "The Music of the Schumann Piano Concerto." *Current Musicology*, 15 (1973), 83–87.

Fromm, Marie. "Some Reminiscences of my Music Studies with Clara Schumann." *Musical Times*, 73 (1932), 615–16.

Fuller Maitland, John Alexander. *Masters of German Music*. London: Osgood, McIlvaine, 1894.

Gal, Hans. *Johannes Brahms: His Work and Personality*. Trans. Joseph Stein. New York: Knopf, 1963. First published in German, 1961.

Geiringer, Karl. *Brahms: His Life and Work*. 2d ed., rev. and enl. New York: Anchor Books, 1961.

————. "Schumanniana in der Bibliothek von Johannes Brahms." In *Convivium Musicorum: Festschrift Wolfgang Boetticher*, ed. Heinrich Hüschen and Dietz-Rüdiger Moser, pp. 79–82. Berlin: Merseburger, 1974.

Gerber, Ernst Ludwig. *Neues historisches biographisches Lexikon der Tonkünstler*. 4 vols. Leipzig: Kühnel, 1812–14.

Gerig, Reginald. *Famous Pianists and Their Techniques.* 2d ed. Washington, D.C.: R. B. Luce, 1974.

Greene, Harry Plunkett. "Leonard Borwick: Some Personal Recollections." In *Music and Letters*, 7 (1926), 17–24.

Grove, Sir George. "Clara Schumann." In *Grove's Dictionary of Music and Musicians*, ed. H. C. Colles, 3d ed., 6 vols., 4:645–48. New York: Macmillan, 1935.

Gutman, Robert. *Richard Wagner: The Man, His Mind, His Music.* New York: Harcourt Brace Jovanovich, 1968.

Haight, Gordon S. *George Eliot: A Biography.* New York: Oxford University Press, 1968.

Hallmark, Rufus. *The Genesis of Schumann's Dichterliebe: A Source Study.* Ann Arbor, Mich.: UMI Research Press, 1979.

Hanslick, Eduard. *Am Ende des Jahrhunderts 1895–1899. (Die Moderne Oper, pt. 8.)* 2d ed. Berlin: Allgemeiner Verein für deutsche Literatur, 1899.

———. *Aus neuer und neuester Zeit. (Die Moderne Oper, pt. 9.)* 3d ed. Berlin: Allgemeiner Verein für deutsche Literatur, 1900.

———. *Concerte, Componisten und Virtuosen der letzten fünfzehn Jahre, 1870–1885.* Berlin: Allgemeiner Verein für deutsche Literatur, 1886.

———. *Geschichte des Concertwesens in Wien.* Vienna: Wilhelm Braumüller, 1869.

Harwood, Gregory. "Robert Schumann's Sonata in F♯ Minor: A Study of Creative Process and Romantic Inspiration." *Current Musicology*, 29 (1980), 17–30.

Henschel, Sir George. *Musings and Memories of a Musician.* New York: Macmillan, 1919.

———. *Personal Recollections of Johannes Brahms.* Boston: R. G. Badger, 1907.

Hiller, Ferdinand. *Aus Ferdinand Hillers Briefwechsel (1826–1861).* Ed. Reinhold Sietz. Cologne: Arno Volk-Verlag, 1958.

Hirschberg, Leopold. "Robert Schumann und der Davidsbündler Fritz Friedrich: Mit einer Auswahl bisher unveröffentlicher Briefe J. P. Lysers an Schumann." *Velhagen & Klasings Monatshefte*, 24 (1909–10), 85–91, 241–47.

Hirst, Margaret. *Life of Friedrich List and Selections from His Writings.* London: Smith, Elder, 1909.

Hofmann, Kurt. *Die Bibliothek von Johannes Brahms.* Hamburg: Wagner, 1974.

———. *Die Erstdrucke der Werke von Johannes Brahms.* Tutzing: Schneider, 1975.

———. *Die Erstdrucke der Werke von Robert Schumann.* Tutzing: Schneider, 1979.

Hohenemser, Richard, "Clara Wieck-Schumann als Komponistin." *Die Musik*, 5 (1905–6), 113–26, 166–73.

Holborn, Hajo. *A History of Modern Germany, 1648–1840.* New York: Knopf, 1964.

Holde, Artur. "Suppressed Passages in the Joachim–Brahms Correspondence Published for the First Time." *Musical Quarterly*, 45 (1959), 312–24.

Huebner, Rudolf. *A History of Germanic Private Law.* Trans. Francis S. Philbrick. Boston: Little, Brown, 1918.

Jahresbericht des Dr. Hoch'schen Conservatoriums zu Frankfurt am Main. Frankfurt am Main: C. Adelmann, 1879 . . . 1921.

Jansen, Gustav F., ed. *Robert Schumanns Briefe: Neue Folge.* 2d ed. Leipzig: Breitkopf & Härtel, 1904. 1st ed. (1886) published in English as *The Life of Robert Schumann as Told in His Letters.* Trans. May Herbert. London: Richard Bentley, 1890.

Joachim, Joseph. *Briefe von und an Joseph Joachim.* Ed. Johannes Joachim and Andreas Moser. 3 vols. Berlin: Julius Bard, 1911–13. Published in English as *Letters from and to Joseph Joachim.* Trans. Nora Bickley. London: Macmillan, 1914.

Joss, Victor. *Der Musikpädagoge Friedrich Wieck und seine Familie; Mit besonderer Berücksichtigung seines Schwiegersohnes Robert Schumann.* Dresden: Oscar

Damm, 1902. 2d enl. ed. of *Friedrich Wieck und sein Verhältnis zu Robert Schumann.* Dresden: Oscar Damm, 1900.

Kalbeck, Max. *Johannes Brahms.* 4th ed. 4 vols. Berlin: Deutsche Brahms-Gesellschaft, 1921. Used here are reprints (Tutzing: Hans Schneider): vol. 1, 4th ed. (1921); vol. 2, 3d ed. (1921); vol. 3, 2d ed. (1912); vol. 4, 2d ed. (1915).

Kämper, Dietrich. "Zur Frage der Metronombezeichnungen Robert Schumanns," *Archiv für Musikwissenschaft,* 21 (1964), 141–55.

Kast, Paul, ed. *Schumanns rheinische Jahre.* Düsseldorf: Droste, 1981.

Kehler, George, ed. *The Piano in Concert.* Metuchen, N.J.: Scarecrow Press, 1982.

Klassen, Janina. "Recht Brahms, ernst und humoristisch: Noch ein paar Bemerkungen zu Clara Schumann und Johannes Brahms." In *Brahms-Phantasien: Johannes Brahms-Bildwelt, Musik, Leben, 18. September bis 26. Oktober 1983,* 7–10. Catalogue Kunsthalle, Christian-Albrechts-Universität, Kiel, 1983.

Kneschke, Emil. *Das Conservatorium der Musik in Leipzig: Seine Geschichte, seine Lehrer und Zöglinge.* Leipzig: Breitkopf & Härtel, 1868.

Köhler, Karl-Heinz. "Felix Mendelssohn (Bartholdy)." In *The New Grove Dictionary of Music and Musicians,* ed. Stanley Sadie, 20 vols., 12:134–59. London: Macmillan, 1980.

Kohut, Adolph. *Friedrich Wieck: Ein Lebens- und Künstlerbild.* Dresden: Pierson's, 1888.

Krebs, Carl. "Clara Schumann." In *Allgemeine Deutsche Biographie,* 54:262–68.

Kreisig, Martin, "Einige Briefe Clara Schumanns." *Neue Musik-Zeitung,* 41 (1919), 35–36.

Kross, Siegfried, ed. *Briefe und Notizen Robert und Clara Schumanns.* Bonn: Bouvier, 1978.

Lara, Adelina de. "Clara Schumann's Teaching." *Music and Letters,* 26 (1945), 143–47.

Laux, Karl. "Dresden ist doch gar zu schön." In *Robert Schumann: Aus Anlass seines 100. Todestages,* ed. Hans Joachim Moser and Eberhard Rebling, 25–42. Leipzig: Breitkopf & Härtel, 1956.

Leo, Sophie Augustine. "Musical Life in Paris, 1817–1848: A Chapter from the Memoirs of Sophie Augustine Leo." Trans. Oliver Strunk. *Musical Quarterly,* 17 (1931), 259–71, 389–403.

Leven, Louise W. "Clara Schumann's First Visit to England." *Musical Times,* 97 (1956), 190–91.

Lippman, Edward. "Robert Schumann." In *Die Musik in Geschichte und Gegenwart,* ed. Friedrich Blume, 12:272–326. Kassel: Bärenreiter, 1965.

Liszt, Franz. *Correspondance de Liszt et de Madame D'Agoult.* Ed. M. Daniel Ollivier. 2 vols. Paris: Grasset, 1933.

———. *Franz Liszts Briefe.* Ed. La Mara. 2d ed. 8 vols. Leipzig: Breitkopf & Härtel, 1893–1902.

Litzmann, Berthold, ed. *Clara Schumann: Ein Künstlerleben nach Tagebüchern und Briefen.* 3 vols. Leipzig: Breitkopf & Härtel, 1902–8. Abr. ed. published in English as *Clara Schumann: An Artist's Life, Based on Material Found in Diaries and Letters.* Trans. Grace E. Hadow. 2 vols. London: Macmillan, 1913.

Loesser, Arthur. *Men, Women, and Pianos: A Social History.* New York: Simon & Schuster, 1954.

Löhner, Wilhelm, ed. "Clara Schumann: Unbekannte Briefe an Emilie Steffens." *Zeitschrift für Musik,* 97 (1930), 177–79.

Lowder, Jerry. "Friedrich Wieck as a Teacher." *Clavier,* 8 (1969), 42–43.

Lyser, Johann Peter. "Clara Wieck." *Caecilia* (Hamburg), 1 (1833), 253–58.

May, Florence. *The Girlhood of Clara Schumann: Clara Wieck and Her Time.* London: Edward Arnold, 1912.

————. *The Life of Johannes Brahms*. 2d ed. 2 vols. London: William Reeves, 1905.

Meichsner, Anna von. *Friedrich Wieck und seine beiden Töchter, Clara Schumann, geb. Wieck, und Marie Wieck: Biographische Notizen über dieselben nebst ungedruckten Briefen von H. v. Bülow, Czerny, R. Schumann, Carl Maria von Weber usw.: Ein Familiendenkmal*. Leipzig: Heinrich Matthes, 1875.

Mendelssohn, Felix. *Felix Mendelssohn Bartholdy: Briefe aus Leipziger Archiven*. Ed. Hans-Joachim Rothe and Reinhard Szeskus. Leipzig: Deutscher Verlag für Musik, 1972.

————. *Felix Mendelssohn-Bartholdys Briefwechsel mit Legationsrat Karl Klingemann in London*. Ed. Karl Klingemann. Essen: Baedeker, 1909.

Moser, Andreas. *Joseph Joachim: Ein Lebensbild*. Rev. and enl. ed. 2 vols. Berlin: Deutsche Brahms-Gesellschaft, 1908.

Müller-Reuter, Theodor. *Bilder und Klänge des Friedens: Musikalische Erinnerungen und Aufsätze*. Leipzig: Wilhelm Hartung, 1919.

Munte, Frank. "Robert und Clara Schumann in Hamburg." In *Brahms-Studien*, ed. Helmut Wirth, 2:7–45. Hamburg: Wagner, 1977.

————. *Verzeichnis des deutschsprächigen Schrifttums über Robert Schumann*. Hamburg: Wagner, 1972.

Newman, William. *The Sonata since Beethoven*. 2d ed. New York: W. W. Norton, 1972.

Niecks, Frederick. *Robert Schumann*. London: J. M. Dent, 1925.

Ostwald, Peter. "Florestan, Eusebius, Clara, and Schumann's Right Hand." *Nineteenth-Century Music*, 4 (1980), 17–31.

————. *Robert Schumann: The Inner Voices of a Musical Genius*. Boston: Northeastern University Press, 1985.

Perenyi, Eleanor. *Liszt: The Artist as Romantic Hero*. Boston: Little, Brown, 1974.

Pettler, Pamela Susskind. "Clara Schumann's Recitals, 1832–50." *Nineteenth-Century Music*, 4 (1980), 70–76.

Plantinga, Leon B. *Schumann as Critic*. New Haven: Yale University Press, 1967.

Ramshorn, Carl. *Leipzig und seine Umgebungen*. Braunschweig: George Westermann, 1841.

Rehberg, Paula, and Walter Rehberg. *Robert Schumann: Sein Leben und sein Werk*. 2d ed. Zurich: Artemis, 1969.

Roesner, Linda Corell. "Studies in Schumann Manuscripts: With Particular Reference to Sources Transmitting Instrumental Works in the Large Forms." Ph.D. dissertation, New York University, 1973.

Rudolphi, Caroline. *Gemälde weiblicher Erziehung*. Heidelberg: Mohr & Winter, 1815.

Sagarra, Eda. *A Social History of Germany*. New York: Holmes & Meier, 1977.

Sams, Eric. "Brahms and His Clara Themes." *Musical Times*, 112 (1971), 432–34.

————. "Schumann and the Tonal Analogue." In *Robert Schumann: The Man and His Music*, ed. Alan Walker, 390–405. London: Barrie & Jenkins, 1972.

————. "Schumann's Hand Injury." *Musical Times*, 112 (1971), 1156–59.

————. *The Songs of Robert Schumann*. 2d ed. London: Eulenburg, 1975.

Schauffler, Robert Haven. *Florestan: The Life and Work of Robert Schumann*. New York: Henry Holt, 1945.

Schindler, Anton. *Beethoven as I Knew Him*. Ed. Donald W. MacArdle. Trans. Constance S. Jolly. New York: W. W. Norton, 1966.

Schlotel, Brian. "Schumann and the Metronome." In *Robert Schumann: The Man and His Music*, ed. Alan Walker, 109–19. London: Barrie & Jenkins, 1972.

Schonberg, Harold C. *The Great Pianists from Mozart to the Present*. New York: Simon & Schuster, 1963.

Schoppe, Martin. "Schumann-Interpretation Clara Schumanns (Tageskritik und

Konzertbericht)." In *3. Schumann-Tage des Bezirkes Karl-Marx-Stadt, 1978*, 17–24. Zwickau: Robert-Schumann-Gesellschaft, 1978.

———— and Gerd Nauhaus. *Das Robert-Schumann-Haus in Zwickau*. Zwickau: Robert-Schumann-Haus, 1973.

Schubert, Franz Peter. *Erlkönig: Facsimile of the Autograph Manuscript*. New York: Pierpont Morgan Library, 1978.

Schumann, Alfred. *Johannes Brahms, der Vater von Felix Schumann: Das Mysterium einer Liebe. Eine sehr ernste Parodie auf die Erinnerungen von Eugenie Schumann*. Von Titus Frazeni (pseud.). Bielefeld: Manfred, 1926.

Schumann, Clara, and Johannes Brahms. *Clara Schumann–Johannes Brahms Briefe aus den Jahren 1853–1896*. Ed. Berthold Litzmann. 2 vols. Leipzig: Breitkopf & Härtel, 1927. Abr. ed. published in English as *Letters of Clara Schumann and Johannes Brahms, 1853–1896*. Trans. Grace Hadow. London: Edward Arnold, 1927.

———— and Robert Schumann. *Clara und Robert Schumann, Briefwechsel; Kritische Gesamtausgabe*. Ed. Eva Weissweiler. Vol. 1, 1832–1838. Basel: Stroemfeld/Roter Stern, 1984.

Schumann, Eugenie. *Erinnerungen*. Stuttgart: Engelhorn, 1925. Translated into English by Marie Busch and published as *The Memoirs of Eugenie Schumann* (London: William Heinemann, 1927) and as *The Schumanns and Johannes Brahms: The Memoirs of Eugenie Schumann* (New York: Dial, 1927). References in this book are to the translation (New York edition), for several reasons: the book is not abridged, Eugenie Schumann knew English well, and since the translation was completed during her lifetime, I believe it to be a reliable version.

————. *Robert Schumann: Ein Lebensbild meines Vaters*. Leipzig: Koehler & Amelang, 1931. Excerpts from the marriage diary in Eugenie Schumann's work have appeared in English as "The Diary of Robert and Clara Schumann," trans. G. D. H. Pidcock, *Music and Letters*, 15 (1934), 287–300; 16 (1935), 40–49.

————. "Über das letzte Werk ihres Vaters Robert Schumann." *Schweizerische Musikzeitung*, 1938, 8–10.

Schumann, Ferdinand. "Brahms and Clara Schumann." *Musical Quarterly*, 2 (1916), 507–15. A translation of Ferdinand Schumann, "Erinnerungen an Brahms," *Neue Zeitschrift für Musik*, 82 (1915), 225–28, 233–36, 241–43.

————. *Reminiscences of Clara Schumann as Found in the Diary of Her Grandson Ferdinand Schumann of Dresden*. Ed. June M. Dickinson. 2d ed. New York: Musical Scope, 1973. A translation probably based on Ferdinand Schumann, "Erinnerungen an Clara Schumann," *Neue Zeitschrift für Musik*, 84 (1917), 69–72, 77–80, 85–88, 93–96, 101–4.

Schumann, Robert. *Erinnerungen an Felix Mendelssohn Bartholdy: Nachgelassene Aufzeichnungen*. Ed. Georg Eismann. Zwickau: Predella, 1947.

————. *Gesammelte Schriften*. 3d ed. Leipzig: Wigand, 1875.

————. *Jugendbriefe von Robert Schumann: Nach den originalen mitgeteilt*. Ed. Clara Schumann. 2d ed. Leipzig: Breitkopf & Härtel, 1886. Published in English as *Early Letters*. Trans. May Herbert. London: G. Bell, 1888.

————. [Klavierwerke]. Ed. Hans Joachim Köhler. Leipzig: Peters, 1973–. The piano works of Robert Schumann issued in separate volumes with extensive commentary.

————. *Robert Schumann: Thematisches Verzeichnis sämtlicher im Druck erschienenen musikalischen Werke mit Angabe des Jahres ihres Entstehens und Erscheinens*. Ed. Kurt Hofmann and Siegmar Keil. 5th ed., enl. and rev. Hamburg: J. Schuberth, 1982.

————. *Tagebücher (1827–1838)*. pt. 1. Ed. Georg Eismann. Leipzig: Deutscher Verlag für Musik, 1971.

————. *Tagebücher*. Pt. 3, *Haushaltbücher (1837–1856)*. Ed. Gerd Nauhaus. 2 vols. Leipzig: Deutscher Verlag für Musik, 1982.

Robert und Clara Schumann: Dokumente zum Düsseldorfer Musikleben. Ed. Joseph Kruse. Düsseldorf: Heinrich-Heine-Institut, 1976.

Searle, Humphrey. "Franz Liszt." In *The New Grove Dictionary of Music and Musicians*, ed. Stanley Sadie, 20 vols., 11:28–74. London: Macmillan, 1980.

Shitomirski, Daniel Wladimirowitsch. "Schumann in Russland." In *Sammelbände der Robert-Schumann-Gesellschaft*, 19–46. Zwickau: 1961.

Slater, Eliot. "Schumann's Illness." In *Robert Schumann: The Man and His Music*, ed. Alan Walker, 406–17. London: Barrie & Jenkins, 1972.

Smith, Julia. *Master Pianist: The Career and Teaching of Carl Friedberg*. New York: Philosophical Library, 1963.

Smyth, Ethel. *Impressions That Remained*. New York: Knopf, 1946.

Sonneck, Oscar, ed. *Beethoven: Impressions of Contemporaries*. New York: G. Schirmer, 1926.

Spohr, Louis. *Lebenserinnerungen*. Ed. Folker Göthel. Tutzing: Schneider, 1968.

Stargardt-Wolff, Edith. *Wegbereiter grosser Musiker*. Berlin: Bote & Bock, 1954.

Stephenson, Kurt. *Clara Schumann, 1819–1969*. Bonn/Bad Godesberg: Inter Nationes, 1969.

Susskind, Pamela. "Clara Schumann as Pianist and Composer: A Study of Her Life and Works." Ph.D. dissertation, University of California, Berkeley, 1977.

Suttoni, Charles. "Piano and Opera: A Study of the Piano Fantasies Written on Opera Themes in the Romantic Era." Ph..D. dissertation, New York University, 1973.

Verne, Mathilde. *Chords of Remembrance*. London: Hutchinson, 1936.

Wagner, Cosima. *Cosima Wagner's Diaries*. Ed. Martin Gregor-Dellin and Dietrich Mack. Trans. Gregory Skelton. New York: Harcourt Brace Jovanovich, 1978, 1980.

Walker, Alan. "Schumann, Liszt, and the C Major Fantasie, Op. 17: A Declining Relationship." *Music and Letters*, 60 (1979), 156–65.

Wasielewski, Wilhelm Joseph von. *Robert Schumann: Eine Biographie*. 3d enl. ed. Leipzig: Breitkopf & Härtel, 1880. Published in English as *Life of Robert Schumann*. Trans. A. L. Alger. Boston: Ditson, 1871.

Wieck, Friedrich. *Briefe aus den Jahren 1830–1838*. Ed. Käthe Walch-Schumann. Cologne: Arno Volk-Verlag, 1968.

————. *Clavier und Gesang: Didaktisches und Polemisches*. Leipzig: F. Whistling, 1853. Published in English as *Piano and Singing: Didactical and Polemical for Professionals and Amateurs*, trans. H. Kreuger (Aberdeen: H. Krueger, [1875]), and *Piano and Song: How to Teach, How to Learn, and How to Form a Judgment of Musical Performances*, trans. Mary P. Nichols (Boston: Ditson, 1875; reprint, New York: Da Capo, 1982).

Wieck, Marie. *Aus dem Kreise Wieck-Schumann*. 2d rev. and enl. ed. Dresden: v. Zahn & Jaensch, 1914.

Wirth, Julia Stockhausen, ed. *Julius Stockhausen, der Sänger des deutschen Liedes: Nach Dokumenten seiner Zeit*. Frankfurt: Englert & Schlosser, 1927.

Index

Index

Index